Competition Law as Regulation

Competition Law as Regulation

Edited by

Josef Drexl

Director, Max Planck Institute for Innovation and Competition, Munich, Germany

Fabiana Di Porto

Associate Professor of Law, University of Salento, Lecce, Italy

ASCOLA COMPETITION LAW

Edward Elgar
PUBLISHING

Cheltenham, UK • Northampton, MA, USA

Published by
Edward Elgar Publishing Limited
The Lypiatts
15 Lansdown Road
Cheltenham
Glos GL50 2JA
UK

Edward Elgar Publishing, Inc.
William Pratt House
9 Dewey Court
Northampton
Massachusetts 01060
USA

A catalogue record for this book
is available from the British Library

Library of Congress Control Number: 2015940686

This book is available electronically in the **Elgar**online
Law subject collection
DOI 10.4337/9781783472598

MIX
Paper from responsible sources
FSC® C013056
www.fsc.org

ISBN 978 1 78347 258 1 (cased)
ISBN 978 1 78347 259 8 (eBook)

Typeset by Columns Design XML Ltd, Reading
Printed and bound in Great Britain by TJ International Ltd, Padstow

Contents

Contributors

Emanuela Arezzo, PhD in Law and Economics (Luiss Guido Carli University, Rome), LL.M. (Rotterdam); Assistant Professor of Law at the University of Teramo, Faculty of Law, Italy.

Adi Ayal, PhD in Economics (UC Berkeley), PhD in Law (Bar Ilan University); co-chair of the Program for Fostering Excellence at the Faculty of Law, Bar Ilan University, Israel.

Marco Botta, PhD in Law (European University Institute), LL.M. in European Business Law (Leiden University); Assistant Professor at the Institute for European Integration Research, University of Vienna, Austria.

Fausto Caronna, PhD in Law (University of Rome, 'La Sapienza'), LL.M. in International Business Law (University College London); Senior Attorney (Cleary Gottlieb Steen & Hamilton LLP).

Fabiana Di Porto, PhD in Law (Perugia and Strasbourg), MSc (London School of Economics); Associate Professor of Law at the University of Salento, Italy; Co-Director of the journal *Concorrenza e mercato. Antitrust, Regulation, Consumer Welfare, IP.*

Michal S. Gal, Professor and Director of the Forum of Law and Markets, University of Haifa, Faculty of Law, Israel.

Tamar Indig, PhD student and research assistant (University of Haifa, Faculty of Law); senior law clerk for the honourable Justice Noam Sohlberg, Supreme Court of Israel.

Krystyna Kowalik-Bańczyk, LL.M. (Bruges), DEA (Toulouse); Associate Professor at the Institute of Law Studies, Polish Academy of Sciences, Warsaw, Poland.

Björn Lundqvist, LL.D. (EUI), LL.M. (Michigan); Associate Professor of Competition Law, Law Department, Copenhagen Business School; and Senior Lecturer of European Law at Stockholm University, Sweden.

Mariateresa Maggiolino, MS in Economics (Bocconi University), JD (State University of Milan), LL.M. (Iowa University); Assistant Professor of Business Law at Bocconi University, Italy.

Nicoletta Rangone, Professor of Economic Law and Administrative Law at LUMSA University, Rome, Italy.

Mario Siragusa, LL.M. (Harvard), Diploma of High European Studies (College of Europe – Bruges); Partner at Cleary Gottlieb Steen & Hamilton LLP; Professor of Law of the EU and Intellectual Property at the College of Europe (Bruges).

Yane Svetiev, JSD, LL.M. (Columbia); Bocconi University, Department of Legal Studies; European University Institute, Law Department.

Alexandr Svetlicinii, PhD (EUI), M.Res. (EUI), LL.M. (CEU); Assistant Professor at the University of Macau, Faculty of Law (Macao SAR, China).

Toshiaki Takigawa, MBA (UC Berkeley), LL.B./Law (Kyoto University); Professor, Faculty of Law, Kansai University, Osaka, Japan.

Rolf H. Weber, PhD in Law (University of Zurich); Professor of Civil, Commercial and European Law at the University of Zurich and Visiting Professor at the University of Hong Kong; Attorney-at-law; Director of the European Law Institute and the Center for Information and Communication Law and member of the Research Priority Program about Financial Market Regulation at the University of Zurich, Switzerland.

Preface

This book assembles various contributions that are based on talks given at the 8th Conference of the Academic Society of Competition Law (ASCOLA), which was held at the University of Salento, Lecce (Italy) on 22–23 May 2013. By raising the thought-provoking question of 'Competition Law as Regulation?', ASCOLA's 2013 conference, based on a call for papers, aimed at discussing the emergence of a 'regulatory approach' to competition law and thereby tried to advance scholarship on the relationships between competition law and regulation.

While there is a lot of literature on market regulation and regulated industries, legal and economic writing has not yet sufficiently addressed the more recent trend of competition law and competition law enforcement to develop mechanisms and tools that *go beyond* mere protection of competition against restraints, but try to improve the market conditions in a *forward looking approach*, which is more typical for market regulation. The 8th ASCOLA Conference reacted to this trend by launching a scholarly debate on its causes and consequences, as well as the advantages and disadvantages of this new 'regulatory approach' of competition law. Accordingly, the conference concentrated on what competition agencies and courts are doing when they apply competition law and not so much on what specialized regulatory agencies are doing. Like the conference, this book is highly topical and at the same time original, because by going beyond the traditional view that competition law is essentially an *ex post* intervention that only reacts to competition restraints whereas regulation intervenes *ex ante*, it provides a much more complex picture. Even authors who analyse the interaction of competition law with regulation in general (Kowalik-Bańczyk, Siragusa and Caronna, Svetlicinii and Botta) or in specific markets, such as telecommunications (Takigawa) from the point of view of a specific jurisdiction, reach the conclusion that regulation is far from disappearing. This insight helps us overcome the much simplified vision of regulation as gradually disappearing in the wake of sunsetting provisions and being replaced by *ex post* competition law enforcement.

The book addresses the topic in five parts. Part 1 explores the foundations of the complex relationship of competition law and regulation and provides definitions and declinations of the 'regulatory approach' of competition law. Part 2 is devoted to new forms of advocacy powers of competition agencies, namely 'market inquiries' and the 'competition impact assessment', and shows how agencies may do a lot more to promote competition and help regulation be pro-competitive than just condemning undertakings for violating competition laws. Parts 3 and 4 deal with competition law in regulated industries, although with different approaches. Part 3 focuses on such industries in general and develops a general approach to them, mostly against the backdrop of different jurisdictions, while Part 4 pertains to regulation and competition in the information and telecommunications markets, and compares specific national approaches with those of the US and the EU. Finally, Part 5 explores the intersection between competition law and regulation in IP-related markets.

Part 1 opens with a contribution by Mariateresa Maggiolino defining what a 'regulatory approach' means. This consists of competition law not (anymore) being neutral with regard to market outcomes: instead, it proactively aims to bring markets to the competitive equilibrium. Accordingly, the 'regulatory approach' does not limit itself to pure *ex post* enforcement of legal prohibitions; rather, it may even include *ex ante* establishment of detailed rules that shape the market structure and define its economic outcome. Decisions with some regulatory flavour are hence decisions based on competition law that do not just eliminate an anticompetitive practice but modify the market.

When dealing with consent decrees and commitment decisions, some European duty-to-deal cases, and those rule-of-reason cases where competition law enforcers prohibit a practice holding that the parties in question could have concluded a less restrictive deal, one gets the impression that current competition law agencies and even judges do not escape from *bringing markets* to the competitive equilibrium. From a perspective of traditional competition law scholarship, such an approach can be viewed with scepticism and qualified as a sort of *regulatory distortion* of competition law.

But is it really so? Maggiolino's 'it depends' answer could not be better suited to open the debate. Her chapter conceptualizes the differences between competition law and economic regulation, so as to make sense of the dichotomy. This leads the author to reconsider a two-pole situation, where competition law and economic regulation pursue different goals and apply different means. The two archetypical poles of this dichotomy are indeed best represented by the Chicagoan conceptualization of US antitrust law of the 1970s, on the one hand; and the diffuse US 'sector-specific, rate-and-entry' economic regulation, emerging in the 1960s, on the other. The latter is categorized as what we would nowadays call 'command and control' regulation, which sets entry conditions, defines (product, process or target) standards, prohibits some conduct or compels a certain course of action, or controls prices charged to consumers or profits earned by the industry. Maggiolino summarizes this extreme as one where 'independent authorities' would act to attain 'economic welfare', economic growth and the 'public interest' by making *ex ante* detailed decisions that 'fully … manage and control private affairs'.

In contrast, the competition law pole is conceptualized as a tribute to neoliberalism that only prohibits those practices that harm 'the competitive *status quo*', i.e. neither the process nor the effect, but the *natural* functioning of the market, 'by looking at the performance of total welfare'.

If these are the two 'pure' versions of regulation and antitrust, melting starts – as Maggiolino claims – when competition law begins pursuing political and social goals and does not let the *natural* market work alone (e.g., when it starts changing the market structure or imposing positive obligations to act instead of merely banning certain conduct).

The preference competition law enforcers have long accorded to the Chicagoan position, according to Maggiolino, can be explained by its 'reassuring nature': due to the intrinsic limitations it poses on enforcers' discretion. This archetype is reassuring in that it seems to be neutral, because it preserves competition authorities from pandering to political ideals, ceding to external interference, and producing false positives when enforcing the law. However, Maggiolino deconstructs the neutrality claim of Chicagoan antitrust. Markets and their *status quo* are not neutral, nor are they value-free, and neither are their theoretical foundations (which is true for all the social sciences).

The following chapter by Adi Ayal reaches very similar conclusions by assessing the 'worrisome' trend of antitrust 'expansion' in deregulated markets as well as in markets characterized by networks and platforms serving as essential facilities in large parts of the modern economy. Ayal starts with a thorough description of regulatory concerns and the types of agencies used to implement them. He then distinguishes between competition and industry-specific regulation and elaborates on the characteristics they share and their main relevant differences. He further discusses regulatory failures, delving into a major challenge for the trends towards deregulation: that of economy-wide network effects and the anti-competitive implications of platforms and bottlenecks. The dynamics of markets showing such effects challenge antitrust oversight, making it especially broad. Ayal discusses the dangers deriving from antitrust's over-inclusiveness, one being the antitrust agencies' lack of time and expertise to 'delve into details and assess market characteristics beyond the broad generalizations of micro-economic theory'. Like Maggiolino, Ayal also posits that such an expansion of antitrust oversight may be dangerous, if 'similar to any governmental regulation, antitrust has never been completely immune' to capture by private interests and to failure. The author's analysis, though, should not be taken to mean that antitrust oversight is harmful *per se*, or should always be avoided in favour of sector-specific regulation; rather, it points out inherent pitfalls and recommends context-specific examination.

In the third chapter of Part 1, Yane Svetiev adopts a teaching by Sparrow: that law enforcers in different domains are regulatory professionals and should 'glance sideways' at their regulatory peers. Dialogue between enforcers and regulators can thus benefit competition agencies, by enriching their enforcement activities with a 'broader range of "compliance-management and behaviour-modification techniques", as well as regulatory structures that could be adapted to controlling or remedying certain types of harms more effectively compared to habitual reliance on inherited mechanisms in various legal and regulatory fields'. Indeed, Svetiev contends that current practices in the implementation of competition law by the European Commission and national agencies already display important features of the 'problem-solving approach'. For instance, this can be seen in the evolution of certain standard mechanisms for implementing competition policy, such as the deliberative peer review of solutions to competition problems within the European Competition Network (ECN) and the growth of remedial enforcement at both the EU and the national level. Concerning the latter, Svetiev underlines how an increasing number of prohibition as well as commitment decisions at the EU level impose on undertakings positive obligations to act to achieve a specific objective similar to problem-solving regulatory decisions.

Commitment-based remedies in particular are not simply an expression of regulation, Svetiev contends, but they 'dissolve the distinction between regulation, law enforcement and market conduct', not least because they 'extend in some respects the autonomy of business conduct of market actors, while simultaneously limiting it'. Once again, the traditional tenet that sees regulation in liberalized markets as a temporary phenomenon, and overwhelming antitrust only acting *ex post*, is overturned. In turn, competition law should be seen as 'a species of economic regulation' that, by making use of the 'problem-solving approaches … either through deliberations with peer agencies or through dialogue with undertakings in remedial enforcement – may seek to dissolve the distinction between *ex ante* and *ex post* implementation'. The main advantages of such an extended variety of tools consists in the ability to quickly adjust implementation strategies and to increase the chances, although not the discretion, to adopt decisions that are more effective and more transparent.

Adopting a regulatory approach to competition law poses challenges not only from a substantive point of view, but also from an institutional one. The contributions in Part 2 discuss the institutional challenges faced by competition agencies when they exercise their advocacy powers. In their chapter, Tamar Indig and Michal Gal analyse market inquires by focusing on the powers competition authorities dispose of when they conduct market inquires. In the following chapter, Nicoletta Rangone focuses on a relatively new sort of power that competition authorities are entrusted with, namely, the power to control anti-competitive or restricting regulation, enabling them to take part in the 'competition assessment' performed by regulators.

Market inquiries allow for in-depth studies of 'market failures that do not necessarily result from competition law infringements'. By analysing the benefits and limitations of market inquiries in detail, Indig and Gal provide an insightful assessment of such powers. The theme is particularly relevant for the regulation/competition intersection because with market inquiries, competition agencies, much like regulators, may apprehend what the obstacles to competition are, 'whatever their roots' (be they market or regulatory failures), even if competition law was not infringed. Moreover, following investigations, competition authorities may, like regulators, adopt structural as well as behavioural remedies, but can also advise the legislature to change the regulatory framework. Market inquiries also allow competition authorities to proactively step into the market at a stage prior to the violation of competition rules; finally, decisions following market inquiries, like regulation, affect all participants in the market and not only those that are addressed by a competition law decision.

Should we then accept competition authorities performing market inquiries? Or should we limit them because they strengthen the 'regulatory approach'? Do they really alienate competition agencies from their 'core' (antitrust enforcement) business? And, as Indig and Gal put it, do they effectively make competition agencies 'move from eliminating anti-competitive conduct into the field of *increasing* competition'? Do market inquiries 'break the lines between *ex post* and *ex ante* regulation'? As a general rule, Indig and Gal suggest that market inquiries should be conducted by competition authorities only if there is a 'comparative advantage' (i.e., if sector-specific regulators cannot effectively perform a market inquiry). More specifically, the solution depends on whether a *supervisory* model of market inquiry is available instead of purely an *advisory* one. In the former case, competition authorities are allowed to adopt measures instead of just proposing them to politicians.

Drawing from the legal literature on coordination mechanisms in shared regulated spheres, Indig and Gal recommend coordination of both advisory and supervisory forms of market inquiries with sector regulation. According to them, such coordination provides some promise for 'overcoming concerns of dysfunctions'. However, while such coordination is very welcome in the 'market analysis phase' (i.e., the first part of the market inquiry), as it allows for cost savings regarding information-gathering and helps to overcome budgetary constraints, it could be problematic when policy conclusions and remedies ought to be drafted (i.e., in the final part of market inquiries), because of the risks of capture, blame-shifting or cross-vetoes in the regulatory arena.

Discussing the merits and pitfalls of the advisory and supervisory models, Indig and Gal conclude that the choice between the two strictly depends on the existence of specific conditions. A supervisory model should be preferred whenever the market inquiry only deals with competition issues and does not imply a balance of competition and non-competition considerations. Also, it should be preferred if 'the inquiry is focused on the efficacy of some form of regulation or its scope; where the inquiry is anticipated to provoke strong pressure groups and change is critical to avoid welfare-reducing stagnation; and where a high level of corruption and a low level of professionalism can be assumed in higher levels of government'. On the other hand, the advisory model should be preferred if 'it is important to gain the acceptance of other regulators, the government or the public for the recommendations; or where the decision is multifaceted and involves not only competition but other considerations such as security, environmental concerns, employment or strengthening the weaker parts of society'.

In her chapter, Nicoletta Rangone explores the question of how best to increase the effectiveness of competition advocacy activities in order to improve competition-friendly regulation, an objective that is shared by both regulators and competition authorities. In this framework, three tools are analysed and compared: the use of competition concepts in rule-making; traditional regulatory advocacy interventions (such as advice, market inquiries, etc.); and 'competition impact assessment'. The chapter concludes that both *ex ante* and *ex post* competition impact assessment might be considered a new advocacy tool and probably the most effective among those entrusted to regulators. Its effectiveness is related to the intrinsic characteristics of this tool, which is used before a formal rule-making is adopted; it is based on an economic analysis, and it always takes into consideration the option not to intervene through regulation. However, competition impact assessment's effectiveness depends on some procedural choices and upon the circumstance that it is not used in a formalistic or even ritualistic way. Rangone also underlines that the involvement of competition agencies in performing competition assessment might increase its effectiveness, even though some issues remain unsolved – one of the most important being how best to balance the role of regulators and competition agencies.

Part 3 is devoted to the general problems arising when competition law is enforced in regulated industries. As mentioned above, it was in the archetypical world of traditional antitrust (Chicago) versus traditional regulation that the notional distinction between the two categories was forged: competition law consists in *ex post* enforcement of rules, while regulation entails *ex ante* intervention prescribing positive obligations to act.

Mario Siragusa and Fausto Caronna picture a system where a 'regulatory drift' of competition law can be observed not only inside antitrust's substantive rules, but also in the law protecting consumers against unlawful unfair commercial practices (which, in the Italian system, is enforced by the same – competition – authority). It is the 'convergence' – not the melting nor assimilation – of the two tools, from a substantive though not institutional point of view, that makes regulation and competition law become 'complementary' in the eyes of EU Courts and the European Commission. In turn, 'complementarity' implies that sector-specific regulation and EU competition law can be enforced in parallel, in a cumulative way, as the *Deutsche Telekom* and *Telefónica* cases teach us. It follows that competition law must find a way to avoid jurisdictional conflicts and regulatory inconsistency. Indeed, the cumulative approach may lead to disproportionate outcomes, putting a heavy burden on the firms operating in regulated industries.

Moreover, divergent outcomes resulting from the application of EU competition rules and national regulation urgently need to be overcome. One possible solution, in Siragusa and Caronna's view, is the *lex specialis* principle as applied in the US (particularly in the *Trinko* and *Linkline* cases), whereby the availability of a regulatory remedy should pre-empt antitrust enforcement (it is the 'mutually exclusive' or antitrust immunity model). However, the authors caution that transplanting that principle into the EU legal system would not be an easy task, due to the principle of supremacy of EU competition rules over national regulation, which would impede any attempt to disregard the application of competition law. The *lex specialis* principle would only work in the exceptional cases where there is precise coincidence between allegations made by a competition authority and the regulated conduct; because, conversely, where regulation requires anticompetitive conduct, firms should not be fined. To conclude, Siragusa and Caronna suggest enhancing coordination between competition authorities and regulators, through the adoption of memoranda of understanding, combined with the publication of the results of that coordination.

In the second chapter of Part 3, Krystyna Kowalik-Bańczyk investigates whether a regulatory approach to competition law is applied by the Polish competition authority. Within the 'regulatory approach', she distinguishes those cases where the authority applies competition law to regulated sectors from cases where it acts 'as the regulator'. Theoretically, the author adheres to the traditional 'sequentiality' pattern, according to which – as already stressed by Siragusa and Caronna – regulation is in place in a given market only until competitive structures have emerged in the market. It follows that regulation is temporary and exceptional (although not special, as Siragusa and Caronna contend). However, Kowalik-Bańczyk admits that under specific circumstances (e.g., as regards services of general economic interest), competition law alone would probably not suffice and regulation should remain in place.

From a more practical perspective, Kowalik-Bańczyk finds cases of a 'regulatory approach' mainly in the authority's commitment decisions; and, more specifically, as regards commitment decisions in cases on local monopolies and services of general economic interest where infrastructures and essential facilities are at stake and where competition law enforcement coincides with sector-specific regulation (telecommunications, transport, energy, etc.). In these situations, the authority is engaged in 'opening markets to competition or surveying consumer welfare rather than just restoring competition'. Kowalik-Bańczyk contends that this approach is consistent with the very 'roots of the American idea of regulation as a part of the law created to guarantee the state's influence on "business affected with a public interest"'. In these specific circumstances, competition law intervention very much resembles regulation, in terms of the goals pursued and the tools employed.

However, Kowalik-Bańczyk recognizes that the overlap is only partial: firstly, regulation also pursues other public interests (e.g., the protection of the environment). Secondly, a distinction is to be made between the creation, establishment or development of competition on the one hand, and its protection on the other. Interestingly, though, the author does not attach excessive importance to this difference, as supporters of the traditional '*ex ante* versus *ex post* intervention dichotomy' advocate. By observing that the Polish authority enjoys the statutory powers of both 'developing' and 'protecting' competition, she argues that some proactive actions to introduce competition in a particular market is legitimate, at least in Poland.

Although legitimate, these doubled competences of the competition authority do present some pitfalls, which are only partially diminished by the self-restrictive attitude of the authority. Firstly, legal certainty for undertakings may be jeopardized because 'commitments' are 'individual and voluntary' and 'are based on the mere plausibility of infringement of competition'. Secondly, because regulation has wider goals, para-regulatory decisions by the authority risk providing only limited protection to the non-competitive goals. Thirdly, regulators may perceive their work as a failure anytime the competition authority proactively intervenes in the same market, while the competition authority might not necessarily possess the required expertise to perform these interventions. Instead of engaging in institutional competition, Kowalik-Bańczyk advises the competition authority and the sector-specific regulators to cooperate, thereby safeguarding their respective sphere of independence.

In the third chapter of Part 3, Alexandr Svetlicinii and Marco Botta analyse the patterns of enforcement of Article 102 TFEU and the respective national rules on dominance in network industries by the National Competition Authorities (NCAs) of 'new' and candidate EU Member States. Their comparative study takes into consideration nine jurisdictions, namely, Albania, Bosnia and Herzegovina, Bulgaria, Croatia, the Republic of Macedonia, Moldova, Montenegro, Romania and Serbia. In spite of the different stages of EU integration, these jurisdictions share a number of common features. While the EU Commission enforces Article 102 TFEU in the context of its pro-market liberalization agenda, NCAs of the selected jurisdictions enforce it in order to protect final consumers. In particular, while the EU Commission focuses its enforcement strategy in network industries on exclusionary conducts and adopts both structural and behavioural remedies via commitment decisions, the NCAs of the selected jurisdictions mainly impose fines to sanction unfair commercial practices of incumbent operators. They thus rely on Article 102 TFEU as a means to 'regulate' network industries: by sanctioning as 'excessive' and 'unfair' the tariffs and contractual conditions adopted by incumbent operators, they often *de facto* 'replace' NRAs' action.

The problematic relationship between regulation and competition law becomes especially visible when Svetlicinii and Botta analyse sectorial experiences. Here the Internet, broadband networks and information *per se* become the stage where the complex relationship is tested in its multi-faceted appearances.

The main question that Rolf H. Weber addresses in the first chapter of Part 4 relates to the relationship between competition law and regulation in the digital sector of the Internet. Firstly, the author claims that with regard to the Internet it is still inappropriate to speak of regulation, given that the debate over its governance is still open and the solutions proposed vary substantially (ranging from 'cyber-national-sovereignty', with states eager to submit Internet management to governmental control, to supporters of a privately organized regime allowing the free flow of information without national interference). Mostly, the Internet is still about self-regulation by international standard-setting organizations (SSOs), while the nation-states are trying to harness it and set some rules based on net neutrality principles, security needs and other public interest rationales.

The online world is therefore a land of conquest for both governments and companies, the latter trying to make profits out of it, while governments try to guarantee widest access or to limit its use, especially when security issues are at stake. Ironically, both online firms and states can adopt commercial strategies or establish rules that shape the market by changing its structure. So, for instance, as regards private actors, a question may arise whether online sellers can exploit lock-in effects caused by high costs for switching from one platform to another and therefore foreclose the market for competing platforms. In the search engine market (Yahoo! and Google), issues of multi-sided markets, new gatekeepers and bottlenecks arise (or of multi-homing in the social networks market), putting at the forefront the question of whether long established standards of antitrust liability are still applicable. In a still unstable and changing world, no one-fits-all solution is emerging: thus, the EU is taking a harder line compared to the US competition authorities (as demonstrated by the diverging results of the Google investigations of 2010 and 2011). In Weber's view, the reason for such divergence resides in Google's super-dominant position (with 90 per cent in the search engine market), which exists in the EU and not in the US (70 per cent).

While the advertising market has not changed due to the advent of the Internet, the same is not true for social platform markets, where competitors struggle 'for user attention', and not just their wallet. In such markets, Weber contends, Schumpeterian competition prevails, with one giant replacing the other. Network effects (that create high entry barriers) and market concentration, however, tend to shape the web world. Should competition law or regulation intervene? In Weber's view regulation is not legitimate and should therefore be excluded, provided that barriers to entry 'are not insurmountable nor non-transitory' and because a mix of elements should be reflected in the product and/or service definition (such as data portability or the value of personal data, which seems to be increasing).

The author supports the notion that general competition law should normally apply, as the online world does not present any new forms of anticompetitive behaviour. However, he cautions that some adjustments are welcome with regard to the definition of the relevant product market and the assessment of market power. For instance, he stresses that the time dimension should be given special emphasis, since incumbents can more quickly be replaced in the online world.

In the second chapter of Part 4, Toshiaki Takigawa analyses the application of competition law in innovation-intensive industries, and especially as regards broadband networks, products and services (i.e., mobile devices and services). His first thesis is that, when dealing with innovation-intensive industries, competition law and competition law enforcement should adapt to the specificities of such markets. This applies, for instance, to the definition of market power, since market shares only provide a static picture, while these markets are characterized by dynamic competition. It follows that competition agencies need to put more emphasis on securing incentives to innovate than on controlling temporary pricing power. Takigawa mainly analyses unilateral conduct in broadband markets and advises antitrust agencies to apply a cautious approach to interventions against unilateral conduct. Agencies should avoid pursuing short-term static efficiency gains at the cost of diminishing dynamic efficiency. Yet he strongly argues that competition law should safeguard competitive pressure from potential market entry, as this incentivizes incumbents to innovate. Therefore, competition agencies should intervene in the market foreclosure strategies of dominant companies that have the potential of blocking market entry.

After an analysis of the evolution of US regulation of broadband access, moving from a 'common carrier' principle (whereby network operators are subject to interconnection and unbundling duties, no matter whether dominant or not) to 'regulatory forbearance' of 2005 (relaxing the afore-cited duties in the name of dynamic efficiency), Takigawa provides insights on the Japanese system. Here the telecoms regulator enforces both interconnection obligations and unbundling duties (as in the US) regarding both narrow and broadband networks operators. Both duties can be exempted, as in the US system, by the regulatory agency upon request from the carriers, and based on considerations of efficiency gains. The main difference resides in the statutory duty of the regulatory agency to establish that a network operator is dominant any time a 50 per cent market share is attained or exceeded.

On the intersection between regulation and competition law, Takigawa strongly favours reliance on competition law rules to govern innovation-intensive broadband markets. The main arguments supporting this position are: firstly, the traditional view about competition law as an *ex post* intervention, as opposed to regulation that steps in *ex ante*, thus putting an excessive burden on individual autonomy; secondly, the argument that competition authorities are less prone to capture than regulators, since they apply the law across all sectors of the economy; and thirdly, the argument that these markets no longer exhibit the characteristics of a natural monopoly and that, by now, competitive structures have emerged in these markets.

The chapter continues with a thorough review of the leading cases in the US and Japan regarding unilateral conduct. Thereby, Takigawa highlights three policy implications regarding the enforcement of competition law in innovation-intensive industries: firstly, competition authorities are advised to use the requirement of market power 'as a safeguard against overregulation of unilateral (exclusionary) conduct'; secondly, they need to base their examination of a refusal to deal (or a price squeeze) regarding access to a broadband network on a standard that balances innovation incentives against chances of new entries; and thirdly, telecom regulators should be allowed to impose behavioural remedies for antitrust violations, provided that such remedies lead to administrative efficiency and that the same regulatory standard is shared between the competition authority and the telecoms regulator. In fact, the author recommends that, if regulatory standards differ, the competition law standard should prevail. However, as competition spreads across the industry, the competition authority should become the sole regulator of competition in the telecoms sector.

In the third chapter of Part 4, Fabiana Di Porto focuses on another set of cross-cutting issues: namely, the relationship between abuses of dominance and information sharing as it arises from EU, Italian and US case-law. Firstly, she explains how informational monopolists (or super-dominant firms) may infringe competition law by three different forms of 'informational abuses': (i) through actual or constructive refusals to exchange information; (ii) through the misuse of information provided to public regulators performing some pro-competitive regulatory procedures; and (iii) through collusion to provide misleading information (outside a regulatory procedure). Secondly, she points out that many cases on Article 102 TFEU (or national unilateral conduct rules in other jurisdictions) are enforced by imposing complex behavioural remedies that mandate an exchange of information. Such behavioural remedies resemble much traditional regulation, as regards the rationale of intervention, the institutional resources employed (e.g., they require continuous monitoring of commitments, strong sectorial expertise and dedicated resources) and the powers exercised. As a consequence, she calls them 'para-regulatory' remedies, thereby distinguishing them from pure, traditional regulatory interventions. In particular, these para-regulatory remedies can conflict not only with already existing information-based regulation, but also with the traditional suspicious approach that competition law applies when it comes to transparency and the enforcement of Article 101 TFEU on restrictive agreements.

Finally, Part 5 of this book discusses the problematic relationship between competition and intellectual property. Both chapters in this part question whether competition law could be seen as a regulatory tool, namely, as regards strategic patent filings and standard setting. Emanuela Arezzo starts her analysis by noting that, in contrast to restrictive agreements, no further guidance is provided as to how EU competition law is to be applied to mergers and unilateral conduct involving intellectual property rights. According to her, especially in the field of unilateral conduct, there is a need for a common core of guiding principles concerning the intersection of competition law and IP, considering not only that 'the number of abusive practices involving the use of IPRs has recently increased, but also that new kinds of practices have emerged, posing increasingly complex issues to analyse'. Among such new practices, Arezzo then focuses on so-called 'strategic patent filings', whereby dominant firms try to keep competitors out of the market by applying for patents, thereby achieving an artificial extension of market dominance based on IP protection. Cases of this kind particularly originate from the pharmaceutical sector. The assessment of these cases is particularly complex because, on the one hand, the act of strategic patenting relates to behaviour which may actually be legal under patent law. In addition, the question is whether even the very acquisition of an intellectual property right – in contrast to its use – can be considered an abuse of market dominance. Arezzo sets the scene by clarifying the relationship between market power and IPRs, and then analyses the potential anti-competitive effect of strategic patent filings. She then describes the interplay between competition law and IP law by differentiating between the 'existence' and the 'exercise' of an IPR and by providing a thorough analysis of the pertinent EU and Italian case-law (*AstraZeneca* and *Ratiopharm v. Pfizer*). Arezzo welcomes the intervention of competition law enforcers – as 'IP watchdogs' – in IP-related markets, which is needed to 'constrain the expansionist trend recently experienced by IP legislation and courts worldwide'. However, she also argues that competition law intervention in IP-related cases should remain balanced and should avoid incurring the risk of diminishing innovation. Especially strategic-patenting cases must be analysed much more thoroughly than traditional refusal-to-deal cases or, in general, cases where dominance does not arise from mere IP ownership but rather from a combination of the IP right and a complex set of market factors such as network effects. When such market-related 'plus-factors' are absent and dominance exceptionally arises only from IP ownership, the application of competition law will be in need of very careful consideration of the specific circumstances of the case. Intervention should only take place in the exceptional case where there is proof that the IP system has been misused for the exclusive purpose of restricting competition with no real consumer benefits in terms of innovation.

In the second chapter of Part 5, Björn Lundqvist looks at the relationship between competition law and the setting of technological standards by standard-setting organizations (SSOs). According to him, 'standard-setting collaborations' and 'unilateral conduct under standards' pose new challenges to competition agencies and regulators. Comparing the practice in the EU and the US regarding SSOs, Lundqvist claims that competition law should scrutinize more thoroughly the standard-setting procedures and the SSOs' organizational rules.

Lundqvist is well aware that using competition law to control standard-setting processes and rules and the activity of SSOs would mean, especially in the US system, setting an unusual rule of primacy of competition rules over regulation. However, he also argues that, in principle, competition law should not scrutinize standards *per se* unless they pose an anticompetitive harm by themselves. So, for instance, for the sake of legal certainty and clear guidance, safe harbours should be identified for those standard-setting collaborations whose anticompetitive effects are limited; competition law immunities, in both the EU and the US, should be accepted for those SSOs that comply with sound principles of good governance and transparency.

For the standard-setting world, and following most prominent case-law, Lundqvist supports the idea that competition law can intervene if the market is able to support competing standards and if the SSO has been misused in the standard-selection phase, or the SSO's governance rules have been gamed, provided that that such conduct has the potential to exclude competitors.

This also means that competition law should not intervene where an SSO sets an 'infrastructure standard' or an 'interoperability standard' under the condition that such markets can only hold one standard. Precisely in these cases, however, Lundqvist explains the major role competition law has to play in guaranteeing that individual members of SSOs respect the rules set by the SSO. In sum, Lundqvist suggests that competition agencies should oblige SSOs, as bodies of private self-regulation, to design their organizations and procedures in a competition-compliant manner. Thereby, competition agencies obviously act as regulators of SSOs.

This book would not have been possible without the conference held at University of Salento, Lecce. Therefore, the editors would like to thank the Rector, Professor Domenico Laforgia and Professor Alessandra Chirco, Director of the Department of Economic Sciences of the University of Salento; the City of Lecce, the Istituto di Studi Giuridici 'Michele De Petro' of Lecce, Monte Paschi di Siena and Hart Publishing as sponsors of the conference. They all recognized the potential of the Conference and provided a unique opportunity to bring together academics from different nations and universities. We are also grateful to the chairs of the sessions of the ASCOLA conference, who made the debate so lively and interesting: Joël Monéger, Wolfgang Kerber, Dimitris Tzouganatos and Paul Nihoul. As regards the burden of organizing the conference, the editors would also like to thank, from the University of Salento, Professors Stefano Adamo, former Dean of the Faculty of Economics, and Marialuisa Zuppetta. Special thanks also go to Anna Maria Casilli, Anna Maria Pezzuto, Anna Maria Muci, Donato Giannuzzi and Marcello Sozzo for their valuable organizational support. A special thanks goes also to Rupprecht Podszun, treasurer of ASCOLA, for always being available for solving financial issues.

Some other people were involved in the preparation of this book to whom the editors are greatly indebted. The editing of the book took place at the Max Planck Institute for Innovation and Competition in Munich, where Delia Zirilli collected the contributions and brought them into a uniform style. Most important and time consuming was the work done by Allison Felmy. She reviewed all the contributions by the non-native speakers from a linguistic point of view. Last but not least, the editors are very grateful to Edward Elgar Publishing and its staff, including, in particular, John Paul McDonald, who strongly supported the book with a lot of patience throughout the time of its coming into existence.

February 2015
Fabiana Di Porto
Josef Drexl

Abbreviations

ADSL	Asymmetric Digital Subscriber Line
AGCM	Autorità Garante della Concorrenza e del Mercato (Italian competition authority)
AGCOM	Autorità per le Garanzie nelle Communicazioni (Italian communications regulatory authority)
Am. Econ. Rev.	American Economic Review
Am. Soc. Rev.	American Sociological Review
Antitrust Bull.	Antitrust Bulletin
Antitrust L.J.	Antitrust Law Journal
APCC	Act on Protection of Competition and Consumers (Poland)
Bell J. Econ. & Manag. Sci.	Bell Journal of Economics and Management Science
Berkeley Tech. L.J.	Berkeley Technology Law Journal
B&H	Bosnia and Herzegovina
Boston College L. Rev.	Boston College Law Review
Brit. J. Crim.	British Journal of Criminology
Bus. L. Int'l	Business Law International
CA	competition authority
Cal. L. Rev.	California Law Review
CAO	Civil Aviation Office (Poland)
Cardozo L. Rev.	Cardozo Law Review
CC	Competition Commission (UK)
C.D. Cal.	US District Court, Central District of California
CFR	Code of Federal Regulations (US)
Cir.	US Court of Appeals, Circuit Court
CJEU	Court of Justice of the European Union
C.M.L.R.	Common Market Law Reports
C.M.L. Rev.	Common Market Law Review
Colum. Bus. L. Rev.	Columbia Business Law Review
Colum. J. L. & Arts	Columbia Journal of Law and the Arts
Colum. L. Rev.	Columbia Law Review

Comp. L. Rev.	Competition Law Review
Comp. Pol.	Comparative Politics
Comp. Pol. Int'l	Competition Policy International
Comp. Pol. Newsletter	Competition Policy Newsletter
Comp. & Reg. Netw. Ind.	Competition and Regulation in Network Industries
Computer L. Rev. Int'l	Computer Law Review International
CONSOB	Commissione Nazionale per le Società e la Borsa (Italian Stock Market Authority)
Cornell L. Rev.	Cornell Law Review
COVIP	Commissione di Vigilanza sui Fondi Pensione (Italian authority for the control of pension funds)
Crim. & Pub. Pol'y	Criminology and Public Policy
Current Leg. Probs.	Current Legal Problems
D. D.C.	US District Court of the District of Columbia
DoJ	US Department of Justice
Duke L. CiCLOPs	Duke Law Center for International and Comparative Law Occasional Papers
Duke L.J.	Duke Law Journal
EC	European Community; (former) European Community Treaty (Amsterdam version)
E.C.L.R.	European Competition Law Review
ECN	European Competition Network
Econ. J.	Economic Journal
Econ. & Pol.	Economics and Politics
Econ. Pol'y	Economic Policy
Econ. Thought	Economic Thought
ECR	European Court Reports
EEC	European Economic Community
ERRA	Enterprise and Regulatory Reform Act (UK)
EPC	European Patent Convention
EPO	European Patent Office
EPO OJ	Official Journal of the European Patent Office
ERO	Energy Regulation Office (Poland)
ETSI	European Telecommunications Standards Institute
EU	European Union
Eur. Comp. J.	European Competition Journal
Eur. Energy & Environ. L. Rev.	European Energy and Environmental Law Review
Eur. L.J.	European Law Journal

Eur. L. Rev.	European Law Review
Eur. Pub. L.	European Public Law
Eur. Rev. Priv. L.	European Review of Private Law
F.2d	Federal Reporter, 2nd Series
FCC	Federal Communications Commission (US)
F.C.C.R.	Federal Communications Commission Record (US)
Fed. Comm. L.J.	Federal Communications Law Journal
Fla. L. Rev.	Florida Law Review
Fordham Int'l L.J.	Fordham International Law Journal
Fordham L. Rev.	Fordham Law Review
FRAND	fair, reasonable and non-discriminatory
F. Suppl.	Federal Supplement
FTC	Federal Trade Commission (US)
GC	General Court (EU)
Geo. L.J.	Georgetown Law Journal
George Mason L. Rev.	George Mason Law Review
Harv. J. L. & Pub. Pol.	Harvard Journal of Law and Public Policy
Harv. J. L. & Tech.	Harvard Journal of Law and Technology
Harv. L. Rev.	Harvard Law Review
Hastings L.J.	Hastings Law Journal
Hofstra L. Rev.	Hofstra Law Review
Houston L. Rev.	Houston Law Review
ICANN	Internet Corporation for Assigned Names and Numbers
ICA	Italian Competition Authority
ICN	International Competition Network
ICRA	Italian Communications Regulatory Authority
IEC	International Electronic Commission
Ind. L.J.	Indiana Law Journal
Intereconomics – Rev. Eur. Econ. Pol.	Intereconomics – Review of European Economic Policy
Int'l Econ. & Econ. Pol.	International Economics and Economic Policy
Int'l. J. Accounting	International Journal of Accounting
Int'l J. Ind. Org.	International Journal of Industrial Organization
Int'l Rev. IP & Comp. L.	International Review of Intellectual Property and Competition Law
Int'l Travel L.J.	International Travel Law Journal
IO	information obligations
Iowa L. Rev.	Iowa Law Review

IP	intellectual property
IPR	intellectual property right
ISO	International Organization for Standardization
IT & Soc.	IT and Society
Ital. J. Pub. L.	Italian Journal of Public Law
ITRs	International Telecommunications Regulations
ITU	International Telecommunications Union
IVASS	Istituto per la vigilanza sulle assicurazioni (Italian Insurances Surveillance Authority)
J. Antitrust Enf.	Journal of Antitrust Enforcement
J. Comm. Mark. Stud.	Journal of Common Market Studies
J. Comp. L. & Econ.	Journal of Competition Law and Economics
J. Corp. L.	Journal of Corporation Law
J. Corp. L. Stud.	Journal of Corporate Law Studies
J. Econ. & Manag. Strat.	Journal of Economics and Management Strategy
J. Econ. Persp.	Journal of Economic Perspectives
J. Eur. Comp. L. & Prac.	Journal of European Competition Law and Practice
J. Eur. Econ. Ass.	Journal of the European Economics Association
J. Eur. Pub. Pol'y	Journal of European Public Policy
J. Intel. Prop., Inf. Tech. & Elec. Comm. L.	Journal of Intellectual Property, Information Technology and Electronic Commerce Law
J. Int'l Econ. L.	Journal of International Economic Law
J. L. & Econ.	Journal of Law and Economics
J. Leg. Stud.	Journal of Legal Studies
J. Netw. Ind.	Journal of Network Industries
J. Phil.	Journal of Philosophy
J. Pol. Anal. & Manag.	Journal of Political Analysis and Management
J. Pol. Econ.	Journal of Political Economy
J. Pub. Pol.	Journal of Public Policy
J. Reg. Econ.	Journal of Regulatory Economics
J. Socio-Econ.	Journal of Socio-Economics
J. Telecomm. & High Tech. L.	Journal on Telecommunications and High Technology Law
JFTC	Japan Fair Trade Commission
John Marshall J. Computer & Inf. L.	John Marshall Journal of Computer and Information Law
JOP	Journal of Politics
JRC	Joint Research Centre (EU)
L. & Contemp. Probs.	Law and Contemporary Problems

L. & Pol.	Law and Policy
L. & Soc. Rev.	Law and Society Review
Loy. U. Chi. L.J.	Loyola University of Chicago Law Journal
Maastricht J. Eur. & Comp. L.	Maastricht Journal of European and Comparative Law
Medit. Comp. Bull.	Mediterranean Competition Bulletin
MI	market inquiry
MIC	Ministry of Internal Affairs and Communications (Japan)
Mich. L. Rev.	Michigan Law Review
Mich. Telecomm. Tech. L. Rev.	Michigan Telecommunications and Technology Law Review
MIR	market investigation reference (UK)
MoC	memorandum of cooperation
Mod. L. Rev.	Modern Law Review
NCAs	national competition authorities
N.C. J. L. & Tech.	North Carolina Journal of Law and Technology
N.C. L. Rev.	North Carolina Law Review
N.D. Cal.	US District Court, Northern District of California
NMa	Nederlandse Mededingingsautoriteit (Dutch competition authority)
NRAs	national regulatory authorities
Nw. J. Int'l L. & Bus.	Northwestern Journal of International Law and Business
Nw. U. L. Rev.	Northwestern University Law Review
N.Y. L.J.	New York Law Journal
N.Y. L. School L. Rev.	New York Law School Law Review
N.Y.U. L. Rev.	New York University Law Review
OEC	Office of Electronic Communications (Poland)
OECD	Organization of Economic Cooperation and Development
OFT	Office of Fair Trading (UK)
OJ C	Official Journal Part C (European Union)
OJ L	Official Journal Part L (European Union)
OMB-OIRA	Office of Management and Budget-Office of Information and Regulatory Affairs (US)
OPCC	Office of Protection of Competition and Consumers (Polish competition authority)
PAEs	patent assertion entities
Phil. & Pub. Aff.	Philosophy and Public Affairs

P.L.	Public Law (US)
PMNE	price-mediated network effects
Pol. Options	Policy Options
Pub. Admin.	Public Administration
Pub. Admin. Rev.	Public Administration Review
Pub. L.	Public Law
Qu. J. Econ.	Quarterly Journal of Economics
RAND J. Econ.	RAND Journal of Economics
R&D	research and development
Reg. & Gov.	Regulation and Governance
Res. Pol'y	Research Policy
Rev. Econ. Stud.	Review of Economic Studies
Rev. Mod. Phys.	Reviews of Modern Physics
Rev. Netw. Econ.	Review of Network Economics
RIA	regulatory impact assessment
Riv. Dir. Ind.	Rivista di Diritto Industriale
Riv. Ital. Dir. Pub. Com.	Rivista Italiana di Diritto Pubblico Comunitario
RTO	Railway Transport Office (Poland)
SAC	Supreme Administrative Court (Bulgaria)
San Diego L. Rev.	San Diego Law Review
S. Cal. L. Rev.	Southern California Law Review
SCM	standard cost model
S. Ct.	Supreme Court Reporter
SDO	standard development organization
SEPs	standard-essential patents
SME	small and medium-sized enterprise
SPC	supplementary protection certificate
SSNIP	small but significant and non-transitory increase in price
SSO	standard-setting organisation
Stan. L. Rev.	Stanford Law Review
St. John's J. Leg. Comm.	St. John's Journal of Legal Commentary
Sw. J. L. & Trade in the Americas	Southwestern Journal of Law and Trade in the Americas
TAR	Tribunale Amministrativo Regionale (Regional Administrative Court; Italy)
TBT Agreement	Agreement on Technical Barriers to Trade
Telecom. Pol.	Telecommunications Policy
Tex. L. Rev.	Texas Law Review

TFEU	Treaty on the Functioning of the European Union
TRIPS	Agreement on Trade-Related Aspects of Intellectual Property
TUF	Testo unico delle disposizioni in materia di intermediazione finanziaria (Italian Law on Financial Services)
U. Chi. L. Rev.	University of Chicago Law Review
UC Irvine L. Rev.	University of California Irvine Law Review
UCPs	unfair commercial practices
UCPD	Unfair Commercial Practices Directive (EU)
UEAPME	European Association of Craft, Small and Medium-Sized Enterprises
U. Ill. L. Rev.	University of Illinois Law Review
U. Pa. L. Rev.	University of Pennsylvania Law Review
U.S.	United States
U.S.C.	United States Code
Utah L. Rev.	Utah Law Review
Va. L. Rev.	Virginia Law Review
Vanderbilt J. Tansnat'l L.	Vanderbilt Journal of Transnational Law
Vanderbilt L. Rev.	Vanderbilt Law Review
VOIP	Voice Over Internet Protocol
Wash. & Lee L. Rev.	Washington and Lee Law Review
Wash. U. L. Rev.	Washington University Law Review
WCIT	World Conference on International Telecommunications
West Eur. Pol.	West European Politics
William & Mary L. Rev.	William and Mary Law Review
World Comp.	World Competition
WTO	World Trade Organization
Yale L.J.	Yale Law Journal
Yale J. Reg.	Yale Journal on Regulation
Yearbook Antitrust & Reg. Stud.	Yearbook of Antitrust and Regulatory Studies Yearbook of Antitrust and Regulatory Studies
Yearbook Eur. L.	Yearbook on European Law
ZWeR – J. Comp. L.	Zeitschrift für Wettbewerbsrecht – Journal of Competition Law

PART 1

Foundations of the complex relationship of competition law and regulation

1. The regulatory breakthrough of competition law: definitions and worries

Mariateresa Maggiolino

1. INTRODUCTION

Today, many antitrust scholars note the great change that competition law is undergoing. Some criticize the law's resemblance to economic regulation; others register with alarm its new regulatory nature.[1] Yet, there is room to argue that the terms 'competition law' and 'economic regulation' are simple labels that relate to wavering ideals and a dynamic maze of diverse and overlapping phenomena (Section 2). Thus, to maintain that current competition law is taking the shape of a piece of economic regulation and support criticism of this transformation, we should address at least three questions. We should: (i) refer to some specific forms of economic regulation and competition law, so as to identify the many contours along which they can overlap or differentiate (Section 3); (ii) verify whether and how this multi-dimensional metamorphosis is taking hold in competition law (Section 4); and (iii) indicate what competition law loses – or is assumed to lose – because of the regulatory makeover it is purportedly undergoing (Section 5).

The chapter intends to accomplish these three goals without neglecting some critical thoughts about the idea that, unlike economic regulation, competition law is (or could be) a matter of pure (economic) technique, totally detached from value choices and political decisions (Section 6).

[1] E.g. P. Areeda and H. Hovenkamp, *Antitrust Law: An Analysis of Antitrust Principles and Their Application* (Aspen Publ.: 3rd edn 2008) 770 et seq., and V. Korah, 'The Interface between Intellectual Property and Antitrust: The European Experience' (2002) 69 *Antitrust L.J.* 801, 832.

2. ECONOMIC REGULATION AND COMPETITION LAW – TWO WIDE-RANGING NOTIONS

The mere idea that current competition law is taking the shape of a piece of economic regulation presupposes at least one insight: that competition law and economic regulation may be conceptualized as two separate phenomena that approach or move away from each other. However, as the following paragraphs show, since economic regulation is a multiform experience and competition law has no specific shape, there is not any *a priori* division between the two.

2.1 Economic Regulation as a Cubist Painting

Only a cubist rendition would be capable of showing on a single plane what current economic regulation is – a *kaleidoscopic* object whose many facets result from more than thirty years of continuous theoretical and practical changes.

Since the late 1970s, when industrialized states embarked upon the so-called neoliberal programme, the experience of economic regulation that already characterized western states has been undergoing a surprising process of expansion and transformation[2] that today is still in progress at national and international levels.[3] While privatizing the assets

---

[2] As a matter of practice, no form of substantial deregulation matched the privatization tide and the liberalization bandwagon that took the scene from the 1980s onwards. Rather, the years of neoliberalism witnessed a real process of 're-regulation' that involved states, markets and societies. See, e.g., I. Ayres and J. Braithwaite, *Responsive Regulation: Transcending the Deregulation Debate* (Oxford University Press 1992) 7. After all, scholars talk about the neoliberal 'programme' just in order to remark how the political practice significantly departed from the theoretical model that neoliberalism supported. For analogous opinions see S.K. Vogel, *Free Markets, More Rules: Regulatory Reform in Advanced Industrial Countries* (Cornell University Press 1996) and D. Levi-Faur and J. Jordana, 'The Rise of Regulatory Capitalism: The Global Diffusion of A New Order' (2005) 598 *The Annals of The American Academy of Political and Social Sciences* 12.

[3] See, for instance, J. Braithwaite and P. Drahos, *Global Business Regulation* (Cambridge University Press 2000) 604, who argue that, although every single state exhibits specific regulatory courses and experiences, it would be a mistake to lose sight of the fact that many of the fundamentals of regulation are global. In addition, this homologation wave took place because, outside Europe and the United States, middle-sized countries are 'rule-takers' and because globalization has made states' territorial boundaries no longer coincide with the

owned by key industries, liberalizing the provision of many goods and services and loosening their grip on tariffs, quotas, rates and market entrance, industrialized states repeatedly adopt a host of regulatory techniques to maintain a sort of arm's length oversight over certain activities and industries, such as transport and infrastructure; power, gas, water and postal services; communication and broadcasting; finance, pollution, public health, labour safety and product quality.[4] In other words, while questioning the reasons justifying and explaining the very existence of regulation (economic regulation included),[5] western countries did experience fifty years of 'regulatory capitalism' – they did become 'regulatory states and societies',[6] willing to control the risks and

---

limits of political authority over economy and society. In this regard, see S. Strange, *The Retreat of the State: The Diffusion of Power in the World Economy* (Cambridge University Press 1996).

[4] E.g. R. Baldwin, M. Cave and M. Lodge, 'Introduction: Regulation – The Field and the Developing Agenda' in R. Baldwin, M. Cave, M. Lodge (eds), *The Oxford Handbook of Regulation* (Oxford University Press 2010) 3, 7.

[5] In brief, neoliberalism considered the market as the best tool to promote both private freedom and economic productivity. As a consequence, it affirmed the need to liberate individual entrepreneurial skills within an institutional framework characterized by, on the one hand, strong private property rights and free trade and, on the other hand, a minimum level of government actionism. In other words, neoliberalism held that governments should never interfere with the private order except in cases when, absent the market, they had to create property rights and distribute legal entitlements – as, for example, in areas such as water, education, health care, social security or environmental pollution. Neoliberalism held that the situation is different when markets already exist. Here any state intervention would cause two kinds of problems, at least: first, it would risk reducing efficiency, productivity and innovation, by harming the self-regulating mechanism that underpins markets; second, unless consistent with the Pareto criterion, state intervention would also collide with individuals' self-determination. Therefore, neoliberalism wanted sectors formerly run or regulated by the state to be turned over to the private sphere, freed from any interference, and left to competition. See, e.g., D. Harvey, *A Brief History of Neoliberalism* (Oxford University Press 2005); H. Overbeek and B. van Apeldoorn (eds), *Neoliberalism in Crisis* (Palgrave Macmillan 2012); H. Macartney, *Variegated Neoliberalism: EU Varieties of Capitalism and International Political Economy* (Routledge 2011); and G. Duménil and D. Lévy, *The Crisis of Neoliberalism* (Harvard University Press 2011).

[6] In essence, the concepts of 'regulatory capitalism', 'regulatory state', and 'regulatory society' are analytical constructs seeking to catch the changes which occurred throughout the 1980s and 1990s. Notably, the first two focus, respectively, on the *economic* and *institutional* facets of the displacing process that

hazards that economic activities entail,[7] by implementing a new division of labour within the diverse components of the state and between the state and the society.[8]

For instance, without totally forgetting direct actions and design solutions,[9] and following the motto 'steering is better than rowing',[10] industrialized countries almost totally abandoned red-light prohibitions,

---

brought modern capitalist democracies away from public ownership and centralized planning, towards a new array of mechanisms of governance, steering and facilitation under the control of independent authorities. See, e.g., G. Majone, 'The Rise of the Regulatory State in Western Europe' (1994) 17 *West Eur. Pol.* 77; D Wincott, 'European Political Development, Regulatory Governance, and the European Social Model: The Challenge of Substantive Legitimacy' (2006) 12 *Eur. L.J.* 743, 750–51; J. Braithwaite, *Regulatory Capitalism. How it Works, Ideas for Making it Work Better* (Edward Elgar Publishing 2009) vii–viii; K. Yeung, 'The Regulatory State', in R. Baldwin, M. Cave and M. Lodge (eds), *The Oxford Handbook of Regulation* (Oxford University Press 2010) 64. The idea of the regulatory society, instead, is less focused on the relationship between states and citizens, but looks at co-coordinating, influencing and balancing interactions between actors and systems, and at the process of creating new patterns of interaction which enable social actors and systems to organize themselves. See, e.g., J. Black, 'Decentring Regulation: Understanding the Role of Regulation and Self-Regulation in a "Post-Regulatory" World' (2001) 54 *Current Leg. Probs.* 103.

[7] M.K. Sparrow, *The Regulatory Craft* (Brookings Institution Press 2000); R. Baldwin and J. Black, 'Really Responsive Regulation' (2001) 71 *Mod. L. Rev.* 59 (2001); R.H. Thaler and C.R. Sunstein, *Nudge* (Yale University Press 2008); and C. Hood, H. Rothstein and R. Baldwin, *The Government of Risk, Understanding Risk Regulation Schemes* (Oxford University Press 2001) 3 and 29.

[8] J. Braithwaite, 'The New Regulatory State and the Transformation of Criminology' (2000) 40 *Brit. J. Crim.* 222, 225; M. Power, *Organized Uncertainty: Designing a World of Risk Management* (Oxford University Press 2007) 188; C. Hood, O. James and C. Scott, 'Regulation of Government: Has It Increased, Is It Increasing, Should It Be Diminished?' (1999) 78 *Pub. Admin.* 283; and M. Moran, *The British Regulatory State: High Modernism and Hyper Innovation* (Oxford University Press 2003) 9–10.

[9] 'Direct actions' take shape when governments use their public resources to create what is materially necessary (such as premises or infrastructures) for the achievement of specific results. 'Design solutions', on the other hand, take place when governments intervene in market structure in order to prevent a specific mischief from arising.

[10] E.g. D. Osborne and T. Gaebler, *Reinventing Government: How the Entrepreneurial Spirit is Transforming the Public Sector* (Addison-Wesley Publishing Company 1992) 25.

command and control regulations[11] for green-light orders,[12] tax/subsidy and right/liability schemes,[13] disclosure regimes,[14] and some diverse combinations thereof.[15] Via varied forms of self-regulation,[16] western

---

[11] Command and control regimes take form when governments impose prohibitions and obligations by employing legal rules backed by administrative enforcement and penal sanctions.

[12] E.g. C. Harlow and R. Rawlings, *Law and Administration* (Cambridge University Press 2009).

[13] By and large, 'tax/subsidy, and right/liability schemes' pivot around the same idea: that governments may use different tools to affect the cost-benefit analysis that economic agents are assumed to develop for deciding whether to undertake a specific detrimental or beneficial behaviour. Within the 'tax/subsidy schemes' governments affect the cost-benefit analysis by allocating expenses and gains. Therefore, they impose negative taxes so as to discourage detrimental activities, or deploy grants, subsidies, forms of public compensation and social insurance to encourage beneficial practices. In contrast, within a 'right/liability scheme' governments affect the cost-benefit analysis by allocating property rights and contracts, or by designing liability, whereby different patterns of rules originate, respectively: either fluxes of expenses or fluxes of gains.

[14] 'Disclosure regulations' usually prohibit the supply of false or misleading information and require mandatory disclosure of some pieces of information towards consumers, public agencies or governmental officials. Systematic mechanisms for surveillance, public scrutiny and accountability, as well as codes of conduct, management systems, corporate reporting systems and third-party certification schemes, have thus become very popular. Today, indeed, 'big corporations are just as subject to red tape and excessive internal regulation as they are to external regulation'. See D. Levi-Faur and J. Jordana (n. 2 above) 21. In other words, re-regulation also witnessed a potent infiltration of public law values, like transparency, into the private ordering. See J. Freeman, 'Extending Public Law Norms Through Privatization' (2003) 116 *Harv. L. Rev.* 1285.

[15] The so-called 'regulation by contract' could be a good example of that. Suppose that the state wants to guarantee a minimum wage. As with direct actions, government departments or agencies can use their wealth and spending powers to conclude contracts only with firms that will pay their employees the required minimum wage. In this way, the state can impose a regulatory standard across all firms contracting with it without employing a specific command, but by distributing legal entitlements (in this case, the contract), as the right/liability scheme would require.

[16] Self-regulation may appear to lack any state involvement, but in reality: (i) it can be adopted in pursuit of public policy tasks; (ii) its process may be constrained by statutory rules or within authorization systems and other mechanisms of participation or accountability; and (iii) its rules may enjoy full legal force even when enacted by self-regulators. The latter, then, may address all the economic agents operating in a given industry, or just those that take part in the self-regulatory process; furthermore, they may discharge several tasks, from

states focused less on mere deterrent and top-down approaches in favour of more persuasive and bottom-up strategies.[17] Having acknowledged that citizens perceived their ministerial apparatuses as arbitrary and technocratic, they delegated regulatory functions not only to independent authorities – whose transparency and social accountability were however to be improved[18] via meta-regulation[19] – but also to third-party non-governmental bodies such as corporations' gatekeepers, industrial associations or international networks of experts.[20] In sum, during half a

---

the promulgation of rules, to the enforcement of these on the ground, to the monitoring of the whole regulatory process. For instance, Braithwaite (n. 8 above) 231 argues that the proliferation of new self-regulatory techniques is a consequence of the development of more complex and globalized economies.

[17] Indeed, according to the so-called 'responsive regulation' and 'smart regulation' models, governments should pursue firms' compliance through persuasion. For this purpose, self-regulation and regulations involving third entities, like professional bodies and industry associations, should be considered as the most effective tools. See, in this regard, N. Gunningham and P. Grabosky, *Smart Regulation* (Clarendon Press 1998).

[18] E.g. M. Power, *The Audit Society* (Oxford University Press 1997); M. Power, 'The Audit Society – Second Thoughts' (2000) 4 *Int'l J. Accounting* 111; M. Power, 'Evaluating the Audit Explosion' (2003) 25 *L. & Pol.* 185 (using the expression 'audit society' to claim how governments had extended financial auditing and other monitoring mechanisms, such as ethics codes, across a variety of regulatory matters like health care, education, finance and welfare, in order to increase the (real and perceived) accountability of their own administrations. Thus, the author argues, 'formalized accountability', i.e. the kind of accountability that could be formally verified and certified, has become a 'ruling principle' for the whole society, i.e. for the job of regulators as well as for the claims of the regulatees). In addition, see C. Hood, O. James, G. Jones, C. Scott and T. Travers, *Regulation Inside Government: Waste-Watchers, Quality Police and Sleaze-Busters* (Oxford University Press 1999) (creating the label 'Regulation Inside Government' to address the new methods of control under which a range of independent regulatory agencies could check their own quality and effectiveness).

[19] The expression 'meta-regulation' addresses just the case of internal regulatory techniques adopted by regulators, regulatees and other subjects (such as gatekeepers, private parties, whistleblowers, or regulated companies' employees) to monitor their compliance with the given regulation and thus to guarantee a greater transparency and social accountability. D. Levi-Faur and S. Gilad, 'The Rise of the British Regulatory State: Transcending the Privatisation Debate' (2004) 37 *Comp. Pol.* 105, 113; C. Parker, 'Regulator-Required Corporate Compliance Program Audits' (2005) 25 *L. & Pol.* 221; C. Coglianese and D. Lazer, 'Management Based Regulation: Prescribing Private Management to Achieve Public Goals' (2003) 37 *L. & Soc. Rev.* 691.

[20] Levi-Faur and Jordana (n. 2 above).

century western states created many and various pieces of regulation that promoted the achievement of different economic, political and social goals in relation to specific sectors and issues, while at the same time combining the job of public and private enforcers, implementing legal, social and economic rules, imposing proscriptions as well as prescriptions and affecting such diverse targets as market structure, legal entitlements, economic incentives, information spread and firms' behaviour.

As a consequence, our current perception of economic regulation cannot be anything but wide and far-reaching[21] – so wide and far-reaching that even competition law can be soundly characterized as a piece of economic regulation. For instance, it can be deemed as a market-harnessing mechanism that, in the interest of the public, realizes a form of legal control on businesses.[22] Thus, to argue that *current* competition law is today *taking the shape* of a piece of economic regulation does not make much sense. In order to talk about 'the regulatory breakthrough' of competition law, we need to put aside any description of what happened in the de-regulation era, as well as any resulting broad and multiform notion of economic regulation. We need to consider a narrower, more specific and detailed conceptualization – in fact, a historically determined conceptualization – of what economic regulation is.

---

[21] To be sure, this broad perception of what economic regulation is should not astonish. Actually, the inability to understand economic regulation is inherent in the very definition of what 'the market' is. On the one hand, the market itself can be regarded as the result of choices and decisions that take the form of legal and social rules, so that almost any rule could be said to affect market practices, even contract, criminal and tort rules that set the general standard of private negotiations. On the other hand, because of the so-called 'commoditization approach', any practice can be conceptualized as an 'economic practice', i.e. as behaviour that requires and entails the use of something that we can commercialize in exchange for something else. Therefore, almost any behaviour subject to rules could be deemed as an economic practice.

[22] E.g. R. Baldwin, M. Cave and M. Lodge, *Understanding Regulation: Theory, Strategy and Practice* (Oxford University Press: 2nd edn 2012) 114 et seq. On the convergence between competition law and economic regulation see C. Leslie, 'Antitrust Law as Public Interest Law' (2013) 2 *UC Irvine L. Rev.* 885; M. Handler, 'Regulation Versus Competition' (1973–1974) 43 *Antitrust L.J.* 277; and U.S. Court of Appeals, *Town of Concord v. Boston Edison Co.*, 915 F.2d 17, 22 (1st Cir. 1990), *cert. denied*, 499 U.S. 931 (1991), where Justice Breyer observed that economic regulation and antitrust law pursue 'similar goals – i.e., low and economically efficient prices, innovation, and efficient production methods'.

2.2 Competition Law as a Liquid Concept

Notwithstanding the few US and EU provisions that directly associate competition law with *anticompetitive arrangements* and *monopolistic conduct*, our conception of what competition law is has changed over time according to the different goals that policy makers and scholars have assigned to it.[23] Think, for example, of the rules applied to monopolistic conduct. During different periods, both US courts and EU antitrust institutions have interpreted and enforced them as if competition law was called to: (i) protect small businesses against the 'dictatorship' of big, concentrated and vertically integrated businesses; (ii) ensure fairness, justice, equity and redistribution; (iii) guarantee the process of competition; (iv) preserve economic welfare; and, in the sole case of the European Union, (v) support the creation of the Single Market.[24]

More generally, over the past fifty years or so antitrust scholars and practitioners have been divided between those who think that competition law can be used aggressively to achieve perfectly competitive markets and those who believe that, in practice, competition law can make only a modest contribution to the goal of protecting effective competition.[25] Indeed, competition law provisions are so flexible and open-ended that they can mirror – and indeed have mirrored – the cultural insights as well as the political concerns and values of our social and political communities.[26] For example, the transatlantic past preference for the welfare of small businesses (and, hence, for dominant firms' rivals) was fed by the *laissez faire* alarm about bigness as such, the economic misconception that good business performances rest only with non-concentrated markets, and by the concern that economic power concentration would

---

[23] See R. Bork, *The Antitrust Paradox* (Simon & Schuster 1978) 50 (arguing that 'antitrust policy cannot be made rational until we are able to give a firm answer to one question: What is the point of the law – what are its goals? Everything else follows from the answer we give').

[24] E.g. M. Maggiolino, *Intellectual Property and Competition Law: A Comparative Economic Analysis of US and EU Law* (Edward Elgar Publishing 2011) 63–71; M.S. Gal, 'Monopoly Pricing as an Antitrust Offense in the U.S. and the EC: Two Systems of Belief About Monopoly?' (2004) 49 *Antitrust Bull.* 343.

[25] R.A. Cass, 'Competition in Antitrust Regulation: Law Beyond Limits' (2010) 6 *J. Comp. L. & Econ.* 119, 120.

[26] A.I. Gavil, W.E. Kovacic and J.B. Baker, *Antitrust Law in Perspective: Cases, Concepts and Problems in Competition Policy* (West Law 2008) 16, argue that even when it comes to the identification of the economic goals of competition law, 'we look to what society expects to achieve through the operation of private markets'.

impair free markets and democracy.[27] Likewise, the currently dominant idea according to which competition law consists of a set of legal rules that aims at preventing those business practices that may harm economic welfare – never mind whether total or consumer welfare[28] – can be traced back to the neoliberal programme that the Chicago School embraced in the 1970s.[29]

In sum, competition law is a liquid concept. Therefore, in order to conceptualize the regulatory breakthrough of current competition law we must, first, assume that there exists a form of competition law – perhaps just a theoretical one – whose shape has nothing to do with a piece of economic regulation, and, second, verify that the shape of current competition law is taking on some regulatory contours. Further, if we want to explain the alarm that this regulatory transformation of competition law is producing, we must also show whether and how competition law loses something important when it is poured into a 'regulatory container'.

3. THE POSSIBLE REGULATORY CONTOURS OF COMPETITION LAW

Behavioural and social phenomena are often understood 'in terms of a purposeful selection of facts from a far wider range of ways of looking at things'.[30] Therefore, in order to grasp the terms under which competition law can become a regulatory enterprise – or a *more* regulatory enterprise – the following paragraphs go to the antipodes. They briefly consider and compare two extreme species of economic regulation and competition

---

[27] D.I. Baker and W. Blumenthal, 'Ideological Cycles and Unstable Antitrust Rules' (1986) 31 *Antitrust Bull.* 323; W. Möschel, 'Competition Policy from an Ordo Point of View', in A. Peacock and H. Willgerodt (eds), *German Neo-liberals and the Social Market Economy* (Macmillan 1989) 146; E.T. Sullivan, *The Political Economy of the Sherman Act: The First One Hundred Years* (Oxford University Press 1990); E.M. Fox, 'We Protect Competition, You Protect Competitors' (2003) 26 *World Comp.* 149, D.J. Gerber, *Global Competition: Law Markets and Globalization* (Oxford University Press 2010).

[28] L. Kaplow, 'On the Choice of Welfare Standards in Competition Law', in D. Zimmer (ed.), *The Goals of Competition Law* (Edward Elgar Publishing 2012) 3.

[29] M. Motta, *Competition Policy: Theory and Practice* (Cambridge University Press 2004) 30.

[30] R. Popkin, 'The Function of Definitions in Social Science' (1943) 40 *J. Phil.* 491, 495.

law, that is to say: (i) those sector-specific, rate-and-entry pieces of economic regulation that the US government actually 'enforced' in the United States until the end of the 1960s; and (ii) the notion of competition law that the Chicago School 'theorized' at the beginning of the 1970s. Indeed, these heterogeneous examples of economic regulation and competition law are optimal 'sparring partners' to reveal the possible lines along which competition law can assimilate to, or differentiate itself from, a piece of economic regulation.

3.1 Government 'Actionism' and Sector-Specific, Rate-and-Entry Regulations

Since the second half of the 19th century and, in particular, for the period from the 1930s to the 1970s, in the United States the term 'economic regulation' was often used to denote what we today call command and control regimes.[31] By using rigid rules backed by administrative enforcement and penal sanctions, independent governmental agencies presided over firms' market actions in many sectors, such as trucking, airlines, telephone services, electricity, radio, television and natural gas. These agencies could prohibit certain forms of conduct, but also demand some positive actions by, say, prescribing the goods and services to be rendered, indicating the market to be served, deciding when plants needed to be built or modernized or determining how much should be invested in developing new technologies. Furthermore, those independent agencies could lay down conditions for entry into a sector, by determining which firms or individuals (or types thereof) were allowed to engage in which activities, and by controlling not only the quality of a production technique or of a service, but also the allocation of input and output, as well as the prices charged to consumers, or the profits made by enterprises.

In brief, by the end of the 1960s the regulatory programmes implemented in the United States required independent authorities to act for a better future – i.e. to promote economic welfare, economic growth and

---

[31] After the end of the Second World War, in the United States and in European countries the label 'economic regulation' was used to describe diverse phenomena. Especially in Europe, where governments preferred to do the job themselves instead of assigning it to bodies of commissioners, the expression economic regulation covered cases of industrial reorganization and planning as well as cases of national states acting as 'entrepreneurs'. See, e.g., D. Swann, *The Retreat of the State: Deregulation and Privatization in the UK and US* (Harvester-Wheatsheaf 1988) 28.

the public interest – by imposing on firms what conduct to undertake and by taking in advance manifold detailed decisions on the market equilibria that these independent authorities believed were to be achieved. These programmes were made up of proscriptions as well as prescriptions, whereby public agencies were entitled to fully decide, manage and control private affairs.[32]

3.2 Neoliberalism and Chicagoan Conception of Competition Law

At the beginning of the 1970s, the Chicagoan conception of competition law was totally defiant of government 'actionism'. Because of its support for neoliberalism, the Chicago School called for the abolition of competition law, by endorsing full faith in the automatic free-market system it maintained that the government was the problem and not the solution.

Then, if competition law was to be somehow tolerated, antitrust enforcers were to play a very residual role. They had to prohibit the sole business practices that harmed the competitive *status quo*, i.e. that produced a negative impact on the 'natural functioning' of the market.[33] Further, enforcers had to identify the 'natural functioning' of the market by looking at the performance of total welfare, i.e. in full accordance

---

[32] S. Breyer, 'Regulation and Deregulation in the United States: Airlines, Telecommunications and Antitrust', in G. Majone (ed.), *Deregulation or Re-Regulation* (Frances Pinter 1990) 7–8 and 12–15. According to Breyer, 'in the United States – at least "economic regulation" broadly conceived – typically refers to governmental efforts to control individual price, output, or product quality decisions of private firms, in an avowed effort to prevent purely private decision-making that would take inadequate account of the "public interest"'.

[33] In sum, the contrast between sector-specific, rate and entry regulations and Chicagoan antitrust law can be analogized to that between a steady cure aimed at treating a chronic disease and a surgical intervention adept at excising specific illnesses. For this analogy see F.M. Scherer and D. Ross, *Industrial Market Structure and Economic Performance* (McGraw Hill 1990) 12. Furthermore, see A. Devlin, 'Antitrust as Regulation? (2012) 49 *San Diego L. Rev.* 823, 825 and 830; N.B. Grzegorek, 'The Price of Admission: How Inconsistent Enforcement of Antitrust Laws in America's Live Entertainment Sector Hurts the Average Consumer' (2010) 44 *J. Marshall L. Rev.* 261, 269; R.A. Cass, 'Competition in Antitrust Regulation: Law beyond Limits' (2010) 6 *J. Comp. L. & Econ.* 119, 122; A.D. Melamed, 'Antitrust: The New Regulation' (1995–1996) 10 *Antitrust* 13; and S. Breyer, *Regulation and its Reform* (Harvard University Press 1982) 156–57.

with the main teachings of mainstream economics,[34] and without pandering to political ideals or specific interests. In addition, and here, too, in order to limit government 'actionism', the Chicago School wanted antitrust enforcers to intervene only when there was no risk of making false positive mistakes. Therefore, they had to take their 'hands off' of any case, such as the monopolization cases, where the alleged harmful effects were somehow questionable and speculative. Also, just to control the negative consequences that could follow a wrong intervention, their remedies had to consist in mere cease-and-desist orders and injunctions,[35] as the traditional US model of private enforcement envisaged.[36]

In brief, the overall conceptualization that the Chicago School made of competition law was thought to limit as much as possible the interference of public powers in private affairs. The neoliberal programme, indeed, assumed that the market mechanism made up of preferences, choices, transactions and contracts was alone capable of guaranteeing economic welfare, individuals' self-determination and the aggregate sum of subjective value satisfactions.[37]

---

[34] M. Maggiolino, 'The Economics of Antitrust Law and Intellectual Property Rights', in S. Anderman and A. Ezrachi (eds), *Intellectual Property and Competition Law: New Frontiers* (Oxford University Press 2011) 73.

[35] E.g., D.L. Rubinfeld, 'On the Foundations of Antitrust Law and Economics', in R. Pitofsky (ed.), *How the Chicago School Overshot the Mark* (Oxford University Press 2008) 51; F. Easterbrook, 'The Limits of Antitrust' (1984) 63 *Tex. L. Rev.* 1, 3.

[36] The enforcement of U.S. competition law is mainly up to judges. Therefore, in the United States antitrust enforcers are thought to be much more passive than regulators. Consider, for example, that judges are to decide only the cases that come before them, whereas regulators control their own agendas and can leap from one spot to another within the whole sector over which they preside. In addition, because of the rules of the adversarial system, it is the conflict between plaintiffs and defendants that shapes judges' decision-making. In contrast, reciprocal consent and negotiation are the usual 'key words' of the decision-making process that regulators develop. Finally, courts are a poor forum for reflecting and balancing democratic values, whereas regulators are institutionally expected to reconcile diverse interests and values.

[37] R. Nozick, 'Distributive Justice' (1973) 1 *Phil. & Pub. Aff.* 3; F. von Hayek, *The Constitution of Liberty* (University of Chicago Press 1960). In addition see *Northern Pacific Ry. v. United States*, 356 U.S. 1, 4 (1958) (arguing that such a conception of antitrust law rests 'on the premise that the unrestrained interaction of competitive forces will yield the best allocation of our economic resources, the lowest prices, the highest quality and the greatest material progress, while at the same time providing an environment conducive to the preservation of our democratic political and social institutions').

3.3 So Far, So Close

In the light of the above terms of comparison, we can elicit many of the conditions under which the shape of competition law can acquire some regulatory contours.

In general, the 'regulatory metamorphosis' of competition law happens – or starts happening – when competition law changes its goals, that is to say, when it does not limit itself to protecting total welfare, but pursues political and social aims, or even an economic goal other than the mere protection of the market's 'natural functioning'. For example, antitrust law may work to set the stage for better market equilibria and for higher levels of competition – it can work to maximize total and/or consumer welfare.

In the latter scenario, then, antitrust law changes for another reason – because it modifies its targets. It focuses not only on those business practices that can harm total welfare, but also on the structure of the markets at stake, on the existing distribution of incentives and legal entitlements, on the spread of information and on business practices that do not maximize total and consumer welfare.[38] In other words, a form of competition law that pursues different goals also puts the spotlight on different economic variables.

When antitrust enforcers modify their targets, they accordingly use different tools and approaches – they impose not only bans, but also positive obligations establishing what economic agents should do in order to set the stage for better market equilibria.[39] They abandon a mere *ex post*, backward-looking and facts-based attitude focused on the protection and the restoration of the *status quo*, to endorse a more *ex ante*,

---

[38] The focus on a specific market makes antitrust rules less universal than they should be according to the Chicago archetype. The latter wants antitrust law to catch any economic agent, just considering it as the 'seller' or the 'purchaser' of the product in question and, thus, regardless of its identity, its 'history of meritorious competitive acts', or its social *status*. A more regulatory conception of antitrust law, in contrast, allows enforcers to deal with the specific protagonists of the market at stake; their reasons, interests, merits and faults.

[39] A more regulatory approach to antitrust law asks the latter to identify what the optimal market equilibrium should be and to target those economic variables and procompetitive activities that can facilitate its achievement over time. See, e.g., D.W. Carlton and R.C. Picker, 'Antitrust and Regulation' (2006), 3, available at: http://ideas.repec.org/p/nbr/nberwo/12902.html (accessed 9 March 2014).

forward-looking and theory-laden position aimed at fostering market development.[40]

In brief, competition law may experience a regulatory breakthrough as long as it moves away from the minimalist archetype of the Chicago School – away from its goals, targets, tools and approaches. Or, at least, this is the 'theoretical framework' into which a regulatory transformation of competition law can be inserted.

4. THE TERMS OF THE PRESENT 'REGULATORY METAMORPHOSIS' OF COMPETITION LAW

The above theoretical map of what might give a regulatory mould to competition law does not necessarily mean that such a transformation is actually taking place. Indeed, the mere existence of this theoretical map does not necessarily imply that this transformation has ever taken place – the Chicagoan notion of antitrust law is still influencing the US and EU practice, but it has never been fully endorsed, especially in the European Union. Therefore, one could argue that competition law has always been a sort of regulatory enterprise.

However, this is not the place to make such a historic analysis. Moreover, this is not the place to discuss the many circumstances in which current US antitrust law and EU competition law look like a piece of economic regulation – the following chapters are devoted to thoughtful analysis of this twofold subject.

Nevertheless, some clear facts suggest that today's competition enforcers – and especially the EU Commission – are available to play a more active role in promoting the maximization of economic welfare (i.e. in pursuing a different goal), by affecting not only business conduct, but

---

[40] While antitrust law – and, in particular, the provisions about anti-competitive arrangements and monopolistic conduct – is thought to work as an *ex post* means, i.e. as a surgeon's knife that eradicates the evil that is actually plaguing the market, economic regulation is meant to serve as an *ex ante* tool, i.e. to dictate in advance what prophylaxis the market should follow to avoid any pain that medicine says will or could occur. In particular, while the *Chicagoan* conception of competition law cannot but be backward-looking and fact-based, i.e. focused on what the involved firms did (or are doing) and on what specific market scenarios characterized (or still characterize) their acts, sector-specific, rate-and-entry regulations are also forward-looking and theory-laden, i.e. focused on what firms are expected to do, and on what events are expected to happen according to the economic theory called on to explain how markets function and develop.

also market structures, the existing economic incentives, and the given legal entitlements (i.e. by targeting different variables). Hoping to set the stage for better market equilibria (i.e. endorsing a more *ex ante* approach), current antitrust enforcers are now more willing than they were in the past to 'negotiate' the content of their decisions (i.e. they are less subordinate to the results coming from the adversarial system) and to use sophisticated economic models[41] to make educated guesses about future market developments (i.e. they are liable to be more theory-laden and to carry their assessment into the long run). Not by chance, indeed, do expressions such as 'competition promotion', 'negotiated remedies', 'forward-looking decisions', 'market reorganization' and 'continuous monitoring' belong to the vocabulary of today's antitrust enforcers.[42] For example, consider what the EU Commission does in duty-to-deal cases such as the *Microsoft* saga.[43] In these cases, for the sake of what the Commission considers to be the public interest, it decides how to reshape property rights and distribute the incentives to compete and innovate among the players of the industries at stake. Thus, in duty-to-deal cases the Commission clearly acts as a regulator: it establishes where to drive markets on the basis of specific economic theories, such as the defensive leverage theory;[44] it endorses a clear forward-looking perspective; and it imposes not only equitable relief and cease-and-desist orders, but also positive obligations impinging on structural variables. In so doing, the Commission takes into account the 'industrial identities' of the involved firms, that is to say, their history of meritorious competitive acts, whether

[41] Melamed (n. 33, above) 15, argues that 'today's economists – using the tools of both price theory and game theory – are able to imagine all sorts of anticompetitive strategies, private market failures, and remedies for them. As a result … government antitrust officials sometimes ask, not whether the defendant violated a legal norm, but whether constraining the defendant's use of its property might improve or ensure its contribution to consumer welfare. In effect, economic analysis lends itself to a kind of prospective analysis that is in substance a regulatory inquiry, not a law enforcement inquiry.'

[42] E.g. M. Szydło, 'Sector-Specific Regulation and Competition Law: Between Convergence and Divergence' (2009) 15 *Eur. Pub. L.* 257.

[43] E.g. M. Maggiolino (n. 24 above) ch. 5.

[44] See, in general, R. Cooper Feldman, 'Defensive Leveraging in Antitrust' (1990) 87 *Geo. L. J.* 2079, and, in relation to the *Microsoft* saga, C. Genakos, K. Kühn and J. Van Reenen, 'Leveraging Monopoly Power by Degrading Interoperability: Theory and Evidence from Computer Markets' (2011) National Bureau of Economic Research, Working Paper 17172, available at: http://www.nber.org/papers/w17172 (accessed 1 September 2014).

they were previous state monopolists, or whether they deserve their market position or their intellectual property rights.[45]

In addition, consider the more frequent commitment decisions. They grant a great regulatory leeway to antitrust enforcers.[46] Indeed, in issuing commitment decisions the EU Commission – not unlike the US agencies that adopt consent decrees – works as a mediator between the parties, knowing their diverse interests and facilitating the negotiation and conciliation of their opposite positions.

Finally, do not forget that, according to some scholars, any antitrust agency or authority that adjudicates a case adopting the rule of reason is actually acting as a regulator that substitutes its economic evaluations for those of entrepreneurs. Namely, establishing whether a restriction is reasonable entails, *inter alia*, considering whether there could be a less restrictive alternative, that is to say, making an educated guess about how best to achieve a better market equilibrium: by using the option chosen by the entrepreneur or by using another option that the antitrust agency or authority envisages.[47]

In sum, there is room to argue that current competition law does not have the shape of the Chicago archetype. And this creates a sort of alarm.

5. THE REASSURING NATURE OF THE CHICAGO ARCHETYPE

Probably, antitrust scholars are very fascinated by the Chicagoan notion of competition law because they were trained during the years of the Chicago bandwagon. Probably – and this is my personal belief – their diffidence towards a more 'regulatory approach' to competition law arises from the reassuring nature of Chicago antitrust, i.e. from the fact that the Chicago concept of competition law shelters – or seems to shelter –

---

[45] Often it has been noticed that those firms that achieve a dominant position because of network effects do not really deserve it – see, e.g., G.J. Werden, 'Network Effects and Conditions of Entry, Lessons from the Microsoft Case' (2001) 69 *Antitrust L.J.* 87 – or that some of the IPRs used to defend a dominant position should have not been granted in the first place – see e.g. I.S. Forrester, 'EC Competition Law as a Limitation on the use of IP Rights in Europe: Is there Reason to Panic?', in C. Ehlermann and I. Atanasiu (eds), *European Competition Law Annual 2003: What is an Abuse of Dominant Position?* (Hart Publishing 2003) 506.

[46] E.g. H. First, 'Is Antitrust "Law"?' (1995–1996) 10 *Antitrust* 9; Melamed (n. 33 above).

[47] E.g. Devlin (n. 33 above) 837.

enforcers from the risk of enjoying too much discretion. Let me briefly elaborate the details of the argument.

Basically, regulators enjoy a great leeway. They can establish (or interpret) what the public interest is and what rules could help to pursue it.[48] Yet, information asymmetries as to present market scenarios, as well as limited knowledge as to possible and future market developments, inexorably affect regulators' ability not only to identify what the optimal market equilibrium should be, but also to determine what changes to market structure, initial endowments and original entitlements should be continuously promoted so as to accommodate the dynamic achievement of this equilibrium. Therefore, regulators may make mistakes in defining (or interpreting) their goals and in elaborating and applying the rules that, over time, should allow these goals to be accomplished.

In addition, the very same ignorance that increases the risk of making mistakes exposes regulators to another twofold risk – that of being manipulated and that of making value choices to the detriment of individuals' self-determination. For example, technocrats themselves may try to influence the notion of public interest in order to preserve or expand their power and jurisdictional turf. In this way, they can deepen their intervention into the affairs of the regulated enterprises and control issues and firms more than necessary.[49] Or, looking for better information to draw up and enforce their rules, regulators can be captured[50] – they may fall under the spell of the regulatees and, thus, consider some rules to be in the public interest, although in fact these rules fulfil the interest of specific groups of firms.[51] And even away from these species of

---

48 For the controversial notion of public interest see, e.g., M. Feintuck, 'Regulatory Rationales Beyond the Economic: In Search of the Public Interest' in Baldwin, Cave and Lodge (eds) (n. 6 above) 39.

49 E.g. L. Loevilger, 'Regulation and Competition as Alternatives' (1966) 11 *Antitrust Bull.* 120.

50 Consider that the so-called 'capture theory', together with the 'public choice' and 'special interest group' theories, are generally associated with what is called the 'economic theory of regulation' elaborated within the walls of the same Chicago School that forged the current notion of competition law. See, e.g., S. Peltzman, 'Towards a More General Theory of Regulation' (1976) 19 *J. L. & Econ.* 211.

51 J. Stigler, 'Theory of Economic Regulation' (1974) 2 *Bell J. Econ.* 3; R.A. Posner, 'Theories of Economic Regulation' (1974) 5 *Bell J. Econ.* 335; W.A. Jordan, 'Producer Protection, Prior Market Structure and the Effects of Government Regulation' (1992) 15 *J. L. & Econ.* 151. In particular, scholars have elaborated a number of versions of the capture theory. The 'bribery' and 'revolving doors' models rely on the idea of a regulator induced to be lenient

manipulations, since regulators have no objective standard to establish what the public interest is and what rules could help in pursuing it, their decisions may, however, side with specific visions of the world. Their decisions are not neutral – they are value choices, at least partially.

In contrast – and in a very reassuring way – the Chicago conception of competition law would have antitrust enforcers act like mere technicians who, by doing only what the economic technique tells them to do, can stay away from any form of discretion and are thus sheltered from mistakes, manipulations and conflicts of interests and values. Namely, suppose that the market is a *cosmos* – i.e. a 'natural, spontaneous and necessary' order governed by universal, unchangeable and objective rules that technicians may know and calculate.[52] Assume, then, that economics is the domain of these rules – it is like a hard science that describes what the 'natural' functioning of the market is. In the light of these assumptions, as long as antitrust law 'translates' these economic rules into the legal realm – as the Chicago School wanted it to do – the risk of making mistakes is low and there is little room for manipulations, conflicts of

---

with respect to regulated firms through offers of monetary transfers or future employment. Other models assume regulator-regulatee proximity as the trigger that induces leniency. The 'life-cycle' explanation suggests that, after great expense of effort and resources to be independent, lonely and isolated regulators become the protectors of the regulated industry; the 'interest-group' accounts stress the extent to which regulators can be influenced by the claims coming from either political or powerful business lobbies.

[52] F. von Hayek, *The Confusion of Language in Political Thought: With Some Suggestions for Remedying It* (The Institute of Economic Affairs 1968) 15 and 28: '[t]he ordered structure which the market produces is … not an organization but a spontaneous order or *cosmos*' subject to *nomoi*, by which term 'we shall describe a universal rule of just conduct applying to an unknown number of future instances and equally to all persons in the objective circumstances described by the rule, irrespective of the effects which observance of the rule will produce in a particular situation … Such rules are generally described as "abstract" and are independent of individual ends. They lead to the formation of an equally abstract and end-independent spontaneous order or *cosmos*.' In particular, von Hayek contrasts this with *taxis*, i.e. an artificial order that results from political choices, tries to pursue specific objectives, and is subject to specific rules named thesis. Indeed, 'we shall use thesis to mean any rule which is applicable only to particular people or in the service of the ends of rulers. Though such rules may still be general to various degrees and refer to a multiplicity of particular instances, they will shade imperceptibly from rules in the usual sense to particular commands. They are the necessary instrument of running an organization or *taxis*.'

interests and diverse political views.[53] In other words, as long as antitrust enforcers pursue the protection of total welfare by forbidding the sole business practices that mainstream economics say harm it, their approach and tools are so tailored to the evil to be removed that they are little suited for anything else.

True, one could argue that economics does not always supply definitive answers to be easily translated into the antitrust realm. Consider, for example, the case of antitrust decisions dealing with the duration and scope of monopolies and IPRs. Economics does not know where to strike the proper inter-temporal balance between creating and disseminating the incentives to compete and innovate. In such a situation, hence, the lack of an economic rule to be translated into the legal field could open the gate to mistakes, manipulations and value choices.

To rebut this argument the Chicago School would argue that in those cases antitrust enforcers must take their hands off any negotiation or any other intrusive decision envisaging what the public interest could be. In the absence of any clear-cut economic rule to be translated into the antitrust realm, leaving things as they are, leaving markets free to polish themselves, should be the best way to limit the risks of prosecuting harmless conduct, of being at the mercy of a specific group of interests and of espousing a particular vision of the world.

In brief, the less, the better. By conditioning antitrust enforcement to what mainstream economics teaches, and by supporting the 'hands-off approach' any time economics is not capable of formulating precise economic rules to qualify business behaviour, the Chicago archetype claims to limit as much as possible enforcers' discretion and, as a consequence, the risks of making mistakes, of being manipulated, and of making value choices. In other words, the more competition law limits itself to replicate the most certain teachings of economics, the more it becomes a safe game – i.e. a matter of 'truth' – and this is something that

---

53 This reproduces in the legal field the idea that microeconomics, in contrast to macroeconomics, identifies a scientific endeavour devoid of politics. Since the mid-1930s 'the high priests and authorities of economics pronounced Anathema, in the sacred name of Science, on value judgments. ... The Anathema on value judgment was obscurantist. The obeisance to the positivist rules of science was epistemologically incongruous and self-deceiving. The economic discourse could not and did not dispense with value judgement': R.A. Solo, 'Values and Judgments in the Discourse of the Sciences' in R.A. Solo and C.W. Anderson (eds), *Value Judgment and Income Distribution* (Praeger 1981) 31 and 34; and R.J.R. Peritz, *Competition Policy in America, 1888–1992: History, Rhetoric, Law* (Oxford University Press 1996) 241.

no form of regulation, and no form of a more regulatory approach to competition law, can ever be.[54]

Yet, this narrative is misleading.

6. DEBUNKING THE REASSURING NATURE OF THE CHICAGO ARCHETYPE

It may actually happen – as the Chicago School maintains – that some economic rules (and their layman rehashes) offer a true description of how markets work. In this case, anchoring antitrust law to economics really limits enforcers' discretion as well as the consequences that this discretion is said to bring about in terms of mistakes, manipulations and value choices.

Yet, even setting aside the case of economic rules that are too sophisticated to offer a realistic description of how competition develops,[55] there are economic rules that, though correct and sound, depend so much on some detailed hypotheses that they do not offer one single applicable conclusion for the specific antitrust case at stake.[56] Moreover, as seen above in the discussion about the duration and scope of

---

[54] G. Minda, 'Towards a More "Just" Economics of Justice – A Review Essay' (1989) 10 *Cardozo L. Rev.* 1855, 1857 (addressing competition law as a 'technocratic legal discourse based on the conceptual framework of market exchange') and D.N. McCloskey, 'The Rhetoric of Law and Economics' (1988) 86 *Mich. L. Rev.* 752, 760–67 (arguing that detachment from value judgments, i.e. objectivity of observations and explanations, is one of the requirements of sciences and, hence, of those social disciplines that try to be scientific). Interestingly enough, Peritz attested to Posner just this attempt to morph its ideology into a science. Peritz (n. 53 above) at 238, argues that 'Posner was obsessed with convincing his readers that his project was positive, not normative; scientific, not ideological. He was not arguing, he insisted, that economic efficiency *ought* to be the beacon guiding public policy and legal rule-making. He was, instead, testing a hypothesis, a scientific theory, about the way human institutions *actually* work.'

[55] M. Blaug, 'Ugly Currents in Modern Economics' (1997) 17 *Pol. Options* 3 (modern economics 'has increasingly become an intellectual game played for its own sake and not for its practical consequences for understanding the economic world'); T. Lawson, 'Mathematical Modeling and Ideology in the Economics Academy: Competing Explanations of the Failings of the Modern Discipline?' (2012) 1 *Econ. Thought* 3.

[56] This is the case of the most recent, and very complicated, industrial organization models implementing game theory.

monopolies and IPRs, there are cases where no economic rule can definitively establish what the 'natural functioning' of the market is.

Hence, in these two cases, any antitrust decision translating one of those economic rules into the legal field is no longer a matter of pure technique.[57] When there is no single and definitive economic rule to implement, antitrust enforcers also enjoy discretion – an amount of discretion that, notably, even the Chicagoan 'hands-off approach' cannot manage in a technical way.

Indeed, the Chicagoan 'hands-off approach' shelters the system from manipulation because it does not leave any room for negotiation. Yet, it is not error-free, because if the natural course of the market is unknown, leaving things as they are can be as wrong as changing them. Moreover, the 'hands-off approach' is not value-free for at least two reasons. First, assuming that false positive mistakes are more serious than false negative mistakes means siding with the (neoliberal) belief that markets can refine themselves better than any government action can. Second, when dealing with a specific case, leaving things as they are may mean siding with specific interests and values – those interests and values that the particular *status quo* at stake reflects. For example, the choice not to impose a duty to deal on monopolists holding IPRs endorses two questionable theses – that judges and antitrust administrative authorities cannot second guess (IP) legislators' choices, and that the overall level of innovation increases leaving the lead to dominant IP holders rather than to tiny followers.

Besides, to test the neutrality claim of the Chicago School against more radical observations,[58] it must be acknowledged that, as such, the

---

[57] A. Devlin and M. Jacobs, 'Antitrust Divergence and the Limits of Economics' (2010) 104 *Nw. U. L. Rev.* 253, 282–83, for instance, argue that, 'in the absence of a useful economic theory, or a workable metric, the foundations of… [the US and EU approaches towards refusals to deal] are inevitably political, valid for each system on its own terms, and somewhat informative for others, but hardly 'correct' in some provable fashion. … if economic analysis does not dictate the choice of a legal rule in this area, something else outside of economics must – in other words, something political'.

[58] To be sure, scholars at the time elaborated many critiques other than that discussed in the text, notably: (i) the liberal critique of Ronald Dworkin (contesting the equivalence between social interest and the mere aggregation of individual interests, arguing that the latter overlooks the differences among people): R. Dworkin, 'Is Wealth a Value?' (1980) 9 *J. Leg. Stud.* 191; (ii) the sociological critique of Robert C. Ellickson (observing that individuals who choose for themselves in private transactions are not really conscious of their true interests and values): R.C. Ellickson, 'Of Coase and Cattle: Dispute Resolution

'existing competitive status quo' that Chicagoan competition law is intended to protect (in this case, by using the 'hands-off approach') is not neutral – it does reflect a mixture of value choices and political decisions. Indeed, competitive equilibrium is not simply 'given', like flowers and electromagnetic forces may be. Each competitive equilibrium results from the combination of many building blocks, such as individual preferences and the willingness to pay,[59] which are determined in large part by the original distribution of wealth and legal entitlements that, in turn, result from many political choices, social pressures, and legal rules.[60] Therefore, it cannot be neglected that markets move from, and result in, scenarios that are not value-free and neutral.[61] As a consequence, if the competitive *status quo* is not neutral, *a fortiori*, the

among Neighbors in Shasta County' (1986) 38 *Stan. L. Rev.* 623; and (iii) the legal realist critique of Arthur A. Leff (focusing on formalism and reductionism as two features of economics that could, as a consequence, create problems once driven into the legal field): A.A. Leff, 'Economic Analysis of Law: Some Realism about Nominalism' (1974) 60 *Va. L. Rev.* 451.

[59] E.g. J. Dewey, *The Quest for Certainty* (1929) 259, 265, 272–73 (claiming that there is a need for critical reflection on the 'conditions under which objects are enjoyed' and on the 'consequences of esteeming and liking them').

[60] E.g. C.R. Sunstein, *After the Rights Devolution: Reconceiving the Regulatory State* (Harvard University Press 1990) 41–42; C.R. Sunstein, *Free Markets and Social Justice* (Oxford University Press 1997) 4–5 (observing that 'in any society, existing preferences should not be taken as natural or sacrosanct'). As a matter of fact, the initial assignment of a right can affect the wealth of the parties, which, in turn, can affect how parties valuate the right as well as the ultimate use of the resource that comes with that right. See further C.E. Baker, 'The Ideology of the Economic Analysis of Law' (1975) 5 *Phil. & Pub. Aff.* 3, 13 (arguing that the 'initial assignment normally affects the relative wealth of the parties. … In addition, since a person's wealth affects how much that person is willing and able to pay for a specific desired right, the effect on a person's wealth of the initial assignment of that right will influence how much the person "values" the right. In these cases, the initial assignment may determine who "values" the right the most.' See also R.D. Willig, 'Consumer's Surplus without Apology' (1976) 66 *Am. Econ. Rev.* 589; G. Calabresi and A.D. Melamed, 'Property Rules, Liability Rules, and Inalienability: One View of the Cathedral' (1972) 85 *Harv. L. Rev.* 1089: 'When a loss is left where it falls in an auto accident, it is not because God so ordained it. Rather, it is because the state has granted the injurer an entitlement to be free of liability and will intervene to prevent the victim's friends, if they are stronger, from taking compensation from the injurer.'

[61] Sunstein, *Free Markets and Social Justice* (n. 60, above) 5, maintains that 'markets should be understood as a legal construct, to be evaluated on the basis

Chicagoan decision not to modify it is likewise not neutral. The latter is a political choice – to say the least, it is a conservative choice – that, as such, must submit to comparison with alternative options, i.e. with other, more progressive approaches.[62]

To be sure, the Chicago conception of competition law may well choose to protect the *status quo* without paying any attention to the possibility of changing it. In addition it may also choose – as is commonly recalled – to say nothing about the ways prosperity is used or distributed, arguing that those are matters for other pieces of law.

Yet, in doing so, the Chicago notion of competition law cannot hide the political value of its choices. Notwithstanding the ostensibly neutral and technical set of principles that it uses, the foundations of the Chicago approach are politically determined. More, we cannot believe that these choices are more neutral than the ones underpinning some pieces of economic regulations. Hence, since the reassuring nature of the Chicago conception of competition law is questionable, we cannot use it to justify our alarm towards the alleged regulatory breakthrough of contemporary competition law.

7. CONCLUSION

As often happens when we are confronted with complex social phenomena, the boundaries of the definitions that we use to address those

---

of whether they promote human interests, rather than as part of nature and the natural order, or as a simple way of promoting voluntary interactions'.

[62] The so-called 'conservative bias' is just one of the many critiques elaborated against economic analysis and its attempt to reconstruct individual liberalism on market terms. See, in this regard, M. Kelman, *A Guide to Critical Legal Studies* (Harvard University Press 1987) 114. For an analogous opinion see S. Kelman, *What Price Incentives? Economists and the Environment* (Auburn House 1981) 27 (observing that, by ignoring the extent to which individuals' values are socially determined, the possibility that institutions can affect the formation of private preferences is neglected). See further, A.T. Kronman, 'Change in the Common Law: Legal and Economic Perspectives' (1980) 9 *J. Leg. Stud.* 227, 242: 'social institutions, including the law, should be used to mitigate the effects of the natural lottery; for the law to intensify them is perverse. A theory which legitimates the chance effects of the natural lottery treats persons as if they were things by giving moral significance to those aspects of our lives over which we have no control. Such a theory fails to recognize that persons are moral beings precisely because they have a capacity for rational action which puts them, in a limited but important way, beyond the reach of nature's indifferent power.'

phenomena are blurred. Therefore, in order to understand what we really mean when we talk about the 'regulatory breakthrough' of present competition law, we need to clarify the exact meaning of the terms 'economic regulation' and 'competition law'. This chapter has explored the scope of these two labels and, using two specific forms of economic regulation and competition law as benchmarks, developed two theses. First: we do not err if we argue that competition law acquires 'regulatory contours' whenever its goals, targets, tools and approaches distance themselves from those of the Chicago archetype. Second: the main concerns about this 'regulatory breakthrough' are rooted in a fallacy – that, in contrast with economic regulation and any sort of regulatory conception of competition law, only the Chicago archetype guarantees neutrality. In fact, the chapter has shown that the Chicagoan theorization of competition law as well as the Chicagoan recipes to support it are value-laden, just as are any other kind of competition law and any example of economic regulation.

2. Anti-anti regulation: the supplanting of industry regulators with competition agencies and how antitrust suffers as a result

Adi Ayal

1. INTRODUCTION

Regulatory endeavours come in many shapes and sizes. In the broadest sense of the term, any government action (and many a non-governmental action) regulates the behaviour of individuals and firms. In the narrower formulation, regulation encompasses actions conducted by specialized governmental units, appointed to oversee specific industries exhibiting inherent market failures, and relying on expertise regarding the inner workings of associated technologies and public interests. In between these extremes, regulatory action encompasses economic and social concerns, is applied by specialized and generalist agencies, and is conducted in the shadow of judicial and political oversight.

This chapter focuses on one trend in the world of regulation, the curtailment of specific-industry regulation in favour of cross-market competition regulation. This trend stems both from specific regulation falling into disrepute due to political and industry influence and from market forces replacing government as a source of constraint on firm behaviour. Those in favour of deregulation often cite governmental imperfections and a belief in market forces. Yet state involvement is not necessarily reduced, as competition regulation steps in to fill the gaps left by deregulation. Both competition agencies and courts in the framework of private litigation enforce antitrust rules, sometimes replacing direct regulation and sometimes encroaching upon its domain. As will be elaborated below, this dynamic is problematic on several levels, both as to industries requiring more specific knowledge than competition agencies normally have, and as to the effect on antitrust law itself. Antitrust aficionados should be wary of the expansion their field is experiencing.

While much of the field's popularity is based on a general appreciation of the benefits of competition and the professionalization of its agencies, expansion comes at a cost.

This chapter is structured as follows: Section 2 introduces regulatory concerns and the types of agencies used to implement them. Section 3 distinguishes between competition and industry-specific regulation, elaborating on the characteristics they share and their main relevant differences. Section 4 discusses regulatory failures, setting up the discussion in Section 5 of their implementation within each type of regulation. Section 6 delves into a major challenge for the trends towards deregulation, that of economy-wide network effects and the anticompetitive implications of platforms and bottlenecks. These influence economic behaviour well beyond the classic and well-known network markets, making antitrust oversight especially broad. Section 7 focuses on the dangers to antitrust itself from its over-inclusiveness, discussing dynamics of concern to competition agencies and those who rely on them. A conclusion follows.

2. REGULATION, BROADLY CONSIDERED

Regulation comes in many forms. At its base it can be defined as a 'sustained and focused control exercised by a public agency over activities that are valued by the community'.[1] Beyond the 'focused control' associated with classic regulation by industry-specific regulators, much of the effect of regulation stems from non-governmental agencies relying on informal monitoring and using either the judiciary (enforcing general legal norms) or the public arena (relying on political pressure). This led to a broadening of the terms used to define regulation, and perhaps the effectiveness of control itself. In its broadest conception, regulation can be seen as 'all the efforts of the state, by whatever means, to control and guide the economy and society'.[2]

The broad definition of regulation encompasses the idea that the state controls private actions through a myriad of means, some direct and some indirect. This formulation may be useful to avoid biases inherent in examining only specific types of rules, while other norms influence the

---

[1] P. Selznick, 'Focusing Organizational Research on Regulation' in R.G. Noll (ed.), *Regulatory Policy and the Social Sciences* (University of California Press 1985) 363.

[2] D. Levi-Faur, *Handbook of the Politics of Regulation* (Edward Elgar Publishing 2012) 4.

same behaviour. In order to overcome such biases, some prefer to use terms such as 'regulatory regime' or 'regulatory space' to denote the environment which influences both the formation and enforcement of such legal norms.[3]

For the purposes of this chapter, I focus on specific regulatory regimes, i.e. those dealing with industries subject to direct agency review, and contrast them with a general regime enforced by competition agencies based on antitrust law. Industry-specific regulation is associated with the rise of the 'administrative state', increasing governmental intervention in the economy and reducing judicial oversight by focusing on expert institutions using 'command and control' methods.[4] While current consensus might be that such regulation was excessive and is in the process of reduction, it should be noted that such cycles of increasing and then decreasing state intervention have been occurring periodically, usually with economic booms increasing trust in markets (and inducing calls for less regulation), and with downturns and depressions pushing in the opposite direction.[5] Deregulation is often associated with an increased role for competition agencies, many citing antitrust as a substitute for industry-specific regulation, a claim that will be assessed in more detail below.[6]

Most studies of regulatory agencies focus on three main types of activities such agencies employ: information gathering, standard setting

---

[3] See e.g. M.A. Eisner, *Regulatory Politics in Transition* (JHU Press: 2nd edn 2000); C. Scott, 'Analysing Regulatory Space: Fragmented Resources and Institutional Design' (2001) *Pub. L.* 329; D.W. Drezner, *All Politics Is Global: Explaining International Regulatory Regimes* (Princeton University Press 2007); M. Thatcher and D. Coen, 'Reshaping European Regulatory Space: An Evolutionary Analysis' (2008) 31 *West Eur. Pol.* 806.

[4] G. Lawson, 'The Rise and Rise of the Administrative State' (1994) 107 *Harv. L. Rev.* 1231; J.L. Grisinger, 'Law and the Administrative State' in S.E. Hadden and A.L. Brophy (eds), *A Companion to American Legal History* (Wiley-Blackwell 2013) 367. For differing views on the rule of law and legitimacy of the regulatory endeavour, see R.A. Epstein, 'The Perilous Position of the Rule of Law and the Administrative State' (2012) 36 *Harv. J. L. & Pub. Pol.* 5; P.M. Shane, 'The Rule of Law and the Inevitability of Discretion' (2012) 36 *Harv. J. L. & Pub. Pol.* 21.

[5] R.H.K. Vietor, *Contrived Competition: Regulation and Deregulation in America* (Harvard University Press 1994); H. Hovenkamp, 'Antitrust and the Regulatory Enterprise' (2004) *Colum. Bus. L. Rev.* 335.

[6] R.D. Cudahy, 'The Folklore of Deregulation (with Apologies to Thurman Arnold)' (1998) 15 *Yale J. Reg.* 427.

and behaviour modification.[7] Information gathering is necessary for an understanding of the industry and problems plaguing it; standard setting is the formation of legal norms and guidelines which firms and individuals subject to the regulatory agency must follow; and behaviour modification refers to enforcement measures aimed at those failing to follow said rules.

Despite the current focus on regulatory enforcement, it is important to note that much of the effect of regulation stems from self-regulation. This is due to businesses' eagerness to avoid later prosecution, or the importance of public perception and the reputational capital associated with the appearance (or reality) of 'good citizenship'. Thus, literature abounds on hybrid forms of regulation, such as requiring firms to form internal codes of conduct or enforcement mechanisms.[8] In these situations, the public agency monitors only the exterior contours of internal regulation, such as the *existence* of such a code or the appointment of an internal compliance officer. Such measures create a legally binding contract (e.g., if encoded in a firm's bylaws) or the public perception of such (e.g., if declared as company policy). Internal compliance measures can thus be self-enforcing and a regulatory agency requiring them, but not enforcing them, can still make a large difference in eventual behaviour.

The current study does not attempt to disentangle the different measures employed by agencies, nor does it dwell on distinctions between 'classic regulation' consisting of 'hard law' rules and directives formed by administrative bodies and 'meta-regulation', which includes 'soft law' and the chilling effects that result from firms attempting to avoid strict scrutiny. I mention them in order to use the different types of regulation in our discussion below, and stress the breadth of regulation in practice. I shall assume that both specific industry regulation and competition regulation employ some means of both types, and focus on the general distinctions between types of agencies rather than types of regulation as such. In so doing, I consciously paint in broad strokes, hopefully illuminating the 'big picture' while noting that often, 'the devil is in the

---

[7] C. Hood, H. Rothstein and R. Baldwin, *The Government of Risk: Understanding Risk Regulation Regimes* (OUP 2001) 21.

[8] I. Ayres and J. Braithwaite, *Responsive Regulation: Transcending the Deregulation Debate* (OUP 1992) 106. Some refer to such measures as a private case of meta-regulation or meta-monitoring; see C. Parker, *The Open Corporation: Effective Self-regulation and Democracy* (Cambridge University Press 2002); P.N. Grabosky, 'Using Non-governmental Resources to Foster Regulatory Compliance' (1995) 8 *Governance* 527.

details'. Nonetheless, it is my contention that such broad generalizations play a large part in the public understanding of the shifts our regulatory regime is experiencing, and their effect not merely on perception, but in actual enforcement and judicial interpretation. Thus, 'soft law' and stereotypical generalizations influence 'hard law' implementation to a significant degree.

3. DISTINGUISHING BETWEEN SPECIFIC REGULATION AND COMPETITION POLICY

> Antitrust is not another form of regulation. Antitrust is an *alternative* to regulation and, where feasible, a better alternative.[9]

> Regulation does not diminish demand for antitrust, but should boost it. ... [R]egulation and antitrust are complements – not substitutes.[10]

> Regulation and competition policy are very close relatives. As you probably all know, relationships between close relatives can be quite complicated.[11]

Both antitrust and regulation aim for similar ends, though use different methodologies and are appropriate in different types of markets. Achieving marginal cost pricing, efficiency in production, and innovation along all possible paths of improvement are appropriate targets for regulators, whether these use competition policy or industry-specific regulation to achieve their aims.[12] Of course, when average costs are downward-sloping, pricing at marginal cost is a losing endeavour, attractive in the short run, but sure to lead to financial ruin for the firm in question and remove it as a competitor from the field. Where stability is important and volatility costly, or national interests in having local firms serving the market are important, the public might be better off paying efficiency costs for long-term gains. In other words, industry-specific regulation can

---

[9] S.G. Breyer, 'Antitrust, Deregulation, and the Newly Liberated Marketplace' (1987) 75 *Cal. L. Rev.* 1005, 1007 (original emphasis).

[10] T.J. Brennan, 'Essential Facilities and *Trinko*: Should Antitrust and Regulation be Combined?' (2008) 61 *Fed. Comm. L.J.* 133, 141.

[11] N. Kroes (then EU Commissioner for Competition), 'The Interface Between Regulation and Competition Law', Speech given at the Bundeskartellamt Conference on Dominant Companies – The Thin Line between Regulation and Competition Law (28 April 2009), available at: http://europa.eu/rapid/press-release_SPEECH-09-202_en.htm?locale=en (accessed 31 December 2013).

[12] Breyer (n. 9 above) 1006.

be useful for markets where competition is unavailable – or for those where competition produces harmful results.

While many treatises cover reasons for choosing between antitrust and industry-specific regulation in different circumstances, this section focuses not on which is appropriate where, but on the differences in their *application* and the perceptions associated with each. It is the perceptions, among both the public and professionals, that are at least partially responsible for the trend of preferring competition to 'classic' regulation. I outline below some of the main differences between modes of regulation, to return later on to the dangers associated with overly optimistic views of competition policy relative to regulation, and the dangers to coherence of antitrust when following deregulatory instincts.

It is easy to distinguish between competition and non-competition regulation on the basis of agencies employed or statute enforced. On the surface, competition statutes are general in their equal application to (almost) all industries and their focus on provisions dealing with restraints on trade, rather than the details of what goods or services are traded and on what terms. Industry regulation, on the other hand, usually creates specialized agencies focusing on one industry at a time, dealing with information-intensive rules applied to the content of business behaviour rather than its form.

Some distinguish between economic regulation, which deals with market behaviour, costs incurred and prices charged, and social regulation, which focuses on health effects or safety considerations, or on specific content thought to be beneficial or detrimental to the consuming public (e.g., broadcasting guidelines). Economic regulation is aimed at promoting competition where possible, or emulating its expected results where competition is unlikely to emerge. Social regulation focuses mostly on risk or harm reduction where profit-seeking competition is unlikely to constrain them due to the lack of successful internalization mechanisms.[13]

While such distinctions are helpful, they also obscure cross-pollination effects, whereby competitive pressures may either increase or decrease risk and non-economic harm, due to the specifics of the market considered. Competition policy, the paradigmatic form of purely economic regulation, creates strong incentives for firms to focus on those attributes that consumers are most likely to base their purchases on, creating a myriad of biases due to consumer myopia or irrationality, and ignoring

---

[13] S. Breyer and S. Jasanoff, *Breaking the Vicious Circle: Toward Effective Risk Regulation* (Harvard University Press 1993).

those attributes where information is missing or responsibility is difficult to ascertain.[14]

Competition regulation is likely to create both economic and social effects, though its preferred mode of operation can be categorized and contrasted to industry-specific regulation. Competition regulation is almost purely *ex post*, in that business behaviour is constrained by punishing commercial agreements after their implementation, with the notable exception of merger review.[15] This is not to say that antitrust lacks *ex ante influence*, as surely firms expecting *ex post* review limit themselves in order to avoid it. Still, relative to industry-specific regulation, which focuses on clear and direct rules of conduct and limits on permissible modes of behaviour, competition policy stands out as an *ex post* regime.[16]

Competition policy is also more permissive than most forms of economic regulation, in that firms are assumed to be able to determine their mode of conduct and innovate in business practices, with regulators stepping in only when the outer boundaries are breached, which is usually determined by competitive effect rather than procedural form.[17] This may be due to the fact that competition policy is often an additional constraint on firms that are already regulated at the industry level. Still, similar dynamics exist in non-regulated industries as well as those

---

[14] M.E. Stucke, 'Is Competition Always Good?' (2013) 1 *J. Antitrust Enf.* 1; A.P. Reeves and M.E. Stucke, 'Behavioral Antitrust' (2011) 86 *Ind. L.J.* 1527; D.H. Ginsburg and D.W. Moore, 'The Future of Behavioral Economics in Antitrust Jurisprudence' (2010) 6 *Comp. Pol. Int'l* 89; A. Tor and W.J. Rinner, 'Behavioral Antitrust: A New Approach to the Rule of Reason after Leegin' 2011 *U. Ill. L. Rev.* 805.

[15] Kroes (n. 11 above), characterizing deregulation and subjection to competition policy as a move from *ex ante* to *ex post* review.

[16] Shelanski makes this point with regard to telecommunications, contrasting *ex ante* rules designed to inhibit monopolies by forcing them to comply with rules of conduct with *ex post* enforcement aimed only at behaviour proven harmful: 'As the benefits of ex ante regulation diminish with competition, the more targeted approach of ex post competition enforcement becomes more appropriate.' See H.A. Shelanski, 'Adjusting Regulation to Competition: Toward a New Model for U.S. Telecommunications Policy' (2007) 24 *Yale J. Reg.* 55, 104.

[17] This is not unique to antitrust, and some promote a similar focus in regulation generally; see C. Coglianese and D. Lazer, 'Management-based Regulation: Prescribing Private Management to Achieve Public Goals' (2003) 37 *L. & Soc. Rev.* 691; P.J. May, 'Regulatory Regimes and Accountability' (2007) 1 *Reg. & Gov.* 8; P.J. May, 'Performance-Based Regulation' in D. Levi-Faur (ed.), *Handbook on the Politics of Regulation* (Edward Elgar Publishing 2012) 373.

experiencing de-regulatory tendencies, whether completely absolving them of specific regulatory oversight or limiting it in line with current trends towards trust in markets rather than appointed officials.[18]

It should be stressed that industry-specific regulation and competition policy are not necessarily substitutes. Indeed, in many industries both operate *in tandem*, whether in parallel or in direct interaction between the relevant agencies, facilitating cooperation and holistic application.[19] Specific regulation and antitrust can thus be seen as complements, and some argue that such complementarity is beneficial not merely to the industry and consumers it serves, but to the agencies themselves.[20]

Nonetheless, competition regulation seems to have a better public perception than industry regulation, whether because of the history of regulatory failure, or because antitrust is perceived as objective and professionally managed. Both aspects will be assessed below.

4. REGULATORY FAILURE: REAL AND PERCEIVED

> One cannot mention regulatory agencies without adding the observation that, of course, such agencies are likely to be 'captured' by the interests they are supposed to regulate. To suggest that matters are any different from this is to mark oneself as hopelessly naïve, or even disingenuous.[21]

Industrial regulation seems to be a favourite punching bag for critics of the administrative state and proponents of free markets. To be fair, the history of modern regulation has given critics much to work with, as human frailties and economic incentives combine to make the power of

---

[18] On the other hand, regulation is often seen as *a response* to a lack of oversight by elected officials, lending professionalism to an otherwise political and ineffective regime. See G. Majone, 'From the Positive to the Regulatory State: Causes and Consequences of Changes in the Mode of Governance' (1997) 17 *J. Pub. Pol.* 139.

[19] See, in general, G. Majone, 'Strategy and Structure: The Political Economy of Agency Independence and Accountability' in OECD, *Designing Independent and Accountable Regulatory Agencies for High Quality Regulation* (2005) 126.

[20] See e.g. OECD, *The OECD Report on Regulatory Reform: Synthesis* (1997), which stresses the difficulty of simultaneously serving different types of policy goals. According to this view, regulatory overlap allows for specialization of each agency, while relying on others to 'take up slack' regarding other goals. It is thus the combination of regulations that serves the ultimate good, while each individual agency is 'partially blind' to concerns outside its purview.

[21] J.Q. Wilson, *The Politics of Regulation* (Basic Books 1980) ix.

the state an attractive target for use in manipulating the market and outright rent seeking.[22] This section sets out the main sources of regulatory failure, though it does not presume to completely cover such a rich topic. Instead, I focus on those issues sure to arise in any discussion comparing industry-specific to competition regulation, in order to assess the trend of preferring the latter to the former.[23]

The most prevalent of complaints against industry regulation is that of regulatory capture. This broad term encompasses many sub-topics, but is generally taken to entail having the regulatory board indebted to (if not outright run by) industry insiders. This can occur due to the standard public-choice problem: industrial concerns are better motivated to lobby politicians and regulators because their main source of income is subject to state-imposed limitations, while consumers and the general public are affected marginally and indirectly.[24] It can also stem from the fact that industry is comprised of relatively few and large firms, whereas the public is dispersed. The regulated firms are thus better equipped (and incentivized) to concentrate their lobbying efforts, while the public suffers from 'rational apathy', whereby each individual is better off shirking than contributing to public oversight of the matter at hand.[25]

---

[22] Classic studies include: G.J. Stigler, 'The Theory of Economic Regulation' (1971) 2 *Bell J. Econ. & Manag. Sci.* 3; R.A. Posner, 'Theories of Economic Regulation' (1974) 5 *Bell J. Econ. & Manag. Sci.* 335; S. Peltzman, 'Toward a More General Theory of Regulation' (1976) 19 *J. L. & Econ.* 211. For an overview see D.C. Mueller, 'Public Choice: An Introduction' in C.K. Rowley and F. Schneider (eds), *The Encyclopedia of Public Choice* (Kluwer 2004) 32.

[23] Competition policy is not immune to such concerns, as it is also a source of state-sanctioned power that can be employed selectively and subject to private interests of regulators – or the politicians funding them. See R.L. Faith, D.R. Leavens and R.D. Tollison, 'Antitrust Pork Barrel' (1982) 25 *J. L. & Econ.* 329. On the other hand, since competition law enforcement is subject to judicial review, it may be better situated than other forms of regulation given that judges usually enjoy long and secure tenures, and are thus more prone to favour public interests. See F.S. McChesney, 'Economics Versus Politics in Antitrust' (1999) 23 *Harv. J. L. & Pub. Pol.* 133, text at notes 26–28.

[24] See generally D.A. Farber and P.P. Frickey, *Law and Public Choice: A Critical Introduction* (University of Chicago Press 1991). For a critique focusing on empirical non-regularities in the production of regulation, see H. Hovenkamp, 'Legislation, Well-Being, and Public Choice' (1990) 57 *U. Chi. L. Rev.* 63.

[25] Such rational apathy is also well known in other contexts. Corporate law assumes this dynamic and corrects for it by levying personal fiduciary duties on officers and directors, just as securities legislation takes pains to induce markets for control rather than relying on voting mechanisms which individual shareholders ignore.

Of course, regulators are not blind to this dynamic, and may employ multiple strategies for de-biasing the information they are presented with.[26] Non-governmental agencies and consumer groups may step in to fill the void, though these are also subject to biases plaguing funding and public support. Even if funding is available absent personal gain, or volunteerism is sufficient to place well-meaning and competent actors as representative of public interests, such groups can be formed with industry support as well, replicating the previously discussed asymmetry between public and private interests.[27]

Beyond the general incentive-alignment issues plaguing public deliberation and action, industry regulation is replete with more blatant usurpations conducted by industry insiders who take over the regulatory bodies.[28] Regulators often come from within the subject-industry itself, with obvious associated problems of divided loyalty (if not worse). This might seem overtly wrong, but should be interpreted in light of the expertise and practical experience required for effective regulation. Those possessing the most relevant background for effective oversight are often the same ones educated in the matter at hand through 'coming through the ranks' and working in the regulated industry. Ideally, practical experience can be transplanted from the field to the regulatory office without it being accompanied by old habits and loyalties. Realistically, one should be wary of expecting too much from mere humans.

Even if the regulators themselves are independent thinkers, most of their decisions will need to be based on information garnered from the regulated firms.[29] Obviously, details such as cost data, available technologies, realistic alternatives, etc. are best known by the firms themselves. But even beyond private information from firm records, those with the most expertise in the relevant practicalities are the same ones implementing them in practice. Expertise is developed through investment of time and effort, usually conducted by those seeking to further

---

[26] R.L. Calvert, 'The Value of Biased Information: A Rational Choice Model of Political Advice' (1985) 47 *JOP* 530.

[27] S Lohmann, 'Information, Access, and Contributions: A Signaling Model of Lobbying' (1995) 85 *Public Choice* 267.

[28] This is not unique to industry-specific regulation, but can be achieved through litigation as well, even in the context of competition laws being usurped in order to subvert their very aim. See W.J. Baumol and J.A. Ordover, 'The Use of Antitrust to Subvert Competition' (1985) 28 *J. L. & Econ.* 247 and J.C. Miller III, 'Comments on Baumol and Ordover' (1985) 28 *J. L. & Econ.* 267.

[29] H.A. Shelanski, 'Justice Breyer, Professor Kahn, and Antitrust Enforcement in Regulated Industries' (2012) 100 *Cal. L. Rev.* 487, 490.

their material goals. While general knowledge can often be found outside of the regulated firms, not always are 'book smarts' a good substitute for being 'street smart'.

Even assuming the abovementioned problems were solved or minimized, incentive effects plague current regulators, as their most promising career path after their stint in government lies in joining the firms they have just finished overseeing.[30] This 'revolving doors' phenomenon can stem from firms making direct promises of future rewarding jobs while regulators are in office, but most often such crudeness is unnecessary. Even without discussing the issue, regulators are well aware that current subjects of their decisions are future potential employers, thus self-censorship is to be expected. In other words, regulators might take care not to infringe upon an implicit understanding that 'hand washes hand' dynamics operate inter-temporally, i.e. current solicitude will be met with future compensation.

Regulatory capture is not merely in the interest of regulated firms, but often sought by regulators as well. These may seek the material gains of future jobs or current contributions towards re-election campaigns (if not outright bribes). They might prefer industry support to its antagonism and associated negative publicity (as industry might influence newspapers no less than governmental organizations). They might even prefer to bask in the warm glow of being surrounded by executives and lobbyists appreciative of their wisdom and understanding. They might be seeking recognition even without being aware of doing so, as cognitive dissonance is a powerful force, and humans have a knack for self-justification and persuasion.[31] They might even use academic support for the contention that 'selling out' is not merely in their private interest, but ultimately serves the public as well.[32] It might seem that regulators, like politicians, will need to 'choose sides', determining whether their integrity is for sale and sticking to one preferred position, but research shows they will actually be better off walking a fine line between extreme positions, keeping themselves in the 'median voter' position whereby

---

[30] Y.K. Che, 'Revolving Doors and the Optimal Tolerance for Agency Collusion' (1995) 26 *RAND J. Econ.* 378; D.J. Salant, 'Behind the Revolving Door: A New View of Public Utility Regulation' (1995) 26 *RAND J. Econ.* 362.

[31] J. Hanson and D. Yosifon, 'The Situation: An Introduction to the Situational Character, Critical Realism, Power Economics, and Deep Capture' (2003) 152 *U. Pa. L. Rev.* 129.

[32] P.T. Spiller, 'Politicians, Interest Groups, and Regulators: A Multiple-Principals Agency Theory of Regulation, or "Let Them Be Bribed"' (1990) 33 J. L. & Econ. 65; J.M. Snyder, 'On Buying Legislatures' (1991) 3 *Econ. & Pol.* 93.

their support is fledging – thus in need of constant encouragement.[33] The public-choice perspective thus predicts that regulators will act in a very human way: incentive-compatible, boundedly rational, and hopelessly indeterminate.

5. COMPARING ANTITRUST TO REGULATION

Competition policy is often compared to regulation on uneven terms. While regulatory failure and capture theory are well known and perceived to be prevalent, antitrust is often presented as being aimed solely at efficiency, and thus in the general interest. One may question the general equivalence between efficiency and equity, i.e. whether increasing efficiency indeed allows all concerned to enjoy its rewards.[34] One may also question whether increasing the role of competition in society necessarily increases its welfare, as wealth is far from determinative of well-being and individualistic preferences do not necessarily outrank communitarian benefits.[35] These issues, though, merit deeper consideration than the scope of this chapter permits. Thus I shall focus here on more direct concerns, applicable even within the wealth-maximization framework.[36]

A number of issues stand out in questioning the superiority of antitrust to industry-specific regulation, including the role of expertise, reaction times, the focus on rules versus standards, and precedential value. This section will sketch out the main critiques of supplanting regulation with

---

[33] T. Stratmann, 'Are Contributors Rational? Untangling Strategies of Political Action Committees' (1992) 100 *J. Pol. Econ.* 647.

[34] See generally L.A. Bebchuk, 'The Pursuit of a Bigger Pie: Can Everyone Expect a Bigger Slice?' (1979) 8 *Hofstra L. Rev.* 671; D. Kennedy, 'Cost-Benefit Analysis of Entitlement Problems: A Critique' (1981) 33 *Stan. L. Rev.* 387; L.H. Tribe, 'Constitutional Calculus: Equal Justice or Economic Efficiency?' (1985) 98 *Harv. L. Rev.* 592; J.R. Hackney, 'Law and Neoclassical Economics Theory: A Critical History of the Distribution/Efficiency Debate' (2003) 32 *J. Socio-Econ.* 361. But see R.O. Zerbe, 'Is Cost-Benefit Analysis Legal? Three Rules' (1998) 17 *J. Pol. Anal. & Manag.* 419, arguing that distribution is considered within the cost-benefit framework, and the values promoted stem from legal, not economic, sources.

[35] M.E. Stucke, 'Should Competition Policy Promote Happiness?' (2013) 81 *Fordham L. Rev.* 2575; D. Lewinsohn-Zamir, 'The Objectivity of Well-Being and the Objectives of Property Law' (2003) 78 *N.Y.U. L. Rev.* 1669.

[36] Elsewhere I discuss in depth the broader issues regarding 'what society wants' from antitrust. See A. Ayal, *Fairness in Antitrust: Protecting the Strong from the Weak* (Hart Publishing 2014).

antitrust, setting up the discussion in Section 7 on the dangers to antitrust should this trend continue.

Expertise: Competition agencies are generalist institutions, with authority covering all types of industries and diverse market structures. Given such a broad purview, they obviously cannot accumulate much specific knowledge regarding any single industry. Since their focus is on protecting competition, lack of specificity is often seen as a minor issue, and detailed knowledge of the markets they regulate as irrelevant for policing the broader issues of concentration, anti-competitive agreements and unilateral restraints of trade. This approach assumes that competition issues are independent from nuanced details of the industry in question, an assumption that may be more or less appropriate depending on the circumstances. In the context of deregulation, there is good reason to deem this assumption overly optimistic and simplistic, as industries that were regulated to begin with usually suffer from a variety of market failures, some of which caused initial regulation and some of which were exacerbated by regulatory history.

One of the most vexing problems is that of partial deregulation, where some aspects remain regulated while others are subjected to competitive pressures.[37] For example, in the telecommunications industry it has long been common to view dominant carriers as natural monopolies, leading to rate regulation and compulsory universal service. As some customers are more profitably served, universal service creates cross-subsidization issues, which rate regulation enforces as state policy. When competition is introduced, entrants obviously aim for the more profitable urban market segments, requiring regulatory attention to ensure that rural areas are not cut off. At the same time, entrants often require access to local loops and to network facilities owned by incumbents. The result is mandated access, whereby incumbents are forced to rent facilities to their competitors, facilitating the very entry they resent and fear. Regulators are thus forced to determine access to bottleneck facilities, which requires a great deal of information regarding technical and cost details. This dynamic, of industry-specific regulation operating side by side with competition regulation, led the U.S. Supreme Court to limit antitrust

---

[37] The resulting regime has been called 'synthetic competition', whereby regulators foster entry in order to create possibly inefficient competition. See D.H. Ginsburg, 'Synthetic Competition' in F. Leveque and H. Shelanski (eds), *Antitrust and Regulation in the EU and US: Legal and Economic Perspectives* (Edward Elgar Publishing 2009) 1, for an argument that this focus on viable competitors rather than efficient production requires courts to adopt more lenient standards of adjudication in such industries.

intervention in such cases.[38] Vigorous debate abounds on the appropriate judicial response, but it is obvious that, without specific knowledge, neither competition agencies nor generalist courts are sufficiently informed or experienced to determine access regulation.

Reaction Time: Competition agencies require time to learn a case and bring it before a court. Courts are notoriously slow to decide complex cases, and implementation of judicial determinations can often stretch out over years of additional deliberation, appeal and enforcement. Industry-specific regulation, while far from being perfect itself, is usually set up to handle the issues before it in a much more timely manner, in no little part due to accumulated experience in similar matters. When a legal claim involves financial remuneration alone, tardiness can be forgiven, as *ex post* compensation can be adjusted to reflect both the monetary value of delay and risk versus reward considerations. When the issues at hand include reputation, access to essential facilities and the like, time is not merely money, but may constitute the difference between survival and demise in an unforgiving market. Entrants in telecommunications industries, for example, require constant access not just to physical assets, but protection of service and constant technical upkeep in order to offer their customers a quality-sufficient alternative to that of the incumbent monopoly. *Ex post* compensation cannot be an alternative to timely determination of constantly changing issues.

Rules Versus Standards and the Role of Precedent: Antitrust has experienced a shift away from standards and towards rules, as part of a more general tendency in the direction of technocratic decision-making.[39] Rules offer clarity of application and predictability, with limited discretion afforded to decision-makers. Standards allow for flexible implementation and balancing between competing values, though at the cost of increasing discretion and vagueness.

When industry-specific regulation determines rules of conduct, they are often revisited regularly, while antitrust rules are determined with no specific industry in mind and applied broadly. Furthermore, the mechanism of antitrust dictates that judicially determined rules stay in place for a long time, as appeals are few and far between and litigation is lengthy. The technocratic shift in antitrust thus makes its application problematic to industries requiring context-specific application and constant updating,

---

38 See *Verizon Communications v. Law Offices of Curtis V. Trinko, LLP*, 540 U.S. 398 (2004).

39 D.A. Crane, 'Technocracy and Antitrust' (2007) 86 *Tex. L. Rev.* 1159; D.A. Crane, 'Rules Versus Standards in Antitrust Adjudication' (2007) 64 *Wash. & Lee L. Rev.* 49.

and creates avoidable problems of misapplication when standards are announced that allow for contextual implementation.

The problem of technocratic rules applied across industries becomes more apparent when the precedential value of antitrust decisions is taken into account. Competition agencies constrain themselves by using written guidelines that favour uniform application across context and time. This forms procedural precedent, even where not formally binding. Courts hear antitrust cases rarely, and use them to define key concepts and burdens of proof that are carried on and applied over decades without significant change before the next major case is heard and the precedent reassessed.[40]

6. NETWORKS AS ESSENTIAL FACILITIES

Network industries are the modern equivalent of the classic natural monopolies. Similarly exhibiting increasing returns to scale and path dependence, such markets are resistant to competition and grant a substantial first-mover advantage. When network effects are significant, an initially successful network owner becomes an entrenched incumbent, able to persist even when better alternatives come along. This section outlines the main characteristics of network markets, from the classic formulation to newer and more advanced models showing how firms may impede innovation and deter entry by manipulating the network effects associated with their products. While initially this may seem a strong argument for interventionist competition policy, recent developments in communication technologies and the proliferation of internet-based social media are prohibitive of such a conclusion. As more and more of society is affected by the networks we are engulfed in, competition becomes both more necessary and more difficult to procure.

[40] A striking example is the U.S. Supreme Court's ruling in *Leegin Creative Leather Prods., Inc. v. PSKS, Inc.*, 551 U.S. 877, 127 S. Ct. 2705 (2007), which submitted resale price maintenance to rule-of-reason analysis, after almost a century of per-se review (and several decades of slowly eating away at the rule). Though the Court finally overruled the per-se interpretation of *Dr. Miles Medical Co. v. John D. Park & Sons Co.*, 220 U.S. 373, 31 S. Ct. 376 (1911), the mere existence of a century-long precedent was sufficient to spark a vigorous dissent by Justice Breyer, citing *stare decisis* as a central judicial concern.

6.1 Classic Network Effects: Direct and Indirect

A network of users exists whenever the product in question becomes more valuable as more customers use it. The most commonly known types of user networks are those where consumers communicate amongst themselves using the product in question. The classic examples include telecommunications, software and the internet. In all cases customers buy a product not merely for the direct utility gained from its use, but for its ability to allow them to exchange information with other customers. The word processor used to write this chapter, for example, was chosen not merely for its functionality, but for its prevalence, which makes sharing files easier. An author considering which software program to use would then take into consideration not merely his own convenience, but also the probability that other potential readers (and journals) have a similar product and will easily be able to access the document.

The classic formulation of the type of network effects created by user communication goes along these lines:

$$U = \alpha + \beta N$$

Where α denotes 'inner' utility from the product itself, and β denotes the strength of network effects, i.e. the utility gained from each additional user of the same product. N denotes the number of users. This formulation makes clear that purchasing a product bestows utility upon the consumer from both independent product characteristics and from the existing network of users. Obviously, choice of product takes into consideration not merely the current network of users, but the expected growth pattern of said network as well. Thus a purchaser of a network product essentially predicts the size of the network in order to assess which product to buy. As the classic literature on the subject shows, early adopters creating an installed base of users may very well determine the growth pattern of competing networks, with a significant first-mover advantage potentially outweighing later product improvements.[41] Thus an initially successful network (perhaps because it was first on the market) will garner sufficient 'network utility' (βN, in the above formulation) to outweigh even significant improvements offered by competitors along internal product characteristics. More formally:

---

[41] For a comprehensive survey, see J. Farrell and P. Klemperer, 'Coordination and Lock-In: Competition with Switching Costs and Network Effects' in M. Armstrong and R.H. Porter (eds), *Handbook of Industrial Organization*, Vol. 3 (Elsevier 2007) 1967.

$$U_1 = \alpha_1 + \beta N_1 > U_2 = \alpha_2 + \beta N_2$$
$$\textit{despite } \alpha_1 < \alpha_2$$
$$\textit{because } N_1 > N_2$$

When direct network effects (due to user interactions) are large, one may fear that inefficient standards retain market success, despite better products coming along. Competition, then, is insufficient to assure efficiency.

Indirect network effects create similar results, though due to different dynamics. The best-known examples of indirect network effects include shopping malls, video game consoles and, again, software products. Consider shopping malls: a proprietor of a shop selling fashionable clothes deliberates where to situate a new store. He could find a nice location along a main street, or he could rent a store in a popular shopping mall. The street venue allows for more choice regarding distance from competitors, while the mall is sure to be packed with similar shops competing for the same customers. In theory, geographical distance from competitors is supposed to serve his interests, but indirect network effects suggest the opposite. If a concentration of similar shops is appealing to shoppers, the proprietor might do well to choose the shopping mall although he is sure to face stiffer competition indoors and close by. The reason is simple: more shops selling fashionable clothes create a preferred venue for shoppers looking to purchase such products. The enhanced competitive pressure created by similar products being offered nearby is thus offset by the increased traffic generated by that very concentration of competitors. The proprietor, while suffering from competitive pressure, is simultaneously enjoying the fruits of this competition, and either effect may dominate.

The video game and software examples create similar dynamics. A manufacturer of a video game (or computer application) must choose which platform to aim for. A game working on Sony Playstation is programmed differently from one planned to work on Microsoft X-Box. Similarly, a word processor planned for Windows is different from one planned to run Apple's OS-X. In both video games and computers, the program runs as an application using the operating system (or console hardware) as a platform. When deciding which platform should form the basis of an application, many considerations are relevant, but chief among them is the future demand expected, which will generate profits for the developer. Indirect network effects in this scenario entail the developer choosing the platform expected to 'do best' in the market, with the number (and popularity) of other applications as a strong indicator of future success. The result is that the developer actually prefers to aim for the more 'crowded' platform, essentially choosing to locate close to potential competitors for the same consumers' demand.

Indirect network effects are similar to direct ones in that a platform that is able to garner initial success, leverages this popularity to attract additional users (competitors), creating a potentially never-ending cycle which hinders competing platforms' ability to enter the market. While initially the 'chicken-and-egg' problem plagues network products attempting to create an installed base of users, once popular support begins, it creates a 'vicious circle' (or wonderful one, depending on the commentator's perspective) whereby success breeds success, sometimes even in the face of later improvements that are unable to garner a sufficient network to make themselves attractive to users. In other words, the problem of excessive inertia exists in all network markets, whether direct or indirect. Both exhibit demand-side economies of scale, in that demand is subject to a self-fulfilling prophecy. As more consumers *believe* a specific network will become dominant, they flock to it in order to enjoy the network effects it will exhibit as its size grows. As consumers flock to a network, they convince others that the initial belief was well-founded, thus convincing other consumers to choose this network over its alternatives. An initial belief thus creates the groundwork for its own materialization, and an initial movement creates the swell that follows it. These effects are akin to demand-side economies of scale, as the product's future utility (determining its demand) increases with its current demand – precisely the snowballing effect referred to above.

This dynamic was made famous in the Microsoft trials of the 1990s, and generated much scholarship and controversy.[42] Obviously the description above is partial and superficial compared to the intricacies and complexities in real-world markets, yet the dynamic described may

---

[42] See e.g. F.M. Fisher, 'The IBM and Microsoft Cases: What's the Difference?' (2000) 90 *Am. Econ. Rev.* 180; S.J. Liebowitz and S.E. Margolis, *Winners, Losers & Microsoft: Competition and Antitrust in High Technology* (Independent Institute 1999); R.J. Gilbert and M.L. Katz, 'An Economist's Guide to US v. Microsoft' (2001) 15 *J. Econ. Persp.* 25; J.E. Lopatka and W.H. Page, 'Microsoft, Monopolization, and Network Externalities: Some Uses and Abuses of Economic Theory in Antitrust Decision Making' (1995) 40 *Antitrust Bull.* 317; D.L. Rubinfeld, 'Antitrust Enforcement in Dynamic Network Industries' (1998) 43 *Antitrust Bull.* 859; D.S. Evans, A.L. Nichols and R. Schmalensee, 'An Analysis of the Government's Economic Case in US v. Microsoft' (2001) 46 *Antitrust Bull.* 163.

be prevalent and powerful enough to forestall effective competition absent governmental intervention.[43]

6.2 Strategic Network Effects: Strengthening First-Mover Advantage

The classic formulation of network effects applies to those products which, due to their connectivity or interaction effects, exhibit demand-side economies of scale. Beyond these classic 'network products' lie a multitude of products and markets in which firms can strategically invest in strengthening the network effects, creating the dynamics outlined above. Where such investment is possible, firms enjoying an initial first-mover advantage (unrelated to network effects) can build upon it to create formidable barriers to entry and impede future competition.

Two general types of strategic investment in creating network effects exist, technology-based and price-mediated investment. Both qualify as 'voluntary network effects' due to their being non-deterministic and wholly dependent on voluntary considerations by the appropriate firms. I shall outline their general characteristics below, though in condensed form as they are but one aspect of the general concern this section aims to elucidate.[44]

Technologically induced voluntary network effects are best understood by expanding upon the example of video game consoles above. Initially, such games were sold via disk for installation and use on one specific console at a time. In this formulation, the games are subject to indirect network effects, as described above; thus some platforms are more attractive to developers because they have already developed an installed base of users (owners of the console) who are potential customers for newly developed games. The market could potentially be monopolized by a successful console manufacturer, but could also support a number of consoles, creating an oligopolistic market of several consoles, each boasting a variety of games. Competition in the market for consoles would be limited, as additional consoles fragment the market, limiting the number of games offered on each. Alternatively, console manufacturers could aim for expanding the variety they offer by paying developers to offer games compatible with their platform. Note, though, that this strategy entails multiple fixed costs, as each version requires investment

[43] But see S.J. Liebowitz and S.E. Margolis, 'Network Externality: An Uncommon Tragedy' (1994) 8 *J. Econ. Persp.* 133, for a view of network effects as more prevalent in theory than practice.

[44] For a more detailed and nuanced version, see A. Ayal, 'Monopolization via Voluntary Network Effects' (2009) 76 *Antitrust L.J.* 799.

of funds and effort. Thus, offering a single game on multiple platforms would be more expensive than limiting its distribution to one (or a few) consoles.

A console manufacturer able to attract more users would thus need to compensate developers to a lesser extent, as he essentially pays them not with money for development, but with customers potentially buying the game once it is offered. Console manufacturers thus compete for users not merely for the financial remuneration paid at the store counter, but for their bolstering developers' incentive to focus their efforts on this console, rather than another. This dynamic, of consumers exhibiting a positive externality on console manufacturers, is precisely the network effect outlined above, and this same dynamic creates a tipping effect that makes concentration (if not outright monopoly) in the console market predictable.

Now assume that one console manufacturer recognizes that the indirect network effect which occurs naturally in the market induces concentration, but is insufficient to cause tipping to monopoly.[45] This manufacturer may invest in developing a technological add-on which facilitates user connectivity, allowing users ('gamers') to play games online with other gamers using the same console. Online gaming is now a reality, prevalent through many platforms. Thus it may be difficult to imagine a console manufacturer choosing to develop this concept for strategic reasons. Still, the initial choice to develop this capability has both internal and network-related reasons. Internal product characteristics have to do with a networked product being more highly valued by consumers and thus able to justify a higher price. Network-related reasons (using the terminology of β above), have to do with transforming the market from one where relatively robust competition exists to one where a strong network effect induces tipping. If network effects are sufficiently strong (and this depends on the benefits users receive from online gaming, dependent in part on the manufacturers' efforts and investment), the market could

---

[45] This could occur due to heterogeneous consumers, each type of which prefers different console characteristics, or due to fixed costs of development being significant, but not to an extent which limits developers to focus exclusively on one platform. It may even be due to developers' strategic considerations, recognizing that if they limit themselves to one version they enjoy lower production costs, but subject themselves to console monopoly later on. Developers might, then, choose to invest in current production costs in order to lower future monopoly price. The choice to focus exclusively on one standard or on many is generally referred to as single vs. multi-homing. See Farrell and Klemperer (n. 41 above).

exhibit 'race for the market' characteristics, allowing monopoly to flourish and severely limiting entry or competitor survival.

The video game example is but one possibility that is easily comprehended due to on-line gaming being a reality familiar to many. The same dynamic could be imagined within any other product category that has the potential of user connectivity (for direct network effects) or platform basis (for indirect network effects). The main point is that investment in technological add-ons to existing products may enhance existing network effects or create new ones. While online gaming may be profitable in and of itself (due to consumers' attraction to its internal benefit), the added network effect may transform such an add-on from the 'nice to have, but too expensive' category to 'worth investing in for future monopoly'. From an antitrust perspective, investment aimed at transforming a relatively competitive market into monopoly is precisely the type of monopolization that is punishable in some jurisdictions, and problematic when carried out by dominant firms in others.[46]

Price-mediated network effects are similar in effect, though they operate through a different source. Here, a tipping dynamic is created by offering consumers rebates dependent either on the number of buyers they bring with them or on the number of consumers in the entire network. The basic idea is similar to that behind purchasing groups or 'friends and family' clubs.[47] If firms are able to offer rebates or price reductions to consumers according to the number of other consumers, this replicates the positive user externality generating standard (direct) network effects. Such tactics can be used in order to generate sufficient interest by early adopters to jump-start a new network product or create herd behaviour by consumers using popularity as a proxy for quality. In and of itself, price-mediated network effects (PMNEs) are unprofitable as

---

[46] See M. Gal, 'Monopoly Pricing as an Antitrust Offense in the US and the EC: Two Systems of Belief about Monopoly?' (2004) 49 *Antitrust Bull.* 343. See also C.C. Rudaz, 'Did *Trinko* Really Kill Antitrust Price Squeeze Claims? A Critical Approach to the *Linkline* Decision through a Comparison of E.U. and U.S. Case Law' (2010) 43 *Vanderbilt J. Transn'l L.* 1077, for an application to regulatory intervention in transforming markets. See also P. Larouche, 'Contrasting Legal Solutions and the Comparability of EU and US Experiences' in Leveque and Shelanski 2009 (n. 37 above).

[47] The market for frequent flyer miles has increased dramatically since its inception; see L. Hoffman, 'The Frequent Flyer Mile Frenzy' (2003) *Int'l Travel L.J.* 201. S. Storm and J.F. Larsen, 'Frequent Flyer Programmes in the EU: Competition Issues and Regulatory Framework' (2000) *Int'l Travel L.J.* 211, assess such loyalty programmes as anti-competitive due to their increasing switching costs and creating barriers to entry.

a monopolization device, because a source of revenue is needed to finance such rebates, and if consumers do not generate true positive externalities, the firm is essentially financing its clientele. Still, if production exhibits returns to scale, or an installed base of consumers is important for network or fashion-related reasons, PMNEs are a strong tactic allowing for generating tipping in an otherwise competitive market.[48]

Both types of voluntary network effects are constrained in application, as the relation between costs and network benefit depends on parameters specific to application. Their effectiveness as a technique of monopolization is thus dependent on context and case-by-case analysis is necessary to determine their anticompetitive effect.[49] Still, cases of such application can be discerned in real-world data and theory gives good reason to take care when examining such cases.[50] As a general issue, voluntary network effects show that tipping and platform issues merit concern. Since tipping markets exhibit a specific type of barrier to entry that is reminiscent of essential facilities and troubling to competition policy, one might ask whether courts' seeming disdain for essential facilities claims underestimates the competitive harm present in today's highly networked world.

6.3 Networked World: Proprietary Versus Global Network Effects

Many describe today's world as 'a global village', where manufacturers and consumers are linked across national boundaries, with globalization a

---

48 See S. Borenstein, 'Repeat-Buyer Programs in Network Industries' in W. Sicel and D.L. Alexander (eds), *Networks, Infrastructure, and the New Task for Regulation* (University of Michigan Press 1996) 137.

49 Frequent flyer miles, for instance, were found to be beneficial to dominant carriers and unimportant for non-dominant ones, when examined on a per-airport basis. See M. Lederman, 'Do Enhancements to Loyalty Programs Affect Demand? The Impact of International Frequent Flyer Partnerships on Domestic Airline Demand' (2007) 38 *RAND J. Econ.* 1134.

50 Loyalty programmes are rampant in the marketplace, and vigorous debate ensues as to their increasing switching costs, reducing entry and facilitating tacit collusion. For various perspectives on the issue, see R. Caminal and A. Claici, 'Are Loyalty-rewarding Pricing Schemes Anti-competitive?' (2007) 4 *Int'l J. Ind. Org.* 647; D. Reitman and P. Greenlee, 'Distinguishing Competitive and Exclusionary Uses of Loyalty Discounts' (2005) 50 *Antitrust Bull.* 441; Y.F. Fong and Q. Liu, 'Loyalty Rewards Facilitate Tacit Collusion' (2011) 20 *J. Econ. & Manag. Strat.* 739; G. Faella, 'The Antitrust Assessment of Loyalty Discounts and Rebates' (2008) 4 *J. Comp. L. & Econ.* 375.

dominant force. In a sense, this mental picture of a global network seems to alleviate antitrust concern, as competition is assumed to come not only from local businesses, but internationally and in real time. Still, one must not confuse proprietary networks with those open to all, and compatible versus fragmented standards.

Proprietary networks are those referred to above in the discussion of network effects and the ensuing tipping to monopoly. Implicit in the analysis is an assumption that in order to enjoy the benefits associated with the network, one must buy the product offered by the network owner. These can include the specific brand of game console, the dominant shopping mall, or the airline alliance offering frequent-flyer or 'friends and family' programmes to those flying on its member airlines.[51] When network effects are proprietary, one cannot enjoy the benefits associated with membership without actually becoming a member, and this entails purchase of the networked product.

Non-proprietary (global) network effects are different. When the network is open to all, everyone joining enjoys the benefits created by other members, without the necessity of purchasing a specific brand of product. For example, when considering whether to purchase a handheld phone, a major benefit is associated with the number of potential calling partners, which includes all those owning any kind of phone. One may use a landline to call a mobile and vice versa, and one may purchase any kind of mobile phone to place such calls. This may seem obvious today, but in the early days of telecommunications, purchasing decisions were very different. In the U.S., if one purchased a phone from AT&T, one could use it to call only other subscribers of the same service.[52] Different

---

[51] Loyalty programmes have an effect on competition through creating an incentive towards concentration of individual firms seeking to create a proprietary network larger than their own set of customers, and offering more choice in exercising accumulated benefits. This is one of the reasons for leading airlines to join alliances which operate as semi-proprietary networks – including multiple independently run firms viewed as one 'group' by consumers, who can use transfer and loyalty coupons issued by one firm and honoured by others within the group. Essentially, this can be seen as a partial merger, and it raises similar questions, though obviously the issues at hand are much broader than merely the loyalty programmes they give rise to. See J. Reitzes and D. Moss, 'Airline Alliances and Systems Competition' (2008–2009) 45 *Houston L. Rev.* 293.

[52] C. Aubert and J.J. Laffont, 'Designing Infrastructure Regulation in Developing Countries' in P. Beato and J.J. Laffont (eds), *Competition Policy in Regulated Industries: Approaches for Emerging Economies* (Inter-American Development Bank 2002) 1, 8; G.W. Brock, *The Telecommunications Industry: The Dynamics of Market Structure* (Harvard University Press 1981).

cities were served by different companies, and a major part of AT&T's competitive strategy was to offer long-distance calling only to its own subscribers. In the terminology set out above, in order for a customer of a local landline to use AT&T's long distance, he would have to 'multi-home', i.e. add an AT&T line to his existing local one, physically keeping two (or more) phones on his desk, each for calling subscribers of that specific phone company.

The transformation of proprietary telecom networks into global ones was brought about by governmental intervention, forcing AT&T to allow other phone companies access to its network, well after many such companies were forced to leave the market (directly or by selling their business to AT&T). Describing a network as proprietary or global is thus not merely a fact of nature, but dependent on legal standards which themselves are subject to revision.

The role of proprietary versus global networks is even more pronounced in technical standards. When firms introduce standards, a network of users is created by employing said standards in the manufacture of other products. When a standard is proprietary, all firms wishing to use it in new products must reach commercial agreements with the standard-creating firm. Royalties are usually paid, and oftentimes the standard becomes a source of contention when firms are charged (what they deem) excessive prices, or are denied use altogether.[53] Such proprietary standards are not merely sources of monopoly pricing, but often serve as *de facto* essential facilities, with the network of products based upon them serving as a barrier to entry for other firms.

Due to this dynamic, standard-setting organizations are often formed specifically in order to allow all firms in the industry not merely to choose the best standard, but to ensure that one global network be formed rather than fragmenting into several distinct ones.[54] Of course, this does not guarantee success, as firm heterogeneity creates different incentives for different firms according to their status in the industry, size of consumer and supplier networks, and ability to succeed as stand-alone businesses rather than network members. Cases have been known where firms introduce technical standards and convince others to employ them,

---

[53] D.G. Swanson and W.J. Baumol, 'Reasonable and Nondiscriminatory (RAND) Royalties, Standards Selection, and Control of Market Power' (2005) 73 *Antitrust L.J.* 1; J. Farrell, J. Hayes, C. Shapiro and T. Sullivan, 'Standard-Setting, Patents, and Hold-Up' (2007) 74 *Antitrust L.J.* 603.

[54] M.A. Lemley, 'Intellectual Property Rights and Standard-Setting Organizations' (2002) 90 *Cal. L. Rev.* 1889.

only to assert ownership once sufficient installed base has been generated.[55] This grants them monopoly power, with pricing and limiting terms determined accordingly.[56]

The dividing line between proprietary and global networks lies in compatibility. When products of different firms are perfectly compatible, users of different brands may interact and complementary products to each brand become complements to them all. In such cases, even if different brands exist, users (both consumers and manufacturers of complements) need not choose a brand according to how popular it is (or is expected to become), but according to 'internal' benefits, price, availability, or other relevant attributes. From a network-effects perspective, compatibility increases welfare, as full benefits can be assimilated by all. From the individual firm's perspective, on the other hand, compatibility is a mixed blessing – or more accurately, a heterogeneously distributed one.

Firms with large installed bases do well on their own, especially when consumers value connectivity highly. Such firms will attract consumers due to their network of users or suppliers, increasing the installed base even more. Compatibility mitigates this advantage in the marketplace, as from the new user's perspective the relevant network includes all firms' customers and suppliers. A new consumer can purchase the product of a small firm which is new to the market, relying on compatibility to facilitate interaction with existing users and products. The small firm is thus at no (network) disadvantage to the large. This may seem to be fair and allow 'competition on the merits', but might mask the disadvantage plaguing the firms that invested initially to create the market or the technical standard, only to see their profits dissipate in *ex post* competition.

Viewing the issue from an *ex ante* perspective, forced compatibility might create disincentives for investment, as firms have no chance for recoupment of sunk and fixed costs. This is reminiscent of the classic 'increasing returns to scale' argument which explains the creation of natural monopoly or highly concentrated oligopolistic markets. There, production economies of scale justify non-marginal pricing, as, when average cost declines with increasing production, selling at marginal cost entails ultimate losses. Industries with high fixed costs require incentives

---

55 G.S. Cary, L.C. Work-Dembowski and P.S. Hayes, 'Antitrust Implications of Abuse of Standard-Setting' (2007) 15 *George Mason L. Rev.* 1241.

56 T.J. Muris, 'Looking Forward: The Federal Trade Commission and the Future Development of U.S. Competition Policy' (2003) *Colum. Bus. L. Rev.* 359, 395–96.

for *ex ante* investment, and these usually occur due to *ex post* concentration allowing for oligopolistic pricing. Full compatibility essentially makes each firm's network the property of all, thus creating cross-subsidization whereby early movers finance later adopters. Firms anticipating dissipation of returns from investment in network creation will thus refrain from this investment, leaving everyone worse off.[57]

Network theory is often cited in the regulation and antitrust literature when dealing with 'network industries', such as telecommunications, railroads, airlines, etc. The internet revolution gave prominence to network issues, and extended them beyond the obvious industries. Essentially, the internet is a global network allowing multi-media communication between all users – the ultimate form of global network effects.[58] One of the insights developed in the study of previous network industries, and even more relevant within internet connectivity, is that owners of platform products are happy to allow others to develop complements to their products, making the network even more beneficial to its users, but are wary of substitutes.[59] This dynamic becomes all the more problematic the more necessary the platform becomes, and leads to cries for enforcement of the essential facilities doctrine to impose duties to deal with rivals on neutral terms. Examples include the antitrust trials of Microsoft (viewing the interoperability information included in its operating system as a type of essential facility), the debate regarding network neutrality, and the (unsuccessful) claim that Google should be subject to search neutrality.[60] As Hovenkamp states: 'The best solution for global market dominating networks such as the telecom system is to let the network itself attain the size and shape that will achieve all

---

57 D.F. Spulber and C.S. Yoo, 'Network Regulation: The Many Faces of Access' (2005) 1 *J. Comp. L. & Econ.* 635.

58 The internet includes both new forms of communication, e.g. social media of various types, as well as a physical platform combining previous forms of communications within a new technological means of conducting them, e.g., VOIP. Both forms make the medium important and strengthen the case for viewing internet access as a very essential facility indeed. See J.E. Nuechterlein and P.J. Weiser, *Digital Crossroads: American Telecommunications Policy in the Internet Age* (MIT Press 2005).

59 See e.g. H. Hovenkamp, 'Antitrust and the Costs of Movement' (2012) 78 *Antitrust L.J.* 67, 85–86.

60 B. Frischmann and S. Weber Waller, 'Revitalizing Essential Facilities' (2008) 75 *Antitrust L.J.* 1; A. Renda, 'Competition–Regulation Interface in Telecommunications: What's Left of the Essential Facility Doctrine' (2010) 34 *Telecom. Pol.* 23; R.W. Hahn, R.E. Litan and H.J. Singer, 'The Economics of Wireless Net Neutrality' (2007) 3 *J. Comp. L. & Econ.* 399; D.A. Crane, 'Search

available economies of scale and scope, but then to use legal policy to preserve competition within the network.'[61] Yet implementation is complex. What legal policy should be used? How broad are the duties to deal with rivals and how should monopoly be defined in a dynamic and innovative context, especially one as multifaceted as the internet and its dominant (for now) platforms? Or, in the limited context this chapter presumes, which type of institution should make such choices, competition agencies, generalist courts, or industry regulators?

Deciding how to impose competition on a network involves considerations not only with regard to the importance of such competition, or the extent of access competitors require, but determinations as to the architecture of the network itself.[62] The internet exhibits 'small worlds' characteristics, whereby nodes are heterogeneous with regard to the amount of links they possess, and this network is constantly evolving due to both the premeditated strategy of those vying for more influence and non-directed phases of growth and decline of various spheres within the network.[63] Implications cover technological sectors, the promulgation of innovation and ideas, and the structure of society itself.[64] Some fear internet connectivity is associated with the decline of communal interaction, while others promise more nuanced communities, moving beyond geographical and traditional social ties.[65] Models of interaction within networks promise connectivity as a solution for a myriad of social ills, creating a naturally evolving cooperative environment impossible in a

---

Neutrality as an Antitrust Principle' (2012) 19 *George Mason L. Rev.* 1199; M. Law, '"Neutral" Search as a Basis for Antitrust Action?' (2013) 26 *Harv. J. L. & Tech.* 1.

61 Hovenkamp (n. 59 above) 87.

62 Y. Benkler, *The Wealth of Networks: How Social Production Transforms Markets and Freedom* (Yale University Press 2006).

63 R. Albert and A.L. Barabási, 'Statistical Mechanics of Complex Networks' (2002) 74 *Rev. Mod. Phys.* 47; D.J. Watts and S.H. Strogatz, 'Collective Dynamics of "Small-world" Networks' (1998) 393 *Nature* 440.

64 M. Castells, *The Rise of the Network Society: The Information Age: Economy, Society and Culture* (Wiley: 2nd edn 2010); B. Wellman, 'The Rise of Networked Individualism' in L. Keeble (ed.), *Community Networks Online* (Taylor & Francis 2001); M. Castells and G. Cardoso (eds), *The Network Society: From Knowledge to Policy* (Center for Translantic Relations 2006).

65 B. Wellman, J. Boase and W. Chen, 'The Networked Nature of Community: Online and Offline' (2002) 1 *IT & Soc.* 151; B. Wellman, 'The Rise (and Possible Fall) of Networked Individualism' (2002) 24 *Connections* 30.

non-networked world.[66] Social capital, always an important subject, becomes all the more so when it is determinative of an ever-increasing part of the benefits individuals receive from society, making access to the quintessential social network all the more important.[67]

Network effects have thus become applicable to interests well beyond a few specified industries, or economic concerns alone. Society itself is determined by the networks it allows to flourish, as the place of individuals within society depends to an ever-growing extent on their ability to participate in the network activities and speak its language. Universal access thus becomes all the more important, both on a physical level and as to the technological literacy of different segments of the population.[68]

When the issues are as diverse and as culturally important as this, competition policy should either incorporate the non-economic concerns involved, or give way to regulatory agencies, which are more able to balance conflicting interests and address non-quantifiable concerns. Of course, regulation is far from perfect, and as shown above, suffers from various failures and biases; thus a regulatory solution might seem overly optimistic. Still, as antitrust becomes more rule-oriented and technocratic, its insulation from political influences is not necessarily a virtue. The internet functions as more than an economic platform exhibiting increasing returns to scale; it functions as a platform for society itself. Maintaining its global network effects may be a competition-oriented issue, which can arguably be addressed by antitrust. Maintaining and promoting its social implications and potential for disruptive ideas side-by-side with disruptive technologies goes beyond the competence and comparative advantage of competition agencies. Arguments ensue as

---

[66] E. Pestelacci, M. Tomassini and L. Luthi, 'Evolution of Cooperation and Coordination in a Dynamically Networked Society' (2008) 3 *Biological Theory* 139; S. Van Segbroeck, F.C. Santos, J.M. Pacheco and T. Lenaerts, 'Coevolution of Cooperation, Response to Adverse Social Ties and Network Structure' (2010) 1 *Games* 317. But see G. Topa, 'Social Interactions, Local Spillovers and Unemployment' (2001) 68 *Rev. Econ. Stud.* 261, for an empirical assessment suggesting such social ties are more important where self-sufficiency fails, such as in low-income and minority groups, and less important for affluent and educated job-seekers.

[67] M. Marsili, F. Vega-Redondo and F. Slanina, 'The Rise and Fall of a Networked Society: A Formal Model' (2004) 101 *Proceedings of the National Academy of Sciences of the United States of America* 1439.

[68] P. Xavier, 'Universal Service and Public Access in the Networked Society' (1997) 21 *Telecom. Pol.* 829. See generally Castells (n. 64 above).

to whether or not (and how) the internet should be regulated.[69] The discussion above addressed some of the complexities involved, arguing that competition agencies are overtly single-minded with respect to what the benefits of their involvement should be. Regulating a dynamic cultural platform as merely a competition issue is thus problematic. The next section generalizes the claim, stressing the flip side of the debate: not that competition agencies are ill-prepared for such regulation, but that they themselves should fear it. The dangers are thus not only for the object of regulation, but for the regulators themselves.

7. ANTITRUST DANGERS: WHEN COMPETITION POLICY TURNS REGULATORY

Successful networks are significant inputs to the production of complementary products, becoming both platforms and bottlenecks able to exploit users and foreclose competitors. It would seem, then, that the essential facilities doctrine would impose upon them a duty to deal, one becoming more and more important in our networked society. Yet precisely this claim was relegated to 'the outer boundaries of Section 2 claims' by the U.S. Supreme Court, while it simultaneously relegated antitrust intervention as secondary to industry regulation.[70] Of course, one could read the decision differently, as preferring industry regulation *only where it already exists*, thus not taking a stand on which is preferable, but merely limiting parallel enforcement of two different types of regulation. The Court, according to this view, signals its trust in industry regulators while limiting not competition regulators, but the agents of private enforcement exploiting antitrust rules when they should be petitioning the regulators in charge.[71] According to an even more

---

[69] T.M. Lenard and R.J. May (eds), *Net Neutrality or Net Neutering: Should Broadband Internet Services be Regulated?* (Springer 2006); N.P. Dickerson, 'What Makes the Internet so Special? And Why, Where, How, and by Whom Should its Content Be Regulated?' (2009) 46 *Houston L. Rev.* 61; S.R. Salbu, 'Who Should Govern the Internet?: Monitoring and Supporting a New Frontier' (1997) 11 *Harv. J. L. & Tech.* 429; Spulber and Yoo (n 57 above); S. Weber Waller, 'Antitrust and Social Networking' (2012) 90 *N.C. L. Rev.* 1771.

[70] *Verizon Communications Inc. v. Law Offices of Curtis V. Trinko, LLP*, 540 U.S. 398, 124 S. Ct. 872 (2004). For criticism of the Court's view, see e.g. H.A. Shelanski, 'The Case for Rebalancing Antitrust and Regulation' (2011) 109 *Mich. L. Rev.* 683.

[71] See A.E. Kahn, 'Telecommunications: The Transition from Regulation to Antitrust' (2006) 5 *J. Telecom. & High Tech. L.* 159.

limiting reading, the Court never decided anything regarding institutional advantage, preferring merely the centralization of decision-making within one institution, and choosing industry regulators since they already have jurisdiction on the issue.[72]

Trinko, together with the *Credit Suisse* decision[73] handed down after it, are generally read as supportive of regulatory oversight and limiting simultaneous enforcement of competition standards by specific regulators and antitrust plaintiffs. Nonetheless, it is important to remember that they apply only within industries subject to active specific regulation and thus do not expressly limit antitrust enforcement within unregulated network industries. As shown in Section 6 above, networks are also prevalent outside of such contexts, and are growing in importance as the internet and social media become dominant platforms. The disillusionment with classic regulation, together with a belief in market-induced innovation, make subjecting such networks to appointed regulators unlikely, with cries for antitrust oversight growing. This section thus outlines the dangers inherent in expanding antitrust purview in order to supplant industry regulation where the latter is being downsized, as well as to oversee emerging markets where networks constitute essential facilities. The analysis should not be taken to mean that antitrust oversight is harmful *per se*, or should always be avoided, but to point out inherent pitfalls and recommend context-specific examination.

7.1 Antitrust as Subject to Regulatory Failures

Antitrust is often described as focused on aggregate efficiency and less prone than regulation to favour specific constituents or special interests.[74] The history of antitrust tells a slightly different story. Passed at the behest

---

[72] See T.J. Brennan, 'Essential Facilities and *Trinko*: Should Antitrust and Regulation be Combined?' (2008–2009) 61 Fed. Comm. L. J. 133. For a similar reading of *Trinko*'s 'sister case', *Credit Suisse v. Billing*, 551 U.S. 264, 127 S. Ct. 2383 (2007), see J.A. Kling, 'Securities Regulation in the Shadow of the Antitrust Laws: The Case for a Broad Implied Immunity Doctrine' (2011) 120 *Yale L.J.* 910.

[73] *Credit Suisse v. Billing*, 551 U.S. 264, 127 S. Ct. 2383 (2007).

[74] D.W. Carlton and R.C. Picker, 'Antitrust and Regulation' in N.L. Rose (ed.), *Economic Regulation and Its Reform: What Have We Learned?* (University of Chicago Press 2014) 25; S.L. Dogan and M.A. Lemley, 'Antitrust Law and Regulatory Gaming' (2009) 87 *Tex. L. Rev.* 685, go further, arguing not only that antitrust is less susceptible to private interests, but that non-economic goals furthered by specific regulation are inherently more prone to capture than economic goals.

of small businesses, the Sherman Act initially aimed to protect competition mostly for the sake of competitors, rather than consumers.[75] At the time, large business concerns were gaining dominance in multiple markets, both due to their efficient use of size and new business methods, and due to their employment of anticompetitive practices. Over time, U.S. competition policy was streamlined to enhance efficiency and focus on collective (rather than private) concerns, but anticompetitive uses of competition law were never completely eradicated.[76] Enforced by state and federal agencies, political influence over agency decisions was exerted both through funding and through appointment of officials. Some argue that the reason for the expansion in federal antitrust enforcement was precisely in order to limit excessive private interest litigation in some states, which was aimed at curtailing out-of-state entry and expropriating benefits from non-local firms.[77] In short, power attracts influence and, similar to any governmental regulation, antitrust has never been completely immune to this propensity.

Of course, regulation may very well be more prone to failure than antitrust, due to the latter's economic focus, which generates objective standards by which to judge it, yet where economic analysis is multifaceted, discretion in its application yields some control of its results. Judicial review by generalist judges may help in this matter, yet imperfectly. Firstly, generalist judges are imperfect arbiters of economic science, and should not be expected to successfully discriminate among competing claims supported by expert economic witnesses, especially

---

75 R.H. Lande, 'Wealth Transfers as the Original and Primary Concern of Antitrust: The Efficiency Interpretation Challenged' (1982) 34 *Hastings L.J.* 65; D.J. Boudreaux, T.J. DiLorenzo and S. Parker, 'Antitrust Before the Sherman Act' in F.S. McChesney and W.F. Shughart (eds), *The Causes and Consequences of Antitrust: The Public-Choice Perspective* (University of Chicago Press 1995) 255; see also R.B. Ekelund, M.J. McDonald and R.D. Tollison, 'Business Restraints and the Clayton Act of 1914: Public- or Private-Interest Legislation?' in the same volume, p. 271, arguing similarly for the Clayton Act.

76 W.J. Baumol and J.A. Ordover, 'The Use of Antitrust to Subvert Competition' (1985) 28 *J. L. & Econ.* 247; D.D. Sokol, 'The Strategic Use of Public and Private Litigation in Antitrust as Business Strategy' (2012) 85 *S. Cal. L. Rev.*; D.A. Crane, 'Optimizing Private Antitrust Enforcement' (2010) 63 *Vanderbilt L. Rev.* 675.

77 J.S. Wiley Jr., 'A Capture Theory of Antitrust Federalism' (1986) 99 *Harv. L. Rev.* 713.

when the economic methods are complex.[78] Secondly, much of antitrust (at least in the U.S.) is enforced through private litigation, which is subject to a selection bias. Since plaintiffs bring only those cases from which they expect to benefit, litigation incentives are skewed. Cases benefitting the public will generally be brought only by governmental agencies, with the large majority of private litigation being initiated by competitors seeking to use legal means to secure market success. Some of these competitors have rightful claims, but a large part of them should be expected to be furthering their own aims rather than aggregate welfare.

7.2 Antitrust as Losing Focus and Diluting Expertise

As explained in Section 5 above, expertise plays a large role in industry regulation, while antitrust focuses on broad arguments implementable universally by generalist judges and agencies. Expanding the application of competition law to deregulated industries, and to network markets subjected to competition regulation in lieu of creating regulatory agencies, is likely to be challenging in this regard. Whereas in these sectors industry specifics matter, antitrust agencies have neither the time nor the expertise to delve into details and assess market characteristics beyond the broad generalizations of micro-economic theory.

A useful example is provided by New Zealand's regulatory experiment in the telecommunications industry. There, regulation was placed solely in the hands of the competition authority, with no industry regulator in place. While competition in telecommunications is obviously important, commentators generally agree that lack of expertise prevented effective regulation, and the market suffered as a result. Phil Weiser, for example, focused his critique on the need for industry-specific knowledge to accurately determine access rules, an issue of interest for our examination of networks and platforms more generally.[79] Aubert and Laffont, while surveying developing economies more generally, agree with the critique, pointing out that New Zealand has since changed direction, adding specific regulation to its competition oversight of the telecommunications

---

[78] M.R. Baye and J.D. Wright, 'Is Antitrust Too Complicated for Generalist Judges? The Impact of Economic Complexity and Judicial Training on Appeals' (2011) 54 *J. L. & Econ.* 1.

[79] P.J. Weiser, 'The Relationship of Antitrust and Regulation in a Deregulatory Era' (2005) 50 *Antitrust Bull.* 549.

sector.[80] A survey of New Zealand's policy in the matter that compared it with the U.S. industry regulation paradigm and the Australian mixed version came to similar conclusions, albeit with a preference for Australia's interconnected agency framework over U.S.-style competition between regulators.[81] There seems to be a broad agreement on the 'difficulty of ensuring competition in the absence of regulation', even without delving into the additional non-economic goals and equity considerations which sector-specific regulators ensure.[82] Some even use the language of monopoly to describe regulatory output, lauding even duplicative efforts by different agencies, as each pushes the other to deliver higher output and quality, benefitting the regulated firms and the public at large.[83] Regulation, like other products, improves with competition.[84]

Part of the allure of competition regulation stems from an implicit assumption that it relies less on case-specific analysis and industry-relevant expertise than industry-specific regulation does. Instead, it uses context-free micro-economic models that are seemingly generally applicable in different markets. Such context-free application of general rules shifts the focus to what may be described either as general themes or as the lowest common denominator, depending on the interpreter's perspective. Antitrust focuses on prices, with the objective of increasing benefits to consumers and, through them, society in general. Best-case assessment points to lower prices leading to increasing demand, making production more efficient, and with firms investigating which product attributes best serve consumers' preferences. Worst-case scenarios involve quality depreciation, firms preying on consumer biases, and short-term thinking

---

[80] Aubert and Laffont (n. 52 above). See also New Zealand Ministry of Economic Development, *Ministerial Inquiry into the Electricity Industry* (2000).

[81] M. Kerf and D. Geradin, 'Controlling Market Power in Telecommunications: Antitrust vs. Sector-specific Regulation: An Assessment of the United States, New Zealand and Australian Experiences' (1999) 14 *Berkeley Tech. L.J.* 919; see also M.N. Williams, 'Comparative Analysis of Telecommunications Regulation: Pitfalls and Opportunities' (2003) 56 *Fed. Comm. L.J.* 269.

[82] J.J. Laffont and J. Tirole, *Competition in Telecommunications* (MIT Press 2001) 34.

[83] W. Blumenthal, 'Models for Merging the US Antitrust Agencies' (2012) 1 *J. Antitrust Enf.* 1.

[84] A similar result is reached by other means when focus is on the public choice perspective. There, simultaneous regulation by two self-interested governmental bodies is shown to reduce rent-seeking. See J.J. Laffont and D. Martimort, 'Separation of Regulators Against Collusive Behavior' (1999) 30 *RAND J. Econ.* 232.

crowding out long-term investment.[85] The upside of modern antitrust is its economic focus, though the price paid includes the non-economic goals industry regulation routinely assesses. In the telecommunications example, universal service and culture-preserving content are routinely considered by regulators, while competition would most likely view these as cross-subsidies which raise prices for urban customers only to benefit the rural, and interfering in the market process of determining product characteristics by letting consumers decide for themselves. Given the technological drift that makes networks (especially, but not only, in communication) so much more central to modern life, focusing on competition regulation alone is likely to further reduce the applicability of traditional regulation's contextual analysis, for better and for worse. Knowing an industry's inner workings does not guarantee beneficial regulation, as our discussion of regulatory failure above demonstrated, but it does present opportunities for contextual analysis which competition regulation overlooks, due both to its intellectual focus and to the simple fact that expertise is diluted when attention is spread over multiple markets and contexts.[86]

7.3 The Return of Public Choice to Antitrust

The expansion of competition regulation increases the influence of the officials involved, and the power of their discretionary enforcement. With influence comes power, and with power – lobbying and political pressure. Competition policy has developed exacting intellectual standards and economic focus, partly insulated from political pressure due to its broad applicability and lack of specific influence on any given industry. Paradoxically, the concomitant expansion of its purview with the contraction of specific regulation shifts the focus towards antitrust agencies, as they become not only more influential, but also generate economies of scale and scope in political lobbying. When competition intervention was

---

[85] X. Gabaix and D. Laibson, 'Shrouded Attributes, Consumer Myopia, and Information Suppression in Competitive Markets' (2006) 121 *Qu. J. Econ.* 505. Elsewhere I review and implement such models, showing how firms' exploitation of consumer biases survives competition and may even present opportunities for tacit collusion. See A. Ayal, 'On Consumers' Freedom of Choice: Lessons from the Cellular Market' (2011) 74 *L. & Contemp. Probs.* 91.

[86] A.F. Abbott and S.B. Sacher, 'Avoiding the "Robin Hood Syndrome" in Developing Antitrust Jurisdictions' in N. Charbit, E. Ramundi, A. Chehatova and A. Slater (eds), *William E. Kovacic: An Antitrust Tribute – Liber Amicorum* (Institute of Competition Law 2013).

sporadic, concentrating firm resources (including money, effort and political clout – all limited and spent with trepidation) on antitrust made little economic sense. As competition regulation becomes more dominant and effectively governs multiple industries, investing in the ability to shift agency concentration becomes more profitable. This dynamic affects both firms aiming to divert antitrust attention away from their business and firms hoping influence will enhance their ability to direct attention towards their competitors.[87]

Expanding antitrust at the expense of specific regulation facilitates repetitive interaction with the competition agency. Firms and conglomerates in semi-regulated sectors become repeat players in the regulation game, shifting their focus towards those influencing their future and present profitability. Repeated interaction creates both incentives and means for attempting influence, subjecting antitrust regulators who hitherto had been relatively (but not completely!) insulated from such pressures to increased scrutiny. Such scrutiny could be applied during the appointment of key officials, in budget deliberations, and even during political debates regarding amendments to relevant statutes and procedures.

8. CONCLUSION

Antitrust is expanding in response to deregulation and the proliferation of networks and platforms serving as essential facilities to much of modern commerce and speech. While seen as a boon from the perspective of believers in the doctrines of competition law and those disappointed by the history of regulatory failures, this trend is worrisome. Anti-regulatory antitrust expansion ignores imperfections in competition policy, including its susceptibility to regulatory failures and institutional factors making antitrust unfitting for some of the contexts in which classic industry regulation operates. Even more worrying to antitrust aficionados should be the dynamic effects expected to plague competition policy and its agencies once their influence and discretion increases. As competition agencies gain power and prominence, they become more likely candidates for political and commercial pressures, raising public choice issues and threatening the intellectual honesty and rigor that (mostly) characterized antitrust as we know it.

---

87 See n. 29 above for such private-interest uses of antitrust.

The pitfalls of anti-regulatory antitrust expansion do not mean that classic regulation is always better suited to the tasks modern commerce and communications put before us. They do, however, remain causes for concern that should be carefully assessed on a case-by-case basis, making deregulation and concomitant competition regulation a cautious endeavour. Enthusiasm for antitrust notwithstanding, humility and trepidation are recommended.

3. (Re-)Joining the regulatory fold? Problem-solving innovations in competition enforcement

Yane Svetiev*

1. INTRODUCTION

In a recent contribution commenting on innovations in the practices of enforcement agencies, Malcolm Sparrow has argued that the police force – as the quintessential example of a law enforcement agency – has 'much to gain by recognizing its kinship with a broad range of regulatory professions' and by 'glancing sideways' to the activities of regulatory peers.[1] In particular, he suggests that a dialogue between them can be fruitful because of a number of commonalities between the objectives and problems faced by enforcers and regulators. Such commonalities include the fact that both types of agencies are tasked with protecting society from a variety of harms and the fact that they do so by 'constraining the behaviour of citizens and industry'. Enforcers and regulators also face similar problems of designing institutions and intervention mechanisms that adequately address multi-dimensional harms (including novel and unanticipated types or sources of harm), while protecting values related to efficacy and fairness that may sometimes compete, but that society holds dear. One of the greatest potential benefits from such 'glancing sideways' is to discover a broader range of 'compliance-management and behavior-modification techniques',[2] as

* The author acknowledges the support of the ERC-funded project on European Regulatory Private Law hosted at the EUI Law Department, within the ambit of which this contribution was written, as well as the comments from the editors and the research assistance of Tilahun Kassahun, with the usual disclaimer.

1 M. Sparrow, 'Crime Reduction through a Regulatory Approach: Joining the Regulatory Fold' (2012) 11 *Crim. & Pub. Pol'y* 345, 346.

2 Ibid., 351.

well as regulatory structures that could be adapted to control or remedy certain types of harms more effectively compared to habitual reliance on inherited mechanisms in various legal and regulatory fields.

While Sparrow explicitly cabins off 'agencies of economic regulation' that aim to 'preserve competition' or 'efficient market function' from the ambit of his observations,[3] in this contribution I argue that the implementation of EU competition policy has provided a setting for testing and blending different types of techniques for improving the operation of markets. Current practices in the implementation of competition law by the European Commission and national agencies disclose important features of the problem-solving approaches, which according to Sparrow were pioneered by social regulation agencies that aim to protect society from different types of harms, such as pollution, occupational hazards, food contamination or unsafe commercial products, discrimination, etc. Such developments suggest that the benefits of dialogue between regulatory crafts may extend to the area of economic regulation. This is not least because 'glancing sideways' can also be useful in the process of error-correction to the extent that we identify shortcomings in how these new, sometimes hybridized techniques work in practice, either in achieving the objectives assigned to them or in safeguarding rights and values that society holds dear. After a brief account of the evolution of the standard mechanisms for implementing competition policy in both the US and the EU (Section 2), I will outline two factors that mark the emergence of problem-solving approaches in EU competition law (Section 3), including the deliberative peer review of solutions to competition problems within the European Competition Network (ECN) (Section 3.1) and the growth of remedy-based enforcement at both EU and national level (Section 3.2), before concluding.

2. ENFORCING COMPETITION LAW

US antitrust law has always been an important source of inspiration and comparison and thus a benchmark for the evolution of EU competition law. At its inception, long before the creation of the US federal administrative and regulatory state, US antitrust law both in its public (enforcement by the Department of Justice) and its private (tort-like suits by harmed private parties) dimension was rooted in a law enforcement model. While there has been considerable debate about whether any

[3] Ibid., 349 (especially at n. 4).

coherent social and economic theories (or ideologies) underpinned the US antitrust laws,[4] the Sherman Act has been described as a 'delegating' statute that implemented a new policy in very imprecise terms and that was to be elaborated by the courts following the common law case-by-case method.[5] Thus, through the traditional tools of judicial reasoning by analogy and distinction and through doctrinal elaboration, courts could over time distil the essential characteristics of both joint and unilateral anticompetitive conduct, which would in turn give shape to the law and provide guidance to market actors.

Importantly, as also argued by Maggiolino in her contribution to this volume, the growing influence of economics on US antitrust from the 1970s onwards did not seek to fundamentally change the law enforcement antitrust paradigm. In relying upon economics-based arguments, Chicago School proponents of an economics-based antitrust simply sought to point out the potential beneficial effects of types of restrictions or conduct treated as anticompetitive, as well as identifying economic forces that could undermine market power even in the absence of antitrust enforcement. As such, the suggestion to infuse economics into the law was not a programme for ambitious economic regulation to promote efficiency through antitrust policy. As I have contended elsewhere, the Chicago arguments – particularly as evidenced in the programmatic statements of Chicago antitrust[6] – were based as much on an acknowledgment of the limits of economics as of the limits of law.[7] Since Chicago scholars and judges were in favour of the maintenance of the law enforcement model for implementing antitrust, but did not see courts as an appropriate venue for economic regulation, the main effect of economics on US antitrust has been through procedural law that removes cases from consideration by courts at an early stage of the proceedings, so as to minimize the burdens of discovery and the unpredictability of decision-making by generalist judges or juries.[8]

---

4 E.g., E.M. Fox and L. Sullivan, 'Antitrust – Retrospective and Prospective: Where Are We Coming From? Where Are We Going?' (1987) 62 *N.Y.U. L. Rev.* 936.

5 P. Leval, 'Trademark: Champion of Free Speech' (2003) 27 *Colum J. L. & Arts* 187, 197.

6 R. Bork, *The Antitrust Paradox* (Free Press 1978); F. Easterbrook, 'The Limits of Antitrust (1984–1985)' 63 *Tex. L. Rev.* 1.

7 Y. Svetiev, 'Antitrust Governance: The New Wave of Antitrust' (2007) 38 *Loy. U. Chi. L.J.* 593, 606.

8 Ibid., 615. The argument there was made by reference to the use of the economics of predation to refine the US standard on summary judgment,

Such a conception of the proper division of labour between antitrust and regulation and the appropriate modes of implementation for antitrust law continues to have currency in the US. This can be seen not only in the pronouncements of US courts[9] and in academic debate,[10] but also in broader public policy debates. Thus, in commenting on the enforcement innovations introduced by Christine Varney – upon her departure as Assistant Attorney-General for Antitrust – the *Wall Street Journal* observed that 'Ms. Varney faced criticism that the remedies she fashioned ... effectively having the government monitor a company's behavior for a lengthy period ... threatened to turn the Justice Department into a regulator from a law-enforcement agency'.[11]

In the EU context, it may be useful to draw a distinction between the EU and the national level. Vestiges of competition enforcement existed at national level in various European countries even prior to the advent of EU competition law; however, these involved largely informal interventions into market structure and conduct by executive actors,[12] oftentimes based on political balancing of various objectives including producer and labour interests, industrial policy and even overt redistribution, typically with limited or no court involvement.[13] As Majone has argued, this model was not transferred to the EU level – notwithstanding

---

allowing the court to determine the matter without the jury having to decide material factual disputes. Since then, the Supreme Court has gone further to use similar reasoning to support dismissal of cases even at the pleading stage on a motion to dismiss prior to discovery. *Bell Atlantic Corp. v. Twombly*, (2007) 550 U.S. 544. Given that these are cases decided under general law of civil procedure, they may amount to a broader self-abnegation of the courts' role in resolving social as well as economic conflicts, though this is a matter for a different occasion. E.g., R. Bone, '*Twombly*, Pleading Rules, and the Regulation of Court Access' (2008) 94 *Iowa L. Rev.* 873; R. Effron 'The Plaintiff Neutrality Principle: Pleading Complex Litigation in the Era of *Twombly* and *Iqbal*' (2009) 51 *William & Mary L. Rev.* 1997.

9 E.g., *Verizon Communications, Inc. v. Law Offices of Curtis V. Trinko LLP* (2004) 540 U.S. 398.

10 E.g., D. Melamed, 'Antitrust: The New Regulation' (1995–1996) 10 *Antitrust* 13.

11 T. Catan and G. Chon, 'Antitrust Chief to Step Down' *The Wall Street Journal* (7 July 2011).

12 R. Kelemen, *Eurolegalism: The Transformation of Law and Regulation in the European Union* (Harvard University Press 2011); cf. D.J. Gerber, *Law and Competition in Twentieth Century Europe: Protecting Prometheus* (Oxford University Press 2001).

13 See on this point M. Maggiolino, 'The Regulatory Breakthrough of Competition Law: Definition and Worries', in this volume.

the fact that an administrative actor was given primary responsibility – where the Commission was to implement competition policy on the basis of the enforcement of neutral rules and subject to judicial review by the EU courts.[14] Holding up competition law as a prime example, Majone argues that an important achievement of the EU economic constitution was the separation of politics and economics, or redistribution and efficiency, with the latter delegated to the EU level and left in the hands of the Commission, which was not explicitly subject to political pressures to decide on non-efficiency grounds.[15] The mere structure of the implementation of EU competition law, whereby the Commission had to identify a violation before implementing a remedy to the violation identified, reflected a law enforcement paradigm. Moreover, both the Commission in its own decision-making, as well as the EU courts, strived to develop a corpus of jurisprudence that delineated the different essential elements of the violations contained in the Treaty competition articles.

An important milestone in the evolution of EU competition policy was the implementation of institutional reforms as part of the 2004 enlargement under the guise of the 'modernization package'. While the modernization reforms involved no changes to the substantive legal provisions, nor any attempt at pruning or codification of the then-existing doctrinal outgrowth, they did widen the scope of direct applicability of EU competition law, thus also empowering national competition agencies (NCAs) and courts to apply EU law in cases that come before them. In a further nod to the *ex post* law enforcement paradigm and away from a regulatory one, the ability to notify and obtain *ex ante* administrative clearance for inter-firm arrangements under Article 101 from the Commission was also removed and not reallocated elsewhere. Such an

---

[14] G. Majone, 'State, Market, and Regulatory Competition in the EU: Lessons from the Integrating World Economy' in A. Moravcsik (ed.), *Centralization or Fragmentation? Europe Facing the Challenges of Deepening, Diversity and Democracy* (Brookings Institution Press 1998) 94, 97–98.

[15] It is worth noting that those who more closely followed the detail of EU competition decision-making might not agree that the separation was so neatly achieved. G. Monti, 'Article 81 EC and Public Policy' (2002) 39 *C.M.L. Rev.* 1057; G. Monti, 'Managing the Intersection of Utilities Regulation and EC Competition Law' (2008) 4 *Comp. L. Rev.* 123. Moreover, political scientists, such as Wigger and Nölke, suggest that EU competition decision-making, as EU economic regulation more broadly, has been heavily (and presumably asymmetrically) influenced by business lobbying. A. Wigger and A. Nölke, 'Enhanced Roles of Private Actors in EU Business Regulation and the Erosion of Rhenish Capitalism: The Case of Antitrust Enforcement' (2007) 45 *J. Comm. Mark.Stud.* 487, 488.

expansion of the legal model of enforcement also to the Member States by co-opting not only their competition authorities, but also the national courts, could in turn limit the autonomy of the Member States to fashion their own variants of both substantive competition law and instruments with which to implement it. Writing in the aftermath of the implementation of the modernization reforms and stressing the Commission's declared objective to stimulate more private antitrust suits at national level, Kelemen suggests that EU competition law is a prime example of an emergent 'Eurolegalism', a distinct EU form of juridification.[16] Along similar lines, Wigger and Nölke argue that the reforms shifted the balance towards an *ex post* litigation model for EU competition law, akin to US Chicago-style antitrust and contrary to the administrative tradition of some Member States; going on to suggest that it would lead to further erosion of the Rhenish in favour of the Anglo-Saxon liberal variety of capitalism.[17]

But another possible path was suggested in the literature, based on the contemporaneous efforts to make EU competition law more economics-based and focused on market effects. This involved moves by the Commission to bolster the Competition Directorate's capacities for economic analysis by building up an internal Chief Competition Economist unit, to be involved in the analysis and elaboration of all cases investigated by the Commission.[18] The Competition Directorate also delivered soft-law guidelines about the application of the economics-based approach to various areas of competition law.[19] Particularly in the light of the leeway traditionally afforded by the courts to the Commission in its analysis of complex facts and economic evidence,[20] this could herald a reorientation of EU competition enforcement towards an even more ambitious kind of economics-based approach compared to US

---

[16] Kelemen (n. 12 above) 194.

[17] Wigger and Nölke (n. 15 above) 492–495.

[18] D. Neven, 'Competition Economics and Antitrust in Europe' (2006) 21 *Econ. Pol'y* 741.

[19] Most prominently, Communication from the Commission – Guidance on the Commission's Enforcement Priorities in Applying Article 82 of the EC Treaty to Abusive Exclusionary Conduct by Dominant Undertakings, [2009] OJ C 45, p. 7, but also earlier Commission notice – Guidelines on Vertical Restraints, [2000] OJ C 291, p. 1. N. Petit, 'From Formalism to Effects? The Commission's Communication on Enforcement Priorities in Applying Article 82 EC' (2009) 32 *World Comp.* 485.

[20] H. Schweitzer, 'Judicial Review in EU Competition Law', in D. Gerardin and I. Lianos (eds), *Handbook on European Competition Law* (Edward Elgar Publishing 2013) 491.

cases.[30] The logic of evolution through concrete problem-solving, rather than through doctrinal elaboration, may be detected in both the agency interactions within the ECN and in the transformation of the enforcement approach of the European Commission (but also the national competition authorities – NCAs) since the coming into force of Regulation 1/2003.[31] While such a development may have been inevitable in light of the shortcomings of both standard models of enforcement, I would argue that it has been hastened as a consequence of both legal harmonization and the influence of economics on the analysis of competition cases.

3.1 The European Competition Network: Peer Review of Solutions to Local Problems

On the legal front, the shift towards problem-solving methods in implementing competition law may be viewed as an unanticipated consequence of the decision not to amend the substantive competition law as part of the modernization reforms and to extend its direct applicability. At first glance, extending direct applicability would seem to produce a harmonizing effect by widening the applicability of the uniform EU text and reducing the scope of operation for the national laws. But such a harmonizing effect would likely have been minimal, since the national laws of the various Member States had already both textually and conceptually spontaneously converged on the European template, both formally and through informal pressures.[32] Yet, the textual harmonization could have an important influence on the nature of deliberations in the ECN by shifting the focus from text to context:

> By requiring the direct application of European law both by the Commission and by the NCAs, … the scope for informed divergence and mutual learning is neither based on, nor confounded by, textual diversity among national laws, but on comparison of how the common European law is applied to particular

---

[30] Cf. J. Drexl, ‘Real Knowledge is to Know the Extent of One’s Own Ignorance: On the Consumer Harm Approach in Innovation-Related Competition Cases’ (2010) 76 *Antitrust L.J.* 677.

[31] Council Regulation (EC) No 1/2003 of 16 December 2002 on the implementation of the rules on competition laid down in Articles 81 and 82 of the Treaty, 2003 OJ L 1, p. 1.

[32] E.g., F. van Waarden and M. Drahos, ‘Courts and (Epistemic) Communities in the Convergence of Competition Policies’ (2002) 9 *J. Eur. Pub. Pol’y* 913.

> problems, the methodology of analyzing the antitrust concerns, and the remedial action, if any, that was taken to correct the problem.[33]

This effect is further enhanced by the failure either to intervene in the text of the competition provisions or to legislatively incorporate or amend some of the legal doctrine and standards that had emerged over the years in the decision-making of the Commission and the courts, not even to reflect novel competition concerns and priorities, nor to codify new methodologies of an economic effects-based approach. The likely consequence of a failure to update the text, as in the case of any 'delegating' statute enacted long ago, is that the implementing agencies are less likely to consider the text or even past doctrinal outgrowth to always be useful guides to their contemporary enforcement tasks. This may lead them to work backwards from problems to tools.

Furthermore, on the methodological front, the shift of focus away from the essence of anticompetitive practices or conduct and towards their economic effects can also favour a transition to a problem-based approach. Arguably, the most important result of the economic-inspired attention to the objectives of competition law and the effects of allegedly anticompetitive conduct was to shift the deliberations of implementing agencies towards the theories of possible *harm* that could result from impugned practices.[34] Such a focus on harm makes economic regulation authorities, such as competition agencies, more akin to what Sparrow calls agencies of social regulation, which have pioneered problem-solving approaches to protecting society from risks by innovating implementation through compliance management and behaviour-modification techniques that address *potential* harms. Having to deal with new and unpredictable risks, agencies tasked with food, pharmaceutical or occupational safety face difficulties when relying on the enforcement of pre-existing rules through classic public law sanctioning, opting

---

[33] Y. Svetiev, 'Networked Competition Governance in the EU: Delegation, Decentralization or Experimentalist Architecture?', in C. Sabel and J. Zeitlin (eds), *Experimentalist Governance in the EU: Towards a New Architecture* (Oxford University Press 2010) 79, 110–111.

[34] W. Kerber, 'Should Competition Law Promote Efficiency? Some Reflections of an Economist on the Normative Foundations of Competition Law', in J. Drexl, L. Idot and J. Moneger (eds), *Economic Theory and Competition Law* (Edward Elgar Publishing 2008) 105.

instead for more collaborative and exploratory engagement with regulated entities with all of the advantages and concerns associated with such an approach.[35]

Moreover, the focus on potential harms of conduct may further compound the uncertainty faced by agencies in fulfilling their competition mandate by leading them down a path of reflecting on a cascade of further questions. Even if the initial focus of an agency case team is only on the likely short-run effects on output and consumer prices, when faced with a specific type of conduct in a particular context, the case team will immediately face the limits of economic knowledge that have already been alluded to by asking whether there is current economic consensus about the likely effects of a practice such as resale price maintenance or loyalty discounts or margin squeeze. Second, even if there is some degree of consensus, the case handlers might further ask whether such consensus is context-sensitive and whether there are features of the particular setting – either of the product/industry itself or of the particular production and distribution arrangements of the local market analysed – that indicate specific problems or challenges affecting the analysis of likely effects.[36] Shifting towards the prediction of future effects, the case team will ask whether there are any dynamic forces at play that are likely to influence the market in a way that makes anticompetitive effects more or less likely over time, analysis that is also largely based on conjecture. In the face of such uncertainty, the case team might wish to explore the possibility of introducing relatively minor modifications in the conduct or practice that would either allay or at least test any possible concerns about anticompetitive effects.

Finally, by inducing such a cascade of inquiry, a focus on harm would likely also lead to questions about other types of harm falling outside of the narrow economic analytic framework. Thus, it is not unusual to hear the argument that local public policy objectives or values falling outside of the narrow economic domain can be adversely affected by the uniform application of EU competition law.[37] If the Commission were to decide such a case, the pressure to adopt a uniform approach – which in the end

---

[35] E.g., M. Sparrow, *The Regulatory Craft: Controlling Risks, Solving Problems, and Managing Compliance* (Brookings Institution Press 2000).

[36] E.g., J. Vickers, 'Competition Law and Economics: A Mid-Atlantic Viewpoint' (2007) 3 *Eur. Comp. J.* 1, 6.

[37] To pick one example, see C. Schmid, 'Diagonal Competence Conflicts between European Competition Law and National Regulation – A Conflict of Laws Reconstruction of the Dispute on Book Price Fixing' (2000) 8 *Eur. Rev. Priv. L.* 153, at 155.

disregards the particular local sensitivities – would be stronger, given that the decision may be applied as a precedent across the internal market in different national and industry contexts. A national agency, by contrast, particularly when embedded in a monitoring and peer review architecture such as the one provided by the ECN, may be more likely to dislodge a *Solange*[38]-like dialogue by fashioning solutions that aim either to pursue both goals simultaneously or at least to demonstrate that the pursuit of the local policy objective can be done with little or no impact on the common competition or efficiency goals.[39]

In fact, notwithstanding predictions about the Commission's continued or even strengthened dominance in competition enforcement resulting in further homogenization of competition law and enforcement across the EU,[40] there is emergent appreciation in the literature that national authorities have become an important force and key players in shaping EU competition enforcement, not least through their role in the ECN.[41] Bender, for example, suggests that 'both DG Competition and the NCAs enjoy levels of discretion that are not limited by the ECN' and that the ECN is 'not the hierarchical control tool that it may have seemed',[42] while Smith reports the persistence of divergent practices and emphasis among different national authorities in the jurisdictions studied, notwithstanding increasing 'institutionalization' of competition enforcement

[38] Bundesverfassungsgericht (29 May 1974) 37 Entscheidungen des Bundesverfassungsgerichts [BVerfGE] 271, 2 CMLR 540; Bundesverfassungsgericht (22 October 1986) 73 Entscheidungen des Bundesverfassungsgerichts [BVerfGE] 339, 3 CMLR 225.

[39] C. Joerges, 'Europeanization as Process: Thoughts on the Europeanization of Private Law' (2009) 1 *Duke L. CICLOPs* 17, 32–35, also available at: http://scholarship.law.duke.edu/faculty_scholarship/1939/ (accessed 31 December 2014).

[40] E.g., A. Riley, 'EC Antitrust Modernisation: The Commission Does Very Nicely – Thank You! Part Two: Between the Idea and the Reality: Decentralisation Under Regulation 1' (2003) 24 *E.C.L.R.* 657; S. Wilks, 'Agency Escape: Decentralization or Dominance of the European Commission in the Modernization of Competition Policy?' (2005) 18 *Governance* 431.

[41] P. Ibáñez Colomo, 'Three Shifts in EU Competition Policy: Towards Standards, Decentralization, Settlements' (2013) 20 *Maastricht J. Eur. & Comp. L.* 363, 381–383.

[42] B. Bender, 'Experimentalist Governance in the European Competition Network' in J. Bailleux and A. Vauchez (eds), *Exploring the Transnational Circulation of Policy Paradigms: Law Firms, Legal Networks and the Production of Expertise in the Field of Competition Policies* (EUI Robert Schuman Centre 2014) 6, 20 (by reference to interview evidence).

along the lines of an EU template and under EU influence.[43] Moreover, even in settings where the ECN appears to present a cohesive front – such as the opinions of the Advisory Committee on Restrictive Practices and Dominant Positions,[44] which typically report unanimous agreement of the NCA representatives on the Committee with the Commission's proposed decision – interviewed national officials have suggested that certain NCAs tend to provide considerable input influencing the outcome of the Commission's decision or the remedy in the deliberations prior to the case being formally considered by the Advisory Committee.[45] Finally, Member States have also been engaging in institutional innovation in competition enforcement, such as through amalgamating agencies with previously narrowly specialized mandates and objectives, in part with the objective of an integrated focus on problems, rather than pre-existing task allocations.[46]

While the foregoing observations relate principally to the more established and well-resourced authorities of the larger Member States, Botta and Svetlicinii report that even authorities who are more recent arrivals to the world of EU competition enforcement have been contextualizing the uniform law to local conditions, by rediscovering the unfair pricing provisions of abuse of dominance law that have been long forgotten and disfavoured in mainstream enforcement.[47] The decisions by such authorities relying on the excessive pricing provision of Article 102, which is contrary to the current practices by the Commission, may be regarded as

---

[43] A. Smith, 'When "Chicago" meets London and Paris: Competition Elites and the Regulation of Restrictive Practices' in Bailleux and Vauchez (n. 42 above) 40 (with reference to France and the UK).

[44] The Committee is made up of representatives of the national competition authorities that are part of the ECN and must provide its opinion on any decision issued by the Commission. See Article 14(1) Regulation 1/2003.

[45] Interview with Official of the German Bundeskartellamt (Bonn, July 2009). See Y. Svetiev, 'Beyond Law *versus* Economics: Competition Policy as a Learning Platform', Paper Presented at the Centre for European Law and Governance Seminar – University of Amsterdam (8 November 2011).

[46] A. Ottow, 'Erosion or Innovation? The Institutional Design of Competition Agencies – A Dutch Case Study' (2014) 2 *J. Antitrust Enf.* 25 (describing the creation of a merged authority with responsibility for competition, consumer protection, communications and energy regulation and suggesting the problem-solving approach was used as the basis for the integration). This can be one method for mediating between competition and other public policy objectives; see notes 37–39 above and accompanying text.

[47] M. Botta and A. Svetlicinii, 'Article 102 TFEU as a Tool of Market Regulation: Excessive Enforcement Against Excessive Pricing in the New EU Member States and Candidate Countries' (2012) 8 *Eur. Comp. J.* 473.

an adaptation of competition enforcement to local problems in those jurisdictions, including the fact that newer authorities may not have sufficient resources and experience to engage in more sophisticated economic-effects analysis or to remedy exclusionary conduct. It may also reflect the fact that local markets may be small or isolated and therefore unattractive for entry, which necessitates reliance on more direct controls of dominant firm pricing. Precisely the discursive and peer review architecture of the ECN can provide a discipline that ensures that such local divergence in enforcement reflects an adaptation to local problems, rather than either reliance on habitual forms of analysis and decision-making or capture by local interests.

3.2 Problem-Solving Remedies

Even if we focus on the Commission's own enforcement practices in resolving cases coming to its attention, the noted shift away from applying rules or elaborating precedential doctrines may also be interpreted as a growing emphasis on resolving concrete problems. There is evidence of such emphasis even in cases where the Commission follows the standard enforcement approach to competition law through a formal violation finding followed by the implementation of a remedy (subject to the ordinary procedures of judicial review). Thus, in describing the Commission's approach to the formulation of remedies in cases decided under the standard Article 7 violation procedure, its officials have suggested that the preferred approach is to ask the corporate defendant to 'undertake appropriate measures to achieve specific objectives' rather than to rely on injunctive remedies specifying forms of proper conduct or elements of market structure.[48] In other words, the Commission specifies the objectives to be achieved by the remedy, leaving it up to the undertaking to choose the appropriate measures for achieving those objectives. This discloses a highly functional approach focused on resolving problems or potential harms, whereby the remedy does not necessarily appear to be closely hemmed in either by the rules and precedents of competition law or by the violation finding itself.[49]

---

[48] P. Hellström, F. Maier-Rigaud and F. Bulst, 'Remedies in European Antitrust Law' (2009) 76 *Antitrust L.J.* 43, 60.

[49] Cf. I. Lianos, 'Competition Law Remedies in Europe: Which Limits for Remedial Discretion?' (2013) CLES Research Paper 2/2013, 41, available at: http://papers.ssrn.com/sol3/papers.cfm?abstract_id=2235817 (accessed 31 December 2014).

This approach to remedial formulation is mirrored in the most significant shift in the enforcement approach of the Commission since the modernization reforms, namely the use of commitment decisions pursuant to Article 9 of Regulation 1/2003. The reliance on commitments is the most widely noted aspect of the Commission's current practice, with scholars observing that it has become the dominant enforcement approach for EU competition law.[50] This development is viewed with considerable and even growing concern, particularly by the community of competition lawyers and legal scholars, not least because of the spectre of US-style plea-bargaining and settlements[51] foreign to some Member States' legal cultures. In the area of competition enforcement, where the Commission already enjoys substantial power and discretion, there is also substantial sensitivity about the possibility of abuse of administrative discretion.

Elsewhere I have argued that part of the concern about the extensive use of this procedure is generated by the assimilation of commitment decisions to litigation settlements for case closure as viewed from the vantage point of the law enforcement approach to competition enforcement.[52] Instead, the commitment decisions approach can be viewed as an attempt to overcome the shortcomings of both the law enforcement and the regulatory approach to implementing competition law in the face of the uncertainties identified earlier. The law enforcement approach requires reliance on rules that capture the essence of anticompetitive conduct in all its possible variants and contexts. A regulatory approach requires expertise being employed on a case-by-case basis to predict the likely effects of impugned conduct, including in cases where conduct has both potentially beneficial and negative effects and where the full effects of conduct are not yet apparent. This approach is constrained by the methodologies available to experts to make predictions with some degree of confidence, including in new market and industry settings, as well as

---

[50] This reflects both the fact that commitment decisions are outnumbering standard violation decisions, as well as the fact that increasingly important cases are being resolved through negotiated commitments. E.g., F. Wagner-von Papp, 'Best and Even Better Practices in Commitment Procedures After *Alrosa*: The Dangers of Abandoning the "Struggle for Competition Law"' (2012) 49 *C.M.L. Rev.* 929; also Ibáñez Colomo (n. 41 above) (characterizing it as one paradigm shift in enforcement).

[51] Thus the procedure is often described as a US legal transplant. G. Georgiev, 'Contagious Efficiency: The Growing Reliance on U.S.-Style Antitrust Settlements in EU Law' (2007) *Utah L. Rev.* 971, 986 and 998.

[52] Svetiev (n. 22 above).

ones where technological innovation is rapidly changing market boundaries. In such cases, it is still possible to develop hypotheses or theories of possible harm. It may also be possible to dismiss some of them out of hand, but otherwise the effects of conduct might depend on the unfolding developments in the market at issue. Furthermore, with certain behaviour modifications, the possibilities of harm could potentially be minimized (though even this may be just a matter of hypothesis).

As such, the design of the Article 9 commitments procedure enables the agency to proceed with resolving the case by gradually relaxing the knowledge constraints under which it is operating and to access the superior private knowledge of the investigated undertaking, by exploiting the undertaking's incentive to resolve the concerns about harm while preserving its business objectives.

The procedure involves no finding of violation and is deemed inapplicable in cases where a fine would be appropriate,[53] thereby excluding it as a vehicle for the resolution of cases where a law enforcement approach should be adequate. Moreover, it is a vehicle for the tentative closure of the case because the proceedings can be reopened in the light of new information or market developments. The reopening of the proceedings can lead to amendment of the remedies; alternatively, the Commission can opt to go down the path of a formal enforcement procedure for a violation finding.[54] As such, the procedure may be viewed as a mechanism for dissolving the distinction between *ex ante* and *ex post* intervention. If we observe the evolution of competition enforcement in the EU, we could argue that competition intervention is being gradually shifted to a later point in time. Starting from the *ex ante* notification procedure under Article 101, where the enforcer had to act as a classic regulator and vet the practice even before it was implemented in the market, under the law enforcement approach with direct applicability, intervention shifts to a point at which the conduct or practice has been implemented, but its full effects are not appreciable. Finally, when coupled with commitments it turns into a procedure which tests contemporaneously both the theories of harm and the possible remedies to ameliorate such harm.

To the extent that we might distinguish competition cases that involve investigative challenges (to uncover clearly outlawed harmful practices) and those that involve analytical challenges in understanding the nature of the conduct in its context and over time, the use of commitments

---

53 Recital 13 to Regulation 1/2003.

54 Svetiev (n. 22 above).

matches the latter types of cases. Thus, I have argued that the Commission's commitments practice 'coincides with areas involving business model innovation and partial integration that present analytical challenges because future effects may depend upon how the arrangements are put into practice as well as market developments'.[55] These include cases of dominant firm conduct in fast-moving technologies, strategic alliances or collaborative innovation, as well as concerted standard-setting in sports leagues or industries relying on modular production architectures.[56] Arguably, such cases present problems in which it is typically difficult to isolate the efficiency objective from other public policy objectives. Nowhere is this more evident than in the cases involving the energy sector,[57] where it is difficult to isolate the implementation of competition objectives from other objectives, including market integration and the related need for infrastructure investment, security and diversification of supply, and even environmental objectives in relation to the use of renewable sources or international strategic goals.

Moreover, as Ibáñez Colomo observes, a similar approach is also noted on the investigative side, where not only settlements, but also the leniency policy is being used as a form of accessing private information to identify and prosecute cartels.[58] We could speculate that cartel cases may themselves over time become analytically difficult, given that in a number of informal interviews competition officials have suggested that the number of new cartel notifications and investigations is apparently falling. Cartel cases are likely to become increasingly analytically difficult, either because situations of competitor coordination present problems engaging multi-dimensional policy objectives,[59] or because

---

[55] Ibid.

[56] M. Mataja, 'Regulating the Regulators through Competition Law: Voluntary Private Regulation as an Alternative to Direct Enforcement?', paper presented at the Harvard European Law Association Workshop 'Informal Enforcement of Competition Law: Perspectives from the U.S. and Europe' (March 24, 2014); cf. Svetiev (n. 7 above) 651–653.

[57] The use of commitments in the energy sector has been one of the most commented-on aspects of the Commission's commitment practice; e.g., M. Sadowska, 'Energy Liberalization in an Antitrust Straitjacket: A Plant Too Far?' (2011) 34 *World Comp.* 449.

[58] Although on the use of cooperative solutions in investigative contexts, consider W. Wils, *Efficiency and Justice in European Antitrust Enforcement* (Hart 2005); see also M. Baer, 'Cooperation's Cost' (2010) 88 *Wash. U. L. Rev.* 903.

[59] J. Fear, 'Cartels', in G. Jones and J. Zeitlin (eds), *Oxford Handbook of Business History* (Oxford University Press 2008) 277.

modern network technology presents production and distribution opportunities which make collusion more difficult to isolate as a phenomenon.[60]

It follows from the foregoing that to evaluate the use of commitment procedures not only by the Commission but increasingly also by national competition authorities,[61] it may be less useful to rely on general concepts and metaphors, such as settlements and transplants. Instead, it may be more helpful to examine the particular reason for which the procedure is used, the market problem and the enforcement problem it may be seeking to overcome and the broader legal and administrative context that constrains the discretion of the relevant authority.

From that perspective, evaluation of their appropriateness must be preceded by distinguishing at least three types of uses of commitment decisions. The first, and the least charitable view, is that this is a mechanism that offers a procedural short-cut, allowing the Commission to intervene even in cases where it has not properly carried out its investigative and analytical work to adopt a formal decision. The competition problem does have a formal legal answer, but it is being resolved in an informal negotiation and prior to a full investigation, therefore possibly wrongly. The second use is in cases where the Commission is convinced of a competitive violation and has demonstrated the evidence of the existence of a violation sufficiently to the defendants, who are consequently prepared to offer remedies in the light of their obvious culpability. Again, the competition problem has a formal legal answer, which is also obvious to the entities and the use of commitments can be justified as a savings of transaction costs. The third situation is use of commitment remedies in cases where there is uncertainty about the competitive significance of the conduct or practice in question. There the problem has neither a legal nor a regulatory answer, and the use of the procedure should be evaluated from the perspective of the policy-learning objective.[62]

Following the highly deferential standard of judicial review for Article 9 decisions announced by the ECJ in *Alrosa*,[63] Wagner-von Papp concludes that the growing use of commitments in enforcement competition law is a lamentable abandonment of the 'struggle for competition law'.[64] Yet such a development may simply reflect the shortcomings of

---

60 Svetiev (n. 7 above) 691.
61 Ibáñez Colomo (n. 41 above).
62 Svetiev (n. 22 above).
63 Case C-441/07 *Commission v Alrosa* [2010] ECR I-5949.
64 Wagner-von Papp (n. 50 above) 961–964.

the legal variant of competition policy and an attempt to overcome them. One view is that the loss of legal rules and precedents in such competition cases may be deemed undesirable in itself. An alternative is to approach the abandonment of the 'search for law' from a problem-based perspective: what are the likely harms of this development and are there corrective mechanisms that can reduce such harms?

One problem of the loss of competition law might be the paucity of relevant rules and updated precedents that provide guidance and legal certainty or predictability to market actors. Whether and to what extent this is a relevant harm depends upon the degree to which undertakings in fact relied on the available precedents as guidance in arranging their affairs and making business decisions. It also depends upon whether there are alternative means through which useful and authoritative guidance can be provided to market actors. Another problem of the shift away from formal violations is the loss of transparency and accountability provided by open formal legal procedures; this contributes not only to constraining administrative discretion but also towards stimulating public and political debate about the use of competition law. Again, the extent to which this is a problem involves an assessment of both the degree to which prior arrangements adequately constrained discretion and made competition decision-making transparent to public debate, and whether there are mechanisms of disclosure and accountability in the new procedures that might be adequate or even an improvement. A third question is whether alternative accountability and transparency mechanisms can be created even in the absence of judicial review.

At the same time, while it is true that commitment remedies disclose a movement away from legal competition enforcement, it may be a mistake to assimilate them too quickly into the world of regulation. As Maggiolino's contribution illustrates, there are many different meanings we can associate with the word 'regulation', which may include any form of public interference in the operations of market actors. But assimilating commitment remedies to the world of regulation may obscure the fact that such mechanisms may be used as a way to overcome the constraints on the regulatory expert-based approach, just as much as those of the legal approach to competition enforcement.[65] Quite apart from the policy-learning dimension, remedies-without-infringement also provide a possible response to the problems of regulatory institutional design.

[65] E. Brosseau and J.-M. Glachant, 'Regulators as Reflexive Governance Platforms' (2011) 12 *Comp. & Reg. Netw. Ind.* 194.

Specialist administrative regulators are more prone to become rule-bound, to follow habitual patterns of decision-making which confuse means with ends and overlook diverse public policy dimensions of the problem.[66] They may even become impermeable to reform.[67] Instead, particularly when observed from a dynamic learning perspective, mechanisms such as the commitments procedure may be interpreted as a problem-based platform for the integration of various specialties, normativities or perspectives in the resolution of problems in the operation of markets *without* the need to create new regulatory institutions.[68] As such, commitment-based remedies are not simply regulation, but they arguably dissolve the distinction between regulation, law enforcement and market conduct,[69] not least because they extend in some respects the business conduct autonomy of market actors, while simultaneously limiting it.[70] It is this boundary-breaking aspect that may make such problem-oriented techniques seem particularly disquieting to some competition lawyers, in part because it does not offer an immediate limiting principle to their use.

4. CONCLUDING REMARKS

The EU legislative packages governing the traditional regulated markets in the networked services sectors, such as that for electronic communications for example, are based on a notion of regulation as (ideally) a temporary phenomenon. Regulatory remedies are to be pursued until

---

66 C.E. Lindblom, 'The Science of "Muddling Through"' (1959) 19 *Pub. Admin. Rev.* 79.

67 E.g., P.J. DiMaggio and W.W Powell, 'The Iron Cage Revisited: Institutional Isomorphism and Collective Rationality in Organizational Fields' (1983) 48 *Am. Soc. Rev.* 147.

68 Y. Svetiev, 'European Regulatory Private Law: From Conflicts to Platforms', in K. Purnhagen and P. Rott (eds), *Varieties of European Economic Law and Regulation* (Springer 2014) 153, 172–173.

69 For another example of an attempt to dissolve the distinction between market conduct and competition enforcement, consider the remedial proposal accepted by the court in the US Microsoft case for the creation of a special committee of independent directors, as well as an internal (antitrust) compliance unit within Microsoft as a way of injecting competition compliance considerations into the highest levels of strategy formulation by the corporate hierarchy. Svetiev (n. 7 above) 670–671 and 680–681.

70 Cf. G. Comparato and H.-W. Micklitz, 'Regulated Autonomy between Market Freedoms and Fundamental Rights in the Case Law of the CJEU' in U. Bernitz, X. Groussot and F. Schulyok (eds), *General Principles of EU Law and European Private Law* (Kluwer 2014) 121.

markets are characterized by sufficient rivalry, which would allow the role of regulation to recede and be replaced by generalist *ex post* antitrust enforcement.[71] This reflects quite a traditional perspective on both the division of labour as between antitrust and regulation and on their respective means of implementation. It is also based on an apparent belief that once market competition is unleashed in such sectors, it will act as a sufficient discipline on market players delivering adequate outcomes along various dimensions of the public interest and thereby reducing the need for regulation. Given such an ambition, it may seem paradoxical that competition enforcers in the EU are increasingly being accused of (re-)joining the regulatory fold.

This contribution seeks to pick up the invitation to 'glance sideways' as a way to reassess both the means and ends of competition policy as a species of economic regulation. Exchanging both 'ideas and tools'[72] across boundaries (such as between different authorities within the ECN or between authorities of different specialization) allows for mutual learning to take place through the observation of both positive and negative experiences and examples. Not only does this avoid the need for good ideas for improving regulatory strategy to be invented multiple times,[73] but it also allows for improvements to build on each other and to exploit identified complementarities in objectives. Moreover, novel instruments for implementation, such as commitment remedies, can strive not only to improve the efficacy of implementation, but they can also be used for raising the level of transparency and accountability of decision-making, or even public input into and participation in such decision-making.

The innovations in the implementation of competition law in the EU discussed in the preceding pages – including both decentralized enforcement and reliance on commitments – may be seen as the result of attempts to overcome the shortcomings of prior models for enforcement,

---

[71] Recital 5 to Directive 2009/140/EC of the European Parliament and of the Council of 25 November 2009 amending Directives 2002/21/EC on a common regulatory framework for electronic communications networks and services, 2002/19/EC on access to, and interconnection of, electronic communications, networks and associated facilities, and 2002/20/EC on the authorization of electronic communications networks and services, [2009] OJ L 337, p. 37 (also known as the 'Better Regulation Directive'), which declares the aim 'progressively to reduce *ex-ante* sector specific rules as competition in the markets develops and, ultimately, for electronic communications to be governed by competition law only'.

[72] Sparrow (n. 1 above) 348.

[73] Ibid.

including the political, legal and regulatory approaches that have been used at different times in different jurisdictions. If this is correct, we should be slow to quickly assimilate them to one of these ideal types, without recognizing precisely what constraints such innovations seek to relax and what new potential problems they give rise to.

I have argued that two factors have contributed to competition agencies both at EU and at national level moving towards problem-oriented approaches to implementation, of the kind practised by some agencies of social regulation. The first factor has been the progressive convergence and harmonization in competition legislation, a process that already preceded the institutional modernization package. Yet at the same time as competition legislation across the EU has converged or even harmonized, the legislative text itself is of decreasing importance as a guide to analysing and deciding cases. As a combined result of these processes, deliberations such as between competition enforcers in the context of the ECN could focus less on text or textual divergences and more on concrete market-operation problems that arise in different industrial or even national contexts, as well as the remedial actions that could be pursued to overcome them.

A second factor has been a perhaps unexpected consequence of the transition towards an economics-based approach of intervention on the basis of a demonstration of market effects. This switch of emphasis has brought the idea of harm to the centre of competition enforcement so that a decision to pursue a competition case ordinarily needs to be supported by a sufficiently plausible theory of harm. In turn, this switch in emphasis away from identifying the essence of anticompetitive conduct towards addressing harm may ineluctably lead enforcement agencies towards two types of follow-up inquiries. One is to ask whether the type of harm identified could be ameliorated through some forms of behaviour modification, even before it eventuates in the market (the logic that appears to underlie the commitments approach). Another is to consider whether different types of harm beyond short-run consumer prices are relevant in the specific case and whether such harms should properly be considered in competition enforcement. Such alternative harms may be pursued by other regulatory instruments, but then the competition enforcer should consider whether the competition intervention has effects that are complementary to, or at odds with, such other instruments.

To the extent that they are effective in attenuating uncertainty for competition enforcers, the problem-solving approaches discussed – either through deliberations with peer agencies or through dialogue with undertakings in remedial enforcement – may seek to dissolve the distinction between *ex ante* and *ex post* implementation by apparently delaying the point of the intervention and allowing possibilities for real-time adjustment in implementation strategy. Such an approach expands the autonomy of undertakings compared to both standard regulatory tools and law enforcement mechanisms, but it also subjects them to more intrusive monitoring and on-going dialogue, not only with agencies but also with other market actors and stakeholders. This may be inconsistent both with any idea of an optimal market structure and with the ordoliberal idea that competition law can establish a set of neutral rules that provides the boundaries within which market actors operate.[74] It may instead require competition agencies, sectoral regulators and even judges to become involved in an on-going process of 'manufacturing of markets' as social institutions that are as conducive as possible to delivering various dimensions of the public interest.[75]

Finally, given the need to cope with uncertainty, problem-solving approaches to competition policy may involve picking and choosing so as to combine specific mechanisms from traditional competition enforcement with certain regulatory instruments and techniques. Consistent with traditional competition enforcement, novel forms of enforcement rely on the general or universal legislative language that applies transversally to all sectors of the economy and that can therefore be used to also resolve novel problems for which there are no specialized rules or regulatory regimes. From the regulators' tool kit they incorporate more elaborate monitoring mechanisms, as well as a variety of approaches to modifying market conduct in the light of the incentives and the kind of private knowledge possessed by different kinds of market actors. And yet compared to rate and entry regulation, problem-based implementation may be less vulnerable to capture, both because it is less institutionally stable[76] and because it requires interaction with a much broader set of market and civil society actors in a way that may re-politicize regulatory decision-making.[77] While resolving some issues, as the literature illustrates, novel implementation mechanisms, such as commitments, lead to

---

74 Christiansen and Kerber (n. 27 above).

75 E. Brosseau and J.-M. Glachant, *The Manufacturing of Markets: Legal, Political and Economic Dynamics* (Cambridge University Press 2014); J. Black, 'Reconceiving Financial Markets – from the Economic to the Social' (2013) 13 *J. Corp. L. Stud.* 401 (arguing for a social conception of financial markets).

76 Svetiev (n. 68 above) 173–174.

77 See generally Brosseau and Glachant (n. 65 above). Cf. also H.-W. Micklitz, 'Do Consumers and Businesses Need a New Architecture of Consumer Law? A Thought Provoking Impulse' (2013) 32 *Yearbook of European Law* 266, 351 and 363.

new and different kinds of concerns and potential problems. To resolve such problems presupposes an understanding of the reasons underlying the process of picking and choosing techniques, and may require further institutional innovation and reallocation of responsibilities, rather than a return to some prior template.

PART 2

New forms of advocacy powers of competition agencies

4. New powers – new vulnerabilities? A critical analysis of market inquiries performed by competition authorities

Tamar Indig and Michal S. Gal

1. INTRODUCTION

In the past two decades the number of competition authorities (CAs) which have been empowered to engage in market inquiries (MIs) has grown significantly. Whereas 20 years ago only a handful of CAs possessed such powers, currently more than 45 authorities can perform MIs,[1] and the number is growing. MIs allow CAs to study in depth market failures that do not necessarily result from competition law infringements.

To be sure, MIs are not a new phenomenon. Data and insights acquired in the study of markets have long enriched and improved legislation and regulation. For example, the US Congress,[2] as well as several executive departments,[3] has inherent market research units, and the EU Joint Research Centre (JRC) serves as a scientific and technical arm of the

[1] Until 2008–2009 at least 40 jurisdictions empowered their competition authorities to perform MIs. ICN Advocacy Working Group, Market Studies Project Report (2009) 18–20, available at: http://www.internationalcompetitionnetwork.org/uploads/library/doc363.pdf (accessed 2 April 2014) (in the following: ICN Report). The number is still growing: ICN Advocacy (Market Studies Project) Working Group, Draft – Market studies Good Practice Handbook (2010), available at: http://www.internationalcompetitionnetwork.org/uploads/library/doc646.pdf (accessed 2 April 2014) (in the following: ICN Draft Handbook).

[2] The Congressional Research Service (2013), available at: http://www.loc.gov/crsinfo/ (accessed 2 April 2014).

[3] Examples include the Office of Financial Research within the US Department of the Treasury, see http://financialresearch.gov/ (accessed 12 June

European Commission.[4] Alongside such permanent research bodies, *ad hoc* ones are sometimes established to perform inquiries into specific issues.[5] The performance of MIs by CAs is also not a new phenomenon.[6] Some authorities have long possessed such powers. For instance, in the US the power dates back to the beginning of the 20th century,[7] in Japan to the late 1940s[8] and in the UK to 1973.[9]

Yet, a clear increase in the number of jurisdictions that empower their agencies to engage in MIs is evident. From a handful in the late 1990s, currently more than one-third of CAs can perform MIs, and additional proliferation is expected. This trend is further strengthened by the revival in some jurisdictions of the power to engage in MIs, which has been dormant.[10] For instance, in the EU the power to launch MIs dates back to

---

2015) or The National Institute of Justice (2013), see http://www.nij.gov/about/welcome.htm (accessed 2 April 2014).

[4] The JRC engages in research and provides the scientific advice and technical know-how to support a wide range of EU policies. See http://ec.europa.eu/dgs/jrc/index.cfm?id=1370 (accessed 2 April 2014).

[5] For a survey of some authorities see the Australia Law Reform Commission, Making Inquiries (Report) A New Statutory Framework (Report 111, 2009) 51–58 and 83–87, available at: http://www.alrc.gov.au/sites/default/files/pdfs/publications/ALRC111.pdf (accessed 2 April 2014).

[6] The descriptive layer of this chapter substantially builds on two studies, namely the ICN Report (n 1 above) and the OECD Directorate for Financial and Enterprise Affairs Competition Committee, Policy Roundtables: Market Studies (Competition Law and Policy OECD 2008), available at: http://www.oecd.org/regreform/sectors/41721965.pdf (accessed 2 April 2014) (in the following: OECD Report). Factual changes might have occurred as of the dates these major comparative studies were completed, due to legislative amendments or policy changes. Absent explicit notes, the factual data mentioned below is thus correct as of 2009 or 2008, respectively.

[7] OECD Report (n. 6 above) 207.

[8] Ibid., 61 and 210.

[9] Ibid., 114 and 222. On 25 April 2013, the Enterprise and Regulatory Reform Act 2013 (ERRA) entered into force. The ERRA changes the regulatory structure and partly the substantial powers. We shall mainly refer to the previous structure.

[10] For instance, the competition regime in Norway dates back to 1993, yet MIs were performed as of 2004. OECD Report (n. 6 above) 89. In Poland the power dates back to 1993, but MIs were performed only from 2007 (ibid., 97). In Spain this power dates back to 1989, yet relatively confined resources were devoted to that task until the entry into force of a new Act in 2007 (ibid., 107, 109).

1962, but the Commission only began to regularly apply it in 2004.[11] Accordingly, it is timely to evaluate this policy tool.

The performance of MIs by competition authorities offers many advantages. It makes use of an authority's expertise in studying the competitive conditions in a market, and allows for a more holistic analysis and remedial suggestions. It can also potentially overcome, at least partially, some of the limitations of sector regulators. Yet, MIs are far from costless. Besides the direct costs bestowed upon an authority and market participants, MIs involve less obvious but nonetheless important price tags through the political economy reactions they generate, given that they strengthen an authority's stand relative to other regulators, thereby tilting the subtle *status quo* within the executive branch. MIs also raise a host of constitutional, democratic and practical issues that should be recognized. Yet, only a few, although insightful, attempts have been made to study these issues.[12]

Accordingly, this chapter analyses MIs from several relevant perspectives in order to reveal their benefits as well as limitations and provide a synergetic analysis. Its road map is as follows. Section 2 describes the scope of powers to perform MIs across jurisdictions. Section 3 focuses on the benefits that empowering CAs to perform MIs may bring. Section 4 explores the possible limitations and downsides such MIs entail. Section 5 focuses on the inter-regulatory effects created, and asks whether adding MIs to CAs' plates improves the overall design of the regulatory system. The analysis builds on and expands the recent administrative law literature that focuses on multi-agency interactions. Section 6 offers some conclusions by way of applying our findings to the two most common models of MIs.

---

[11] A. Jones and B. Sufrin, *EU Competition Law: Text Cases and Materials* (5th edn, Oxford University Press 2014). According to the OECD Report the power to conduct an MI was included in Article 17 of Regulation EEC 17/62, yet MIs are 'recent'. See OECD Report (n. 6 above) 153 and 235.

[12] See e.g. R. Whish and D. Bailey, *Competition Law* (7th edn, Oxford University Press 2012) 451 and 486; H. Andersson and E. Legnerfalt, 'Dawn Raids in Sector Inquiries – Fishing Expeditions in Disguise?' (2008) 29 *E.C.L.R.* 439; D. Ridyard, 'The Competition Commission's Northern Ireland Banking Market Investigation: Some Unanswered Questions on the Role of Market Investigations' (2008) 29 *E.C.L.R.* 173.

2. THE SCOPE OF POWERS GRANTED IN MARKET INQUIRIES

The powers granted to CAs to perform MIs differ from traditional competition law tools. Most importantly, the aim of MIs is to study obstacles to competition, whatever their roots.[13] As a result, MIs allow the CA to use a broad prism, focusing not only on privately erected barriers but also on governmental ones, including an authority's own past interventions. Possible recommendations for change are also much broader than traditional remedies and may include, *inter alia*, structural and behavioural changes in the market and changes to the regulatory system, including the lowering of governmental artificial barriers to entry. Such remedial suggestions are not limited to a predetermined list but rather provide the CA with a broad palate. Furthermore, MIs are not triggered by pre-specified potentially anti-competitive actions of private parties, such as predatory pricing. Hence, they allow the CA to actively step into the scene at an earlier stage. In addition, MIs may potentially affect a much larger number of market participants in comparison to the number of parties involved in a typical enforcement activity.

These traits are common to most MI powers granted to CAs. However, implementation powers often differ across jurisdictions. Below we explore four relevant parameters: the power to initiate MIs; the exact ends MIs serve; investigative powers; and the ability to impose the recommended remedies.

2.1 The Power to Initiate MIs

The power to initiate MIs is often granted to the CA, which has discretion in selecting such inquiries.[14] It is also quite common that the legislature or the executive branch may request the CA to perform an MI.[15] In a small number of jurisdictions MIs can only be externally mandated.[16]

---

[13] OECD Report (n. 6 above) 209.

[14] Examples include the Czech Republic, Poland and Spain. See OECD Report (n. 6 above) 27, 105 and 109.

[15] Examples include the US, Norway, Russia and Greece. Ibid., 142–143, 219, 218, 190 and 215.

[16] Only one authority that participated in the ICN survey reported that MIs are conducted solely at the request of the relevant government ministers. See ICN Report (n. 1 above) 30.

The selection criteria applied to choose the subject of an MI often correspond to the types outlined in the next section. The most common criterion is the malfunctioning of a market.[17] Most jurisdictions apply additional considerations such as the importance of the market to the economy as a whole,[18] or its significance to consumers,[19] as well as the ability to remedy the perceived market or regulatory failures. Certain selection criteria are unique to specific jurisdictions, most notably 'the importance of the industry for the poor' in South Africa,[20] and reaction to an unusual situation in a market following a natural disaster in the US and Canada.[21]

2.2 The Exact Ends to be Served

As the OECD Report notes,[22] MIs are 'a very flexible tool which can accommodate a number of objectives'. Yet three main types of MIs can be identified.[23]

2.2.1 Identification of market failures in a specific market

This is the most common type of MI, which explores and analyses in depth the causes of underperformance or market failures across a whole market or sector. Such MIs attempt to reach a thorough understanding of the nature of the prevalent market conditions and dynamics, and the resultant obstacles to competition, in order to structure (suggested) remedies accordingly.

2.2.2 Enforcement-oriented inquiries

Such MIs attempt to detect generally suspected yet evasive (and thus not sufficient for initiating a formal investigation) anti-competitive conduct

---

[17] In some jurisdictions, such as Italy, the focus is solely on public restrictions or inefficient equilibrium; OECD Report (n. 6 above) 213.

[18] See, for example, OECD Report (n. 6 above) 215 (Romania) and 234–235 (Mexico).

[19] See, for example, OECD Report (n. 6 above) 69 (Korea), 215 (Romania), 143 (US) and 234–235 (Mexico).

[20] Ibid., 217. This led to MIs in the sectors of food, health care and pharmaceuticals.

[21] Ibid., 143 and 229.

[22] Ibid., 8.

[23] Of course, an inquiry can foster more than one end, and partial overlaps exist among the outlined types. Yet each of these types has a clear distinctive core.

that may explain the underperformance of a market. This type is the most closely related to traditional competition law tools.

Jurisdictions substantially vary in their approach to this possibility.[24] Some, including Mexico and Canada, stress the division between MIs and enforcement activities.[25] In others, such as the EU and Italy, the linkage to enforcement is welcome.[26] Other jurisdictions, including the US,[27] UK[28] and Japan,[29] preserve some degree of separation between the different tools, while recognizing their complementarities. As elaborated below, the tension between efficiency and constitutional concerns underlies these different approaches.

2.2.3 Competence-building studies

Such MIs aim at endowing the CA with in-depth knowledge and insights across markets.[30] They may, for example, enhance the CA's familiarity with dynamic and innovative sectors or practices,[31] explore certain aspects of competition policy and its interface with other types of regulation, search for efficient ways of analysing competition problems or test economic theories.[32] As noted by Kovacic, such inquiries may create 'economic precedents' that 'demonstrate the validity of hypotheses' and can be referred to in the future to support specific activities.[33]

Retrospective inquiries are a subset of competence-building inquires. They focus on evaluating the impact of legislative or executive reforms or regulatory interventions on a market. They might also be inwards-looking, aimed at self-evaluation of the wisdom and effects of the CA's

---

[24] ICN Report (n. 1 above) 32–33, 96 and 107.

[25] OECD Report (n. 6 above) 211. In such jurisdictions MIs 'do not commonly lead to law enforcement' and are 'quite separate from law enforcement'.

[26] Ibid., 213–214.

[27] In the US, MIs are not used as a substitute for enforcement. However, there is a frequent targeting of markets where expertise was gained during past enforcement actions. At times MIs reveal information that leads to enforcement, while at times enforcement activities illuminate the need for a specific MI. Ibid., 145.

[28] See UK contribution, ibid., 112–119.

[29] See Japanese contribution, ibid., 210.

[30] ICN Report (n. 1 above) 33 and 94.

[31] OECD Report (n. 6 above) 69, 211, 220 and 227.

[32] ICN Report (n. 1 above) 98.

[33] W.E. Kovacic, 'Measuring What Matters: The Federal Trade Commission and Investments in Competition Policy Research and Development' (2004) 72 *Antitrust L.J.* 861, 865.

past predictions, decisions and performance, and eventually seek to guide future steps.[34] As several scholars observe, constant reassessment of the CA's capacities and efficacy and the upgrading of the theoretical comprehension of rapidly changing market realities is important in order to avoid repeated mistakes and strengthen the CA's abilities.[35]

In this chapter we shall focus mainly on the first type of MI, since here the expansion of the mandate of the CA beyond its traditional mandate is the largest.

2.3 Availability of Investigative Tools and Follow-On Enforcement Actions

An important parameter, which will be analysed in depth below,[36] involves the ability of the CA to use its general investigative powers to obtain data and information while performing an MI. In some jurisdictions, including the EU, Japan, Norway, Italy, Spain and Hungary, the CA may use its regular powers.[37] In others, only the gathering of voluntarily provided data is possible.[38]

A divergence also exists with regard to the ability to use the information gathered in MIs in follow-on enforcement actions. Yet the

---

[34] See, e.g., OECD Report (n. 6 above) 212 and 217– 218 (Norway). In the US, such studies are not performed 'unless there is another enforcement matter in the industry', because they are highly resource-consuming, and causality is difficult to establish absent substantial information. Ibid., 220–221.

[35] W.E. Kovacic, 'Rating the Competition Agencies: What Constitutes Good Performance?' (2009) 16 *George Mason L. Rev.* 903, at 923; W.E. Kovacic, 'The Digital Broadband Migration and the Federal Trade Commission: Building the Competition and Consumer Protection Agency of the Future' (2010) 8 *J. Telecomm. & High Tech. L.* 1, 6 and 14; K. Ewing, *Competition Rules for the 21st Century: Principles From America's Experience* (2nd edn, Kluwer Law International 2006); M. Greenstone, 'Towards a Culture of Persistent Regulatory Experimentation and Evaluation' in D. Moss and J. Cisternino (eds), *New Perspectives on Regulation* (The Tobin Project 2009) 111, 120–122.

[36] This issue is further discussed at 4.3 below, as part of the constitutional dimension.

[37] OECD Report (n. 6 above) 8 and 208 (General discussion), 155 (EU), 65 (Japan), 91 and 218 (Norway), 57 (Italy), 109–110 (Spain) and 226 (Hungary).

[38] The Mexican regime serves as an example. Ibid., 234. In the US, the FTC has investigative powers, while the Antitrust Division lacks them. Ibid., 142, 147 and 229–230.

majority of CAs have used information obtained in MIs to help enforcement activities.[39]

2.4 The Implementation of Recommendations

Two main models can be identified. In most jurisdictions the CA's role is mainly advisory. At the end of the inquiry it presents its findings to the relevant governmental bodies and suggests potential routes to overcome obstacles to competition, such as changes in legislation, regulation or policy, recommendations to change market participants' conduct, or suggestions for consumer education. The EU,[40] US, South Africa, Romania, Mexico, Ireland and Italy[41] adopt the advisory model, to name a few.

More rarely, jurisdictions take a blunter path and adopt a supervisory model, under which the CA is empowered to act in a proactive manner and take active steps to remedy at least some types of market failures, much like a sector regulator intervening and changing market conditions in order to further competition. Adopting such a model creates significant tectonic changes in the regulatory *status quo*, as elaborated below. Given that the supervisory model is the furthest from traditional competition law tools, since it involves at least some degree of market engineering, let us explore some examples.

The Greek CA, for example, can impose 'behavioural or structural measures to improve market performance' at the end of an MI.[42] In Spain the CA is empowered to 'bring actions … against administrative acts and regulations from which obstacles to the maintenance of effective competition in the markets are derived'.[43] More recently, the Italian regime

39 ICN Report (n. 1 above) 70–71 and 105.

40 Jones and Sufrin (n. 11 above) 850–851.

41 OECD Report (n. 6 above) 220 (US), 217 (South Africa), 215 (Romania), 234 (Mexico), 213 (Italy) and 54 (Ireland).

42 Ibid., 215. See also Hellenic Competition Commission (2007), available at: http://www.epant.gr/content.php?Lang=en&id=85 (accessed 2 April 2013).

43 OECD Report (n. 6 above) 110 and 108 ('regulatory recommendations contained in market studies could be followed by further and more drastic actions. Thus, this new instrument gives the [authority's] opinions and calls for action more strength than ever').

has moved towards a supervisory model: the CA is empowered to challenge regulations that infringe competition before administrative courts.[44]

The UK regime offered, until the entry into force of the above-mentioned ERRA legislation in 2014, a mixed model: the Competition Commission (CC) had extended supervisory powers,[45] while the Office of Fair Trading (OFT) had only advisory ones. The CC performs MIs following referral from sectoral regulators with competition powers or from Ministers. The OFT may also issue a market investigation reference (MIR) to the CC, if as a result of an MI the OFT performs, it reaches the conclusion that mandatory remedies, rather than traditional enforcement steps, are needed. An MIR is most likely where serious but potentially remediable barriers to entry and restrictions on rivalry in oligopolistic or monopolistic markets exist. The CC has the power to apply binding remedies which are perceived as necessary to address structural or behavioural elements that prevent, restrict or distort competition. The range of such remedies is very broad, including conduct rules, changing agreements between firms, and divestment of assets. However, fines are not included. The remedial action may be taken by the CC or it may recommend that other governmental bodies take action. The newly legislated Enterprise and Regulatory Reform Act creates the single Competition and Markets Authority.[46] The supervisory powers remain, and are vested in a 'Market Reference Group' that the Authority's chair may establish.[47]

In Israel, in 2011, the CA was empowered to actively change market conditions in economic sectors characterized by a high degree of oligopolistic coordination, even when no competition law offence was

---

[44] Italian Competition Law, Article 21. First, the CA adopts an opinion pointing out the allegedly anti-competitive regulation to the concerned administration. The latter has 60 days to comply with the requirements expressed in the CA's opinion. If it does not change its regulation to conform with the CA's opinion, the latter may challenge the measure before the administrative courts. The authors wish to thank Fabiana Di Porto for providing them with this valuable information.

[45] OECD Report (n. 6 above) 113–118, 129, 139 and 224. The following description builds on the OECD Report.

[46] ERRA, Sections 25–26.

[47] ERRA, Section 133A. The ERRA empowers the CA to make a referral to its chair for the constitution of a market reference group under Schedule 4. Section 133A of the Enterprise Act 2002 as added under Schedule 5, Section 166, sets the functions the market reference group exercises, including 'the duty to remedy, mitigate or prevent the adverse effect on competition'.

found. The CA may act in a proactive manner, *inter alia*, mandating firms that engage in oligopolistic coordination to eliminate or reduce switching costs or to increase transparency in the market. It can also apply to the Competition Tribunal for structural remedies. Where a sector regulator in the relevant market exists, the CA is mandated to consult with it if the CA's aim is to prevent significant harm to competition, and is mandated to receive the agreement of the regulator when it aims to increase competition in the market. The importance of this new power stems from the fact that it enables the CA to overcome one of the most troubling weak spots of competition law: dealing with oligopolistic coordination. This is a big loophole, especially in small economies in which the natural conditions in the market can only support a small number of firms in most of the markets and entry barriers are often quite high. Indeed, other tools attempting to deal with this problem have been problematic. In addition, in March 2014, the Antitrust Act was amended and the CA was empowered by the government to engage in a broader set of MIs. Following the MI, 'the Director General may submit his reasoned conclusions and recommendations to the minister responsible for the sector examined and to the Minister of Treasury, and in a sector that is regulated by another agency – also to the head of that agency'.[48]

Under both models, the (suggested) remedies are not confined to specific firms which have created artificial barriers to competition. This is an important difference when compared to other policy tools at the CA's disposal, such as the EU commitments procedure.[49]

In sum, while diversity exists along different aspects of MIs, they all share an important trait: the ability to comprehensively study the roots of market or regulatory failures even if the competition law was not infringed.

The next two sections focus on the justifiability and efficacy of MIs being performed by CAs: the first analyses the justifications and benefits of such bodies performing MIs, and the second performs a critical analysis of such MIs.

3. JUSTIFICATIONS AND BENEFITS

MIs performed by CAs offer important advantages, by harnessing the authorities' comparative advantages to MIs. This chapter is based on the

---

[48] See Israeli CA's 2014 Annual Report on Competition Policy Developments in Israel, §1.1.4.

[49] Y. Svetiev, '(Re-)Joining the Regulatory Fold? Problem-Solving Innovations in Competition Enforcement', in this volume.

assumption that MIs are a good tool for improving public policy, and only touches upon this assumption if it directly relates to MIs performed by CAs.

One of the main benefits involves the CA's expertise in performing market studies. Although the authority's regular analysis focuses on anti-competitive conduct, it must also often analyse the effects of the general market conditions on conduct and performance. For example, in determining whether to allow a merger, market conditions in the pre- and post-merger situation must be analysed. Performing MIs may strengthen the CA's expertise even further. This is especially true when the CA engages in studies which have implications on related activities, including retrospective and competence-building inquiries.

Let us pause and analyse this argument more carefully. MIs tie the authority's expertise in competition issues to the in-depth study of markets or sectors. Yet a question arises whether this is the main essential capacity for accomplishing successful MIs, or whether the authority's confined expertise in other areas justifies conferring this power on others. CAs might not be well suited to study industries in which highly specialized and on-going knowledge is necessary. In such markets, specialized sector regulators enjoy a comparative advantage with regard to expertise. Perhaps more importantly, since the CA is exclusively oriented towards eliminating anti-competitive behaviour, it might not be able to objectively evaluate all the implications of a change on social policy and might not possess the expertise to weigh all conflicting considerations (e.g., competition v. stability).[50]

In addition, MIs move from eliminating anti-competitive conduct into the field of increasing competition. When the UK authority decides on divestment of assets or the Israeli authority applies the power to give instructions to firms operating in markets characterized by a high degree of oligopolistic coordination, they perform a much more interventionary role than in traditional antitrust. Instead of scrutinizing the decisions of market players, the authority determines some of the market conditions by dictating (or in the advisory model – recommending) a specific business decision intended to increase competition. Such a role necessitates adequate practical business wisdom to choose the optimal path, which the authority's staff might lack.

Yet, these arguments do not lead to the conclusion that MIs should not be performed by CAs, but rather that their scope should be limited in cases in which their comparative advantages are less relevant. Some

---

50 M. Gal and I. Faibish, 'Six Principles for Limiting Government-Facilitated Restraints on Competition' (2007) 44 *C.M.L. Rev.* 69.

examples follow. First, where another regulatory body has expertise in the market, it might be more efficient to require it to perform the MI. If it is assumed that the regulatory body cannot perform it efficiently or effectively, the CA should be required to take active steps to bridge its gap of expertise. The new UK legislation suggests an interesting layout for encountering the issue of MIs that involve public interests other than competition:[51] it grants the Secretary of State extended powers to appoint a 'public interest expert' who has particular knowledge or expertise in the related matters.[52] Yet, the CA retains substantial powers even when broad public interests are involved.[53] In short, the question is whether another governmental entity is preferable in terms of expertise, objectivity and readiness to engage in the MI, across the administrative landscape.

Second, it might be wise to distinguish between the legal and economic analysis of the obstacles to competition performed by the authority, and the remedies it recommends (or attempts to implement). With regard to the former, the authority usually acts in its field of expertise, while in shaping broad remedies it does not. Accordingly, when remedies are challenged, the appellate body might give less weight to the expertise of the CA. Also, minding the democratic concern, where a balancing of competitive and non-competitive considerations is required, this should be performed at a higher level of government.

Endowing the CA with the power to engage in MIs can also potentially overcome, at least partially, some of the limitations often attributed to sector regulators. Such limitations focus on the competence and efficiency of the direct regulator, who may be plagued, *inter alia*, by an inadequate ability to evaluate the real causes of limited competition and the ways to remedy it, by regulatory capture, and by its concern with losing its sphere of influence. In contrast, the CA's expertise lies in competition issues, and its mandate includes a wide range of markets; thus it is not as susceptible to regulatory capture and to concerns with its sphere of influence.[54] Moreover, the authority's enhanced powers and

---

[51] Ibid. ERRA, Section 35.

[52] ERRA, Sections 141, 141A and 141B. See also Gal and Faibish (n. 50 above) 30–32 (for additional powers of the Secretary of State).

[53] ERRA, Sections 146A, 147A, 148A, for instance to decide whether adverse affects on public interests exist, to recommend that other persons take actions, or what actions should be taken. The CA only needs to 'have regard' of the views of a public interest expert that the Secretary of State may appoint.

[54] D.E.M. Sappington and D.L. Weisman, 'Regulating Regulators in Transitionally Competitive Markets' (2012) 41 *J. Reg. Econ.* 19, 31 and 36. Yet the strength of this argument is dependent on the specific circumstances. For

impact also urge other regulators to mind competition considerations in advance. Relatedly, the incentives of pressure groups to invest resources in influencing the regulator might be weakened if they assume that a supervisory agency might undo the effects of such influence.[55]

MIs can also serve as vehicles for providing the empirical and theoretical basis to justify and move along modifications in a long-standing *status quo* in regulated sectors. Along these lines, Stiglitz argues that an important way to prevent regulatory failure is by 'multiple oversight, a broad system of checks and balances. The costs of duplication are far less than the costs of mistakes.'[56]

MIs performed by the CA can also help refute mistaken public assumptions that anti-competitive behaviour is taking place, most notably in cases of price increases. Thus, MIs can prevent mistaken and costly regulatory interventions or public outcries. The UK Agency's power to give an industry a 'clear bill of health' serves this end.[57]

MIs can also create positive reputational effects on both the wider public and the government. For one, MIs serve as valuable opportunities to demonstrate the CA's contribution, professionalism and relevance to economic policy. In particular, MIs that lead to visible and positive changes in market conditions, as well as those that affirm the positive effects of previous CA's interventions, can strengthen its reputation. Such reputational effects, in turn, may contribute to the enhancement of competition in the long run, through increased resources or readiness to take into account the CA's suggestions. However, MIs can also create negative reputational effects. MIs might harm the CA's reputation if it is required to make decisions on issues that involve a non-obvious trade-off among different values. As noted elsewhere, 'distributional issues are inherently more political than might be considered optimal for a body that needs to be regarded as an impartial overseer devoted to advancing the general public welfare'.[58] One way to overcome such effects is to narrow the mandate of the CA to perform only MIs that focus mainly on obstacles to competition.

---

example, a competition authority that is directly subordinated to or headed by a Minister, may be more susceptible to political economy pressures.

[55] J. Freeman and J. Rossi, 'Agency Coordination in Shared Regulatory Space' (2012) 125 *Harv. L. Rev.* 1133, 1186.

[56] J. Stiglitz 'Regulation and Failure' in D. Moss and J. Cisternino (eds), *New Perspectives on Regulation* (The Tobin Project 2009) 13, 20.

[57] OECD Report (n. 6 above) 8, 118 and 233.

[58] Ibid., 8, 218 and 234.

In sum, MIs by CAs entail substantial merits.[59] At the same time, the power to engage in MIs gives rise to some costs that we now turn to evaluate. Acknowledging such costs is essential for ensuring the efficient responsiveness of the regulatory toolkit.

4. POSSIBLE VULNERABILITIES AND DOWNSIDES

Adding MIs to the CA's mandate involves a dramatic change, as it breaks some of the traditional lines between *ex post* and *ex ante* regulation and broadens the CA's powers significantly to include 'market engineering'. This section outlines the possible costs of moving from a reactive model to a proactive one. As elaborated, MIs are far from costless, even in their more benign advisory model form. Beyond the direct costs imposed on both the CAs and market participants, MIs often carry less obvious but nonetheless important price tags which we seek to unveil. The present section focuses on intra-regulatory costs, while the next focuses on inter-regulatory ones. In particular, this section explores capacity constraints (sub-section 4.1), shift of focus (sub-section 4.2), constitutional issues (sub-section 4.3) and regulatory capture (sub-section 4.4).

Two main questions lead our inquiry. The first is whether the CA is the right body to perform the analysis, and the second is whether MIs should be performed only as a last alternative or at least in the most moderate manner possible, where traditional competition law enforcement tools cannot provide a reasonable solution to market failures, or whether once granted MIs stand in the regulatory toolbox in line with all other tools, and the authority may freely choose among them. To answer these questions one must look at all the different aspects that are relevant, and put together the pieces of the puzzle.

4.1 Capacity Constraints

Assuming that adding MIs to the CA's regulatory plate is not accompanied by increased funding, diversifying the authority's toolkit may result in diluting the resources designated to traditional tasks, leading to inferior performance and deterrence.

Several counter-arguments can be raised. First, MIs' broad prism, which does not focus on a specific firm but rather on a sector, a type of agreement, consumer conduct patterns, regulatory frameworks, etc., has a

---

[59] Of course, the exact powers granted to the CA affect such merits. Such specifications are beyond the scope of this chapter.

higher probability of reaching the genuine roots of market or regulatory failures, and allows for more holistic remedial suggestions. Furthermore, MIs can also tailor solutions to market failures that are not dealt with effectively by competition laws. Most importantly, they may deal with the Achilles heel of competition law: oligopolistic coordination in highly concentrated markets. Accordingly, the goal of furthering competition may in some cases be better achieved through MIs.

Second, the new powers create synergies between regulatory tasks. Economic insights derived through MIs may be applicable to the authority's other activities. They provide a solid and thorough knowledge base to draw upon in traditional investigations in the studied markets, thereby reducing asymmetric information problems.[60] Furthermore, general insights and lessons from an MI can carry over to traditional inquiries, as well as improve its advocacy activities by incorporating a wider set of examples that correspond with recognized public concerns and perceptions. Thus, even if diluting the resources vested in each task, MIs may still enrich the authority's expertise and compensate for dividing the resource pie into smaller pieces.

Third, MIs may avert the implementation of costly and lengthy traditional enforcement steps. If firms identify the potential for enforcement steps through an MI that may affect their markets more than traditional enforcement activities, they might even end their anti-competitive conduct to avoid such steps.[61]

4.2 Shift of Focus

A related concern involves a shift in the CA's *modus operandi*. Remedying the ills of a market might be easier and faster through an MI, especially if the authority is operating under the 'supervisory model'. This is especially true in jurisdictions in which the CA cannot impose significant remedies by itself, even in traditional competition law violations, but needs to prove in court that anti-competitive conduct has indeed taken place. Accordingly, it may choose the MI path whenever possible, thereby limiting traditional enforcement activities.

60 Stiglitz (n. 56 above) 15.

61 OECD Report (n. 6 above). The Report provides two examples. In Italy, once the agency opened an investigation into the banking sector, many banks immediately decided to eliminate certain practices. Ibid., 213–214. In the UK, the OFT 'focused on getting the industry to agree to change its practice through a market study', in the context of car warranties, although the situation could have alternatively been countered by using Article 101 of the TFEU. Ibid., 209.

This raises the question whether this is good public policy. No dichotomic answer can be given. A straightforward no is problematic. Oftentimes the first-best solution to limited competitive performance is to lower or eliminate entry barriers and let competition have its way. When barriers are not caught by the competition law (e.g., oligopolistic coordination or government-erected barriers), MIs may be more efficient. A straightforward yes is also problematic, since a regulator may tend to take the easiest path, with short-term visibility and reputational effects and decreased costs of effortful litigation, even if this is not the path that increases social welfare in the long run. Social welfare might be decreased if remedies imposed through an MI are not sufficiently deterrent or because of the level of uncertainty MIs create in the market. Accordingly, a balance must be found between the different regulatory tools based on each tool's comparative advantages and disadvantages.

An additional type of shift of focus occurs when the CA is required not only to prevent specific types of conduct that limit competition, but also to introduce or increase competition in a market. This increases uncertainty in the market: what degree of intervention is warranted and which tools for achieving it are preferable? Conceptually, until all market imperfections are remedied, improvements are possible. MIs actually change the rules of the game from 'everything that is not explicitly forbidden is permitted' to 'certain things that are not forbidden may be subject to authoritative prescriptions (or recommendations)'. Accordingly, moving from the black zone of anti-competitiveness into the grey zone of increasing competition may create a high degree of uncertainty. This, in turn, might negatively affect firms' conduct, especially investment decisions. One counter-argument focuses on the fact that the government's mandate generally allows it to change market conditions where such a change is highly conducive to social welfare, regardless of whether this role is performed by the CA or by another governmental entity.

4.3 Constitutional Issues

Empowering the CA to apply MIs raises some constitutional issues, given that MIs may entail significant social, economic or political consequences which might limit rights such as freedom of occupation and property rights.[62]

---

[62] Of course, the tension between constitutional rights and effective enforcement is not unique to MI. For one excellent analysis in the context of cartel enforcement see W. Wils, *Efficiency and Justice in European Antitrust Enforcement* (Hart Publishing 2008).

At the legislative stage, the question arises whether the authority can engage in MIs which require broad public policy decisions, given its democratic mandate[63] and the fact that the CA is a professional agency, not directly nominated by the public. We argue that the answer partially relies on the way that the power was granted to the agency. Any deviation from its traditional powers should be specifically embedded in clear legislation or in a clear delegation of powers from the government. The relevance of this argument becomes apparent in the light of the ICN survey, which found that 11 per cent of the surveyed jurisdictions (four out of 38) perform MIs without formal powers to carry out such inquiries. Of course, such delegation is especially crucial under the supervisory model. But even under the advisory model MIs can lead to dramatic changes in market conditions.

Once legislated, the question arises whether, from a constitutional point of view, MIs should be performed only as a last alternative. On the one hand, MIs may have significant effects on market players that go well beyond traditional competition law remedies, and might change market conditions radically. Accordingly, one may argue that changing the conditions of the market that are not the result of private anti-competitive conduct changes the rules of the game for market players and thus such steps should be taken as a last resort, if at all. On the other hand, MIs can in some cases be seen as a measure to limit more intrusive regulatory activities, since they may detect the potential for anti-competitive patterns prior to their full realization, and their elimination might necessitate less drastic regulatory steps. Furthermore, MIs do not generally lead to criminal or civil litigation. But most importantly, market players do not have an inherent right to expect that current market conditions will remain unchanged. This is especially true if barriers are artificial.[64] The social contract in a capitalistic society does not promise to protect the *status quo*, but is based on a dynamic model in which firms must deal with changing circumstances to increase social welfare. Yet, this last argument does not imply that constitutional issues are not relevant. Rather, proportionality is required: ensuring that the expected social benefits from MIs outweigh the potential harm from the inquiry itself and its outcomes.

Constitutional issues should also affect the procedural aspects of MIs. An important issue surrounds the investigative powers that can be used in MIs. Such powers can potentially range from collecting information supplied

---

63 We refer only to the first type of MIs; see at 2.2.1 above.

64 A. Ayal, 'Counter-Intuitive Fairness in Antitrust: Protecting the Monopolist and Balancing among Competing Claims' (2012) 8 *J. Comp. L. & Econ.* 627.

voluntarily, through compelling the supply of information, to the use of search and inspection powers. Jurisdictions differ in the point chosen along this spectrum. For instance, in Canada, an amendment to the Competition Law proposed in 2005, which eventually was not adopted, granted the CA formal powers to subpoena documents, but not to search premises.[65] Conversely, the Italian CA has search powers in performing MIs.[66]

We argue that any investigative power, beyond voluntary requests for information, should be specifically granted in the legislation. This implies that the powers to perform inquiries of anti-competitive conduct should not be automatically expanded to apply to MIs. A tougher question regards requests by the CA for voluntary divulgement of information. On the face of it, such requests do not harm any rights, given that market players can simply not comply. Yet, the interaction of market players with the CA is long-term and multifaceted, and such an objection might create negative externalities on the market player, thereby creating incentives to comply with voluntary requests that might impose significant costs.

Accordingly, we argue that such powers should also be legislated and subject to judicial scrutiny and constitutional constraints such as proportionality. In this vein, the legality of 'fishing expeditions' and especially of dawn raids by the European Commission performing MIs has been questioned by Andersson and Legnerfalt.[67] The authors point to the lack of compatibility between the costs and burdens and the utility derived from such steps, and stress not only the immediate costs but also the damage to the integrity of the firms involved.[68] Such costs should be evaluated against the aims to be achieved and the other methods for obtaining information at the CA's disposal, such as obtaining it from other governmental agencies.[69] We also argue that proportionality should also relate to the possibility that in extreme cases MIs might harm competition, if they impose a disproportionately high burden on small firms. In such cases, the CA should apply extra care before requesting the information and should even consider covering some of the expenses of firms. External mechanisms that *ex ante* verify the reasonableness of the

---

65 OECD Report (n. 6 above) 229.

66 Ibid., 57, at para 2, pointing to EC Regulation No. 217/98.

67 Andersson and Legnerfalt (n. 12 above). The paper relates to the European Commission's inquiry into the pharmaceutical market that began by dawn raids despite the absence of any suspicion of wrongdoing by any specific firm.

68 Ibid.

69 OECD Report (n. 6 above) 231; ICN Report (n. 1 above) 39–41.

CA's requests for information may reduce constitutional concerns.[70] Lastly, while preserving the elasticity of the MI tool is legitimate and efficient, as it enables the exact tailoring of the CA's activity to various circumstances, specifying the borders of legitimacy of investigative powers is required. The ICN Draft Handbook advises agencies to be clear about the purposes of the request and the legal constraints on using it.[71]

An important constitutional question involves the transition between the two tools: whether the findings of market inquiries can be used for proving an antitrust violation. This question arises in its strongest form when information is voluntarily supplied. In recognizing the difficulties involved, many jurisdictions adopt some limitations on moving from an MI to traditional enforcement. For example, in the EU the authority cannot use information collected in MIs in subsequent litigation unless it requests it again from the parties.[72] In Italy, when an MI reveals an infringement, the agency must open a separate antitrust investigation into the specific issue.[73] The US CA cannot base enforcement solely on the basis of information collected in an MI and additional information must be gathered through a separate investigation.[74]

Yet, the concern arises that such safeguards are largely lip service, affecting mostly the expediency of the enforcement. Once the information is known, the authority can easily comply with the requirements for issuing new formal demands to deliver a specific document. Accordingly, if MIs lead to actual enforcement, there is a need to apply rules that go beyond such limited safeguards. Such rules should balance the need to adequately exploit public funds with the need to protect the public interest (including from abuse of an MI to reveal information which, it is then argued, cannot be used against the firm providing it). They must additionally consider the faith of market participants who have cooperated with MIs, in the assumption that this vehicle is distinct from enforcement, as well as the interest in creating conditions of certainty and confidence that can facilitate cooperation in future MIs. Accordingly, CAs should be required to seriously evaluate in advance

---

[70] The US regime integrates into the process of crafting a mandatory information request, both an opportunity for the public to comment on draft requests, and a need to gain the clearance of an independent public entity, the Office of Management and Budget (OMB), according to the Paperwork Reduction Act. OECD Report (n. 6 above) 146–151.

[71] ICN Draft Handbook (n. 1 above) 78–79.

[72] OECD Report (n. 6 above) 212.

[73] Ibid., 214.

[74] Ibid., 146.

whether the issue should better be channelled to enforcement or to an MI. Once the decision to engage in an MI is adopted, the CA should avoid a 'zigzag' approach, staying at the edge of enforcement, ready to jump into its deep water whenever possible, unless severe infringements of competition prohibitions are revealed. This, in turn, will also increase motivations to comply with information requests that lead to better and more informed MIs.

4.4 An Increased Risk of Regulatory Capture

It is generally accepted that sector regulators might be more vulnerable to regulatory capture.[75] Yet, as the CA's powers broaden, if it nevertheless falls prey to capture, the implications might be more worrisome.

Three conditions join to facilitate capture: the pressure group has the motivation and ability to engage in it; the public officials are willing to cooperate with capture attempts; and there are practical opportunities to successfully realize capture. MIs increase two of these conditions: the more substantial the implications of a regulatory power, the stronger the motivation of those whose interests are at stake to try and achieve capture. MIs, especially under the supervisory model, may result in significant changes in the market and thus strengthen such motivations. MIs also increase the opportunities to realize capture.[76] Beyond the many ways open to CAs to structure their conclusions and recommendations, MIs enable regulators to enjoy the fruits of capture in a rather concealed way that is harder to detect, does not generally raise resistance and is thus less risky and more tempting.

Yet the relevant question is not whether the CA might be subject to regulatory capture, but rather whether the risk is sufficiently worrisome or larger than under other regulatory alternatives so that MI powers should not be granted. The answer is generally negative. At the same time, recognizing possible capture effects increases the need for devising ways

---

[75] Regulatory capture 'occurs when one particular interest group is able to obtain favors from a legislative body or regulatory agency'. See H. Hovenkamp, *Federal Antitrust Policy: The Law of Competition and its Practice* (2nd edn, West Publishing 1999) 681. For the theory of capture see e.g. G. Stigler, 'The Theory of Economic Regulation' (1971) 2 *Bell J. Econ. & Manag. Sci.* 3; S. Peltzman, 'Toward a More General Theory of Regulation' (1976) 19 *J. L. & Econ.* 3; F. McChesney, *Money for Nothing: Politicians, Rent Extraction, and Political Extortion* (President and Fellows of Harvard College 1997).

[76] OECD Report (n. 6 above) 9, 219, 226 and 241; ICN Report (n. 1 above) 49–51, 59, 61 and 102.

to detect and fight it. One method is to recognize the potential interest groups in each MI and their motivations and aims, and keep them in mind during the inquiry. Stiglitz teaches that caution is necessary even with regard to MIs into theoretical foundations since 'capture also occurs in a more subtle way: through the promulgation of ideas'.[77] He urges agencies to ensure that the voice of those whose interests are likely to be hurt by regulatory failure is well represented in the regulatory procedures.

5. INTRA-REGULATORY EFFECTS

So far the analysis has focused mainly on the ability of CAs to efficiently, effectively and constitutionally perform MIs, given the CA's characteristics. An important, yet often overlooked, aspect of MIs focuses on the intra-regulatory effects they create, that is, their effects on the CA's interactions with other governmental entities as well as their effects on the conduct of such entities. This is the subject of this section. Sub-section 5.1 analyses the effects of MIs on the inter-regulatory status quo. Sub-section 5.2 explores the new administrative law literature regarding coordination mechanisms in a shared regulatory sphere. It critically evaluates the desirability of implementation of coordinated processes, in each of the two relevant models.

5.1 Effects on the Inter-Regulatory *Status Quo*

Empowering the CA to engage in broad MIs that analyse and make (or apply) remedial suggestions for overcoming market and regulatory failures changes the *status quo* within the executive branch. In fact, it enables the CA to act as a 'super-regulator' (or 'super advisor') in markets that are not functioning well. Especially under the supervisory model, it changes the CA's role from Robin (the assistant who acts through advice) to Batman (the super-hero who leads the fight) as it subordinates the other regulators' decisions to those of the CA.

Let us first explore the extent of change in the regulatory *status quo*. Of course, it is most pronounced in markets in which sector regulators operate. In most countries the general *status quo* grants superiority to sector regulation over antitrust in cases of clashes between the two

[77] Stiglitz (n. 56 above) 13 and 20. He notes as one example that 'the financial sector in recent years actively promoted the idea that markets could be self-regulating'.

regimes.[78] Both the advisory and the supervisory models change this situation. In both, the CA is authorized to perform studies and suggest remedies in markets regulated by other governmental bodies. The supervisory model goes further by enabling the CA to determine changes in regulation of the market. Interestingly, as the ICN survey revealed, among the five most studied sectors, four are subject to sector regulation.[79] This may result from the importance of regulated markets to the economy, which justifies additional inquiries in order to find the most effective regulatory path, or from concerns that sector regulation – or a sector regulator – is not functioning well.[80]

A less evident yet still important change in the *status quo* can also be created even when no sector regulator exists in the market. Indeed, the carrying out of an MI resembles the throwing of a pebble into a river, as it creates several widening circles of impact. The relevant ministry, or even the whole government, can be affected by the conclusions of the MI. An MI that points to regulatory shortcomings or to policy decisions that created (or failed to lower) obstacles to competition in the market may well have a negative impact on public perceptions of the government. Such an impact might be stronger if indeed the CA's recommendations are applied in practice and reveal the cost that the public has paid for inefficient regulation.

As a result, a sector regulator may wish to avoid such studies. One way is to pressure the government not to perform MIs in its sector (or at all). Another way is to take active yet covert steps to cut the budget of the CA or to harm its reputation, to ensure that its recommendations are not given much weight by the government or the public.

Conversely, the empowerment of the CA to perform MIs might create positive externalities on other regulators or governmental bodies, as it

---

[78] For such a rule in the US see, e.g., T. Sullivan, H. Hovenkamp and H. Shelanski, *Antitrust Law, Policy and Procedure: Cases, Materials, Problems* (5th edn, LexisNexis 2003) ch. 9 ('Antitrust and Other Forms of Regulation') 981–985; P. Areeda, L. Kaplow and A. Edlin, *Antitrust Analysis: Problems, Text, and Cases* (6th edn, Aspen Publishers 2004) 83–84. Shelanski argues that '[t]he Supreme Court has redrawn the boundary between antitrust and regulation in a way that reduces the applicability of antitrust law in regulated markets'. See H. Shelanski, 'Justice Breyer, Professor Kahn, and Antitrust Enforcement in Regulated Industries' (2012) 100 *Cal. L. Rev.* 487.

[79] ICN Report (n. 1 above) 98.

[80] OECD Report (n. 6 above) 120 (on the UK) and 145 (on the US): 'The purpose of these reports was to create greater public awareness of the costs of regulation and thereby to encourage greater consideration of the benefits of competition and of market-based solutions.'

re-shapes their incentives in a way that may do away with the need to perform some MIs. It strengthens the incentives of other regulators to act more proactively to find solutions to market failures in order to limit scrutiny (or intervention) by the CA.[81]

In sum, an MI may strengthen the standing and prestige of the CA, and may endow competition considerations with increased weight in diverse policies and activities, due to enhanced awareness. Yet, when an MI does not lead to any change, the reputation of the CA might be harmed.

5.2 Coordination Among Regulators?

The following pages explore the applicability to MIs of some of the insights offered by the recent administrative law literature, which takes the focus from a single agency and moves it to multiple agencies' interactions.[82] In their recent paper, Freeman and Rossi praise coordination as the response to the challenges faced when multiple agencies interact in a 'shared regulatory sphere'.[83] This sub-section questions the desirability of applying cooperation mechanisms between the CA and the sector regulators while performing MIs.

Freeman and Rossi describe modern governance as often characterized by a fragmented and overlapping delegation of powers to several agencies, each responsible 'for part of a larger whole'.[84] They contend that in such a reality, coordination 'has significant promise for overcoming concerns of dysfunctions'.[85] Accordingly, we analyse the possibility of integrating coordination into MIs.

The benefits of coordination are contingent on the type of coordination and the initial reasons that have led lawmakers to design the specific shared regulatory space.[86] With regard to the first stage of an MI – the market analysis – CAs can definitely benefit from coordination, which may save information-gathering costs and generate more accurate analysis given the input of those generally involved in regulating the specific market. It also decreases duplication and inconsistency.[87] Coordination facilitates these gains while preserving the independence of each agency,

[81] See, e.g, Sappington and Weisman (n. 54 above) 32.

[82] See E. Biber, 'The More the Merrier: Multiple Agencies and the Future of Administrative Law Scholarship' (2012) 125 *Harv. L. Rev.* 78.

[83] Freeman and Rossi (n. 55 above).

[84] Ibid., 1134.

[85] Ibid., 1136–1137.

[86] Ibid., 1137 and 1144.

[87] Ibid., 1182.

which is important for productive interagency competitiveness and the ongoing operation of distinct laboratories for policy ideas. Another beneficial by-product of coordination is that it inherently involves more individuals that pertain to more than one organization. This guarantees additional independent inspection that can locate, and thus deter and prevent, unconstitutional or otherwise disturbing misuse of MIs. Yet we argue that even at this stage, the CA should keep in mind the political economy limitations that may affect the sector regulator.

A more complicated question arises with regard to policy conclusions and remedies. Coordination might increase the possibility that remedies are workable. Moreover, in case an MI is a fruit of cooperation, the regulator might view the report as partly its own, thereby refuting some of the potential criticisms by indicating that it is open to self-assessment and change, and thereby increasing the prospect of affirmation and actualization. On the other hand, coordination has its costs when criticizing the conduct of a regulator, as it is not simple to simultaneously nourish a cooperative and a competition-prone consciousness. This is because cooperation creates personal affiliation between officials across agencies and a habit of cooperation. Accordingly, coordination in structuring remedies might be least beneficial in regulatory sunset situations, in which changes in the market (most likely technological) suggest a change in the regulatory function towards greater reliance on market forces. As a result, caution is required in order to avoid fostering coordination mechanisms that protect a given inefficient regulatory mechanism. If we expect the CA to advance the realization of conditions that lead to turning the lights off in other regulatory agencies, coordination might in some situations be counter-productive.

In cases in which coordination is beneficial, which tools are most efficient? Freeman and Rossi recognize three types of coordination tools: consultation, agreements and joint policymaking. Consultation seems most applicable to MIs,[88] preserving the CA's lead and limiting the danger of stagnation of regulatory methods. Mandatory consultation[89] may be advisable: requiring the CA to consult, but leaving it with full discretion as to whether to accept the sector regulator's inputs.

In practice, many jurisdictions foster cooperation while performing MIs. For instance, while the Hungarian agency is not obliged by law to do so, in practice it circulates drafts of reports to governmental agencies which operate in the same policy space. It also consults with government

---

88 Ibid., 1192.

89 Ibid., 1157–1161.

institutions, to hear opinions and discuss the draft prior to holding hearings with firms. It finds this approach useful for verifying the soundness of the analysis and improving the final report's quality.[90] Indeed, the ICN Draft Handbook[91] advocates the consideration of cooperation with sector regulators while performing MIs.

Some jurisdictions go further and engage in partly joint MIs, mostly as a way to ensure the provision of information and overcome budgetary constraints.[92] Others adopt an opposing position,[93] warning of negative effects on the public perception of the CA's independence, risks of delays and clash of interests. The ICN Draft Handbook[94] seems to more caution against than encourage joint reports. In our view, much depends on the circumstances. Especially when the core aim of the MI is to consider the continuance of sector regulation or part thereof, joint MIs might lead to a deadlock.

6. INSTEAD OF A CONCLUSION: COMPARATIVE EVALUATION OF THE SUPERVISORY AND ADVISORY MODELS

As this chapter has attempted to show, MIs performed by CAs may create significant benefits. Although MIs create both direct and indirect costs, such costs can largely be reduced by acknowledging them and structuring the MI accordingly. For example, the strengthening of the CA's powers requires taking stronger precautions against regulatory capture than previously applied.

That said, instead of a regular conclusion, we apply the above conclusions to the two main models of MIs: the advisory and the supervisory model, to determine which one is more effective and efficient.[95] Of course, the answer depends, *inter alia*, on parameters that are unique to each jurisdiction, such as the level of performance of other regulators and the extent of corruption. These parameters, which should also be taken into account when making a decision in a specific setting, are beyond the scope of this chapter.

---

[90] OECD Report (n. 6 above) 226.

[91] ICN Draft Handbook (n. 1 above) 33.

[92] See, e.g. the contributions of the following jurisdictions to the OECD Report (n. 6 above) 163 (Chile), 157 (Italy), 227 (France) and 76 (Mexico).

[93] See, e.g., the Irish contribution to the OECD Report (n. 6 above) 50.

[94] ICN Draft Handbook (n. 1 above) 23–24.

[95] Part of the measurements for comparatively evaluating the two models follow the thresholds outlines by Freeman and Rossi (n. 55 above).

The clear tendency worldwide to embrace the advisory model, accompanied by rare exceptions to follow the supervisory one, raises the question of whether the majority miss substantial utilities created by the blunter alternative, whether the minority overlooks important pitfalls of its choice, or whether different circumstances justify different models. We hope to shed light on this question.

As noted, the models differ in the extent to which the CA can independently enforce the remedies it reaches at the completion of the inquiry. Under the advisory model, the CA presents its findings and suggestions to the relevant governmental bodies and has no power to act upon them; while under the supervisory model it is empowered to take active steps to remedy at least some types of market failures. This difference affects the future implications of the inquiry, and also affects, backwards, the process of the inquiry and, sidewards, the interfacing agencies.

With regard to the CA's expertise, both models make use of its analytical capabilities in analysing market failures. The supervisory model further makes use of this expertise when the imposed remedies pertain to introducing more competition, but moves the CA into unknown territory if balancing of competitive and non-competitive considerations is required. Although consultation and cooperation are possible, the supervisory model usually makes less use of the expertise of other governmental bodies in structuring remedies, as it lacks one layer of critical assessment of such remedies by other governmental bodies that is inherent in the advisory model.

The supervisory model proscribes one entity – the CA – as responsible for performance, substantial conclusions, choice of remedies and course of implementation of the MI. This fact stimulates the authority to vest efforts, act professionally, and strive for the best possible result. In addition, the fact that one agency carries out the project from start to end may increase the MI's coherence.

The type of model applied also affects the risks of capture. As elaborated, CAs are assumed to be relatively immune to such risks. Yet, endowing the authority with substantial power over sector regulators implies higher risks of capture, as it is 'most likely to arise where the delegation scheme allows a single agency to block, dominate, or neutralize others'.[96] This risk is of course higher under the supervisory model. In the advisory model, even if the authority is captured, the implementing governmental agencies may negate the capture. Another kind of capture

[96] Ibid., 1186.

relates to political capture, where political entities may wish to make political usage of the CA's substantial powers in order to foster agendas unrelated to competition, especially if MIs can be initiated as a result of a referral by politicians.

Yet, the main difference between the two models regards the MI's effectiveness: the potential that conclusions will turn into actions. Under the advisory model, the risk that important changes will not take place due to their rejection, circumvention or abandonment by other governmental agencies, and the related risk of eroding the CA's relative stand, is higher. Furthermore, as noted in the OECD Report, under the advisory model, when the MI is submitted, the work is not done. Rather, this is often when the hard work starts: explaining and marketing the conclusions and convincing other governmental institutions to act upon them.[97] Moreover, anticipating such a reaction, the CA might have weaker incentives to invest in performing certain MIs altogether. In other cases, it might tailor the remedies to avoid such reactions, even if this implies second-best solutions. The longer timetables for remedying market failure through an advisory model may further reduce incentives, since authorities tend to invest less in projects that will bear fruit in the distant future. Rather, public officials may prefer to pick the fruits of a successful inquiry during their own term. The supervisory model largely avoids such limitations, although expected criticism from other governmental bodies can sometimes have similar but weaker influence.

The importance of this difference depends, *inter alia*, on the frequency and the causes that prevent the actualization of an MI's recommendations. Indeed, the OECD Report finds that potential acceptance of an MI often depends on circumstances that may have nothing to do with the substance and desirability of their conclusions.[98] MIs that result in controversial conclusions have a higher risk of being disregarded, absent supervisory powers. To the extent that this outcome results from the mandate of the government to take into account broader considerations or to have the final word on controversial issues, this is a legitimate and

[97] OECD Report (n. 6 above) 10, 222 and 235.

[98] This reality was described in the Irish contribution to the OECD Report (n. 6 above) 53: 'The effectiveness of market studies as a tool for reform depends on many factors, including the collective policy of the Government of the day, the receptiveness of individual Government Departments to change, the strength and organization of any entities who may wish to resist change and retain the *status quo*, the extent of consumer and other pressure for change, and so on. These dynamics will naturally vary from sector to sector, and from time to time, depending on individual and collective economic circumstances.'

desirable result. But when the political power of those enjoying the current situation leads to stagnation, the advisory model is inefficient.[99] The CA can reduce some of the deficits of the advisory model by creating counter-pressures through the general public. The public may leverage the MI into an action plan by creating political incentives for policymakers to mind the public call for action. An additional tool is requiring the government to respond to the MI recommendations in a limited time frame.[100] While this does not offer any guarantee that the recommendations will be accepted, the mandatory demand to consider them and to explain their rejection, slightly increases the potential for their acceptance. The supervisory model largely avoids such deficits.

The supervisory model spares the CA the burden of persuasion, lobbying or educational activities. Rather, the CA can swiftly implement the proposed changes. Yet, change might often best be achieved through persuasion rather than force. Accordingly, the advisory model may increase the prospects of urging a genuine and durable internalization of the merits of competition, as well as compliance that is based on acceptance as opposed to calculation of risk and sanctions. In addition, the effectiveness of the supervisory model is not necessarily long term. Rather, the shorter way to implementation may turn out to be inefficient. Governmental bodies or pressure groups which oppose the remedies might try to harm the reputation of the CA or use their influence to clip its wings. In recognizing such caveats, the ICN study notes that CAs have developed multiple measures, aimed at the government, the business community and third parties, which may serve to increase the possibility that their recommendations will be adopted.[101]

In sum, each model has strengths and weaknesses. The supervisory model has clear merits. It reduces political economy distortions; it stimulates responsibility and coherence; it strengthens incentives to engage in MIs; it saves resources needed for persuasion following the

---

[99] The OECD report mentions the example of a historical US MI where the 'Congress decided that the competition agency that performed the market study would no longer be allowed to study or report on a sector – the insurance sector – precisely because the incumbents in the market sector applied political pressure on Congress to do so'. Ibid., 208.

[100] As required in nine jurisdictions, according to the ICN Report (n. 1 above) 74.

[101] The Irish contribution to the OECD Report (n. 6 above) 54, puts this forward clearly: 'Market studies also have intangible benefits. If they are drawn up properly, and presented professionally, skilfully and (most importantly) accessibly, they both stimulate public debate on the issue at hand and get people talking about competition issues in general.'

completion of MIs, and it enjoys a higher effectiveness of implementation of remedies. In parallel, the advisory model also enjoys some merits: it allows for external balancing of competition and non-competition concerns by policymakers; it is based on persuasion that results in less resistance, thereby creating a higher potential to achieve genuine and lasting internalization and compliance; it does not entail substantial concerns of political manipulations; and it reduces motivations to harm the reputation of the CA.

Accordingly, it seems to us that each of the models is preferable in a different set of cases.[102] The basic condition for applying the supervisory model, in our opinion, is that the inquiry focuses almost solely on competition and does not require the balancing of competition and non-competition considerations. Once this condition is fulfilled, the supervisory model may work best if the inquiry is focused on the efficacy of some form of regulation or its scope; where the inquiry is anticipated to provoke strong pressure groups and change is critical to avoid welfare-reducing stagnation; and where a high level of corruption and a low level of professionalism can be assumed in higher levels of government.[103]

The advisory model is recommended where it is important to gain the acceptance of other regulators, the government or the public for the recommendations; or where the decision is multifaceted and involves not only competition but other considerations such as security, environmental concerns, employment or strengthening the weaker parts of society. In such cases, democratic considerations mandate that the CA only delivers its suggestion to the government, which is better equipped to balance the competing considerations.

Thus, in order to maximize the utilities of MIs, it is suggested that jurisdictions consider outlining in their legislation the exact conditions under which each of the models may be implemented, instead of adhering to a single model. This increases legal certainty while allowing for the matching of the CA's capabilities to diverse cases.

---

102 This approach follows the idea of 'matching' suggested by Freeman and Rossi (n. 55 above) 1191.

103 One might argue that in such situations the government will not give up its power to decide. Yet the political economy literature indicates that even in such situations the decision-making might be assigned to a professional agency. See, e.g., S. Voigt and E.M. Salzberger, 'Choosing not to Choose: When Politicians Choose to Delegate Powers' (2002) 55 *Kyklos* 289.

5. New frontiers for competition advocacy and the potential role of competition impact assessment

Nicoletta Rangone

1. GOALS AND STRUCTURE OF THE CHAPTER

This chapter will explore the question of how best to increase the effectiveness of advocacy activities in order to improve competition-friendly regulation.

In this framework, three tools are compared: the use of competition concepts in rule-making, i.e. hybridization (at 3.1 below), traditional advocacy interventions (at 3.2 below) and competition impact assessment (at 3.3 below). The analysis is intended to highlight the key components of these tools, to assess their effectiveness in improving regulation and sound competition and to suggest appropriate uses for each.

Then, a more in-depth analysis is dedicated to the role that *ex ante* and *ex post* competition impact assessment can play in order to improve regulation (and in so doing enhance competition), and the crucial part that competition authorities might play in this (at 3.3.1 and 3.3.2).

This chapter concludes that competition impact assessment can be considered as a new advocacy tool, and indeed the most effective such tool (if used at a very early stage, using economic analysis and always taking into consideration the option not to intervene through regulation), provided that the analysis is limited to rules which have been correctly selected according to the proportionality principle and is not applied in a ritualistic way (at section 4 below). It also underlines that the involvement of competition authorities has the potential to increase the effectiveness of competition assessment (by enhancing the robustness of the economic analysis and therefore addressing the above-mentioned ritualistic approach), even though some issues remain unsolved, one of the most important being how best to balance the role of regulators and competition authorities (at section 5 below).

2. THE STARTING POINT: GOOD REGULATION ENHANCES COMPETITION (AND COMPETITIVENESS)

This chapter starts with the hypothesis that high-quality regulation will enhance competition. Therefore the objective of improving a competition-friendly regulatory framework is shared by regulators and competition authorities, and they must cooperate in the search for good regulation.[1]

Good market efficiency (or sound competition) is strictly linked to the quality of regulation.[2] The core elements of good regulation are both the content of regulation and its form. Regulation should indeed be necessary, proportional and consistent, on the one hand, as well as well written and accessible to end users, on the other.[3]

These criteria for good regulation are also valuable tools for pro-competitive regulation. Necessity and proportionality have been the main thrust of regulation in the electronic communications sector in order to reduce *ex ante* sector-specific rules progressively as competition in the market develops, and to choose the regulatory tool which best fits the specific detected problem, according to a case-by-case approach. Necessity and proportionality of regulation are also tested by competition advocacy activities. Moreover, these activities check that regulations are accessible, written in plain language, and easy to understand, in order to free up firms' energies which would otherwise concentrate on understanding and complying with unnecessary burdens, but also in order to limit the uncompetitive practices of bureaucrats and firms.

---

[1] This chapter refers to regulation as both legislation and regulation, i.e. sources of law approved at the political level, administrative provisions adopted by public administrations through discretionary or technical powers and self-regulation delegated by public powers. Indeed, what is relevant for market forces is the regulatory content of a rule, whether expressed in a law, a governmental regulation or an administrative decision.

[2] One example of this generally accepted link can already be found in the title of the European guidelines on competition assessment: *European Commission – Better Regulation: A Guide to Competition Screening* (2005).

[3] An obscurely and ambiguously written rule is not implemented; a rule that is impossible to implement (because economic, social, cultural, organizational conditions are messy) is no more than a slogan; a rule that has unintended consequences could create bigger risks than those it was intended to address; etc. See M. De Benedetto, M. Martelli and N. Rangone, *La qualità delle regole* (Il Mulino 2011) 11.

From a historical point of view, as is well known, the 'dirigiste' state[4] was characterized by large-scale direct public intervention in the economy (through public ownership of key industries) and similarly broad indirect public intervention through 'finalistic' regulation (which indicated to firms what and how to produce). This approach, which had some justification (e.g. the objectives to ensure the universality of networks and services in public utilities), also limited or even suppressed competition in many markets. Therefore, in this period the most relevant constraints on competition came from regulations.[5]

As such, the 'dirigiste state' (or better, its anticompetitive regulation) was questioned by European and international law. These new waves (the 'regulatory state', using Majone's famous expression) redrew the borders of the public sphere and redefined regulatory tools in order to be consistent with supranational principles and regulations.[6] However, poor regulation (unnecessary, anticompetitive or excessively burdensome to end-users) is still one of the main causes of low market efficiency in many countries around the world,[7] where legislation, administrative provisions and bureaucratic attitudes and traditions often still prevent, restrict and distort competition.[8] The legal uncertainty associated with the lack of transparency and accessibility, and the instability and inconsistency of regulation, acting as a *de facto* juridical entry barrier, may also hinder potential newcomers.[9]

---

[4] G. Majone, 'The Rise of the Regulatory State in Europe' (1994) 17(3) *West Eur. Pol.* 77.

[5] See G. Amato and L. Laudati (eds), *The Anticompetitive Impact of Regulation* (Edward Elgar Publishing 2001) and G. Amato and L. Laudati, 'The Protection of Public Interests and Regulation of Economic Activities' in F. Snyder (ed.), *The Europeanisation of Law: The Legal Effects of European Integration* (Hart Publishing 2000) 141.

[6] B. Du Marais, *Droit public de la régulation économique* (Dalloz 2004).

[7] M. D'Alberti, 'Administrative Law and the Public Regulation of Markets in a Global Age' in S. Rose-Ackerman and P.L. Lindseth (eds), *Comparative Administrative Law* (Edward Elgar Publishing 2010) 63.

[8] Much research analyses the effects of anticompetitive regulation on economic growth. See, for instance, E. Allegra, M. Forni, M. Grillo and L. Magnani, 'Antitrust Policy and National Growth: Some Evidence from Italy' (2004) 63 *Giornale degli Economisti e Annali di Economia* 69; A. Alesina, S. Ardagna, G. Nicoletti and F. Schiantarelli, 'Regulation and Investment' (2005) 3 *J. Eur. Econ. Ass.* 791; G. Barone and F. Cingano, 'Service Regulation and Growth: Evidence from OECD Countries' (2011) 121 *Econ. J.* 931.

[9] Comisión Nacional de la Competencia (Spanish competition authority), Recommendations to public authorities for more efficient and pro-competitive market regulation (2008) 6.

The above-mentioned adverse effects on competition are sometimes the result of conscious public decisions, a sort of trade-off between different general interests, i.e. competition on the one hand, and the protection of the environment, the promotion of health and safety or another social interest goal (for instance, job protection), on the other. However, prevention, restrictions and distortions of competition are very often unintended consequences of regulations adopted without any consideration of their impact.

Anticompetitive regulations have strong adverse consequences not only on competition, but even on competitiveness. Concerns about the impact that regulations may have on competitiveness are not new: the key element in ensuring the competitiveness represented by competition-friendly regulation is stressed by many international,[10] European[11] and national documents.[12] Further, in the current economic crisis, as always

[10] A good regulatory framework is an indicator of competitiveness, which is always used in international ranking, showing that poor regulation is a problem in many European and non-European countries. For instance, *Doing Business 2013* stresses that '[a] growing body of empirical research shows that particular areas of business regulation, and particular regulatory reforms in those areas, are associated with vital social and economic outcomes – including firm creation, employment, formality, international trade, access to financial services and the survival of struggling but viable firms'. See *Doing Business 2013: Smarter Regulations for Small and Medium-Size Enterprises* (2012) 20. In sum: 'Smarter business regulation promotes economic growth', at 21. See also *Doing Business 2014: Understanding Regulations for Small and Medium-Size Enterprises* (2013) 20 et seq.; World Economic Forum, *The Global Competitiveness Report 2012–2013* (2012) 4 and 6.

[11] See, for instance, Communication from the Commission of 16 March 2005 to the Council and the European Parliament – Better Regulation for Growth and Jobs in the European Union, 16 March 2005, COM(2005) 97 final.

[12] Under the Australian National Competition Policy reform programme, which aims at implementing the Hilmer Report drafted in 1993 by an Independent Committee of Inquiry, over 50% of 1,700 laws identified have been reviewed, and the federal government pays states for quality of effort in revising regulations (0.1–0.2% of GDP used for incentive payments). This policy has resulted in an increase of the growth rate by 1 to 1.75%. See S. Ennis (OECD) Competition Assessment (12 February 2010) 22, available at: http://www.oecd.org/daf/competition/45048328.pdf (accessed 31 January 2014). See also Government of Canada, Compete to Win, Final Report (2008) 1, available at: https://www.ic.gc.ca/eic/site/cprp-gepmc.nsf/vwapj/Compete_to_Win.pdf/$FILE/Compete_to_Win. pdf (accessed 31 January 2014).

in times of economic distress,[13] the link between good regulation and competitiveness explains the reason for the renewed commitment to better regulation in most OECD countries, at both the national and local level.[14]

3. TOOLS FOR MORE EFFECTIVE ADVOCACY ACTIVITIES: HYBRIDIZATION, TRADITIONAL ADVOCACY, COMPETITION ASSESSMENT

There are many tools that can be used to effect cooperation between competition authorities and regulators in the search for high-quality regulation.

Some are traditional activities of competition authorities (the various advocacy interventions). Another is the use of competition-based concepts in rule-making, so-called regulation hybridization experienced in the field of electronic communications (like the former, it is familiar to scholars and practitioners, though in constant evolution). A further tool is competition impact assessment, which focuses on the impact of drafts or existing rules on competition in affected markets, assessing their advantages and disadvantages (proposed here as a new advocacy tool).

Hybridization, advocacy activities and competition assessment are tools working towards pro-competitive regulation. These three tools, while not mutually exclusive, are of different degrees of efficacy in drawing up pro-competitive regulation and, in general, in improving regulation. Indeed, these tools function in different ways, have different objects and may have a different efficacy in attaining the aim of introducing competition concerns into regulation, and, by doing so,

---

[13] R.A. Posner, *Economic Analysis of Law* (Aspen Publishers 2003) 380; B.J. Wiener 'Better Regulation in Europe' (2006) *Current Leg. Probs.* 455, available at: http://scholarship.law.duke.edu/faculty_scholarship/1586

[14] Pro-competitive regulation is also considered to promote pro-poor economic growth and to this end competition impact assessment might help to assess the pro and anticompetitive effects of specific regulations: E.M. Fox, 'Competition and Poverty Reduction' in OECD Global Forum on Competition, OECD-Doc. DAF/COMP/GF(2013)4 (2013), available at: http://search.oecd.org/officialdocuments/publicdisplaydocumentpdf/?cote=DAF/COMP/GF%282013%294&docLanguage=En (accessed 31 January 2014).

helping to build a competition-friendly regulatory framework (as summarized in Table 5.1 below).[15]

Therefore, competition assessment can play a crucial role in enhancing competition in markets and competitiveness of countries by reducing regulatory restrictions and requiring a justification of any rule that prevents, restricts or distorts competition. However, although some regulators and competition authorities are familiar with competition assessment, others are sceptical or simply not aware of it.

By analysing the role that competition authorities can play in the use of competition assessment, this chapter argues that they can properly perform the assessment and accordingly advise and guide legislators and rule-makers in assessing the flow and stock of rules in the regulation life-cycle. The effectiveness of competition impact assessment is then analysed compared to traditional advocacy activities and to regulation hybridization.

3.1 Hybridization

The hybridization of sectorial regulations experienced in the electronic communications sector has been imposed by the European legislature in order to achieve a more competitive and open internal market. Here, the regulators are the main actors, though they are advised by the competition authorities.

The central thrust of the 2002 directives was to promote the use of competition-based regulatory concepts (relevant market and market power) and to reduce *ex ante* sector-specific rules progressively as competition in the market develops.[16] The regulatory reform process begun in 2007[17] has led to innovative results in several respects (for

---

[15] Therefore, in theory, these tools could complement each other, as they are not mutually exclusive: an advocacy intervention could be addressed to a rule adopted after an *ex ante* competition impact assessment, as well as competition authorities giving their advice (expression of an advocacy activity) on the regulation of the electronic communications sector (currently the unique example of regulatory hybridization).

[16] European Commission Recommendation of 11 February 2003. See F. di Porto, 'La regolazione "geneticamente modificata": c'è del nuovo in tema di rapporti tra regolazione e concorrenza' (2006) *Riv. Ital. Dir. Pub. Com.* 947 with further references.

[17] Commission Staff Working Document, Impact Assessment, Accompanying document to the proposal for a Directive amending Directives 2002/19/EC, 2002/20/EC and 2002/21/EC, proposal for a Directive amending Directives

example, by strengthening the European Regulators Group (ERG) in the Body of European Regulators for Electronic Communications (BEREC) in order to limit non-homogeneous national implementation).[18] It has not, however, changed the main idea that remedies should be informed by concepts borrowed from competition law and should constitute an expression of the proportionality of regulations.

However, as is well known, competition law concepts are not implemented in regulatory laws and competition law in a homogeneous way. Indeed, national regulators should not only promote competition, but also contribute to the development of the internal market, and promote the interests of the citizens of the European Union.[19] This is all the more true since the promotion of investment in new and enhanced infrastructures was introduced as a new regulatory principle[20] (in the sense that it is not

---

2002/22/EC and 2002/58/EC, proposal for a Regulation establishing the European Electronic Communications Markets Authority (13 November 2007) SEC(2007) 1472.

[18] Regulation (EC) No 1211/2009 of the European Parliament and of the Council of 25 November 2009 establishing the Body of European Regulators for European Communications (BEREC) and of the Office, [2009] OJ L 337, p. 1; Directive 2009/136/EC of the European Parliament and of the Council of 25 November 2009, amending Directive No 2002/22/EC on universal service and users' rights relating to electronic communications networks and services, Directive 2002/58/EC concerning the processing of personal data and the protection of piracy in the electronic communications sector and Regulation (EC) No 2006/2004 on cooperation between national authorities responsible for the enforcement of consumer protection laws, [2009] OJ L337, p. 11.

[19] See Article 8 of Directive 2002/21/EC of the European Parliament and of the Council of 7 March 2002 on a common regulatory framework for electronic communications networks and services (Framework Directive), [2002] OJ L 108, p. 33. See P. Larouche, 'What Went Wrong with Telecommunications: The European Perspective', Tilburg Law and Economics Center (TILEC) Discussion Paper No. 2003-01 (2003) 14 ff., available at: http://papers.ssrn.com/sol3/papers.cfm?abstract_id=832464 (accessed 31 January 2014). Moreover, 'the market is usually defined more broadly under sector specific law than under competition', a significant market power 'operator does not necessarily enjoy a dominant position under Article 82 EC', and the significant market power 'designation does not lead, nor presume that the regulated operator has committed any abuse'. See A. de Streel, 'The Integration of Competition Law Principles in the New European Regulatory Framework for Electronic Communications' (2003) 26 *World Comp.* 489, 511.

[20] Article 8(5) European Framework Directive 2002/21/EC (n. 19 above). According to the ECJ, C-424/07 *Commission v Germany* [2009] ECR I-11431, para. 91, it is up to national regulators, 'and not the national legislatures, to

strictly related to the promotion of competition, but is a sort of industrial policy aim), which could, in practice, hinder competition-based regulation.

Moreover, hybridization could be of limited efficacy in reducing regulation (which is not an end in itself). Firstly, if national regulators can choose the remedy that best fits the competition problem to be addressed, they can also hardly avoid adopting a decision: when market power is detected, the alternative remedies cannot be compared to the so-called zero option (Article 16(4) of Framework Directive 2002/21/EC has been interpreted as requiring the adoption of at least one remedy).[21] Secondly, with the new regulatory framework, the idea of a decrease in regulation is abandoned (though not explicitly), due to the increased powers of the European Commission concerning national remedies[22] and of the national regulation authorities, which can impose a functional separation.[23]

---

balance those objectives when defining and analysing a relevant market which may be susceptible to regulation'.

[21] Revised ERG Common Position on the approach to appropriate remedies in the ECNS regulatory framework ('Remedies' document), ERG (06) 33 (May 2006) 1, available at: http://pfs.is/upload/files/erg_06_33_remedies_common_position_june_06.pdf. This is one of the reasons why competition-based regulation in the electronic communications sector cannot be considered to be a sort of regulatory impact assessment (as some national regulators claim) of which competition impact assessment is a part. Another reason is that the analysis is usually intended to adopt an individual decision and not a general one, meaning a rule addressed to an undetermined number of regulated parties. One exception might be 'symmetric regulation' concerning access obligations that regulators could impose on all firms active in a given market irrespective of their individual market position and which complement asymmetric obligations for specific physical bottlenecks (Article 12 of the Framework Directive).

[22] Under the European Framework Directive (n. 19 above), the European Commission is involved in national rule-making by means of an automatic consultation, which could lead to a non-binding letter of comments, a non-binding recommendation, or a veto provision preventing the draft from being adopted (Article 7 of the modified Directive).

[23] An increase in regulation could also be linked to cases where 'the sectorial regulator has more operational tools at its disposal to eliminate broadly anticompetitive practices than the competition authority', and can apply 'a more stringent competitive effects test than might apply under competition law'. See International Competition Network, Antitrust Enforcement in Regulated Sectors Working Group, Subgroup 2: Enforcement experience in regulated sectors, Report to the Third ICN Annual Conference (2004) 11–12, available at: http://www.internationalcompetitionnetwork.org/uploads/library/doc379.pdf (accessed 31 January 2014).

3.2 Competition Advocacy

Advocacy is always construed very broadly as including 'those activities conducted by the competition authority related to the promotion of a competitive environment for economic activities by means of non-enforcement mechanisms, mainly through its relationships with other governmental entities and by increasing public awareness of the benefits of competition'.[24]

Therefore, competition authorities can play an important role in promoting the use of competition-based concepts in rule-making and in *ex post* evaluation of regulations, using a wide range of formal and informal tools.

The formal tools currently used most often can be summarized as follows. Many competition authorities are empowered to:

(a) inform regulators whenever pre-existing or draft legislative and administrative measures promise to create restrictions on competition;
(b) advise national sectorial regulators in their rule-making and decision-making activities (including the electronic communications sector affected by hybridization); and
(c) identify in an annual report all regulations that distort competition.[25]

Competition authorities may also conduct a discretionary analysis of draft or existing sector-specific regulation and should also set general guidelines of regulatory reform.[26]

---

[24] See ICN, Advocacy Working Group, Advocacy and Competition Policy, Report prepared for the ICN's Conference in Naples (2002) 25, available at: http://www.internationalcompetitionnetwork.org/uploads/library/doc358.pdf (accessed 31 January 2013). The ICN, an international body devoted to competition law enforcement and formed in 2001 by antitrust authorities from 14 jurisdictions, is one important forum that supports the primacy of competition over regulation. See M. D'Alberti, 'Competition Law and Regulatory Reform' in P. Pavlopoulos and S. Flogaitis (eds), *Multilevel Governance and Administrative Reform in the 21st Century* (Esperia 2008) 275.

[25] In Italy this power has been reinforced by requiring the government to present parliament with an 'annual law on competition' that incorporates the competition authority's recommendations and specifies where it has decided not to follow them. See Article 47 of Law No. 99 of 23 July 2009.

[26] M. D'Alberti, 'I poteri di advocacy delle autorità di concorrenza in prospettiva comparata' (2013) *Concorrenza e Mercato* 871.

Therefore, competition authorities can act in cooperation with regulators, if not as a supervisor of regulators, where the former has the power to challenge regulation in courts, as does the Italian competition authority.[27]

However, despite the strength of these traditional tools, they can be of limited potential efficacy in avoiding anticompetitive regulation and creating more effective and less burdensome regulation[28] that adheres to the principles of necessity and proportionality and embraces the plain language and accessibility that characterize good regulation. This is due to the fact that competition authorities usually express non-binding opinions to regulators.[29] Moreover, their opinions regard a previously

[27] Section 21*bis* of Italian Law No. 287 of 10 October 1990; introduced by Section 35 of Law Decree No. 201/2011, which was converted with modifications from law No. 214/2011. See M. Clarich, 'I poteri di impugnativa dell'Agcm ai sensi del nuovo art. 21-bis, l. 287/90' (2013) *Concorrenza e Mercato* 865.

[28] The effectiveness of traditional competition advocacy – as well as the proposed competition impact assessment as a new tool – is analysed here from a theoretical point of view, having regard to its characteristics. Indeed, there is no single, reliable way to assess the 'real' impact of advocacy interventions, which depends on numerous factors that can be extremely difficult to take into consideration. For instance, other types of advocacy, such as those of the private sector, may also affect the regulatory outcome. Moreover, even if rule-makers later declare that they relied on recommendations by competition authorities, there is no certainty that such statements are not just 'after-the-fact justifications'. In this sense see J.C. Cooper, P.A. Pautler and T.J. Zywicki, 'Theory and Practice of Competition Advocacy at the FTC' (2005) 72 *Antitrust L.J.* 1105. It may also be inappropriate to assume that in the absence of the initiative by the competition authority, the anticompetitive regulation would have been imposed in its initially proposed form. In this sense see S.J. Evenett, 'Competition Advocacy: Time for a Rethink?' (2006) 26 *Nw. J. Int'l L. & Bus.* 495, 508. Last but not least, regulation is often the result of multilateral (and multilevel) decision-making involving many regulators and end-users, so that it is difficult to say who most influenced the final decision.

[29] A thorough study on the impact of Italian competition advocacy measures shows that 33% of the interventions adopted between 1990 and 1995 were 'successful' in the sense that the anticompetitive regulation was not adopted or was revised after the competition authority initiative. However, in 73% of these successes, this was largely due to a parallel (binding) action of the European Commission. See P.L. Parcu, 'Stato e concorrenza. L'attività di segnalazione dell'autorità antitrust: contenuti, efficacia e prospettive' (1996) *Temi e Problemi no. 4*, available at http://www.agcm.it/trasp-statistiche/doc_download/2636-tp4.html (accessed 31 January 2014). Another detailed survey has been carried out by E. Arisi and F.M. Esposito, 'Un bilancio dell'efficacia dell'attività di

drafted regulation. Therefore, on the one hand, this advising does not take place at a stage when there is scope to influence the policy outcome. On the other hand, it is highly unlikely that the regulator will be convinced to prefer the regulatory option of doing nothing. Furthermore, the advice provided by the competition authorities to regulators is rarely the result of a specific economic analysis concerning the (competition) impact of different regulatory options, even if this is a theoretical ideal.[30]

When competition authorities play a role in assessing the competition impact of regulation, this tool must also be considered as a competition advocacy instrument, whose usefulness and effectiveness will be discussed in the following paragraphs.[31]

3.3 Competition Impact Assessment

Competition authorities can play an important role in promoting competition and the use of competition-based concepts by cooperating with regulators in the framework of their compulsory regulatory impact assessments (RIA) and in their reform of the stock of regulation.

Competition authorities may be involved in different ways and degrees in competition assessment (see Table 5.2):

---

advocacy dell'Autorità garante della concorrenza e del mercato' (2008) 2 *Economia e politica industriale* 140. Based on the period 2001–2006, this survey shows, among other things, that advocacy interventions are more effective when they address a draft regulation instead of an already adopted one.

[30] Increasingly, many competition authorities, such as the British OFT, the DoJ and the FTC in the US, the European Commission and the NMa in the Netherlands, are quantifying the aggregate benefits to consumers of their activities of competition enforcement and advocacy. They do so mostly in order to provide transparency about their activities, and to account for the use of their resources. See OECD, Working Party No. 2 on Competition and Regulation, Evaluation of Competition Enforcement and Advocacy Activities: the results of an OECD survey, OECD-Doc. DAF/COMP/WP2(2012)7/FINAL (20 February 2013). For these purposes, the impact assessment is done annually (i.e. during the following year) and, therefore, its results do not reflect the 'real', more long-term, impact of advocacy interventions.

[31] It is interesting to note that, from a regulatory point of view, this position was already clear in 1995. See OECD Recommendation on improving the quality of government regulation (with checklist for regulatory decision-making), OECD-Doc. C(95)21/FINAL (1995), available at: http://acts.oecd.org/Instruments/ShowInstrumentView.aspx?InstrumentID=128&InstrumentPID=124&Lang=en&Book=False (accessed 31 January 2014).

1. Competition authorities, such as those of the UK,[32] Spain, South Korea,[33] France[34] and Italy,[35] can be given the responsibility for developing competition assessment guidelines for rule-makers and policy-makers, usually organized as checklists.
2. They can be given the responsibility for assessing the competitive impact of new or existing regulations (Mexico, South Korea,[36] Hungary[37]).
3. They may also have the function of advising regulators in competition assessment (the UK,[38] Spain,[39] France[40]).

---

[32] Office of Fair Trading, Completing competition assessment in Impact Assessment – Guideline for policy makers (2007), available at: https://www.gov.uk/government/uploads/system/uploads/attachment_data/file/191489/Green_Book_supplementary_guidance_completing_competition_assessments_in_impact_assessments.pdf; HM Treasury and Office of Fair Trading, Guidance on how to assess the competition effects of subsidies (2007), available at: https://www.gov.uk/government/uploads/system/uploads/attachment_data/file/191490/Green_Book_supplementary_guidance_assessing_compeition_effects_subsidies.pdf (accessed 31 January 2014).

[33] Korea Fair Trade Commission, Competition Assessment Toolkit (2010), available at: http://www.oecd.org/daf/competition/reducingregulatoryrestrictionsoncompetition/46192134.pdf (accessed 31 January 2014).

[34] Autorité de la concurrence, Guide d'évaluation de l'impact concurrentiel de projets de textes normatifs, (2012), available at: http://www.autoritedelaconcurrence.fr/user/standard.php?id_rub=453 (accessed 31 January 2014).

[35] The Italian competition authority has published guidelines on impact assessment and a case study on their implementation at regional level, the sole example of their use to date. See Autorità garante della concorrenza e del mercato, Analisi di impatto della Regolazione sulla concorrenza: Linee guida e applicazione al caso della regione Toscana (2006), available at: http://www.agcm.it/component/joomdoc/doc_download/2651-sr2.html (accessed 31 January 2014). See also L. Cavallo, 'L'Analisi dell'Impatto della Regolazione sulla Concorrenza', *Osservatorio sull'Analisi di Impatto della Regolazione* (2010), available at: www.osservatorioair.it (accessed 31 January 2014).

[36] Korea Fair Trade Commission, Competition Assessment Toolkit (n. 33 above) 3: 'All new or existing regulations requiring regulatory analysis reports must undergo competition assessment by the Fair Trade Commission.'

[37] OECD, Competition Assessment Toolkit, Vol. I: Principles (2011) 28, available at: http://www.oecd.org/daf/competition/46193173.pdf (accessed 31 January 2014).

[38] Section 7.1 of the Enterprise Act of 2002. See also Office of Fair Trading, Completing competition assessment in Impact Assessment (n. 32 above) paras 1.10, 1.11, 2.9, 4.18, 7.6 and 7.8; Office of Fair Trading, Guidance on how to assess the competition effects of subsidies (n. 32 above) para. 4.26.

[39] Comisión Nacional de la Competencia (n. 9 above) 27.

[40] Autorité de la concurrence, Guide d'évaluation de l'impact concurrentiel de projets de textes normatifs (2012) Introduction, available at: http://www.autoritedelaconcurrence.fr/user/standard.php?id_rub=456 (accessed 31 January 2014).

Competition impact assessment can be used to analyse new regulation with a potential significant impact on competition (*ex ante* competition assessment) and to review and modify the stock of existing regulations (*ex post* competition assessment).[41] This tool has proved to be extremely useful by providing evidence to decision-makers about the adverse effects on competition of different regulatory tools.[42] The result could be a re-thinking of the balance between the different public interests involved or of the rule chosen in order to attain them.[43]

The potential effectiveness of this tool and the role of competition authorities, summarized in Table 5.1, will be analysed below.[44] For now, it can be underlined that in competition assessment the impact of the

---

[41] It is generally recognized that regulation must be managed throughout its whole life-cycle: from the design of a single piece of legislation to implementation, enforcement, evaluation and revision. See A. La Spina and G. Majone, *Lo Stato regolatore* (Il Mulino 2000) 103; OECD, The OECD Report on Regulatory Reform: Synthesis (1997) 29–30, available at: http://www.oecd.org/gov/regulatory-policy/2391768.pdf (accessed 31 January 2014). On the policy life-cycle see M. Howlett and M. Ramesh, *Studying Public Policy: Policy cycles and policy subsystems* (Oxford University Press 1995).

[42] OECD, Competition Assessment Toolkit, Vol. II: Guidance (2011) 14, available at: http://www.oecd.org/daf/competition/45544507.pdf (accessed 31 January 2014): 'Rules and regulations may alter the incentives for the market participants, and an important aspect of competition assessments will be to understand what impact regulations might have on the behaviour of market participants and the likely effects on competition.'

[43] For instance, competition impact assessment shows that a rule that limits foreign competition, while temporarily saving jobs at some incumbent firms, could prevent the creation of new jobs.

[44] There are essentially two reasons why this chapter refers to 'potential' effectiveness of competition assessment. On the one hand, competition authorities' advice, requisitioned in the framework of an SME Test or the SCM – as suggested here – is far from being implemented or considered necessary. On the other hand, most of the analysis on the *ex ante* assessment of rules is intended to answer the question of whether RIA has been effective in supporting decision-making, but the effect of competition assessment on the regulatory process is extremely difficult to find. On the European RIA see European Court of Auditors, Impact Assessments in the EU Institutions: Do They Support Decision-Making? Special Report No. 3 (2010) 18 and 19, available at: http://ec.europa.eu/smart-regulation/impact/docs/coa_report_3_2010_en.pdf (accessed 31 January 2014) (with the claim, though without specific data, that RIA has been effective in supporting decision-making within the EU institutions). R. Hahn and P.C. Tetlock, 'Has Economic Analysis Improved Regulatory Decisions?' (2008) 22(1) *J. Econ. Persp.* 67, argue a limited effect of RIA in the US federal regulatory process.

relevant regulatory options (including the zero option) are measured through a specific qualitative and – where possible – quantitative analysis (differently from advocacy activities, including hybridization). Moreover, while neither competition impact assessment nor other advocacy activities and hybridization impose any final choice on regulators, the former requires a detailed justification of final decisions, which includes evidence of quantified potential impact of different regulatory options. Indeed, if a regulator prefers an option that, according to the competition impact assessment restricts competition, its final decision must 'demonstrate benefits [to the community] that outweigh the costs and that no alternative means of achieving the same objective is available'.[45]

Unlike hybridization, competition impact assessment is about rules and not individual decisions (the former being addressed to an undetermined number of regulated parties, whereas individual decisions affect individuals or categories of addressees that have been identified or are identifiable) and is of horizontal application, because it extends the scope of the competition principle beyond economic regulation even to various kinds of social regulation, such as health and safety, as well as environmental regulation.[46] Moreover, whereas according to the regulation of the electronic communications sector a remedy must be adopted wherever market power is detected, the 'do nothing' option is crucial in competition assessment as well as in RIA. It is therefore a comparative exercise that weighs up the option of not altering the status quo (the 'do nothing' or 'baseline' option)[47] against all the feasible regulatory options, showing how incremental deviations from the status quo will achieve results. This step may increase pressure not to intervene through new regulation when it is not clear what is wrong with the current situation or what its specific undesirable effects are.

---

[45] Australian Government, Best Practice Regulation Handbook (2014) 36, available at: http://www.cuttingredtape.gov.au/sites/default/files/documents/australian_government_guide_regulation.pdf (accessed 5 May 2014).

[46] OECD Recommendation on Competition Assessment, OECD-Doc. C(2009)130 (2009), available at: http://acts.oecd.org/Instruments/ShowInstrumentView.aspx?InstrumentID=219&InstrumentPID=215&Lang=en&Book = False (accessed 31 January 2014): 'undue restrictions can occur unintentionally even when … public policies … are not focused on economic regulation and not intended to affect competition in any way'.

[47] See US Federal Office of Management and Budget, Circular A-4: Regulatory Analysis (2003) E 2, available at: http://www.whitehouse.gov/omb/circulars_a004_a-4 (accessed 31 January 2014): 'You need to measure the benefits and costs of a rule against a baseline. This baseline should be the best assessment of the way the world would look absent the proposed action.'

Competition impact assessment in the regulation life-cycle and its result, i.e. competition-based regulation, has many advantages, not only in terms of competition between firms, but also regarding competitiveness between countries. In general, competition impact assessment contributes to domestic competition because – to a greater extent than other advocacy activities – it prevents the adoption of regulations that restrict and distort competition, and provides the basis for the revision of the stock of these regulations. Therefore, competition impact assessment helps to create an environment where firms face strong domestic competition, and in so doing it also helps them to perform better in international markets.[48] It cannot be denied that there can be tension between competition and competitiveness.[49] However, the potential conflict may be solved by RIA: competition and competitiveness are two different economic impacts that are likely to occur and that must be separately analysed in competition impact assessment.[50]

---

[48] Moreover, if we consider competition impact assessment as a tool for good regulation, we must remember the role of the latter in improving competitiveness by offering win-win opportunities: good regulation helps to make countries attractive places to invest in and for citizens to work in. It ensures legal certainty and efficient application and enforcement of rules. It allows for social and environmental objectives to be attained without disproportionate administrative costs. See Communication from the Commission to the Council and the European Parliament – Better Regulation for Growth and Jobs in the European Union, COM(2005) 97 final (16 March 2005) 3.

[49] A recurring theme in many countries is how to balance the need of firms to achieve scale and specialization in order to compete in global markets and concerns about reduced competitive intensity in the internal markets due to industry consolidation and concentration. See, for instance, Government of Canada, Compete to Win, Final Report (2008) 53, available at: https://www.ic.gc.ca/eic/site/cprp-gepmc.nsf/vwapj/Compete_to_Win.pdf/$FILE/Compete_to_Win.pdf (accessed 31 January 2014).

[50] Impact Assessment Guidelines for EU Lamfalussy Level 3 Committees (2008), available at: http://www.esma.europa.eu/nl/system/files/3L3_IA_GUIDELINES.pdf (accessed 31 January 2014). According to the European Commission's Impact Assessment Guidelines, the questions to be raised in order to find economic impacts of a regulatory tool are about competition and competitiveness. See European Commission, Impact Assessment Guidelines, SEC(2009) 92 (15 January 2009) 33, available at: http://ec.europa.eu/smart-regulation/impact/commission_guidelines/docs/iag_2009_en.pdf (accessed 31 January 2014).

Table 5.1 Tools for more effective advocacy activities

	Hybridization	Competition assessment	Advocacy
Object	Individual decisions	Rules	Rules/individual decisions
Type of rule	Regulation	Regulation/ legislation	Regulation/ legislation
Areas	Sector-specific regulation	Any regulation/ legislation	Any regulation/ legislation
Timing	*Ex ante*	*Ex ante/ex post*	*Ex ante/ex post*
Measures impact of regulatory options (including doing nothing)	No	Yes	No
Role of competition authority	Non-binding advice	Non-binding advice/ responsibility	Non-binding advice
Justification of regulation based on empirical result of measurement	No	Yes	No

3.3.1 *Ex ante* competition impact assessment

Competition assessment in RIA Competition assessment is often performed in RIA, which is a systematic and comparative appraisal of the potential economic, social and environmental consequences that rules may have. RIA is a process that prepares evidence for political decision-makers on the advantages and disadvantages of possible regulatory options by assessing their potential impact. The feasible options must be measured by documenting the overall qualitative-quantitative dimension through one or more of the major techniques of economic analysis: cost-benefit analysis, multi-criteria analysis, cost-effectiveness analysis, compliance cost assessment or risk analysis.

The identification and comparison of the impact of relevant regulatory options (including the 'do nothing' option) is intended to identify a 'preferred' option the benefits of which outweigh its disadvantages.

The enrichment of RIA through competition impact assessment, by focusing on the impact of proposed rules on competition in affected markets,[51] is an innovative approach adopted in countries that have been pioneers in preventive economic analysis of regulations, such as the UK,[52] Australia[53] and the USA.[54] The value of this holistic analysis has recently been recognized in other countries, such as Italy[55] and France.[56] At the European level, a specific competition assessment in RIA is required by the European Commission[57] and by the Lamfalussy Level 3 Committees,[58] which have since been transformed into European financial markets authorities.[59] This assessment may be performed by the regulator, by the regulatory body responsible for the RIA (if different), by the competition authority or by the regulator in cooperation with the competition authority (see Table 5.2).

When used in *ex ante* RIA, the approach suggested by many guidelines is to organize the analysis in two steps, which are here of interest in order to frame the potential role of competition authorities.

According to the proportionality principle, an initial assessment may indicate the opportunity to proceed to a more in-depth analysis only

---

[51] Competition impact assessment could, for instance, consider harms to competition as risks whose probability may be analysed in order to give an indication about the possible opportunity to deal with them through regulation, which puts into practice the principle of proportionality.

[52] Office of Fair Trading, Completing competition assessment in Impact Assessment (n. 32 above).

[53] Australian Government, Best Practice Regulation Handbook (n. 45 above).

[54] Executive Order 12866/1993 of 30 September 1993, Regulatory Planning and Review, Section 6(a)(3)(C), available at: http://www.reginfo.gov/public/jsp/Utilities/EO_12866.pdf (accessed 31 January 2014).

[55] The Italian RIA Regulation (Decree of the President of the Council of Ministries No. 170/2008) requires a specific assessment of the impact of proposed governmental rules on competition and competitiveness when major rules are involved.

[56] Autorité de la concurrence (n. 34 above).

[57] European Commission, Impact Assessment Guidelines (n. 50 above). See also the earlier document of the European Commission, Better Regulation: A Guide to Competition Screening (2005).

[58] Committee of European Securities Regulators (CESR), Committee of European Banking Supervisors (CEBS), Committee of European Insurance and Occupational Pensions Supervisors (CEIOPS); the Impact Assessment Guidelines for EU Lamfalussy Level 3 Committees (n. 50 above) 56 calls for a specific analysis of indirect costs, which include a change in the effectiveness of competition.

[59] European Banking Authority (EBA), European Insurance and Occupational Pensions Authority (EIOPA), European Securities and Markets Authority (ESMA).

where the existing or proposed rule has or could have a significant impact on competition (first step). In other words, an assessment has to be made as to whether this regulation has the potential of unduly constraining market activity by: (a) restricting entry for new firms; (b) affecting the ability of firms to compete; or (c) reducing the incentive for firms to compete in the relevant market.[60]

In the full competition assessment (second step), rules are filtered through checklists composed of competition filter questions similar to those mentioned below (regarding direct and indirect entry or exit restrictions for new firms to and from given markets;[61] limitations on the ability of firms to compete;[62] reduction of incentives for firms to compete[63]), which at this stage need more in-depth answers. These filter questions can also be used in *ex post* competition impact assessment.

The core of the competition assessment begins with the second step, because the analyst must identify and compare the competitive effects of the proposed or the existing rules, as well as of the alternative options in the primary market and in any related markets. This step might indeed

---

[60] Similar competition filter questions are to be found in many guidelines. See, for instance, OECD, Competition Assessment Toolkit, Vol. II: Guidance (n. 42 above); UK Office of Fair Trading, Completing competition assessment in Impact Assessment (n. 32 above); Australian Government, Best Practice Regulation Handbook (n. 45 above) 31–37.

[61] Examples of restrictions that raise barriers to entry to, expansion in or exit out of a market are: restrictions based on exclusive (including monopoly) rights to a firm; restrictions on which firms are permitted to compete in the market; restrictions that limit access to essential infrastructure or resources; restrictions that stop the free flow of goods and capital across borders; licensing or educational requirements; regulatory standards that impose a significant cost for compliance (e.g. rigorous product testing requirements or forced adoption of certain technologies); and financing constraints. ICN, Advocacy Working Group, Competition Assessment Project, Discussion Draft (4 April 2013) 2–5, available at: http://icnwarsaw2013.org/docs/icn_awg_discussion_draft_competition_assessment_substantive.pdf (accessed 31 January 2014).

[62] Examples of restrictions that control how firms are allowed to compete in a market are: market regulations that favour certain firms over others; price controls; control of non-price terms of sale; control of quality of goods; restrictions on quantity; and restrictions on advertising. Ibid., 5–7.

[63] Examples of restrictions that shield firms from competitive pressure are: regulations that exempt the activity of a particular industry or group of firms from the operation of general competition law; regulations that permit firms to exchange information; self-regulated professions; restrictions that limit the amount of profits that a firm may collect or the market share it may accumulate; and restrictions that control the choices available to consumers. Ibid., 7–9.

require specific skills:[64] the completion of a comprehensive competition impact assessment typically involves competencies related to market definition and market power. Moreover, whereas the first step is designed as an initial screen to 'qualitatively' assess market interventions that may be relatively problematic and is structured to be conducted in a short timeframe, the second one is designed to fully and 'quantitatively' evaluate those interventions that have the potential of causing significant harm, or to restructure regulations to minimize harm to competition.[65] In this framework, the competition authority's knowledge would be useful in defining the relevant market(s) and assessing the impact on competition of the do-nothing option and other regulatory options (where an in-depth analysis is needed because a regulation has been shown to have the potential of unduly constraining market activity).

Therefore, the OECD, which adopted a Recommendation in 2009 and published a 'Competition Assessment Toolkit' in 2011,[66] has suggested asking the advice of the competition authorities about laws or regulations that are expected to have an economic impact before the provisions in question are enacted.[67] A similar approach was adopted in Spain, where 'legislator is obliged by law to conduct its own assessment, while the Spanish Competition Authority (CNMC) may also conduct its own assessment, which may result in recommendations to the legislator'.[68] In Australia, the Office of Best Practice Regulation (established within the Productivity Commission) has a central role in assisting regulators in competition assessment.[69]

---

[64] OECD Recommendation on Competition Assessment, OECD-Doc. C(2009)130 (2009), available at: http://acts.oecd.org/Instruments/ShowInstrumentView.aspx?InstrumentID=219&InstrumentPID=215&Lang=en&Book=False (accessed 31 January 2014).

[65] The goal here is to quantify the effects the rule or regulation might have, e.g. barriers to entry on new businesses, forced exit of certain types of businesses, higher prices for goods and services, less product or process innovation or significantly higher concentration in the relevant market. See Ennis (n. 12 above) 12.

[66] OECD, Competition Assessment Toolkit, Vol. I: Principles (n. 37 above) and Vol. II: Guidance (n. 42 above).

[67] OECD, Competition Assessment Toolkit, Vol. I: Principles (n. 37 above) 28–29.

[68] ICN, Advocacy Working Group, Framework of Competition Assessment Regimes (2015), 33, available at: www.internationalcompetitionnetwork.org/uploads/library/doc1024.pdf (accessed 30 June 2015).

[69] Australian Government, Best Practice Regulation Handbook (n. 45 above) 10. The ICN has also launched a new project to prepare best practices, good

The SME test The advice of competition authorities can also be useful when the impact of rules on small and medium-sized enterprises is subject to a specific analysis (see Table 5.2). Due to the specificity of problems faced by these firms, the SME test is used by the European Commission[70] and by many countries, such as the UK,[71] Denmark, the Netherlands, the US[72] and Switzerland,[73] as well as the Australian state of Victoria,[74] in order to measure the impact of regulatory options on SMEs and to mitigate them. The test comprises three main steps: (1) preliminary assessment of firms likely to be affected; (2) measurement of the impact of proposed rules on SMEs; and (3) adoption of mitigating measures to soften negative effects on smaller firms wherever this is appropriate. The SME test can be used as a part of RIA – this approach has been adopted, for instance, by European institutions and by the UK – or as an autonomous analysis such as in the US. The competition authorities' opinion could be useful in assessing the impact of proposed rules on competition during the cost/benefit analysis step and the likely

practices or recommended practices for competition authorities in conducting and promoting competition impact assessment and to convey competition impact considerations to policy-makers. See ICN, Advocacy Working Group, Proposal for Competition Assessment Project (2013), available at: http://www.internationalcompetitionnetwork.org/uploads/library/doc862.pdf (accessed 31 January 2014).

[70] According to the 2009 revision of the European Impact Assessment Guidelines, the SME test is a part of RIA, as are competition impact assessment and administrative burdens measurement. See Impact Assessment Guidelines (n. 50 above) 33, 40, 42 and 43.

[71] Office of Fair Trading, Completing competition assessment in Impact Assessment (n. 32 above).

[72] Executive Order No 13272/2002, Proper Consideration of Small Entities in Agency Rulemaking, Section 1, available at: http://www.epa.gov/sbo/pdfs/eo-13272.pdf

[73] The degree to which European institutions and national countries are implementing the 'Think-Small-First' principle is analysed by UEAPME, Think Small Test and SBA Implementation Scoreboard (2012) available at: http://www.ueapme.com/spip.php?rubrique121 (accessed 31 January 2014). National implementation is also analysed by the Directorate-General for Internal Policies, Barriers and Best Practices in SME Test Implementation, Report to the European Parliament (2011), available at: http://www.europarl.europa.eu/RegData/etudes/etudes/join/2011/464437/IPOL-ITRE_ET%282011%29464437_EN.pdf (accessed 31 January 2014).

[74] Small Business Regulatory Impact Assessment Manual (2007); Victorian Guide to Regulation (2011) 7, available at: http://www.dtf.vic.gov.au/publications/victoria-economy-publications/victorian-guide-to-regulation

impact on competition of mitigating measures (which could include exemptions,[75] lighter regulatory regimes[76] or reduced fees).

3.3.2 *Ex post* competition impact assessment

In general, rule-makers pay little attention to *ex post* impact assessment, at least compared to the *ex ante* RIA,[77] and when they do, they rarely provide for specific competition assessment. However, the OECD strongly urges OECD signatory countries to adopt both *ex ante* and *ex post* competition assessment and to conduct *ex post* competition impact assessment in cooperation with the national competition authorities (as practised in Greece[78] and Mexico[79]).

---

[75] For instance, for the new European general Data Protection Regulation the Commission proposes that companies with fewer than 250 workers need not have a data protection officer. See Article 25(2)(b) of the Proposal for a Regulation of the European Parliament and of the Council of 25 January 2012 on the protection of individuals with regard to the processing of personal data and on the free movement of such data (General Data Protection Regulation), COM(2012) 11 final.

[76] When exemptions are not possible, regulatory regimes can still be tailored to the specific needs of SMEs. For instance, according to Article 8(2)(1) of the new Directive 2012/27/EU of the European Parliament and of the Council of 25 October 2012 on energy efficiency, [2012] OJ L 315, p. 1, SMEs are encouraged, but not obliged, to carry out an energy audit. See, in general, Communication from the Commission to the European Parliament, the Council, the European Economic and Social Committee and the Committee of the Regions – Smart regulation – Responding to the needs of small and medium-sized enterprises, COM(2013) 122 final.

[77] This is the case, for instance, in Norway, Germany, Sweden, the UK (on these four countries see OECD, Regulatory Impact Analysis (RIA) Inventory, GOV/PGC/RD(2004)1, para. 30, available at: http://www.oecd.org/regreform/regulatory-policy/35258430.pdf (accessed 31 January 2014)), Italy and recently in the US (see Executive Order 13579, Regulation and Independent Regulatory Agencies (2011), available at: https://www.whitehouse.gov/sites/default/files/omb/memoranda/2011/m11-28.pdf and OMB-OIRA, 2009 Report on Benefit and Costs of Federal Regulations and Unfunded Mandates on State, Local, and Tribal Entities (2010) 41, available at: http://www.whitehouse.gov/sites/default/files/omb/legislative/reports/2010_Benefit_Cost_Report.pdf (accessed 31 January 2014)), and suggested at European level (see, Impact Assessment Guidelines of the European Commission and for EU Lamfalussy Level 3 Committees (at 40) (both n. 50 above).

[78] In Greece, an assessment of regulatory constraints on competition in four sectors (tourism, retail trade, food processing and construction materials) was conducted in 2013 by a project team composed of competition experts, economists and lawyers from the Hellenic Competition Commission and the OECD.

Ex post competition impact assessment of the regulatory baseline Ex post competition assessment could be used for an overall evaluation of existing regulation in the economy as a whole. The so-called guillotine system has been implemented in a few countries, such as Mexico, South Korea and Italy. This implies an analysis of the stock of regulation through such review criteria as legality, necessity, efficiency and administrative cost recovery, which prominently feature market friendliness and an automatic abrogation ('guillotining') of all regulations considered unnecessary in the light of those criteria. Finally, all remaining regulations must be organized into unified texts and simplified (in fact, the guillotine is almost never the end of reform and the reduction of regulation is not an objective in itself). An advanced guillotine mechanism also requires an impact assessment – including an assessment of the impact on competition – of existing rules under evaluation and an involvement of stakeholders. Other countries, such as Australia in 1996[80] and Sweden in 2009,[81] performed an examination of their entire stock of laws for potential restrictions on competition and identified and scheduled them for review without the guillotine automatism.

OECD, Greece: Competition Assessment Project, available at: http://www.oecd.org/competition/greececompetitionassessment.htm (accessed 31 January 2014).

[79] A similar approach was applied in Mexico in 2008 in cooperation with the Mexican Federal Competition Commission (CFC) and the Ministry of Economy of Mexico. The project also pursued regulatory improvement and attained some achievements in terms of regulatory reforms. See E. Pérez Motta, 'New Year, New Project: Turning the Focus to Competition Policy for 2013' *Comp. Pol'y Int'l* (2012), available at: https://www.competitionpolicyinternational.com/assets/Uploads/ICN1-29-2013.pdf (accessed 31 January 2014).

[80] In Australia the National Competition Council was created in 1995 as an independent body 'with responsibility to oversee and report on the performance of review program by the Commonwealth, States and Territories'. See OECD, Government Capacity to Assure to Assure High-quality Regulation in Australia (2010) 12, available at: http://www.oecd.org/australia/44529857.pdf (accessed 31 January 2014).

[81] In 2008, the Swedish Ministry of Economy requested the competition authority to perform a broad review of competitive restraints in the economy, and to evaluate potential effects, economic implications and feasibility. The competition authority produced a report with 60 annexed proposals. See Konkurrensverket (Swedish Competition Authority), Action for Better Competition (2009), available at: http://www.konkurrensverket.se/globalassets/english/publications-and-decisions/action-for-better-competition.pdf

Ex post competition impact assessment of a specific regulation Ex post competition assessment could also be used to assess a given regulation for which RIA has been performed or not. Many countries perform a retrospective and periodic review of existing significant regulations when operational experience is available after implementation (Germany, Norway, Sweden, UK,[82] Italy,[83] USA[84]). The analysis is intended to verify whether the rule is still needed and justified from a competition point of view.[85] The advice of competition authorities could be useful in this context too, in order to evaluate the impact on competition of existing regulation and of suggested reforms.

Administrative burden reduction programmes Lastly, in order to improve a competition-based regulation, administrative burden reduction programmes are crucial. Indeed, it is well known that regulation that is unstable, non-uniform and that imposes unjustified costs on end-users may distort competition between enterprises and harm the competitiveness of countries. This is why competition authorities devote efforts to simplification policies, which are usually the objects of their advocacy activities.[86]

Competition authorities might also be aware that an analysis of the impact on competition of simplification proposed in this framework could be useful. Indeed, the impact of simplifications on competition might be assessed where they result, for instance, in total, partial or temporary exemptions of SMEs from regulation (for instance, through reduced obligations for taxation or record-keeping), or a privileged treatment of small businesses by public administrations (e.g., lower fees, shorter periods for processing applications). In many countries, simplification of unnecessary regulatory burdens are often based on measurement of administrative costs by applying the so-called standard cost model (SCM), which is used to quantify the costs of the time needed to

---

[82] OECD, Regulatory Impact Analysis (RIA) Inventory (n. 77 above) para. 30.

[83] President of the Council of Ministries, Decree No. 212/2009.

[84] Executive Order 13563, Improving Regulation and Regulatory Review (2011), available at: http://www.gpo.gov/fdsys/pkg/FR-2011-01-21/pdf/2011-1385.pdf

[85] In this context, one question often refers to the follow-up of effects on SMEs caused by regulation (for instance in Sweden).

[86] See, for instance, hearing of the president of the Italian competition authority before the Parliament (27 February 2014), available at: http://www.agcm.it/trasp-statistiche/doc_download/4105-audizione-20140227.html (accessed 3 March 2014).

Table 5.2 Potential for contribution by competition authorities

Competition assessment tool	Role of competition authorities	Step containing the relevant contribution
Competition assessment in RIA	Advisory or Responsible	*Full competition assessment:* Definition of the relevance of market(s); doing-nothing and alternative options; impact assessment on competition
SME test	Advisory	*2nd step (cost/benefit analysis):* Assessment of the impact of proposed rules on competition *3rd step:* Assessment of the impact on competition of mitigating measures
Ex post competition assessment of existing regulations	Advisory	*1st step:* Analysis of the stock of regulation through market-friendliness review criterion (where possible an assessment of impacts on competition) *2nd step:* Assessment of the impacts on competition of reforms or proposal of competition friendly reforms
Ex post assessment of a given regulation for which RIA has been performed or not	Advisory	*1st step:* verification of whether the rule is still needed and justified from a competition point of view *2nd step:* Assessment of the impacts on competition of reforms or proposal of competition-friendly reforms
Administrative burden reduction programmes	Advisory	*2nd step:* Analysis of the impact on competition of simplification proposals

accomplish an information obligation by the end-users of a specific regulation.[87] In this case too, the advice of the competition authority would help to assess the impact on competition of proposed simplifications.

4. COMPETITION IMPACT ASSESSMENT: ADVANTAGES AND POTENTIAL DRAWBACKS

Competition impact assessment can improve the quality of regulation by preventing unintended consequences for competition and by allowing public targets to be met without unjustified costs for end-users. The final objective is to have necessary, proportional and consistent rules that, at the same time, are well written and accessible.

Therefore, competition impact assessment should be considered as a new and particularly useful advocacy tool whose effectiveness, as shown above, is mainly related to two factors. Firstly, competition assessment is used at a very early stage in rule-making and the evidence it provides can be decisive for making the final decision, including the option not to adopt any new regulation. Secondly, it is linked to the use of economic analysis to investigate the potential impacts on competition of draft rules and of existing regulation (and their alternatives).

There are also two specific advantages connected to the use of competition impact assessment in rule-making. First, competition impact assessment (and RIA) generally ensures transparency and stakeholder input in rule-making. Indeed, consultations are of great importance in *ex ante* and *ex post* assessments (e.g., regarding the former, they are crucial in order to bring out the need for regulation and to suggest and assess the policy option). The evidence of the impact on competition of a given rule and its transparency (considering that data related to RIA might be published) could increase the awareness of end-users of regulation and

---

[87] The SCM, which was initially developed in the Netherlands, is at present the methodology most widely applied in OECD countries for measuring administrative burdens, i.e. costs of information obligations (IO) that would not be met by businesses or citizens if not required to by law. In this context, IO refers to legal obligations for businesses to provide data on their activities to public authorities or to private parties (for instance, the obligation to notify specific activities or events, submit reports, label products, apply for permits and certificates, register or cooperate with audits and inspections by public authorities). See Standard Cost Model Network, The Standard Cost Model – A framework for defining and quantifying administrative burdens for businesses (2004).

facilitate future reform of this balance or of the regulatory tool chosen. Therefore, it also furthers a better understanding of previously adopted rules and better informs political discussion about reform. From a competition point of view, these features are important because they enable all the market actors to take part in the decision-making by raising and making clear the different problems they deal with.[88] Moreover, transparency and consultations can help SMEs to provide their point of view in competition impact assessment or in a specific SME test.

Secondly, competition impact assessment (and consultation), while not imposing any final choice on regulators, provides evidence for political decision-makers and allows evidence-based decisions, and it requires decision-makers to give reasons for their final choice.[89] Therefore, the role of the competition authority as an advisor could be crucial to increase pro-competitive regulation, by imposing an in-depth justification of regulations on competition concerns, based on the empirical results of measurement. This justification has many aspects. On the one hand, it addresses the preference given to the 'lesser evil': policy options with lesser harm on competition should be preferred, provided they achieve the identified objectives. On the other hand, the proportionality of any restriction on competition must be proven, and any attested lack of competition concerns explained.[90] Lastly, a decision-maker who adopts a rule whose benefits for competition do not outweigh its disadvantages must justify this choice.[91] Indeed, it bears repeating that even if competition assessment seems to be based on the unspoken assumption that more competition is always good, sound competition is only one of the

---

[88] For instance, competition impact assessment limits the number or range of suppliers when it 'significantly raises the costs of new suppliers relative to existing suppliers; significantly raises the costs of some existing suppliers relative to other existing suppliers; significantly raises the costs of entering, or exiting, the affected market'. See Office of Fair Trading, Completing competition assessment in Impact Assessment (n. 32).

[89] In fact, RIA and competition impact assessment provide evidence for political decision-makers and must be considered an 'aid to political decision-making, not a substitute for it'. European Commission, Impact Assessment Guidelines (n. 50 above) 4.

[90] Office of Fair Trading, Completing competition assessment in Impact Assessment (n. 32 above) para 2.6.

[91] This not only increases transparency, but will also 'create a valuable public record' which may facilitate later efforts to reform anticompetitive regulation. See ICN Advocacy Working Group Discussion Draft (n. 61 above).

public interests considered in the rule-making process, and not necessarily the most important one.[92]

Moreover, competition impact assessment should be used with special care in order to avoid its incorrect use, which can result in its being useless and imposing unjustified costs on the rule-making process.[93]

Competition impact assessment is a costly procedure: it complicates the rule-making process (for instance, due to the coordination of rule-makers and competition authorities), it increases the time needed to decide (the European Commission suggests a minimum consultation period of eight weeks),[94] and it imposes direct costs on both the rule-makers and the competition authorities involved (due to the surveys, consultation, etc. needed). Therefore, only important rules with a potential significant impact on competition should be considered. Otherwise, if

---

92 Though outside the scope of this chapter, it must be noted that criticism has been voiced of the current application of competition law to regulated industries, which could harm the regulatory goals. According to G. Monti, 'Managing the Intersection of Utilities Regulation and EC Competition Law' (2008) 4(2) *Comp. L. Rev.* 123, 144, 'there should be instances where competition law gives way to regulation, either because suspending competition law can yield greater efficiency or because it can allow the pursuit of other non-economic policy objectives'.

93 This is not the appropriate place to discuss the weak points of RIA in depth, even if they influence *ex ante* competition impact assessment. However, they can be summarized as follows: experts can influence policymakers through a distorted use of technical instruments (like consultation and cost-benefit analysis). The benefits of regulation might end up being underestimated (see D.A, Faber, 'Rethinking the Role of Cost-benefit Analysis' (2009) 76 *U. Ch. L. Rev.* 1362). When based on cost-benefit analysis, RIA assumes that human behaviour is rational, which is not always true. RIA detects the consequences of a single regulation, but has limited capacity to evaluate the interdependence of very different regulatory strategies and institutions (see R. Baldwin, 'Better Regulation: Tension Aboard the Enterprise' in S. Weatherill (ed.), *Better Regulation* (Hart Publishing 2007) 27, 34–35). However, these aspects will not necessarily impede the usefulness of this tool: benefits can be assessed by a qualitative analysis, which must always complete the quantification; real people's behaviour could be assessed through empirical evidence collected through a cognition-based approach; and agenda-setting might help to coordinate efforts and prevent cumulative burdens (for a more in-depth analysis see N. Rangone, 'The Myth and Reality of Good Quality Regulation Tools' (2012) 4 *Ital. J. of Pub. L.* 1, available at: http://www.ijpl.eu/assets/files/pdf/2012_volume_1/IJPL_volume%201_2012.pdf (accessed 31 January 2014).

94 Communication from the Commission, Towards a reinforced culture of consultation and dialogue – General principles and minimum standards for consultation of interested parties, COM(2002) 704 final.

all the flow and stock of regulation is assessed, the analysis risks being superficial and its costs unjustified. The principle of proportionality must be applied in the use of competition impact assessment to help to avoid costs deriving from too frequent use of economic analysis in all regulatory processes. At the same time, the depth of the assessment (as well as the consultation process) must be proportional to the issues at stake and the resources available.[95]

Moreover, *ex ante* competition impact assessments (as well as other advocacy tools and hybridization) 'are based upon predictions, and predictions in real life often turn out to understate competitive harms or overstate competitive benefits'.[96] For this reason, those carrying out the assessment must organize monitoring activity as well as an *ex post* evaluation, even if an *ex ante* assessment has already been performed.[97]

---

[95] At the European level, although general exceptions have not been made, the concept of 'proportionate level of analysis' for any RIA (and competition impact assessment) has been conceived. This relates to the necessary level of detail of analysis for the different steps of RIA, and is connected to potential impact, political significance and the steps in the process of policy development. See European Commission, Impact Assessment Guidelines (n. 50 above) 12. In the US, at the federal level RIA is only used for rules that may have 'an annual effect on the economy of $100 million or more or adversely affect in a material way the economy, a sector of the economy, productivity, competition, jobs, the environment, public health or safety, or State, local, or tribal governments or communities'. See Section 2(f)(1) of Executive Order 12866, Regulatory Planning and Review (n. 54 above). In the UK, competition impact assessment is applied for regulatory proposals that have a potential significant impact on competition. See Office of Fair Trading, Completing competition assessment in Impact Assessment (n. 32 above). The same approach is advocated by HM Treasury and Office of Fair Trading (n. 32 above) 4 (It 'applies to subsidies that carry the highest risk of distorting competition. These are subsidies of more than £500,000 to an individual firm which has a market share exceeding 5 to10 per cent of the affected market').

[96] OECD, Competition Assessment Toolkit, Vol. I: Principles (n. 37 above) 29.

[97] A final clarification is required in order to guarantee that competition impact assessment (and RIA) be useful and effective. Only rules can be measured through competition assessment (such rules are the so-called policy options or regulatory actions whose impacts are analysed in *ex ante* assessment), meaning the rules that directly affect the end-users by causing a change in their activity, production or organization. As a consequence, competition impact assessment must thoroughly analyse those rules that have a potential relevant impact on competition) and not the full text of a given regulation as such (e.g., legislative decrees or governmental regulations). This approach has concrete consequences. For instance, in Italy RIA reports often confuse the alternative

5. ADVANTAGES AND CHALLENGES OF THE INVOLVEMENT OF COMPETITION AUTHORITIES IN COMPETITION IMPACT ASSESSMENTS

The involvement of competition authorities in competition impact assessments has the potential to produce many positive results.

When competition authorities lead or advise competition impact assessment, the regulatory uncertainty linked to potential non-consistency of rules with competition law and litigation arising from such uncertainty (referring to European[98] and national jurisdictions[99]) can be reduced. For example, the potential clashes between the behaviour of firms adopted in observance of a sectorial regulation and competition law might be prevented by *ex ante* competition impact assessment. This could be achieved by filtering draft regulations through a series of questions. This would mean asking not only whether the rules prevent firms from engaging in autonomous conduct that 'prevents, restricts or distorts competition'[100] or whether such conduct is 'facilitated' by a regulation (as in the competition enforcement);[101] it would also entail the question of whether the regulation might allow regulated firms to misrepresent the compatibility of their behaviour with competition law.[102]

Moreover, the role of competition authorities can be crucial in order to avoid the danger of an incorrect approach to competition impact assessment in response to a legal obligation in name only (in these cases, a time-consuming and costly method such as competition impact assessment is used to no advantage). Indeed, the cooperation of competition authorities and rule-makers might improve the use of economic analysis

---

policy options with the sources of laws so that they conclude that there are no alternatives to laws if a European directive is to be implemented.

[98] As is well known, the European Commission can bring a case against a Member State whose law requires or enables firms to engage in conduct contrary to EU competition law or legitimizes or reinforces the effects of that conduct.

[99] Autorité de la concurrence (n. 40 above).

[100] Joined Cases C-359/95 P and C-379/95 P *Commission and France v Ladbroke Racing Ltd* [1997] ECR I-6301, para. 34.

[101] Case C-198/01 *Consorzio italiano fiammiferi* [2003] ECR I-8079.

[102] Two of the many cases of concurrent application of regulation and competition law that might create uncertainty about the role played by regulators and competition authorities. See Commission Decision of 21 May 2003, Case COMP/C-1/37.451 37.578, 37.579 – *Deutsche Telekom AG*, [2003] OJ L 263/9; Commission Decision of 4 July 2007, Case COMP/38.784 – *Wanadoo España v Telefónica*, available at: http://ec.europa.eu/competition/antitrust/cases/dec_docs/38784/38784_311_10.pdf (Prohibition Decision) (accessed 31 January 2014).

in competition impact assessment, specifically in administrative-law countries, such as Italy and France, where regulators find it hard to overcome a formalistic approach, such as a box-ticking routine.[103] This can improve the quality of regulation, which in turn will enhance competition.

To sum up, cooperation of competition authorities in rule-making processes might help to improve competition-friendly regulation by detecting adverse impacts of rules on competition, as well as by cutting down rule-makers' protectionist arguments.

However, these results could be frustrated if competition impact assessment is done in a ritualistic and formalistic way and is not used according to the proportionality principle.

The danger of formalistic application might be prevented by the involvement of competition authorities in competition impact assessment. This becomes clear when considering the main reasons for the numerous bad regulations: regulators (including politicians) use regulation as the easiest answer to problems; their administrative staff usually lack adequate skills in analysing the advantages and disadvantages of rules; regulators may not be interested in the correct use of a competition assessment that increases participation, transparency and accountability in rule-making; regulators often have fragmented responsibilities that lead to excessive and overlapping rules. Moreover, especially in time of crisis, there is a risk that regulators will consider all rules (and not only anticompetitive or burdensome ones), as well as good-quality regulation tools, such as RIA, competition impact assessment, the SME test and consultations as being obstacles to competitiveness.[104] These reasons for

---

[103] The risk of using RIA as a tick-the-box exercise with no effect on policy choice also exists at the European level. According to Radaelli's and Meuwese's analysis, this risk is related to the very reason for the adoption of RIA: the fundamental disagreement about political control of the European Commission. As a consequence, the choice for RIA might be considered to be an 'agreement to postpone disagreement' about the European Commission's powers. C.M. Radaelli and A.C.M. Meuwese, 'Hard Questions, and Equally Hard Solutions? Proceduralization through Impact Assessment in the European Union', Paper delivered to the Connex Worshop 'Governing the European Union: Policy, Instruments in a Multi-Level Polity' (Norwich, 2008), available at: http://centres.exeter.ac.uk/ceg/research/riacp/documents/Radaelli_Meuwesehardsolutionsfinal.pdf (accessed 31 January 2014).

[104] See H. Mulholland, 'David Cameron Axes Equality Assessments in War on "Red Tape"', *guardian.co.uk* (19 November 2012), available at: http://www.theguardian.com/politics/2012/nov/19/cameron-axe-equality-assessments (accessed 31 January 2014).

bad regulation do not affect competition authorities' activities and their adverse effects can be prevented if competition authorities are involved in competition impact assessments.[105] However, this is only true if the competition authorities are independent from government or exercise their power (and perform competition assessment) impartially.

The second danger, that of disproportionality, might be avoided through procedural choices, for instance, by using competition impact assessment only for most important rules. In order to avoid ossification of the rule-making procedure,[106] competition assessment must be based upon a selective approach concerning its use and the depth of the economic analysis and of the consultations. In this regard, it is important to have continual informal cooperation between regulators and competition authorities, where the advising role of the competition authority is needed on a case-by-case basis or according to a general criterion (e.g., in the full competition impact assessment phase in *ex ante* RIA, when rules with a significant impact on competition are involved).

However, some issues remain unresolved.

Firstly, the task of selecting rules with a significant impact on competition is especially delicate, since the criteria must be both objective and flexible. Therefore, the adoption of these criteria is not easy for rule-makers or legislators.

Secondly, it is up to the legislative or administrative power to decide if and when competition authorities must or should be asked for advice, as well as whether it is compulsory or not to follow this advice. But it is also up to competition authorities to set clear priorities when engaging in the competition screening of rules, for instance, by identifying which types of rules have the most impact on competitive conduct or market structure and by selecting potential critical sectors to be monitored. In this framework, it is not clear how best to balance the role of competition authorities. On the one hand, competition authorities hardly have the

---

[105] See ICN Advocacy Working Group Proposal (n. 69 above) 1: 'The financial crisis and ensuing economic downturn have made it more urgent than ever that competition agencies are equipped to guard against anticompetitive practices generally – addressing private restraints through enforcement actions, and government restraints with advocacy initiatives. Advocacy is potentially more important than enforcement these days in many jurisdictions across the economic spectrum, as trust in markets has been shaken by the economic downturn. This has caused policymakers to be more receptive to protectionist arguments at a time when competitive markets and economic growth is crucial.'

[106] The term is borrowed from T.O. McGarity, 'Some Thoughts on "Deossifying" the Rulemaking Process' (1992) 41 *Duke L.J.* 1385.

human and financial resources necessary to check the flow and stock of regulation. This issue is strictly related to the growth of government and the lack of coordination across their different levels. How could a competition authority manage to advise all the multiple centres of production of rules, even with a significant impact on competition? But if antitrust cannot, who else could? On the other hand, assigning the whole competition impact assessment task to competition authorities could limit the possibility for rule-makers to improve their knowledge in performing competition impact assessment and consequently to improve their sensitivity and skills regarding competition issues.[107]

Thirdly, it is clear that the final competition impact assessment of a rule is greatly influenced by the approach to (and the idea of) competition that characterizes the competition authority involved, when focusing – for instance – on the protection of competitors or on improvement of consumer welfare and innovation. In general, it seems that the approach chosen in evaluating the effects of anticompetitive market distortions should be based on their impact on consumer welfare, which is a common theme for enforcement activities around the world, even if their definition differs from one authority to another.[108] Moreover, the current European competition policy's 'more economics-based approach' (focusing on the effects of firms' actions) might be more consistent with the idea of a preventive analysis of the potential impact on competition of proposed and existing rules, rather than on the form that these actions may take (form-based approach).[109]

In conclusion, competition authorities may have responsibilities for competition impact assessment or their intervention may be limited to an advisory role. In these various ways they act as regulators.

---

[107] Nor should one underestimate the tendency for regulators to be more willing to consider competition concerns if these are presented by their own staff instead of external sources (such as an antitrust authority).

[108] ICN, Competition Enforcement and Consumer Welfare – Setting the Agenda, Discussion document for the 10th Annual Conference, The Hague (2011), available at: http://www.internationalcompetitionnetwork.org/uploads/library/doc857.pdf (accessed 31 January 2014).

[109] The 'more economics-based approach' relates to the assessment of anticompetitive agreements and abusive exclusionary conduct by dominant companies and merger control. See N. Forwood, 'The Commission's More Economic Approach: Implication for the Role of the EU Courts, the Treatment of Economic Evidence, and the Scope of Judicial Review' in C.D. Ehlermann and M. Marquis (eds), *European Competition Law Annual 2009: The Evaluation of Evidence and its Judicial Review in Competition Cases* (Hart Publishing 2011) 255.

Therefore, what is desirable is cooperation and not substitution (which would also be impossible due to the number of regulators and of the rules they enact), because by simply making rule-makers autonomous one can hope that rules will always be informed by the criterion of proportionality and the goal of being as unrestrictive of competition as possible.

Moreover, it is hardly necessary to point out that a competition authority's involvement in competition impact assessment should not bar any subsequent action under the competition laws, such as (traditional) competition law enforcement against restraints based on anticompetitive business conduct. This is appropriate, because competition impact assessment is by definition based upon predictions, and the ultimate effect (on competition) depends on how a rule will be implemented, enforced, interpreted and sanctioned. Therefore, regulation and competition law enforcement must always remain separate, even when a competition authority performs a competition impact assessment, and in this sense is acting as a regulator.

PART 3

Competition law enforcement in regulated industries in general

6. A reassessment of the relationship between competition law and sector-specific regulation

Mario Siragusa and Fausto Caronna

1. INTRODUCTION

Government intervention in markets can impose or forbid firms' behaviour in many different forms. Sector-specific regulation and competition law are a part of this general set of economic rules.

Traditionally, competition law and regulation were considered two opposing categories. Indeed, the former rules 'delimit the choices available to a firm by indicating few forbidden behaviours that cannot be held on the market'.[1] Since competition law entails prohibitions, it can only be enforced *ex post* – which means after the anti-competitive behaviour is discovered.

Sector-specific regulation is more typically characterized by an *ex ante* positive intervention because normally it prescribes what type of actions firms are required to undertake in a certain market. Therefore, an industry is considered 'regulated' or 'unregulated', depending on the degree to which firms are left 'free' to operate in a market.

This distinction, based on the traditional theoretical approach, is no longer quite so clear. Indeed, the well-defined boundaries between competition law and regulation seem to have vanished. This is due to the growing convergence – from a substantive point of view – of competition law and sector-specific regulation, which leads to a gradually increasing overlap between the roles and mandates of national regulatory authorities (NRAs) and the national competition authorities (NCAs).[2]

[1] See P.L. Parcu, 'The Surprising Convergence of Antitrust and Regulation in Europe' (2013) *Concorrenza e Mercato* 321.

[2] See N. Petit, 'The Proliferation of National Regulatory Authorities Alongside Competition Authorities: A Source of Jurisdictional Confusion' (2004)

This point is further stressed by the fact that there is no longer a difference in terms of the timing of the intervention: competition authorities may intervene *ex ante* (as seen in merger control and commitments), while regulators may act *ex post*, especially when NRAs are entrusted with powers enjoyed by the NCAs.

As the former EU Commissioner for competition, Joaquín Almunia, affirmed, 'Competition enforcement and sector regulations are complementary instruments'.[3] Over time, this complementary nature has become a critical issue, multiplying jurisdictional conflicts as well as creating a risk of regulatory inconsistency.

Currently in Italy the solution predominantly adopted to solve the difficult cohabitation of competition law and sectoral regulation provides – in accordance with settled EU case-law – for the simultaneous application of those two sets of rules when: (i) regulation and competition law are aimed at different goals; and (ii) sector-specific regulation leaves room for anti-competitive behaviour.[4]

A contrasting conclusion was recently reached by the Plenary Session of the Council of State with regard to the relationship between general consumer law and sector-specific regulation.[5] Indeed, the Plenary Session held that general consumer protection rules contained in Directive 29/2005/EC (as implemented by the Italian Consumer Code)[6] were not applicable to the electronic communications sector, in so far as the sector is subject to specific regulations, which include, among its primary institutional purposes, the protection of consumers. Therefore, based on

---

Global Competition Law Centre Working Papers Series, no. 02, 3, available at: http://www.coleurope.eu/sites/default/files/research-paper/04b_gclc_working_paper_02-04.pdf (accessed February 2014).

[3] See J. Almunia, 'Competition v Regulation: Where Do the Roles of Sector Specific and Competition Regulators Begin and End?' (23 March 2010), available at: http://europa.eu/rapid/press-release_SPEECH-10-121_en.htm (accessed February 2014).

[4] See at section 2.2 below.

[5] See judgments of the Council of State, Plenary Session, of 11 May 2012, *Telecom Italia SpA v. Autorità Garante delle Concorrenza e del Mercato*, no. 12; *Telecom Italia SpA v. Autorità Garante delle Concorrenza e del Mercato*, no. 13; *Wind Telecomunicazioni SpA v. Autorità Garante delle Concorrenza e del Mercato*, no. 16. Although the same principles have been enunciated in the financial sector as well, the Council of State, Plenary Session, reached a dissenting conclusion in its judgment of 11 May 2012, *AGOS SpA v. Autorità Garante delle Concorrenza e del Mercato*, no. 14.

[6] See Legislative Decree no. 2007/146 (entered into force on 21 September 2007).

the principle of specialty, and in order to guarantee the unity and consistency of sanctioning measures, while avoiding the duplication of enforcement actions, the Council of State ruled that: (i) sector-specific regulation must prevail over general consumer law; and consequently (ii) the Italian Communications Regulatory Authority (ICRA) has exclusive jurisdiction over consumer protection in the electronic communications sector.

Although the Council of State makes it clear that its conclusions do not apply to competition law, these recent landmark decisions call for a reassessment of the established principles on the relationship between competition law and sector-specific regulation, in order to devise solutions capable of better guaranteeing a high level of legal certainty and consistent administrative action, as well as ensuring compliance with the *ne bis in idem* (double jeopardy) principle, while not overlooking the fundamental principle of supremacy that characterizes the competition rules enshrined in the TFEU.

This chapter aims at assessing whether it is necessary to strengthen the actual coordination mechanisms existing in Italy (and elsewhere) between competition law and sector-specific regulation. The chapter is organized as follows. Following this introduction, section 2 deals with the horizontal application of competition law in regulated industries, focusing on significant case-law developments. Section 3 examines the overlap between NRA and NCA functions in the specific field of consumer protection. Section 4 offers concluding remarks.

2. THE HORIZONTAL APPLICATION OF COMPETITION LAW IN REGULATED INDUSTRIES

2.1 EU Law

To address the risk of regulatory inconsistencies and of jurisdictional conflicts, the Court of Justice of the European Union (CJEU) has placed on the NRAs a general duty to observe competition rules (in particular, Articles 101 and 102 TFEU). In the *GB-Inno-BM v. ATAB* case, the CJEU held: 'while it is true that Article 86 EC (now Article 102 TFEU) is directed at undertakings, nonetheless it is also true that the Treaty imposes a duty on Member States not to adopt or maintain in force any measure which would deprive that provision of its effectiveness'.[7]

[7] Case C-13/77 *SA G.B.-INNO-B.M. v. Association des détaillants en tabac (ATAB)* [1977] ECR I-2115, para. 31.

In this regard, the *Consorzio Industrie Fiammiferi* (*CIF*) case made it clear that these obligations rest on various public administrative authorities and entail the duty to set aside national legislation that is contrary to EU law. Indeed, the Court held:

> In accordance with settled case-law the primacy of Community law requires any provision of national law which contravenes a Community rule to be disapplied, regardless of whether it was adopted before or after that rule. The duty to disapply national legislation which contravenes Community law applies not only to national courts but also to all organs of the State, including administrative authorities … , which entails, if the circumstances so require, the obligation to take all appropriate measures to enable Community law to be fully applied.[8]

Therefore, the NRAs may not, on matters falling within the scope of their jurisdiction, frustrate the *effet utile* of the EU competition rules.

Since sector-specific regulation and competition law are 'complementary instruments', they can be enforced in a cumulative way. Indeed, European case-law consistently confirms the horizontal application of competition law in regulated industries.[9]

However, competition law enforcement requires the firm's capability to behave autonomously in the market. If anti-competitive conduct is required by national regulation, competition law can still apply, but no penalties may be imposed on the undertaking 'in respect of past conduct when the conduct was required by the national legislation' (so-called state action defence).[10] Moreover, in the *CIF* case the Court held: 'if a national law merely encourages, or makes it easier for undertakings to engage in autonomous anti-competitive conduct, those undertakings remain subject to Articles 81 and 82 EC and may incur penalties, including in respect of conduct prior to the decision to disapply that national law'.[11]

The *Deutsche Telekom* (*DT*) case provides a good example of the fact that compliance with sector-specific regulation does not shield dominant

---

[8] Case C-198/01 *Consorzio Industrie Fiammiferi (CIF) v. Autorità Garante della Concorrenza e del Mercato* [2003] ECR I-8055, paras 48 et seq.

[9] See R. Whish and D. Bailey, *Competition Law* (7th edn, OUP 2012) 977ff.

[10] Case C-198/01 (n. 8 above) para. 53.

[11] Ibid., para. 56.

companies from facing possible charges for the violation of Article 102 TFEU. The case concerned DT's obligation to unbundle the local loop to allow competitors to offer competing services, and the wholesale price for this was approved by the German telecommunications regulator. Although the charges for wholesale and retail access to the loop were regulated, the Commission found that DT had abused its dominant position by using the margin of discretion left by the regulator to squeeze its competitors out of the market by charging abusive prices to access its local network.

The Commission's reasoning was based on the assumption that 'competition rules may apply where the sector-specific legislation does not preclude the undertakings it governs from engaging in autonomous conduct that prevents, restricts or distorts competition'.[12]

This position, based on the constitutional structure of the Treaty, was confirmed by the *O2* decision, in which the Commission affirmed that the application of Article 101 TFEU in the electronic communications sector is

> subject to the principle of the primacy of Community law [and] the national regulatory framework and the EU competition rules are of parallel and cumulative application. National rules may neither conflict with the EU competition rules nor can compatibility with national rules and regulations prejudice the outcome of an assessment under the EU competition rules.[13]

The Commission's approach was then fully upheld by the General Court ('GC') as well as by the CJEU. Indeed the latter Court held that:

> dominant undertakings have a special responsibility not to allow their conduct to impair genuine undistorted competition on the common market. … In that regard, the mere fact that a dominant undertaking in the telecommunications sector was encouraged by the intervention of a national regulatory authority such as the regulatory authority for telecommunications and post to maintain the pricing practices which led to the margin squeeze of competitors who are at least as efficient as that undertaking cannot, as such, in any way absolve that undertaking from responsibility under Article 82 EC.[14]

---

[12] Commission Decision of 21 May 2003, Case COMP/C-1/37.451, 37.578, 37.579 – *Deutsche Telekom AG*, [2003] OJ L 263, p. 54.

[13] Commission Decision of 16 July 2003, Case COMP/38.369 – *T-Mobile Deutschland/O2 Germany* [2003] OJ L 75, p. 22.

[14] Case C-280/08 P *Deutsche Telekom v. Commission* [2010] ECR I-9555, paras 83 et seq.

These principles were subsequently confirmed in the *Telefónica* case.[15]

As illustrated by these cases, competition law enforcement has the function of eliminating the distortion caused by firms that use the leeway left by the regulator to carry out anti-competitive behaviour. This shows also that the concurrent application of overlapping rules can lead to divergent results. Indeed, the Commission found that:

> There is nothing extraordinary or exceptional in the fact that the Commission and the [national telecommunications regulator] found different results: in the telecommunications sector regulators put in place *ex ante* regulatory mechanisms allowing competition to develop, but can only do this on the basis of market and cost forecasts. In so doing regulators lessen, but cannot entirely eliminate the risk of anti-competitive behaviour. Competition authorities act *ex post*, using historical data on effectively incurred costs. Accordingly, in many Member States, competition authorities have investigated and sanctioned *ex post* anti-competitive conducts in the regulated telecommunications markets, including broadband access.[16]

2.2 Italian Law

Identical principles have been laid down by settled case-law at the Italian level. In 2012, the Regional Administrative Tribunal of Lazio (TAR Lazio) further confirmed that when sector-specific regulation leaves room for anti-competitive behaviour, simultaneous application of both sets of rules is not excluded.

In the *Posta Elettronica Ibrida* case, the TAR Lazio partially annulled a decision by the Italian Competition Authority (ICA), which had fined Poste Italiane for abuse of a dominant position in the liberalized sector of hybrid mail.[17] The alleged abusive conduct concerned: (i) the application of unjustified and discriminatory conditions to access the delivery network, which the ICA contended were not provided for by the applicable Ministerial Decree of 18 February 1999 (hereafter the Decree). In any event, in the ICA's view the Decree was contrary to EU Law and, therefore, had to be set aside; (ii) the adoption of a discriminatory system

---

[15] Commission Decision of 4 July 2007, Case COMP/38.784 – *Wanadoo España Telefónica SA*, available at: http://ec.europa.eu/competition/antitrust/cases/dec_docs/38784/38784_311_10.pdf (accessed August 2014).

[16] See European Commission, 'Antitrust: Commission Decision against Telefónica: Frequently Asked Questions', MEMO/07/274 (4 July 2007), available at: http://europa.eu/rapid/press-release_MEMO-07-274_en.htm (accessed February 2014).

[17] TAR Lazio, judgment of 9 January 2013, *Poste Italiane SpA v. Autorità della Concorrenza e del Mercato*, no. 125.

of charging some important customers; and (iii) the awarding of substantial economic, financial and informational advantages to the subsidiary Postel S.p.A..

The TAR Lazio, while recognizing that the ICA had correctly set aside the national law in conflict with EU Law, found that Poste Italiane's conduct could not have created any additional barriers to competition, in so far as the company had merely applied the regulatory provisions (which were *ex se* characterized by a foreclosure effect) and promptly established the conditions to access its network. However, the TAR Lazio confirmed that, in accordance with the principles established at the EU level, Poste Italiane had a special responsibility, which *inter alia* obliged it to apply transparent, non-discriminatory and cost-oriented economic and technical conditions.

Accordingly, while upholding the above-mentioned allegations, the TAR Lazio held that Poste Italiane was culpable only with regard to the allegation at (iii) above (granting of significant economic and informational advantages solely to its subsidiary Postel). At the same time, the TAR Lazio held that the ICA, when determining the amount of the fine, must take into account the EU principle according to which firms cannot be held responsible for anticompetitive conduct whenever such behaviour constitutes an implementation of clear and unambiguous national legislative provisions. Therefore, in accordance with the *CIF* principles, the TAR Lazio recalculated the amount of the fine imposed by the ICA and granted Poste Italiane a 20 per cent reduction of the fine.

In the recent *Auditel* case, the TAR Lazio upheld the ICA decision, fining Auditel for abuse of dominant position in the regulated market for television audience surveys.[18] In doing so, the TAR Lazio rejected the company's claim regarding the exclusive jurisdiction of the ICRA in the telecommunications sector.

The reasoning of the TAR Lazio is based on the assumption that, in this case, sector-specific regulation and competition law aim for different goals: the ICRA's aim is to ensure the pluralism of information, while the aim of the ICA is to protect effective competition in the market.[19]

According to the TAR Lazio, this is precisely what makes regulation and competition law complementary, and is why they can be enforced simultaneously. Hence, the rules laid down by the regulator must be integrated with the more general antitrust rules, meaning that strict

[18] TAR Lazio, judgment of 6 June 2012, *Auditel Srl v. Autorità Garante della Concorrenza e del Mercato*, no. 5689.

[19] See R. Caponigro 'L'actio finium regundorum tra l'Autorità antitrust e le altre Autorità indipendenti' (2013) *www.giustamm.it* (accessed February 2014).

compliance with the regulations issued by the ICRA does not preclude the ICA's intervention with regard to the abuse of a dominant position.

In this context, the TAR Lazio adopted a slightly different approach in the *Posta Time* case.[20] Indeed, the TAR Lazio annulled a decision of the ICA that had imposed a 39.4-million-euro fine on Poste Italiane for breach of Article 102 TFEU. According to the ICA, Poste Italiane adopted a complex exclusionary strategy aimed at foreclosing complainant TNT Post Italia S.p.A. (TNT) and other competitors from the markets for guaranteed time and date delivery services, and for notification services through messengers.[21]

On appeal, the TAR Lazio annulled the decision, stating that the ICA failed to demonstrate with the required legal standard that the contested practices infringed Article 102 TFEU. In particular, the TAR Lazio ruled that the procedure for handling mail items found in Poste Italiane's network was in compliance with the relevant sector regulation and, thus, could not be considered part of an abusive strategy aimed at excluding its competitors.

Hence, the TAR Lazio concluded that the ICA could not find such conduct to infringe Article 102 TFEU, unless the ICA had previously called into question the compatibility of the applicable sector-specific regulation with the Italian competition law.

Indeed, the TAR Lazio strongly held that even if – in this case – the legal order can be considered inappropriate, the ICA could not substitute itself for the legislature and integrate the regulation, least of all through the exercise of its sanctioning power.

Another interesting case was decided by the TAR Lazio in September 2012.[22] This case arose from an ICA decision of 1999 which fined SNAM – which at the time was not only the operator, but also the owner of the gas pipeline network in Italy – for having abused its dominant

---

20 TAR Lazio, judgment of 25 June 2012, *Poste Italiane SpA v. Autorità Garante della Concorrenza e del Mercato et al.*, no. 5769.

21 In particular, the ICA found that Poste Italiane abused the market power it held on traditional postal services in order to enter newly liberalized markets by: (i) the systematic interception of competitors' mail in order to define strategic actions of 'customers win-back'; (ii) offering its guaranteed time and date delivery services 'PostaTime' – competing with the 'Formula Certa' service offered by TNT – at predatory prices; and (iii) charging predatory prices for time and date delivery services offered in tender procedures held by the Municipality of Milan and Equitalia SpA.

22 TAR Lazio, judgment of 3 September 2012, *SNAM SpA v. Autorità Garante della Concorrenza e del Mercato*, no. 7481.

position through the refusal to grant access to its network, as well as to negotiate freight rates with private producers.

In 1999, by means of interim measures, the TAR Lazio suspended the ICA's decision, holding that it seemed to substantially impose on SNAM the requirement to fully liberalize access to its pipeline network, in contrast with the framework outlined by Law No 9/1991 and with Directive 98/30 EEC, which – at the time – was still being implemented. Indeed, the regulatory framework seemed to require SNAM to implement the contested conduct, since the regulated sector was not yet liberalized.

In 2012, the TAR Lazio affirmed that the ICA had unlawfully made a conscious non-application of the special rules that – at the time – regulated the market. In accordance with the principle of *lex specialis*, those rules necessarily prevailed over the general competition rules.

Therefore, the TAR Lazio held that the ICA's decision to set aside the special regulation was not legitimate. Indeed, the ICA had wrongly classified the SNAM gas network as an essential facility, subject to regulated and non-discriminatory access, and it had consequently applied the general competition rules related to abuse of dominant position.

The TAR Lazio concluded that the ICA tried to impose on SNAM a general obligation to grant unconditional access to its network to anyone that required such access, causing a sudden opening to competition of the gas market that had not yet been introduced by the sectorial legislator. In doing so, the ICA largely disregarded the national legislation as well as EU law, assuming functions assigned to the sector-specific Authority for Electricity and Gas.

2.3 Some Preliminary Concluding Remarks

These cases show how the application and the interpretation of the principles laid down at EU and Italian levels by the Commission and the ICAs and NRAs (as well as by the national courts having jurisdiction) can still lead to divergent and conflicting results. This may cause legal uncertainty and inconsistency in administrative enforcement actions, the burden of which rests with the firms.

Indeed, the cumulative approach adopted both at the EU and at the national levels requires firms to comply with a dual standard: first, with the rules laid down in the sector-specific regulation and, second, with the general principles of competition law. The case-law analysed so far considers it legitimate on condition that: (i) the two sets of rules aim at different goals; and (ii) sector-specific regulation leaves room for anti-competitive behaviour.

By contrast, as the *SNAM* case demonstrates, the cumulative solution cannot be adopted in the exceptional case of a regulated activity not yet liberalized, in so far as competition law does not apply to sectors that are still subject to a state monopoly.

Even when the conditions are fulfilled, the simultaneous application of competition law and sector-specific regulation may still be problematic. First, establishing the primary objectives of the sectorial regulation might be a difficult and risky analysis since it leaves a wide margin of discretion to the NCAs, as well as to courts. Second, the NCAs and the courts enjoy the same degree of discretion in determining to what extent an undertaking enjoys a margin to behave autonomously in the market, which might lead to conflicting results.

This would, *inter alia*, jeopardize the achievement of the objectives set by both competition law and regulation, causing major issues of over-deterrence, while disregarding not only the principle of legal certainty and consistent administrative action, but also the *ne bis in idem* principle.

3. THE OVERLAP BETWEEN NRA AND NCA FUNCTIONS IN THE SPECIFIC FIELD OF CONSUMER PROTECTION

3.1 Preliminary Remarks

Analogous issues have arisen with regard to the relationship between general consumer law and sector-specific regulation.

At the EU level, Directive 2005/29/EC (hereafter the 'Directive'), while introducing the general prohibition of unfair commercial practices (UCPs), clarifies that it

> applies only in so far as there are no specific Community law provisions regulating specific aspects of unfair commercial practices, such as information requirements and rules on the way the information is presented to the consumer. It provides protection for consumers where there is no specific sectorial legislation at Community level.[23]

---

[23] See Directive 2005/29/EC of the European Parliament and of the Council of 11 May 2005 concerning unfair business-to-consumer commercial practices in the internal market (Unfair Commercial Practices Directive), [2005] OJ L 149, p. 22.

Indeed, Article 3, paragraph 4, of the Directive provides that 'in the case of conflict between the provisions of this Directive and other Community rules regulating specific aspects of unfair commercial practices, the latter shall prevail and apply to those specific aspects'. With regard to the enforcement of the UCP rules, pursuant to Article 11 of the Directive, Member States may choose the system which best guarantees their adequate and effective enforcement.

Therefore, EU rules on UCPs play a residual role, completing the *acquis européen* applicable to consumer protection.

The Directive has been almost literally implemented by Articles 18 to 27 of the Italian Consumer Code, which entrusts the ICA with the powers to stand over UCPs, and at the same time leaves open the possibility of private enforcement by individuals (Article 27).

The ICA has carried out extensive and intensive enforcement activity of the UCP rules, focusing primarily on regulated sectors. It is significant that, between 2009 and 2012, the proceedings in the electronic communications, energy, banking and insurance sectors represented almost 60 per cent of the proceedings in the field of UCPs and the related fines have reached almost 70 per cent of the total sanctions imposed by the ICA.[24]

3.2 The Initial Position Taken by the Administrative Courts

The specific focus on regulated sectors in the ICA's enforcement activity of UCP rules exacerbated the well-known concerns of legal uncertainty and inconsistency in administrative action and sector-specific regulation, generating extensive litigation.

These issues were addressed, for the first time, in the immediate aftermath of the implementation of the Directive in Italy. Indeed, in 2008 the Council of State – upon the ICA's request – issued the Opinion of 3 December 2008, No 3999 (hereafter the Opinion), concerning the applicability of the UCP provisions contained in the Italian Consumer Code to the financial sector.

[24] See Circolare Assonime, 'Misure in tema di pratiche commerciali scorrette nel decreto legge n. 95/2012 e nuove regole sui procedimenti per pubblicità ingannevole, pratiche commerciali scorrette e clausole vessatorie', of 15 January 2013, 2, available at: http://www.assonime.it/AssonimeWeb2/dettaglio.jsp?id=243447&idTipologiaDettaglio=451 (accessed August 2014).

In Italy, financial services – even before the implementation of the Directive – were regulated by several legislative acts.[25] These acts contain many provisions which impose a variety of information duties and rules of conduct, the aim of which is to protect 'clients' or 'investors' (not only 'consumers') from abuses.

Accordingly, those legislative acts provide that the violation of these informational duties and rules of conduct is punished with administrative pecuniary sanctions and injunctions, which must be applied by the sectorial enforcement authorities. These are different from the ICA, which is entitled to apply the administrative pecuniary sanctions and the other sanctions laid down in Article 27 of the Consumer Code to an infringement of the prohibition of a UCP with regard to consumers.

In this context, the problem arose because Articles 18 and 19 of the Consumer Code do not exclude – expressly or implicitly – financial services from the scope of application of such provisions.

Therefore, there is a risk that an undertaking may be punished twice – with two different fines applied by two different authorities – for the same conduct. It is precisely to avoid the violation of the *ne bis in idem* principle that the Council of State held that it is necessary to identify a single authority responsible for the application of the above-mentioned rules.

According to the Council of State, the two different sets of rules share the same objective, i.e. consumer protection. Hence, the Council of State held that the TUF, the Italian law on financial services, contains rules of a 'special nature', whereas Articles 18 to 27 of the Consumer Code include the 'general rules'.

Since the TUF is intended to protect 'clients' and 'investors', which are species within the broader category of 'consumers', the general provisions laid down in Articles 18–27 of the Consumer Code do not find application in the field of investment services and activities. Thereby, the Council of State held that the only enforcement authority entrusted – by the *TUF* – with the power to protect efficiency, transparency and loyalty

---

[25] In the field of banking and credit services, see Legislative Decree no. 1993/385 – 'Testo unico delle disposizioni in materia bancaria e creditizia' (TUB), which is a general act containing the rules concerning banks and credits. In the field of investment services, see Legislative Decree no 1998/58 – 'Testo unico delle disposizioni in materia di intermediazione finanziaria' (TUF), which is a general act containing the rules concerning investment services and activities. In the field of insurance services, see Legislative Decree no 2005/209 – 'Codice delle assicurazioni private' (PIC).

in the financial services market is the *Commissione Nazionale per le Società e la Borsa* (*CONSOB*), and not the ICA.

In its opinion, the Council of State was clear: when general consumer law and sector-specific regulation are both aimed at protecting the same interest (i.e. consumer protection), if there is a detailed and complete regulation to be applied by an authority entrusted with significant powers, the principle of specialty must prevail, setting aside the general consumer law.

Nevertheless, the opinion clarified that this solution might be different with regard to other regulated sectors; indeed, assessing the exhaustiveness of each specific regulatory framework requires very careful consideration, and cannot but be based on a case-by-case approach.

Indeed, in the four years after issuance of the opinion, the administrative courts' case-law repeatedly excluded the applicability of the principle of *lex specialis* with regards to other regulated sectors,[26] thus confirming the ICA's powers to enforce UCP rules in all regulated sectors, with the only exception being that governed by the TUF.

3.3 The Decisions of the Plenary Session of the Council of State in May 2012

The scenario radically changed in May 2012, when the Council of State was – once again – called to rule on the so-called *actio finium regundorum* between sector-specific regulation and general consumer law. Indeed, the Plenary Session of the Council of State adopted five decisions (hereafter the *Plenarie*) related to the ICA's jurisdiction to apply the UCP's rules in the telecommunications and financial sectors, which are both subject to specific regulation, having, among its primary institutional purposes, the protection of consumers.[27]

---

[26] See Council of State, judgment of 31 May 2011, *Enel SpA v. Autorità Garante della Concorrenza e del Mercato*, no. 720; TAR Lazio, judgments of 30 June 2010 *Wind Telecomunicazioni SpA v. Autorità Garante della Concorrenza e del Mercato*, nos 14856 and 4931; judgments of 22 June 2010, *Telecom Italia SpA v. Autorità Garante della Concorrenza e del Mercato*, nos 19893 and 14857.

[27] See Council of State, Plenary Session, judgments of 11 May 2012, *Telecom Italia SpA v. Autorità Garante della Concorrenza e del Mercato* and *Autorità Garante della Concorrenza e del Mercato v. Wind Telecomunicazioni SpA*, nos 11 and 15 concern the 'recharge of mobile services, the transparency and the right to withdraw contracts concluded with mobile operators, television and internet services' (ex-Article 1 of the Law-Decree no. 7/2007, as converted, with amendments, by Law no 40/2007). Judgment of 11 May 2012, *Telecom Italia SpA v. Autorità Garante della Concorrenza e del Mercato*, no. 12 concerns

In the first of these decisions, the Council of State clarifies that, in order to address the issue of jurisdiction, it is fundamental to analyse the relationship between general consumer-protection rules and sector-specific regulation. Indeed, according to the Council of State, the settlement of the relationship between substantive rules is the logical first step in properly determining which is the authority having jurisdiction, in so far as there are no doubts that the ICA and the ICRA are entrusted with the power to enforce, respectively, UCP rules (Article 27 of the Consumer Code) and the sectorial regulation (Legislative Decree no. 259/2003, the 'Electronic Communications Code').

The Council of State addresses the 'substantive' issue through the application of the 'principle of specialty'. Indeed, it affirms that Article 19(3) of the Consumer Code – which regulates, in line with Article 3(4) of the Directive, the relationship between the application of the UCP rules and sector-specific regulation – must be read as codifying the 'principle of specialty'. In particular, the Council of State holds that it is impossible to simultaneously apply two different sets of rules governing the same matter when one of them contains all the elements of the other and adds a further element of specificity (either by addition or by qualification).

Furthermore, the Council of State establishes three conditions that must be met to apply the 'principle of specialty': (i) general (consumer) law and sector-specific regulation must be aimed at the same goals, i.e. the protection of consumers; (ii) sector-specific regulation must be detailed and exhaustive; and (iii) there must be a public authority entrusted with significant sanctioning powers that are appropriate to ensure the effective implementation of the regulatory provisions.

With regard to the electronic communications sector all three conditions were satisfied:

1. The Council of State recognizes that the relevant sector-specific regulation includes full protection of 'consumers/users', observing

---

what is called 'repricing', i.e. the communication via SMS to users/subscribers of any changes in the tariff plans of mobile phone subscription. Judgments of 11 May 2012, *Telecom Italia SpA v Autorità Garante della Concorrenza e del Mercato* and *Wind Telecomunicazioni SpA v. Autorità Garante della Concorrenza e del Mercato*, nos 13 and 16 concern 'teleselling', in which an operator solicits prospective customers to buy telephone services (especially through call centers). Judgment of 11 May 2012, *AGOS SpA v. Autorità Garante della Concorrenza e del Mercato*, no 14 concerns financing transactions for the purchase of products sold at retail outlets.

inter alia that the Electronic Communications Code refers to consumer protection in many provisions. Therefore, it rejects the argument put forward by the ICA according to which the Electronic Communications Code only aims at protecting competition effectiveness and guaranteeing information pluralism. The Council of State holds that these objectives go along with consumer protection. To support its argument, it also notes that the ICRA has been designated by the Italian government to the European Commission as the NRA responsible for consumer protection in the electronic communications sector.

2. Then, the Council of State finds that the regulatory framework in the electronic communications sector is exhaustive, thus excluding the possibility of a residual ICA intervention. Indeed, this is shown by the fact that, starting from the general principles, the sector-specific regulatory framework disciplines the details of each specific conduct, thus leaving no space for the application of general consumer law. In addition, the risk of gaps or deficits in protection is further prevented by the general clauses provided by the sectorial legislation. In this regard, the Council of State also rejects the 'case-by-case approach' proposed by the ICA according to which its jurisdiction should be assessed *ex post*.
3. Finally, the Council of State ascertains that the relevant sector-specific regulation entrusts the ICRA with significant sanctioning powers to fine any infringement of the regulatory provisions.

In the Council of State's view, the above conclusions would still be valid even if scrutinized in the light of the specific 'specialty rule' codified in Article 3(4) of the Directive and Article 19 of the Italian Consumer Code. As already seen, pursuant to these provisions, the application of the UCP rules must be ruled out only where they are in 'conflict' with the applicable sector specific provisions. However, the Council of State has it that the notion of 'conflict' must be understood in terms of a 'dissimilarity' that would make illogical the overlap of the two sets of rules. A different interpretation, which would attribute to the notion of 'conflict' the meaning of a real antinomy, would otherwise confine the application of the principle set forth in Article 3(4) of the Directive and Article 19(3) of the Consumer Code to very exceptional (almost impossible) situations of incompatibility between concurrent provisions.

The Council of State also makes clear that its proposed solution best complies with the constitutional principle of good performance of the administration, as well as with the principle of proportionality, the aim of which is to avoid useless conflicting decisions in respect of the *ne bis in idem* principle.

Identical principles have also been enunciated with regard to the banking sector. However, the Council of State reached a different conclusion establishing the ICA's jurisdiction in this sector. Indeed, the Council of State holds that the national regulation applicable *ratione temporis* – the recalled TUB – is aimed at ensuring the proper and transparent functioning of the banking and credit markets, and does not contain specific provisions directly aimed at protecting consumers. In this context, the Council of State clarifies that the rules introduced by Legislative Decree 141/2010 represent the first step towards the transformation of the TUB into an exhaustive sectorial regulation including consumer protection among its primary goals.

3.4 The Latest Developments

The principles and conclusions reached by the Council of State in its landmark judgments of May 2012 have been confirmed by subsequent holdings of the TAR Lazio.

In January 2013, quoting the *Plenarie*, the TAR Lazio established the exclusive jurisdiction of the NRA – the *Istituto per la vigilanza sulle assicurazioni* (*IVASS*, formerly *ISVAP*) – in the field of consumer protection with regard to the private insurance sector.[28]

Moreover, on 18 February 2013, the TAR Lazio confirmed the jurisdiction of the ICRA with regard to consumer protection in the electronic communications sector, setting aside the possible application of the Consumer Code and, therefore, confirming the Council of State's decisions discussed above.[29]

---

[28] In this case, the ICA had fined a firm – operating in the private insurance sector – for having engaged in UCPs. The ICA's jurisdiction was then challenged before the TAR Lazio due to the existence of the Private Insurance Code, established by Legislative Decree no. 209/2005, which, according to the plaintiff, satisfied all three conditions required by the Council of State for the application of the 'principle of specialty'. Indeed, it is aimed at consumer protection; it represents a detailed and exhaustive sector-specific regulation, the application of which is attributed to the NRA (entrusted by the same regulation with appropriate sanctioning powers). See TAR Lazio, judgment of 17 January 2013, *Zuritel SpA v. Autorità Garante della Concorrenza e del Mercato*, no. 535.

[29] In the case concerned, the ICA fined several companies due to the fact that the consumers were not sufficiently informed about the existence of already activated ancillary services on their SIM cards. According to the ICA, the use of such services, if not disabled at the express request of the customer, involved the

In this context, a further development was brought about in 2012 by the Italian government through the adoption of the so-called 'Spending Review' Law Decree,[30] which – with a questionable legislative technique – seemed to be aimed at restoring margins for the enforcement activity of the ICA in regulated sectors.

Indeed, Article 23, paragraph 12-*quinquiesdecies* – while increasing the maximum amount of the fine for the violation of the UCP provisions to five million euros – incidentally specifies that the ICA has jurisdiction to assess and fine violators for UCPs except in cases in which: (i) UCPs concern conduct that is the object of specific regulation at the EU level; (ii) the regulation directly aims at consumer protection; (iii) the regulation must be applied by an authority entrusted with effective sanctioning and inhibitory powers; and (iv) the exception to the ICA general jurisdiction is limited to the regulated aspects of the regulatory framework.

Only when the above four conditions are cumulatively fulfilled can the jurisdiction of NRAs actually displace the application of general consumer law by the ICA.

Even if this new legislative provision might be considered as a challenge to the conclusions reached by the Italian case-law,[31] it is arguably perfectly consistent with the principles laid down in Article 3(4) of the Directive and Article 19(3) of the Italian Consumer Code, as interpreted by the Council of State in the *Plenarie*.

At the EU level, it must also be mentioned that the Commission in its 'First Report on the application of Directive 2005/29/EC' (hereafter the 'Report') – issued on 14 March 2013 – found that:

> where sectorial legislation conflicts with the Directive's general provisions, the corresponding provisions of the *lex specialis* will prevail. ... However, the existence of specific EU rules in a given sector does not exclude the application of the Directive: in these cases and in relation to all the aspects not covered by the *lex specialis*, the UCPD complements these sectorial

payment of specific fees. Therefore, these activities had the effect of exerting undue influence, which restricts considerably and, in some cases, even excludes free choice for consumers. See TAR Lazio, judgment of 18 February 2013, *Telecom Italia SpA v. Autorità Garante della Concorrenza e del Mercato*, no. 1752.

30 See Law Decree no. 95/2012.

31 See Circolare Assonime (n. 24 above) 5ff.

provisions and fills any remaining gaps in the protection of consumers against unfair commercial practices.[32]

This position seems to partially disregard the more extreme conclusions reached by the Council of State in the *Plenarie*, in so far as it appears to support a case-by-case approach. In this context, it must also be mentioned that the Commission – according to Article 258 TFEU – has opened proceedings against Italy for failure to fulfil its EU obligations with regard to the correct implementation of the Directive.[33]

4. CONCLUSION

The case-law analysed at section 2 above confirms that, save in very exceptional circumstances, the application of sector-specific regulation does not prevent the simultaneous application of EU competition law.

In this regard, it must be questioned whether this cumulative approach may, at least in some circumstances, lead to disproportionate results. As we have seen, the *Deutsche Telekom* judgment imposes a heavy burden on firms operating in regulated sectors, exposing them to the risks of double punishment, legal uncertainty and duplication of proceedings.

Since more and more new powers are given to NCAs and NRAs, it appears necessary to identify possible solutions to overcome the concerns raised by the possible overlap between sector-specific regulation and competition law.

It is precisely the desire to minimize these concerns that prompted the Plenary Session of the Council of State to displace UCP rules through the application of the principle of l*ex specialis* in the field of consumer protection.

The same desire drove the US Supreme Court in 2004 to apply the principle of specialty in the *Trinko* case. The Court recognized a sort of 'pre-emption or exhaustion principle in the field of antitrust'.[34] Indeed, competition rules enforcement should be 'exhausted' where a sector-specific remedy exists. The rationale behind this solution lies in the assumption that where a regulatory remedy is available, 'the benefits

---

[32] See European Commission, 'First Report on the application of Directive 2005/29/EC' [2013] http://ec.europa.eu/justice/consumer-marketing/files/ucpd_report_en.pdf (accessed February 2014).

[33] See Commission, IT 2013/2169 JUST, Transposition and application of Directive 2005/29/EC on unfair commercial practices in Italy, *Mise en demeure* 258, of 16 November 2012.

[34] See Petit (n. 2 above) 23.

from antitrust action are likely to be limited and the costs are likely to be significant'.[35]

Furthermore, this reasoning has recently been confirmed in the *LinkLine* case, in which the Supreme Court stated that competition rules must be applied prudently in order not to damage the necessary legal certainty as well as to avoid a situation in which the competition authorities actually become the regulator.[36]

The transposition *tout court* of such solutions on the EU side does not seem possible. If it is doubtful that this is possible with regard to EU consumer law (see at section 3.4 above), it is certain that, on the competition law side, the fundamental principle of supremacy enshrined in the TFEU does not allow authorities to *a priori* disregard the application of competition rules in regulated sectors, as clearly showed by the case-law analysed at section 2 above.

However, in the light of the conditions required by the case-law for the cumulative application of both competition law and sector-specific regulation, should an investigated firm succeed in demonstrating that the allegations raised by the NCA vis-à-vis its conduct pertain precisely to those aspects that are the object of specific regulation – which leaves firms with no discretion over how to carry out their business – that firm could legitimately argue that competition law must be set aside[37] or, at least, that it is not liable for any infringement.

A slightly different conclusion would apply to those exceptional cases in which (the NCAs argue that) the application of sector-specific regulation, notwithstanding its asserted pro-competitive goals, might paradoxically lead to anti-competitive effects. In these circumstances, in line with the principles enunciated in the *CIF* case, no fines should be imposed to restrictive conduct mandated by the regulator.

Pleading for the cumulative application of competition law (and/or of competition fines) even in the above-mentioned circumstances – on the

---

[35] Ibid., 23 et seq.

[36] See J.C. Laguna de Paz, 'Regulation and Competition Law' (2012) 33 *E.C.L.R.* 82.

[37] In such circumstances, firms might even challenge ICA's decisions to initiate antitrust proceedings. See TAR Lazio, judgment of 26 January 2012, *Ferrovie dello Stato v. Autorità Garante della Concorrenza e del Mercato*, no. 864, which held that, although normally acts internal to proceedings do not cause direct and specific injury to the legal sphere of the addressee (and therefore may only be challenged together with the final decision), this is exceptionally not the case when it is alleged that the ICA does not have jurisdiction to open proceedings. Accordingly, in such cases, a decision to initiate proceedings may in itself be the object of an appeal.

ground that this conclusion is mandated by the principle of the supremacy of EU law – would unreasonably jeopardize the fundamental principles of legal certainty and consistent administrative action, as well as violate the *ne bis in idem* principle, while seriously disregarding the principle of proportionality in the exercise of the sanctioning powers.

On a different ground, a better coordination can and should surely be achieved through the adoption of memoranda of understanding between NCAs and NRAs.

In the Italian scenario, for example, there are already memoranda of this kind between the ICA and several NRAs, including between the ICRA,[38] the authorities in the financial sector[39] and the Authority for Electricity and Gas.[40] These memoranda are aimed at promoting and implementing joint initiatives, strengthening the means of mutual cooperation that already exist and coordinating future activities.

In particular, on 22 February 2011, the Bank of Italy and the ICA signed a 'Memorandum of Understanding' in the field of consumer protection in the banking and financial markets. It substantially provides for an exchange of information between the authorities about the proceedings in order to enable them to transmit information about any measures taken regarding the reported cases. It also provides for regular meetings to study important issues, to coordinate their activities and to resolve any issues related to the implementation of the memorandum itself. In addition, it foresees the establishment of temporary working groups to analyse the relevant issues of common interest.

Potentially, greater publicity with regard to the enforcement and output of these cooperation mechanisms would increase their effectiveness. Indeed, the simple adoption of a memorandum is not sufficient to actually achieve results. Therefore, it would be desirable for NCAs and

---

38 See 'Memorandum of Understanding' published on the ICRA's website on 28 January 2004, available at: http://www.agcom.it/documents/10179/540063/Comunicazione+28-01-2004/8998392f-401d-4f5a-b0bf-b716739d158c?version=1.0

39 On 9 June 2010, the Bank of Italy, CONSOB, COVIP, ISVAP (now IVASS) and the ICA signed a 'Memorandum of Understanding' on the financial sector.

40 On 13 September 2012, the Authority for Electricity and Gas and the ICA signed a Framework Protocol which provides: forms of cooperation; reciprocal reports; mutual cooperation; exchange of advice and alerts on issues of common interest; and joint initiatives to control and supervise the market. The Protocol also provides for the mutual and periodic exchange of information between the two authorities on pending proceedings and their conclusions, both in competition law and the law against UCPs.

NRAs to be obligated to publish the data related to the occasions on which the memoranda are used, as well as to the results that have been reached.

7. Regulatory approach to competition law in the practice of the Polish competition authority – a critical assessment

Krystyna Kowalik-Bańczyk

1. INTRODUCTION

The aim of this chapter is to identify whether there is any 'regulatory approach' to competition law in the practice of the Polish Competition Authority, the Office of Protection of Competition and Consumers (hereafter OPCC). This is a huge subject and it requires some reservation as to the scope of the chapter. This text deals only with competition rules and does not touch upon the issues concerned with concentrations. It also leaves aside the on-going reform of the Polish Competition Act.[1]

The analysis of different decisions of the President of the OPCC in recent years allows for identification of two possible ways of understanding the 'regulatory approach'. The OPCC acts either in lieu of or in concert with the regulator. Thus there are situations where the President of the OPCC acts *in* the regulated sectors despite (or in addition to) the actions undertaken by the sectoral regulating authorities, or there are situations where the President of the OPCC acts *as* the regulator in the markets where competition is very weak or needs to be created and not simply protected. Both possibilities touch on the problem of the limits of the OPCC's competences and of the borders between actions undertaken by the regulators and the President of the OPCC.

Apart from presenting the examples of the OPCC President's decisions where either of the two forms of 'regulatory approach' could be

[1] Broader on this reform: K. Kowalik-Bańczyk, 'Reforms of Polish Antitrust Law: Closer to, or Farther From, the European Model?' (2014) 5 *J. Eur. Comp. L. & Prac.* 703.

identified, this chapter critically analyses the legitimacy of this approach in the light of the objectives of the Polish competition law,[2] the Act on Protection of Competition and Consumers 2007 (APCC). There is a need to interpret strictly the powers of any state organ; therefore a question arises of whether the powers of the OPCC can be used in proactive or only reactive ways. Can the OPCC step into the fields reserved for regulators?

Before we begin a more detailed description of the Polish competition reality with the focus on its presumed regulatory twist, two general remarks should be made that influence this analysis as a whole. First and foremost, this chapter presents what is happening in one of the (still) new Member States of the European Union as far as application of competition rules is concerned. The case of Poland is an almost ideal example of a situation where a set of rules set out in the Treaty on the Functioning of the European Union[3] (TFEU, formerly the Treaty on European Community), namely Articles 101 and 102, have been copied to the national legislation – first, the APCC of 2000, and, subsequently, the presently binding APCC of 2007.[4] For instance, respectively, Article 6 APCC mirrors Article 101 TFEU and Article 9 APCC mirrors Article 102 TFEU,[5] not to mention the introduction of both the commitment decisions and the leniency programmes into the APCC in response to the European developments in secondary regulations and the soft law.[6] One

---

[2] Act of 16 February 2007 on competition and consumer protection (Journal of Laws of 2007, No. 50, item 331), available in English at: http://www.uokik.gov.pl/competition_protection.php (accessed August 2014). On the earlier antitrust laws in Poland cf.: S. Sołtysiński, 'Dostosowanie prawa polskiego do wymagań Układu Europejskiego' (1996) 6 *Państwo i Prawo* 4; I, Wiszniewska, 'Dostosowanie polskiego prawa antymonopolowego do prawa europejskiego', (1996) 1-4 *Studia Prawnicze*, 142, T, Skoczny, *Die Angleichung der Wettbewerbsregeln in den neuen und zukünftigen Mitgliedstaaten an das Gemeinschaftsrecht. Polen*, (Nomos 2006).

[3] [2012] OJ C 326, p. 47.

[4] On the Europeanization of Polish competition law in historical perspective see T. Skoczny, 'The Polish Competition Law in the 1990s – on the Way to Higher Effectiveness and Deeper Conformity with EC Competition Rules' in T. Einhorn (ed.), *Spontaneous Order, Organisation and the Law. Roads to a European Civil Society. Liber Amicorum Ernst-Joachim Mestmäcker* (T.M.C Asser Press 2003) 349.

[5] As noted by D. Miąsik, those provisions are so general and imprecise that they resemble provisions of constitutional law. See D. Miąsik, 'Controlled Chaos with Consumer Welfare as the Winner – a Study of the Goal of Polish Antitrust Law' (2008) 1(1) *Yearbook Antitrust & Reg. Stud.* 34.

[6] Cf. Article 12 and Article 109 of the APCC.

can thus presume that the way those national provisions are interpreted and applied in the Polish legal system is greatly influenced by the practice of the European Commission and the jurisprudence of the European courts.[7] It is true that the development of the practice of the Polish OPCC, *toutes proportions gardées*, mirrors greatly the developments undertaken by the European Commission. However, this 'drive to copy' in purely internal situations was mitigated by the Polish Supreme Court as early as 2006, when it stated:

> the provisions of antitrust law form that part of national law which is not covered by the process of harmonisation under Articles 94 and 95 EC [Articles 115 and 114 TFEU]. *There is no obligation of consistent interpretation* of provisions of the Act on the protection of competition and consumers, because the provisions of this Act that concern the protection of competition – as opposed to the provisions on the protection of collective consumer interests … – do not transpose to the Polish law the provisions of Community directives. Therefore the judgments of the ECJ and decisions of the European Commission that touch on Articles 81 and 82 EC [now Articles 101 and 102 TFEU] are – in matters that do not affect trade between Member States and that have been appealed after the decisions of the President of the OPCC – only *a source of intellectual inspiration, an example of legal reasoning and understanding of certain notions* that might be applied to the interpretation of provisions of Polish law, at least because of the fact that the market economy and free competition, and subsequently the law on the protection of competition, have existed in the Republic of Poland only since 1990.[8]

This position of the Supreme Court resulted in a 'selective application' of EU solutions by the Polish OPCC and the courts. This does not enhance legal security.[9] With this reservation in mind, it still can be presumed that any legal development on the European level sooner or later will be

---

[7] Broader on this process see D. Miąsik, 'Solvents to the Rescue – A Historical Outline of the Impact of EU Law on the Application of Polish Competition Law by Polish Courts' (2010) 3(3) *Yearbook Antitrust & Reg. Stud.* 11; M. Kolasiński, 'Influence of the General Principles of Community Law on Polish Antitrust Procedure' (2010) 3(3) *Yearbook Antitrust & Reg. Stud.* 29. This development is becoming visible in the number of 'Polish' cases delivered by EU Courts. For an overview see K. Kuik and A. Mościbroda, '2010 and 2011 EU Competition Law and Sector-Specific Regulatory Jurisprudence and Case Law Developments with a Nexus to Poland' (2012) 6(7) *Yearbook Antitrust & Reg. Stud.* 157.

[8] Judgment of the Supreme Court of 9 August 2006, III SK 6/06, at 35 of the findings. Translation and emphasis by the author.

[9] Miąsik (n. 7 above) 25.

reflected at the national level, perhaps with some local flavour. This 'drive to copy' will also be invoked in the following analysis, because, unlike in the case of the Polish sector-specific regulations, there is no harmonisation involved, and therefore the need for consistent interpretation of national rules with their EU equivalents does not directly occur. It is worth bearing in mind, however, that this 'bottom-up', approach consisting of spontaneous harmonisation, is not a novelty in the European Union.[10]

The second general remark relates to the circumstances in which it is legitimate to use the regulatory tools and who is allowed to do this. It is common knowledge that sector-specific regulation is created to facilitate competition, while competition rules are aimed at minimising the distortions of competition.[11] If regulation should be perceived as a 'supplement' to antitrust rules, being in place in a particular market or sector only until the competition in this market or sector is introduced and fixed, then any 'overspill' of the regulation methods into competition rules should be avoided.[12]

The temporality and the exceptionality were initially perceived as the main features of sector-specific regulation.[13] However, one can also argue that there are sectors, or economic circumstances linked directly to the particular economic reality of a case analysed, where regulation is to stay,[14] as antitrust rules alone would possibly never suffice. In Poland such situations occur mainly for the following reason: even though the

---

[10] H. Ullrich, 'Harmonisation within the European Union' (1996) 3 *E.C.L.R.* 178.

[11] M. Szydło, *Regulacja sektorów infrastrukturalnych jako rodzaj funkcji państwa w gospodarce* (Prawo i Praktyka Gospodarcza 2005) 93.

[12] J. Temple Lang, 'European Competition Policy and Regulation: Differences, Overlaps, and Constraints' in F. Lévêque and H. Shelanski (eds), *Antitrust and Regulation in the EU and US: Legal and Economic Perspectives* (Edward Elgar Publishing 2009) 20; and J. Tapia and D. Mantzari, 'The Regulation/Competition Interaction' in D. Gerardin and I. Lianos (eds), *Research Handbook on European Competition Law* (Edward Elgar Publishing 2013) 588.

[13] In fact, regulation is perceived as necessary where there are important and non-transitory barriers of entry to a market dominated by one undertaking with so-called significant market power. See A.T. Szablewski, *Zarys teorii i praktyki reform regulacyjnych na przykładzie energetyki* (DiG 2003) 11. The drive to introduce *ex ante* regulation and then to refer to general competition law instead can be illustrated by the so-called 'sunset clauses' used in regulatory decisions; cf. S. Piątek, 'Investment and Regulation in Telecommunication' (2008) 1(1) *Yearbook Antitrust & Reg. Stud.* 118.

[14] S. Bishop and M. Walker, *The Economics of EC Competition Law – Concepts, Application and Measurement* (Sweet & Maxwell 2002) 24.

state-owned monopolies have been dismantled, the new private undertakings still need to be overseen by the state because they provide public services (or even so-called services of general economic interest[15]), among them very often services of universal character.[16] Thus there are questions of objectives of any action undertaken by the OPCC in those markets – is the OPCC bound to restore competition only or should it also protect the consistent supply of those vital services and protect consumers (end-users)?

The traditional sets of tools available to the antitrust authorities allow them to react *ex post facto* to competition law infringements. The infringement decisions allow the President of the OPCC to restore competition and to punish infringements of it. Those traditional tools have been broadened – and there the novelty lies – to a new set of instruments, allowing for a more radical and prescriptive intervention of the competition authority into the operation of undertakings in the market, because they imply some positive behaviour by the undertakings.[17] Those relatively new tools – where an element of regulation is very visible – are for the most part commitment decisions. In the decisions of the President of the OPCC issued between 2011 and 2013 they are mainly used in circumstances that resemble the classic 'regulation' situations – namely, to address the local dominant undertakings (which often are *de facto* local monopolies,[18] incumbents or 'public

---

[15] As Jones and Sufrin state, they are 'services that belong to the market, but to which other, "non-market", values are applied'. See A. Jones and B Sufrin, *EC Competition Law* (5th edn, Oxford University Press 2014) 621.

[16] Much more broadly on this problem see G. Amato, *Antitrust and the Bounds of Power: The Dilemma of Liberal Democracy in the History of the Market* (Hart Publishing 1997) 88 et seq. In the purely Polish context on railway and electricity see K. Bobińska, 'The Defense of Monopoly as a Determinant of the Process of Transformation of State-owned Infrastructure Sectors in Poland' (2008) 1(1) *Yearbook Antitrust & Reg. Stud* 131–150. Stressing the development of regulation as 'public utility regulation' in United States cf. Szablewski (n. 13 above) 19.

[17] On this in EU law, see I. Maher, 'Regulating Competition' in C. Parker, C. Scott, N. Lacey, J. Baithwaite (eds), *Regulating Law* (Oxford University Press 2004) 194. Cf. also F. Di Porto, 'Abuses of Information and Informational Remedies: Rethinking Exchange of Information Under Competition Law?', in this volume.

[18] Therefore the proceedings in such cases are mainly led by the so-called Delegations (*delegatury* in Polish) of the OPCC, placed in the following cities: Bydgoszcz, Gdańsk, Katowice, Kraków, Lublin, Łódź, Poznań, Warszawa, Wrocław, according to Article 33 of the APCC and Regulation of the Prime Minister of 1 July 2009 on the local and substantial powers of the Delegations of

undertakings',[19] or undertakings granted special or exclusive rights[20] in the meaning of Article 106 TFEU) providing public services[21] (water supply, sewage disposal, gas and electricity supply, etc.) and holding an infrastructure.[22] The character of those infrastructures as 'essential facilities'[23] might also be an argument for the more regulatory inclination of the OPCC – as it acts as an authority opening markets to competition or

---

the OPCC, Journal of Laws 2009, No. 107, item 887. Out of about 100 decisions of the President of the OPCC concerning practices infringing competition per year, the majority concerns local Polish markets. See M. Krasnodębska-Tomkiel, 'Perspektywy polityki konkurencji w Polsce w 20. Rocznicę powstania UOKiK' in M. Krasnodębska-Tomkiel (ed.), *Zmiany w polityce konkurencji na przestrzeni ostatnich dwóch dekad* (Urząd Ochrony Konkurencji i Konsumentów 2010) 518.

[19] Case 188-190/88 *France, Italy and the UK v. Commission* [1982] ECR 2545. Control by the state occurs either by ownership or by some contractual, structural or financial connection between the state and the undertaking.

[20] Case 30/87 *Bodson v Pompes Funèbres des Régions Libérées* [1988] ECR 2479.

[21] The first example cited in the literature is the OPCC decision of 24 August 2010, Case DOC-7/2010 *ZAIKS* (Polish Copyright Collecting Society). See T. Kozieł, 'Commitment Decisions under the Polish Competition Act – Enforcement Practice and Future Perspectives' (2009) 3(3) *Yearbook Antitrust & Reg. Stud.* 76. To the author's knowledge, based on the Report published by the OPCC in 2012 (available at: https://uokik.gov.pl/ [accessed August 2014]), 29 of 30 of the commitment decisions issued in 2012 were made in cases of presumed abuse of dominant position, including as addressees some public service providers.

[22] This type of development has already been criticised in European law. See G. Monti, 'Managing the Intersection of Utilities Regulation and EC Competition Law' (2008) 4(2) *Comp. L. Rev.* 121. It should be noted that there is a broad jurisprudence where the local municipalities (*Gminy* in Polish; often city communes) are treated as undertakings. See judgments of the Supreme Court of 19 October 1999, Case III CZ 112/99; of 12 June 2000, Case V CKN 48/00; of 7 August 2003, Case IV CZ 90/03; of 5 January 2007, Case III SK 16/06; of 14 November 2008, Case III SK 9/08. See also M. Bernatt, 'The Legal Status of Undertaking – Should Local Governments be Treated more Favorably in Relation to Penalties for Breaching Polish Antitrust Law?' (2008) 1(1) *Yearbook Antitrust & Reg. Stud.* 219.

[23] For a definition of this notion in the jurisprudence of the Polish Courts see judgment of the Court of Competition and Consumer Protection of 7 December 2006, Case XVII Ama 11/06 *Kielce Commune v. President of OPCC*; judgment of the Supreme Court of 14 January 2009, Case III SK 24/08 *R Commune v. President of OPCC*. See also the comment by J. Jeżewska, 'Possible objective justification of a network monopoly's refusal to conclude an agreement on an interconnected market' (2010) 3(3) *Yearbook Antitrust & Reg. Stud.* 271. The notion of 'essential facility' elaborated by the Polish jurisprudence largely

surveying consumer welfare rather than just restoring competition.[24] Thus, the practice of the OPCC goes back to the roots of the American idea of regulation as part of the law created to guarantee the state's influence on 'business affected with a public interest'.[25] The analysis of the emerging Polish practice shows that such local undertakings often avoid fines for antitrust infringements, because they undertake commitments that are accepted and made binding by the President of the OPCC.

2. COMPETITION *VERSUS* REGULATION IN THE POLISH LEGAL SYSTEM

Articles 20 and 22 of the Polish Constitution[26] imply a need to seek a balance between economic freedom and the limitations of that freedom introduced in the public interest.[27] The modern Polish competition law began[28] in 1990 with the Act of 24 February 1990 on Counteracting

corresponds to the EU developments present in the judgment of the ECJ of 25 November 1997, C-7/97 *Bronner* [1997] ECR I-7791.

[24] E. Sage, 'Who Controls Polish Transmission Masts? At the Intersection of Antitrust and Regulation' (2010) 3(3) *Yearbook Antitrust & Reg. Stud.* 161; P. Larouche, *Competition Law and Regulation in European Telecommunications* (Hart Publishing 2000).

[25] Szablewski (n. 13 above) 22 and 30.

[26] Constitution of the Republic of Poland as adopted by the National Assembly on 2 April 1997, available in English at: http://www.trybunal.gov.pl/eng/index.htm (accessed August 2014).

[27] Krasnodębska-Tomkiel (n. 18 above) 517. See more generally M. Szydło, *Swoboda działalności gospodarczej* (C.H. Beck 2005) 6 ff.; C. Kosikowski, 'Wolność działalności gospodarczej i jej ograniczenia w praktyce stosowania Konstytucji RP' in C. Kosikowski (ed.), *Zasady ustroju społecznego i gospodarczego w procesie stosowania Konstytucji* (Wydawnictwo Sejmowe 2005) 37.

[28] In fact, Poland had a cartel regulation from the 1930s: Act of 28 March 1933 on Cartels, Journal of Laws 1933, No. 31, item 270 and Act of 13 July 1939 on Cartel Agreements, Journal of Laws 1939, No. 63, item 418. In 1987, the Act of 28 January 1987 on counteracting monopolistic practices in national economy, Journal of Laws 1987, No. 3, item 18, was issued. See more generally M. Błachucki, *Polish Competition Law – Commentary, Case Law and Texts* (Urząd Ochrony Konkurencji i Konsumentów 2013), available at: http://papers.ssrn.com/sol3/papers.cfm?abstract_id=2257719&download=yes (accessed August 2014).

Monopolistic Practices and Protection of Consumers,[29] which was subsequently replaced by the Act of 15 December 2000 on Competition and Consumer Protection.[30] At present, it is regulated in the APCC. According to its Article 1.1, the APCC 'determines the conditions for the development and protection of competition'. As stated by the Polish Supreme Court, the APCC applies to 'all behaviour of undertakings where the legislature has allowed for the functioning of market mechanisms, leaving the market participants an autonomy as to the choice of their market behaviour'.[31] Article 1.2 of the APCC provides that 'The Act regulates the *principles* and *measures* of counteracting competition-restricting practices'.[32] Thus it seems that the powers granted to the President of the OPCC are regulated in quite an open manner in the APCC, allowing him or her to react to various categories of behaviour of autonomous undertakings in the market.

On the other hand, the Polish sector-specific regulation acts are aimed, just as the EU ones, at regulating the behaviour of undertakings that are either natural monopolies or are acting in circumstances of limited competition, most usually because of their dominant position.[33] Regulatory acts are supposed to 'artificially' correct the situation of limited competition, very often by particularly detailed provisions. Thus, the

---

[29] Act of 24 February 1990 on Counteracting Monopolistic Practices and Consumer Protection, Journal of Laws 1997, No. 49, item 318 with amendments.

[30] Act of 15 December 2000 on Competition and Consumer Protection, consolidated text – Journal of Laws 2005, No. 244, item 2080.

[31] Judgment of the Supreme Court of 3 March 2010, III SK 37/09. For instance, if an undertaking independently sets the tariffs for water supply and those tariffs are only accepted by the municipalities, the undertaking concerned retains autonomy. See C. Banasiński and M. Krasnodębska-Tomkiel, 'Zastosowanie środków prawa antymonopolowego na szczególnych rynkach regulowanych' (2009) 1 *Przegląd Prawa Handlowego* 18.

[32] Emphasis added.

[33] In Poland the previous state monopolies have been gradually dismantled, first by legal privatisation: see first the Act of 13 July 1990 on privatisation of state-owned companies, Journal of Laws 1990, No. 51, item 298. That however excluded the services of general economic interest, like power plants, power stations, railways, telecommunications industry, transmission networks, water boards, gas and oil pipelines, etc. Later came the Act of 30 August 1996 on commercialisation and privatisation of state enterprises, Journal of Laws 1996, No. 118, item 561. Another important act was the Act of 5 February 1993 on ownership restructuring certain state-owned enterprises of special importance to the national economy, Journal of Laws 1993, No. 16, item 69. See Bobińska (n. 16 above) 134.

sector-specific regulation acts 'define – in relation to regulated undertakings – how the monopolist is to behave in order to create as much room for competition as possible'.[34] In the Polish doctrine sector-specific regulation is understood as an instrument allowing the state to influence, by actions of independent authorities – regulators – the behaviours of undertakings that are either monopolists or dominant undertakings possessing some important infrastructure (such as rail tracks, energy or telecommunication networks, etc.). The regulators are said to have greater discretionary powers than any other administrative organs in the Polish legal system.[35]

Historically speaking, Poland began developing new regulatory acts in sector-specific areas around the year 2000 and mainly just before and because of accession to the European Union in 2004. Since Poland's accession to the EU, the introduction of competition in network industries (mainly telecommunication, energy and air transport) has been one of the main objectives of the Polish legislature. As in the whole European Union, the introduction of competition in those markets is supposed to be achieved by establishing special regulators. There are four basic regulators: (1) the Office of Electronic Communications (OEC), which regulates telecommunications and postal services,[36] and together with the

---

[34] A. Stawicki, 'The Autonomy of Sector-Specific Regulation – Is It Still Worth Protecting? Further Thoughts on the Parallel Application of Competition Law and Regulatory Instruments' (2011) 4(4) *Yearbook Antitrust & Reg. Stud.* 115, 124.

[35] W. Hoff, *Prawny model regulacji sektorowej* (Difin 2008) 15.

[36] Act of 16 July 2004 Telecommunication Law, Journal of Laws 2004, No. 171, item 1800 with subsequent amendments. In a historical perspective, Poland adopted the first Telecommunication Law in Central Europe (in November 1990) that was supposed to liberalize the whole sector. It divided the previous state monopoly into two entities: Polish Post and Polish Telecommunication. It formally allowed other undertakings to start providing telecommunication services alongside Polish Telecommunication. However, competition was not easily introduced to this sector. It is quite revealing that out of 107 antitrust decisions by the Polish OPCC President in the telecommunication sector issued in 1991-2002, 103 were directed against Polish Telecommunication. See A. Żołnowski and W. Szymczak, *Polski sektor telekomunikacyjny w świetle działań organu antymonopolowego* (Urząd Ochrony Konkurencji i Konsumentów 2003) 4. In 2000 a new Telecommunication Law was adopted. It was broadly criticised as not corresponding to the European Union requirements and it was soon replaced by the present Act of 16 July 2004, the so-called Telecommunication Law. Already in 2000, an Office of Regulation of Telecommunication was created (in the meantime its name has changed twice, in 2002 and 2006). During the period 2002–2010 its competences were gradually broadened so that it really

State Council of Radio and Television deals with electronic media; (2) the Energy Regulation Office[37] (ERO); (3) the Railway Transport Office[38] (RTO); and (4) the Civil Aviation Office (CAO).[39] In each of these sectors we witness at present a different degree of opening to competition. According to OCCP's report on Polish competition policy, the most advanced state of competition exists in the airways transport sector because it has been greatly liberalised and opened for consumers' needs due to the full implementation of EU law. Effective competition is also advanced in telecommunication markets. Growing effectiveness of competition is attested in the energy sector and in postal services.[40] The smallest degree of competition is observed in railway transport despite the fact that it was fully liberalised in 2007.[41] In each of those sectors the conditions for the creation of competition are different. A big role is attributed to the actual will of the regulator to use its competences in a way that allows for the development of competition. For instance, in the railway sector, the liberalisation process formally started in 1997 with the Railway Transport Act of 1997. Yet it was only the Act of 28 March 2003 on railway transport that introduced competition into the Polish railway industry and established the regulator for the sector, the RTO.[42] It is broadly confirmed, however, that the RTO does not possess enough competences to be able to introduce competition to the railway markets,[43]

---

became a regulator able to introduce competition on the Polish telecommunication markets. See in more detail J. Kubasik, 'Walka o konkurencję na polskim rynku usług telekomunikacyjnych' in C. Banasiński and E Stawicki (eds), *Konkurencja w gospodarce współczesnej* (Urząd Ochrony Konkurencji i Konsumentów 2007) 157, 173.

[37] Act of 10 April 1997 – Energy Act, consolidated text Journal of Laws 2006, No. 89, item 625 with subsequent amendments.

[38] Act of 28 March 2003 on Railway Transport, consolidated text Journal of Laws 2007, No. 16, item 94 with subsequent amendments. This Act replaced the previous Act of 27 June 1997 on Railway Transport, Journal of Laws 1997, No. 96, item 591.

[39] Act of 3 July 2002 – Aviation Law, consolidated text Journal of Laws 2006, No.100, item 696 with subsequent amendments.

[40] OPCC, *Polityka konkurencji na lata 2011–2013* (2011) 7, available at: https://uokik.gov.pl/ (accessed August 2014).

[41] Ibid.

[42] More in detail on this process, see M. Król, 'Liberalization without a Regulator: The Rail Freight Transport Market in Poland in the Years 1996–2009' (2010) 3(3) *Yearbook Antitrust & Reg. Stud.* 166.

[43] See OPCC (n. 40 above) 27.

despite a major reform in 2011 that partly extended those competences.[44] This regulator fails to regulate the market and 'constitutes an instructive example of the regulator's passive approach'.[45] Marcin Król explains it by the lack of independence of this regulator, which is subordinate to the Ministry of Transport, which is said to be 'a ministry of state transport companies.'[46]

2.1 Aims of Polish Competition Rules *versus* Aims of Regulation

The APCC is applied in the 'public interest'; therefore, the OPCC must include an analysis on the public interest protection in each of its decisions.[47] The notion of 'public interest' is defined – in the jurisprudence of the Polish Supreme Court in competition matters – in two possible ways. The public interest is at stake if either the questioned practice 'infringes competition or causes negative effects in the market'[48] or that practice concerns 'a broader audience of market participants'.[49] The Supreme Court has consistently stressed that 'it is not necessary to infringe an interest of an individual to apply the instruments of intervention stipulated in the Competition Act …[50] – the concept of public interest should be interpreted from the perspective of the antitrust axiology',[51] and it should be invoked if competition is restricted, because 'the existence and development of competition on all relevant markets is

---

[44] In more detail see K. Bożekowska-Zawisza, 'Legislative Developments in Railway Transport in 2011' (2012) 6(7) *Yearbook Antitrust & Reg. Stud.* 239.

[45] Król (n. 42 above) 174.

[46] Ibid., 175.

[47] This notion is not constant and unified. The OPCC must consider public interest by analysing the negative impact of controlled practices on a relevant market. See judgment of the Supreme Court of 24 July 2003, Case I CKN 496/01; Krasnodębska-Tomkiel (n. 18 above) 520.

[48] Judgments of the Supreme Court of 27 August 2003, Case I CKN 527/01; of 26 April 2004, Case III SK 1/04; of 5 June 2008, Case III SK 40/07; of 2 April 2009, Case III SK 30/08; of 16 October 2008, Case III SK 2/08.

[49] Judgments of the Supreme Court of 7 April 2004, Case III SK 27/04 and of 5 June 2008, Case III SK 40/07. As underlined by Miąsik (n. 5 above) 42, since 1990 the public interest has become a precondition for application of antitrust rules because of 'a rational need to separate trivial cases from important ones'.

[50] Judgment of the Supreme Court of 7 April 2004, Case III SK 27/04, translation by A. Jurkowska-Gomułka, 'Polish Antitrust Legislation and Case Law Review 2009' (2010) 3(3) *Yearbook Antitrust & Reg. Stud.* 222.

[51] Judgments of 16 October 2008, Case III SK 2/08; of 5 June 2008, Case III SK 40/07, translations by Jurkowska-Gomułka (n. 50 above) 222.

in the public interest'.[52] However, the precise goals of the Polish competition policy are difficult to identify. According to Article 1.1 of the APCC, the Act 'determines the conditions for the development and protection of *competition* as well as the principles of protecting the *interests of undertakings and consumers in the public interest*' (emphasis added). Thus it is in the public interest that the OPCC should protect competition, undertakings and consumers. However, only competition and consumers are really directly protected; there is no construction of Article 1 APCC allowing the assumption that the protection of competitors is an aim in itself, as this task is fulfilled by the unfair competition rules, belonging to private law.

There are varied opinions on the interpretation of Article 1.1 of the APCC.[53] In the Act itself, there is no indication of the essence of the goals and their mutual relationships.[54] It seems that the 'protective function' for competition is the dominant one, as there is no clear suggestion that the President of the OPCC is supposed to set the conditions for competition.[55] Various goals are invoked and treated as equally important in the decisions of the President of the OPCC and further in the jurisprudence of the courts: the increase in economic efficiency, the protection of consumer welfare, the freedom of economic activity, and the protection of independence of undertakings (including the protection of competitors).[56] Sometimes the protection of the *process*

---

[52] Judgment of the Court of Competition and Consumer Protection of 21 March 2005, Case XVII Ama 16/04 *Telekomunikacja Polska v President of OPCC*, translation by Miąsik (n. 5 above) 43.

[53] C. Banasiński and E. Piontek (eds), *Ustawa o ochronie konkurencji i konsumentów. Komentarz* (Lexis Nexis 2011) 16. E. Stawicki, 'Commentary to art. 1' in A. Stawicki and E. Stawicki (eds), *Ustawa o ochronie konkurencji i konsumentów. Komentarz* (Wolters Kluwer Polska 2011) 29–30; K. Kohutek, 'Commentary to article 1' in K. Kohutek and M. Sieradzka (eds), *Ustawa o ochronie konkurencji i konsumentów. Komentarz* (Wolters Kluwer Polska 2008) 42–44; E. Modzelewska-Wąchal, 'Ochrona konsumentów w polskiej ustawie antymonopolowej. Zagadnienia horyzontalne' in M. Krasnodębska-Tomkiel (ed), *Zmiany w polityce konkurencji na przestrzeni ostatnich dwóch dekad* (Urząd Ochrony Konkurencji i Konsumentów 2010) 105–107.

[54] T. Skoczny in T. Skoczny, D. Miąsik and A. Jurkowska (eds), *Ustawa o ochronie konkurencji i konsumentów. Komentarz* (C.H. Beck 2009) 23–25.

[55] Modzelewska-Wąchal (n. 53 above) 105.

[56] Miąsik (n. 5 above) 36–37; Z. Jurczyk, 'Cele polityki antymonopolowej w teorii i praktyce' in C. Banasiński and E. Stawicki (eds), *Konkurencja w gospodarce współczesnej* (Urząd Ochrony Konkurencji i Konsumentów 2007) 36; E. Kosiński, 'Cele i instrumenty antymonopolowej interwencji państwa w gospodarkę' (2004) 3 *Kwartalnik Prawa Publicznego* 40–41.

of competition itself is pointed to as one of the main goals of the APCC.[57] However at present it seems that the 'winner' in this competition of goals is 'consumer welfare', perceived in a very broad and open-ended way as covering not only the final consumers, but all contractors and customers of the undertakings concerned in competition law proceedings.[58] That said, there is a broad margin of appreciation for the President of the OPCC as to which of the possible goals to pursue, which further erodes legal certainty.[59] The recent drive to put consumer welfare at the top of the aims pursued by the OPCC reflects the present European Union policy[60] and this cannot be perceived as accidental.

As for the regulators, depending on the sector concerned, their aims are various. We shall give two examples of the definition of purposes of regulation – first, as far as telecommunication is concerned, and, second, for the energy sector. They illustrate how much broader and richer the aims of the regulators are in comparison to those pursued by the OPCC, and that some of those aims are identical.

Article 1.2 of the Act of 16 July 2004 on Telecommunications states that the purposes of this Act are first and foremost 'to create conditions for supporting equal and effective competition within the scope of providing telecommunications services'. The Act concerns the competition faced by incumbents, existing monopolists in the various telecommunication markets. No effective competition can exist if one undertaking completely dominates the market, and that was initially the case of Polish Telecom. Continuing with the Telecommunication Act, the aforementioned provision lists further purposes of the Act: the development and use of modern telecommunications infrastructure; ensuring order in the management of numbering, frequencies and orbital resources; ensuring the maximum benefit for users in terms of choice,

---

57 Stawicki (n. 53 above) 30.

58 Miąsik (n. 5 above) 33–57; D. Miąsik and T. Skoczny, 'Commentary to art. 1' in T. Skoczny, D. Miąsik, A. Jurkowska (eds), *Ustawa o ochronie konkurencji i konsumentów. Komentarz* (C.H. Beck 2009) 52–53. See also judgment of the Supreme Court of 5 January 2007, Case III SK 17/06 *Kolej Gondolowa*.

59 B. Turno, *Leniency. Program łagodzenia kar pieniężnych w polskim prawie ochrony konkurencji* (Wolters Kluwer Polska 2013) 54–55.

60 P. Lowe, 'Making Markets Work for Consumers: The Challenge in Europe' in M. Krasnodębska-Tomkiel (ed), *Zmiany w polityce konkurencji na przestrzeni ostatnich dwóch dekad* (Urząd Ochrony Konkurencji i Konsumentów 2010) 539. A good example of this attitude in regulated sectors is the Commission Decision of 16 October 2009, Case COMP/39401 – *E.ON/GDF*, [2009] OJ C 248, p. 5 (concerning the energy sector).

price and quality of telecommunications services; ensuring technological neutrality. The aim of guaranteeing the users 'the maximum benefits' also applies to 'consumer welfare'. It allows the regulator to audit the service providers as to whether they do use onerous and abusive clauses in their contracts with end-users (consumers).[61] All of the aims listed in the Telecommunication Act correspond with those set out in Article 8 of Directive 2002/21/EC.[62] Article 1.3 of the APCC states clearly that the provisions of the Telecommunication Act 'shall be without prejudice to the provisions on competition and consumer protection'.

As far as the energy sector is concerned, the regulatory goals are set out in Article 1.2 of the Act of 10 April 1997 on Energy.[63] They are numerous and cover: creating conditions for sustainable development of the country as a whole; providing energy security; assuring safe and rational use of energy and fuels; developing competition; preventing negative effects of natural monopolies; protecting the environment; fulfilling international obligations undertaken by Poland; and keeping the balance between the interests of energy undertakings and end-users. As interpreted by the Polish Constitutional Tribunal, the Energy Act is not only a tool for steering economic processes but also an instrument for securing social interests as it sets limits on economic activity in the public interest.[64] In the sector of production and distribution of energy, the Energy Act clearly provides that one of the main tasks of the President of the ERO is the 'promotion of competition'.[65] Consequently,

---

[61] M. Rogalski and D. Gałecka, *Prawo telekomunikacyjne*, LEX el (Wolters Kluwer Polska 2011).

[62] Directive 2002/21/EC of the European Parliament and of the Council of 7 March 2002 on a common regulatory framework for electronic communications networks and services, [2002] OJ 108, p. 33.

[63] Journal of Laws 2006, No. 89, item 625.

[64] Judgment of the Polish Constitutional Tribunal of 25 July 2006, Case P 24/05; as cited by Z. Muras and M. Swora (eds), *Prawo energetyczne. Komentarz*, LEX el (Wolters Kluwer Polska 2010).

[65] According to Article 23.2 of the Energy Act, the ERO President undertakes several activities to introduce or maintain competition in both wholesale and retail markets, for instance, (1) granting and withdrawing licences; (2) approving and controlling tariff applications for gaseous fuels, electricity and heat, including analysing and verifying costs adapted by the energy enterprises as justified to calculate prices and fees in their tariffs; and (3) establishing the period for the tariff to be in force and correcting factors. The list is not exhaustive. For a full picture of the ERO President's tasks see http://www.ure.gov.pl/portal/en/4/22/Presidents_duties.html (accessed August 2014). For reports on the activity of the ERO's President see http://www.ure.gov.pl/

the Energy Act does not exclude the application of antitrust rules to the energy undertakings.

It can thus be stated that the introduction and maintenance of competition and – equally important – consumer welfare[66] remain the common goals of antitrust and sector-specific regulation. The regulators, however, very often pursue various other goals connected mainly with the stability of supply of certain services and with consumers' safety. As Article 1.1 of the APCC states that the 'development of competition' (and not only the protection of existing competition) belongs to the competences of the Polish OPCC, one can argue that some proactive initiative to 'introduce' competition to a particular market is legitimate in the light of this provision.[67] Therefore, there is a possibility of doubled competences: of the regulator and of the President of the OPCC.[68]

2.2 Institutional Independence of Competition Authorities *versus* Institutional Independence of Regulators

From the point of view of institutional independence, the OPCC is structurally 'more independent' than the regulators, although not fully independent from the government. The OPCC is a central organ of the government administration accountable to the Prime Minister only (the Prime Minister nominates and dismisses the President of the OPCC, and also controls the activity of the office). The President of the OPCC participates in the meetings of the government and can directly influence the legislative initiatives undertaken by the government.[69] All of the regulators mentioned above are less independent institutionally, because they are controlled by the ministers responsible for the particular sectors.[70] Some authors even suggest that the real 'regulation' in Poland took place only in the telecommunication and energy sectors. This is

---

portal/en/17/67/Reports.html (accessed August 2014). For a critical assessment of ERO's activity see R. Guzik, 'Regulacja energetyki w kontekście prawa ochrony konkurencji' in *Amerykański i europejski system ochrony konkurencji* (Urząd Ochrony Konkurencji i Konsumentów 2007) 69.

66 Miąsik (n. 5 above) 33; Sage (n. 24 above) 139.

67 Thus, it resembles the first democratic law on competition protection from 1990, which was called the Antimonopoly Act. See Miąsik and Skoczny (n. 58 above) 29; A. Fornalczyk, 'Początki polityki konkurencji w Polsce' in M. Krasnodębska-Tomkiel (ed.), *Zmiany w polityce konkurencji na przestrzeni ostatnich dwóch dekad* (Urząd Ochrony Konkurencji i Konsumentów 2010) 419.

68 Guzik (n. 65 above) 74.

69 See Article 31.8 of the APCC of 2007.

70 Krasnodębska-Tomkiel (n. 18 above) 516–517.

because in all other domains the regulators do not possess enough independence and legislative guarantees of their powers to truly be able to introduce competition (as already mentioned, the main example of this is in the railway sector, where the regulator deals mainly with the safety rules and not competition matters).[71] The recently published OPCC policy for competition for the years 2011–2013 is supposed to concentrate on developing the competition in network industries, particularly railway transport, post and electronic media.[72]

The regulatory acts in the Polish legal system refer a lot to the notions and terminology of competition law. Because of this, competition law and regulation form two interlinked subsystems of Polish public economic law. However, as stressed by Hoff, under the Polish acts on regulation, the issues of control (Pol. *nadzór*) over undertakings dominate over the competition matters.[73] The Polish model of regulation thus combines two initially opposite ideas – the elements of control and the elements of economic freedom.[74] The sector-specific regulators mainly take into account the existence of market power and view market practices from the point of view of the incumbent and not of other market participants.[75] However, the regulators are not so much concerned with the actual practices undertaken by the incumbents, unlike the OPCC. Their perspective is thus different – they observe the market as such and not the particular behaviour of participants of the market, with the exception of those with significant market power (incumbents).[76] In this context, a paradoxical situation has occurred regarding the implementation of the Electronic Communication Package. Poland had been found liable under Article 258 TFEU[77] for a wrongful transposition of Directive

---

[71] Hoff (n. 35 above) 21. Król even argues that the liberalisation process in the Polish Retail Freight Transport Market occurred not 'because of "effective regulation" but despite its absence'. See Król (n. 42 above) 165. This author further critically assesses that the regulator 'does not even have the "desire to regulate"' and that it exists only 'in theory'. Ibid., 166.

[72] OPCC (n. 40 above) 5.

[73] Hoff (n. 35 above) 35–36.

[74] Hoff (n. 35 above) 46.

[75] Sage (n. 24 above) 147.

[76] Sage (n. 24 above) 151.

[77] Case C-227/07 *Commission v Poland* [2008] ECR I-8403. See also S. Piątek, 'Stopping the Creeping Telecom Regulation. Case Comment to the Judgment of the European Court of Justice of 13 November 2008 – European Commission v Republic of Poland' (2009) 2(2) *Yearbook Antitrust & Reg. Stud.* 229.

2002/19/EC (Access Directive),[78] because the Polish Telecommunication Act in its Article 26 allowed the regulator to impose an obligation on incumbents to negotiate access with a third party without any previous analysis of the scope of the competition on the market concerned. Thus, the regulator imposed an obligation to negotiate access to all telecommunication markets, regardless of the actual position of the incumbent in those markets. Accordingly, and paradoxically, the legal solution allowed for a situation in which the degree of competition was not an issue analysed by the regulator.

Apart from the fact that the OPCC and the regulators have different attitudes towards market participants, the regulators survey the markets themselves while the OPCC surveys the market participants. The Polish legislations concerning the different regulated industries are very different in scope and structure, so no coherent and concise regulatory policy can be identified among sectors.

3. APPLICATION OF COMPETITION LAW TO REGULATED SECTORS

In the traditional US antitrust doctrine, regulation has often been opposed to the antitrust rules.[79] In the EU version of such a relationship this type of opposition has never been clearly present.[80] The echoes of this US/EU division are also visible in the Polish practice. In parallel to the creation of regulatory acts and the introduction of regulators, there are quite often cases of abuse of dominant position in regulated sectors (though mainly in telecommunication).[81] Consequently, a question very much debated in the Polish doctrine is whether the use of sector-specific regulation excludes the use of competition rules, based on the presumption that regulation constitutes a *lex specialis*[82] in relation to competition

---

78 Directive 2002/19/EC of the European Parliament and of the Council of 7 March 2002 on access to, and interconnection of, electronic communication networks and associated facilities [2002] OJ L 108, p. 7.

79 See M. Maggiolino, 'The Regulatory Breakthrough of Competition Law: Definitions and Worries' in this volume.

80 Szablewski (n. 13 above) 19.

81 OPCC (n. 40 above) 5.

82 The source of this position is the resolution of the Polish Supreme Court of 7 December 2005, Case III SZP 3/05, denied in the further jurisprudence. See description by Stawicki (n. 34 above) 120 ff.

rules.[83] The provision in the APCC that might be perceived as allowing for such an interpretation is Article 3, which states: 'The provisions of the Act shall not apply to restrictions of competition allowed by the separate provisions.' This provision is sometimes interpreted as meaning that the APCC is a *lex generalis* to all other Polish legal acts concerning various aspects of competition in the Polish markets.[84] However, such interpretation has been criticised; under Article 3 APCC the behaviour of undertakings is covered by the APCC unless a specific act directly imposes on the undertaking an obligation that clashes with competition rules or directly excludes the application of APCC.[85] Therefore, the Polish antitrust rules should in principle be applied in all aspects of economic activity.[86] This is all the more so because any presumption of treating sector-specific regulation as *lex specialis* is not confirmed by the practice of the OPCC, where competition rules are also applied to regulated sectors, mainly the telecommunication sector.[87]

---

[83] Stawicki (n. 34 above) 117; J. Baehr and A. Stawicki, 'Rozważania wokół równoległego stosowania prawa konkurencji i instrumentów regulacyjnych' in C. Banasiński (ed.), *Ochrona konkurencji i konsumentów w Polsce i Unii Europejskiej* (Urząd Ochrony Konkurencji i Konsumentów 2006), 145; J. Baehr and A. Stawicki, 'Prawo energetyczne jako lex specialis w stosunku do przepisów ustawy o ochronie konkurencji i konsumentów' in C. Banasiński (ed.), *Prawo konkurencji – stan obecny oraz przewidywane kierunki zmian* (Urząd Ochrony Konkurencji i Konsumentów 2006) 132.

[84] See generally E. Kosiński, *Rodzaje i zakres sektorowych wyłączeń zastosowania ogólnych reguł konkurencji* (Wydawnictwo Naukowe UAM 2007) 202; Kohutek (n. 53 above) 80.

[85] D. Miąsik in T. Skoczny, D Miąsik and A Jurkowska (eds), *Ustawa o ochronie konkurencji i konsumentów. Komentarz* (C.H. Beck 2009) 3.

[86] This in fact corresponds to the way in which Articles 101 or 102 TFEU are applied. See Joined Cases C-159/91 and C-160/91 *Poucet and Pistre* [1993] ECR I-637, paras 18–19; Case C-364/92 *SAT Fluggesellschaft* [1994] ECR I-43, para 30.

[87] See judgments of the Supreme Court of 28 October 2003, Case I CK 179/02; of 15 July 2009, Case III SK 34/09; of 19 October 2006, Case SK 15/06. These judgment reflect the practice started by the decision of the European Commission of 21 May 2003, Joined Cases COMP/C-1/37.451, 37.578, 37.579 – *Deutsche Telekom AG*, [2003] OJ L 263, p. 9, confirmed by the former Court of First Instance in T-271/03 *Deutsche Telekom AG v. Commission* [2008] ECR II-477 and the Court of Justice in Case C-280/08 P *Deutsche Telekom AG v. Commission* [2010] ECR I- 9555). See also N. Petit, 'The Proliferation of National Regulatory Authorities alongside Competition Authorities: A Source of Jurisdictional Confusion' in D. Gerardin, R. Muñoz and N. Petit (eds), *Regulation Through Agencies in the EU: A New Paradigm of European Governance* (Edward Elgar Publishing 2005) 180; D. Geradin and R. O'Donoghue, 'The

The President of the OPCC is presumed to possess competences in all competition matters unless specific provisions transferred them to other administrative organs. If a different organ is competent to act, the President should not take action. Most of the Polish provisions on sector-specific regulations are not clear as far as this division of competences is concerned, allowing for 'concurrent application' of both antitrust and regulatory provisions.[88] The Polish Supreme Court has a tendency to perceive the competences of the OPCC President as 'general' and those of regulators as 'specific'.[89]

To add to this, some Polish authors argue that the strict separation between competition and sector-specific regulation renders the two ineffective and that thus they should be combined.[90] This parallel application of competition rules and regulation sometimes leads to a *ne bis in idem* argument and confusing effects, as is very well shown in the EU *Deutsche Telekom* saga. In this case, an undertaking acting in conformity with existing regulation was found guilty of infringing competition rules, despite the fact that it applied rates and prices under a tariff approved by the national regulator. It leaves open the question of whether such an approach does not undermine the very existence of sector-specific regulation, as the undertakings concerned cannot legitimately rely on the regulator's decisions. Rather, a 'certain degree of coordination' is required between the OPCC and the regulators, and certainly any focus on emphasising one's distinctiveness and major importance above the other authority is to be avoided.

The Polish Supreme Court has had an occasion to assess the scope of cooperation between the President of the OEC and the President of the OPCC. According to Article 25.2 of Telecommunication Act of 2004 (in a version before amendment in 2011), the regulatory decisions should

---

Concurrent Application of Competition Law and Regulation: the Case of Margin Squeeze Abuses in the Telecommunications Sector' (2005) 1 *J. Comp. L. & Econ.* 355; M. Szydło, *Prawo konkurencji a regulacja sektorowa* (Wolters Kluwer Polska 2010); C. Banasiński, 'Równoległe stosowanie instrumentów prawa konkurencji i instrumentów regulacyjnych w Polsce' in C Banasiński (ed.), *Prawo konkurencji – stan obecny* (Urząd Ochrony Konkurencji i Konsumentów 2006) 97.

[88] See for instance the judgment of 7 January 2004 of the Court of PCC, Case XVII Ama 24/03 *Polskie Górnictwo Naftowe I Gazownictwo v. President of OPCC* (on the possibility of using both Energy Act provisions and antitrust provisions to the same situation, according to the choice of those interested in the matter).

[89] Judgement of the Supreme Court of 25 May 2004, Case III SK 48/04.

[90] Sage (n. 24 above) 134 and 158; Szydło (n. 11 above) 97 and 315.

have been taken by the President of the OEC 'in agreement' with the President of the OPCC. In fact, the practice consisted of the President of the OPCC giving an assessment of a draft regulatory decision, on the basis of a description provided by the Office of Electronic Communications itself, on both the facts and the merits. Therefore, the regulatory decisions were rarely questioned. The Supreme Court held in 2011 that the mere preparation of an opinion by the President of the OPCC was not enough to treat the regulatory decision as adopted 'in agreement' with the President of the OPCC. The President of the OPCC should have more impact on the decision-making process and should be required to 'accept' the regulatory decision of the President of the OEC.[91] The need for cooperation and coordination of the national competition authorities and regulators is also underlined on the international level[92] so that the two types of authorities apply the same 'competition culture'.[93]

Apart from the problem of cooperation between the OPCC and regulators, there are examples of real parallel exercise of powers of the OPCC and the regulator, where the actions undertaken by the regulator might be described as 'inefficient'. Thus, the Polish telecom incumbent, Telekomunikacja Polska (TP), has been held liable by the President of the OPCC for abusing its dominant position by conduct consisting of imposition of unfair prices in local markets for services of leasing telecommunications' technical channel systems,[94] despite the fact that the regulator should have corrected this type of behaviour. TP has been also held liable and fined for abuse in the market for origination of inter-regional and international connections in fixed telecom networks and in the access market to these connection services.[95] Interestingly, the discussion on the 'competition' of competences between the Polish OPCC and the regulator has been transferred to the European level. On

---

[91] Judgment of the Supreme Court of 2 February 2011, Case III SK 18/10, cited by K. Kosmala, 'Legislative and Jurisprudential Developments in the Telecommunication Sector in 2011' (2012) 5(7) *Yearbook Antitrust & Reg. Stud.* 219. At present, Article 25.1 of the Telecommunication Act merely requires a non-binding opinion from the President of the OPCC.

[92] OECD, Global Forum on Competition, The Relationship Between Competition Authorities and Sectoral Regulators, DAF/COMP/GF(2005)2.

[93] Z. Muras and M. Swora (eds), *Prawo energetyczne. Komentarz*, LEX el (Wolters Kluwer Polska 2010).

[94] Judgment of the Court of Appeals of 27 May 2009, Case VI Aca 1407/08 *Telekomunikacja Polska v President of OPCC.*

[95] Judgment of the Court of Competition and Consumer Protection of 17 June 2009, Case XVII Ama 102/08 (*Telekomunikacja Polska v President of OPCC*). Both judgments are cited by Jurkowska-Gomułka (n. 50 above) 218.

22 July 2011 the European Commission issued its first decision addressed to a Polish company in the telecom sector – *Telekomunikacja Polska*.[96] The European Commission stated that TP abused its dominant position in two Polish markets for wholesale broadband services by refusing to grant access to its fixed telephone network to alternative operators. The national regulation and the EU regulation required of TP, as an operator with significant market power on the fixed public telephone network, that it grant access to alternative operators both to the wholesale broadband and to the local loop and that it publish a so-called reference offer. The European Commission identified TP as the only supplier of wholesale markets for broadband and local loop in Poland. It also found that TP had a high market share in the retail market. The alternative operators were in fact blocked by TP, which proposed *inter alia* unreasonable conditions for access to its network and wholesale broadband products, denied access negotiations and obstructed the implementation of access agreements already signed. It also refused to give alternative operators information on the technical specifications of its equipment that was necessary for the alternative operators to operate.

What is interesting, in the context of this text, is that TP raised several arguments contesting the European Commission's competence to act, because the telecom sector is highly regulated in Polish law and is supervised by the national regulator (the OEC). There existed a set of OEC decisions fining TP for not fulfilling the obligations to grant access to the network and imposing on TP commitments that it would not treat alternative operators in a discriminatory manner. The European Commission invoked the *Deutsche Telekom* case and argued that TP had not changed its behaviour despite the regulator's decisions.[97] The OEC's practice of regulating the tariff for broadband access without a previous market analysis required by the Electronic Communication Framework Directive had been condemned by the European Court of Justice in 2010.[98]

However it should also be underlined that the decisions of regulators can make an undertaking immune from antitrust liability in a way defined

---

[96] Commission Decision of 22 July 2011, Case COMP/39.525 – *Telekomunikacja Polska* [2011] OJ C 324, p. 7. See also D. Kamiński, A. Rogozińska and B. Sasinowska, 'Telekomunikacja Polska Decision: Competition Law Enforcement in Regulated Markets' (2011) 3 *Comp. Pol. Newsletter 3*; Kuik and Mościbroda (n. 7 above) 164–167.

[97] Kuik and Mościbroda (n. 7 above) 167.

[98] Case C-545/08 *Commission v. Poland* [2010] ECR I-53; Kuik and Mościbroda (n. 7 above) 180.

in the European doctrine of the 'state action defence'.[99] In a judgment of 2010, the Polish Supreme Court stated that 'the decision [of the President of the OEC imposing a certain obligation on an incumbent undertaking] caused behaviour judged by the President [of the OPCC] as a practice limiting competition to become an allowable limitation of competition as defined in Article 3 of the APCC'.[100] Thus, if the regulator takes action, its decision imposing obligations on an undertaking might be seen as a 'state action' that immunises an undertaking from antitrust liability, provided that any autonomous behaviour of the undertaking concerned is excluded.

4. APPLICATION OF COMPETITION LAW *AS* REGULATION

For the purposes of this text, the possibility of applying antitrust rules *as* regulation is understood as situations where the President of OPCC issues decisions that can be perceived as having a regulatory character in that they tend to reorganise the market instead of just prohibiting anti-competitive practices. The two previous Presidents of the OPCC confirm, in a joint article, the possibility that competition law might be used to support regulation of the market.[101]

In the Polish practice of recent years (mainly decisions issued in 2012 are analysed) the examples of using antitrust law as a regulatory tool appear mainly in *commitment* decisions of the Polish Competition Authority. Up until 2011 there was no doubt (statistically) that the most frequently used instrument of the OPCC remained the infringement decision, regulated in Article 10 in conjunction with Article 106 of the APCC. However, in 2012 commitment decisions outnumbered infringement decisions, as for 30 infringement decisions there were 37 commitment decisions.[102] An infringement decision establishes a breach of competition law, sometimes imposes positive obligations and often levies fines that fulfil deterrence functions. Thus, it clearly informs the market

---

[99] Very clearly in the judgment of the Supreme Court of 15 July 2009, Case SK 34/08 *Polskie Górnictwo Naftowe i Gazownictwo S.A. v President of OPCC* (in a case of an incumbent's refusal to supply gas).

[100] Judgement of the Supreme Court of 17 March 2010, Case III SK 40/09, at para 7.

[101] Banasiński and Krasnodębska-Tomkiel (n. 31 above) 18.

[102] See Report of the OPCC for 2012, p. 11, available at: http://uokik.gov.pl/sprawozdania_z_dzialalnosci_urzedu.php (accessed August 2014).

participants what behaviour is unacceptable in the eyes of the President of the OPCC. However, obtaining such a decision implies serious enforcement costs.[103] One of the possible negotiated enforcement instruments that allow the OPCC to avoid those costs while restoring competition is the commitment decision (the other is the leniency procedure in cartel cases). The main source of inspiration for introducing commitment decisions in the Polish legal order was Article 9 of Regulation 1/2003.[104] Commitment decisions have been issued by the President of the OPCC since 1 May 2004 and, as then explained, they were presented as a way of restoring effective competition in a more efficient way than by imposition of fines.[105] They were first introduced by an amendment to the APCC of 2000, just before Polish accession to the EU, and at present they are disciplined in Article 12 of the APCC.[106] In the first years of their application, the President of the OPCC issued a surprisingly low number of commitment decisions.[107] At present, their use is gradually growing,[108] probably because the undertakings have learnt how to use this tool and how to propose the commitments.

---

[103] Kozieł (n. 21 above) 74; A. Gill and M. Swora, 'Decyzja zobowiązująca jako metoda rozwiązywania sporów w postępowaniu przed Prezesem Urzędu Ochrony Konkurencji i Konsumentów' (2005) 3 *Kwartalnik Prawa Prywatnego* 107.

[104] Proposal for amendment of the Competition and Consumer Protection Act and several other Acts of 20.02.2004 (Druk Sejmowy no. 2561), point III.4 of the memorandum attached to the proposal.

[105] Ibid. It has to be underlined that in Article 89 of the previous version of the ACPP of 2000 there existed a 'settled solution', consisting of a possibility that the President of the OPCC would not levy a fine in cases of minor violation where an undertaking admitted to having engaged in an anticompetitive practice. See Kozieł (n. 21 above) 75.

[106] It provides in its 1 paragraph: 'In the event that, in the course of antimonopoly proceedings, it has been rendered plausible – on the basis of the circumstances of a given case, information comprised in the notification or information forming the basis for instituting ex officio proceedings – that the prohibition referred to in Article 6 or Article 9 of the Act, or in Article 81 or 82 of the EC Treaty, has been infringed, whereas the undertaking being charged with having infringed such prohibition has agreed to take or discontinue certain actions aiming at preventing those infringements, then the President of the Office may, by way of a decision, impose upon the undertaking an obligation to exercise the undertaken commitments.'

[107] The phenomenon and its possible reasons are described by Kozieł (n. 21 above) 89.

[108] On the basis of yearly reports presented by the OPCC (available at: http://uokik.gov.pl/sprawozdania_z_dzialalnosci_urzedu.php, accessed August

One of the first identified examples of the 'regulatory-like ambitions' of the OPCC can be seen in a commitment decision by its President in the *POLSAT* case, declaring that 'the commitment in question should be regarded in a broader sense as an attempt to create *positive market behaviours* for the transmission of major sporting events'.[109] In this decision the OPCC obliged the Polish TV Station transmitting the 2008 European football championship to buy back the decoders that it first sold and that were necessary for watching the Euro 2008.

As at the EU level, the Polish OPCC is facing a major challenge (and choice) as far as commitment decisions are concerned. This relatively new instrument is close to the private law instruments, with the vital difference that the possible negotiations are conducted between a public authority that is supposed to protect a widely defined public interest and a supposed infringer (or infringers) of competition law. As Florian Wagner-Von Papp puts it, in such circumstances 'there is a danger that the struggle for law is abandoned in favour of discretionary case-to-case negotiations'.[110] The behaviour that might constitute an infringement might pass unnoticed. In July 2012 the Polish Competition Authority

---

2014) the (approximate) numbers are as follows: in 2005 in the general number of 144 decisions there were eight commitment decisions in cases on abuse of dominant position and one decision in a case concerning vertical agreement; in 2006 in the general number of 202 decisions there were seven commitment decisions in cases of abuse of dominant position and one decision in a case concerning vertical agreement; in further years the reports for 2007 to 2011 do not give precise numbers of commitment decisions issued by the President of the OPCC; in 2012, 37 commitment decisions were issued. The general analysis reveals that they were mainly issued in cases of abuse of dominant position and their number per year before 2012 was about 20.

[109] Decision DOK-1/2010 *Cyfrowy Polsat*, p. 40 (emphasis added); cited by Kozieł (n. 21 above) 85.

[110] F. Wagner-Von Papp, 'Best and Even Better Practices in Commitment Procedures after Alrosa: The Dangers of Abandoning the "Struggle for Competition Law"' (2012) 3 *C.M.L. Rev.* 930. The same author explains the reasons why the competition authority might be less reliable as an agent acting for the public interest in such proceedings than in the usual antitrust procedure: (1) the competition authority does not have the benefit of a full investigation into the facts; (2) without this full investigation into the facts, the adequacy and the proportionality of the remedies can be assessed only tentatively; (3) comments by third parties in the market test procedure need not reflect the full extent of the public interest at stake; (4) another distinguishing feature between the infringement procedure and the commitment procedure is the difference in the dynamic interaction that develops in an adversarial setting on the one hand, and a consensual setting on the other hand. Ibid., 946.

issued guidelines on commitment decisions concerning practices limiting competition or practices infringing collective interests of consumers.[111] Limiting ourselves to the part of the guidelines related to competition law, it should be stressed that the declared aim of a commitment decision issued by the President of the OPCC is to 'eliminate such acts of undertakings that infringe competition'.[112]

It is a prerogative of the OPCC to issue commitment decisions, and not an obligation (it is the OPCC's choice whether to use its powers). It is up to the undertakings concerned to formulate the commitments in the first place.[113] Then it is up to the OPCC to accept the commitments, suggest modifications to them or refuse them. However, some authors are of the opinion that 'nothing should prevent the authority from indicating to the investigated company that the case may be solved by committing to refrain from adopting certain actions',[114] thus clearly the autonomy of undertakings in formulating the actual commitments might be in fact less than declared.

The commitment decision is issued once two conditions are fulfilled: (1) there is a probability, exposed during the proceedings, that there is an infringement of Article 6 or 9 of the APCC; and (2) there is a commitment proposed by an undertaking to take or to block certain defined actions in order to prevent infringements. The President of the OPCC can accept a commitment if a violation of competition 'has been rendered plausible'. An infringement does not need to be proven with full certainty; it is enough that its existence is seen as probable and credible. A violation of competition rules is plausible 'if [the OPCC President] considers it to be obviously more probable than any other alternative solution to the practice in question'.[115] The probability of infringement is identified on the basis of circumstances of the case, the information obtained by the OPCC or any other information that influenced the Office's decision to initiate the proceedings concerning a possible

---

[111] OPCC, *Wyjaśnienia w sprawie wydawania decyzji zobowiązującej w sprawach praktyk ograniczających konkurencję oraz praktyk naruszających zbiorowe interesy konsumentów*, available at: https://uokik.gov.pl/ (accessed August 2014).

[112] Ibid., 8.

[113] As underlined in the Polish doctrine, it is one of the main advantages of this procedure from the point of view of market participants. See Kozieł (n. 21 above) 75; Z. Kmieciak, *Mediacje i koncyliacje w polskim prawie administracyjnym* (Zakamycze 2004) 18.

[114] Kozieł (n. 21 above) 77.

[115] Ibid., 78.

infringement of Article 6 or 9 of the APCC. The President is not obliged to lead an extensive investigation to prove the supposed practice; the OPCC should only find out that there is a serious probability that the infringement has taken place.

According to the guidelines, the commitments proposed by an undertaking should lead to the prevention of infringement either by taking up a particular practice or by ceasing a particular practice. The President of OPCC will accept the commitments proposed by an undertaking and impose on it the obligation to fulfil those commitments by a decision only in cases where the realisation (fulfilment) of the proposed commitment would eliminate the supposed practice or its consequences.

The guidelines state clearly that in the cases concerning agreements limiting competition, because of the character of such practices, the commitments can be accepted by the OPCC only in 'exceptional circumstances'.[116] In other cases where commitment decisions can be issued, the OPCC should consider the seriousness of alleged infringement and its actual or potential consequences for the market. Practice shows that the vast majority of commitment decisions concern the presumed abuses of dominant positions and not agreements between undertakings. This results in commitment decisions resembling the decisions issued by the regulators as they are directed towards those who dominate the relevant market and contain positive obligations imposed on those dominating firms. When an undertaking proposes commitments, it should formulate them in a way allowing for elimination of either the alleged practice or its consequences. The content of the commitments should be directly linked with the alleged infringement. In fact, the proposal of commitments should be an answer to the charges posed by the OPCC and it should clearly indicate how the fulfilment of commitments would lead to the elimination of the alleged infringing practice. If the commitment is

[116] This is an important novelty, as before the issue of guidelines, commitment decisions were issued in all kinds of competition restriction, including hard-core violations, e.g. Decision DOK-3/2008 *Xella Polska et al.* (where the removal of a minimum resale price clause was accepted as one of the commitments) as cited by Kozieł (n. 21 above) 82. See also the interpretation of Article 12 APCC suggested by Miąsik (n. 85 above) 740. The guidelines stress that such practices usually have a significant negative influence on competition and the parties to such agreements benefit from them. A commitment decision cannot be issued if the alleged practice consists of: (1) direct or indirect price fixing or other conditions of sale (price cartels); (2) limiting or control of production, sale or technical development or investment (contingency agreements); (3) division of markets (division agreements); (4) agreements concerning bid rigging (bid-rigging cartels).

intended to eliminate the consequences of alleged practice, it is up to the undertaking concerned to indicate what consequences the practice might have for the market and how they would be eliminated by the commitments.

The commitments might include various actions that could lead to the elimination of alleged infringements. But they must remain in direct connection with the practice that is the object of proceedings. If the undertaking concerned is charged with several accusations, the commitments proposed by this undertaking should be defined separately for each of the alleged practices. The commitment cannot consist of a general declaration that the undertaking concerned will in future eliminate the alleged practices. For instance, the undertaking concerned cannot limit itself to a general obligation that it would not abuse its dominant position in the future by imposing onerous terms and conditions on contractors.[117] When analysing the proposed commitments, the OPCC should mainly consider whether they could eliminate the infringements. The Office can – when refusing the proposed commitments – suggest what other form they can take, unless they are strictly necessary for preventing infringements.[118]

An obligatory element of the commitment decision is the setting by the OPCC of an obligation on the undertaking concerned to report in a set timeframe on the fulfilment of commitments so that the OPCC can ascertain itself whether and how the commitments have been fulfilled. Depending on the practices that are the subject-matter of the commitment decision, the decision may consist of imposing an obligation to provide a periodical update on the status of fulfilment of the decision, or it might be just a single notification. The OPCC should inform the undertaking of the type of information (proof) required in the indicated timeframe. The guidelines stress that commitment decisions should aim at eliminating the practices infringing competition and thus forbid the introduction of

---

[117] The term 'onerous terms and conditions' was defined by the Supreme Court in its judgment of 16 October 2008, Case III SK 8/08, as a term that 'constitutes for one party of an agreement a burden bigger than commonly accepted in a certain type of relationships'; as cited by A. Jurkowska-Gomułka, 'Key Legislative and Jurisprudential Developments of Polish Antitrust Law in 2011' (2012) 5(7) *Yearbook Antitrust & Reg. Stud.* 206. See also judgment of 15 July 2011, Case VI Aca 1301/10 *Dolnośląska Spółka Gazownictwa*, where the Court of Appeals confirmed that an onerous term consists of placing on one of the parties a burden heavier than commonly accepted; cited by the same author, p. 207.

[118] Kohutek (n. 53 above) 436; Miąsik (n. 85 above) 745.

commitments not connected with the presumed infringement of competition. This should limit the possibility of widespread use of commitment decisions as regulatory decisions, excluding a too proactive attitude of the President of OPCC.

In its practice, the Polish OPCC has as yet usually issued commitment decisions in cases concerning abuse of dominant position in two sets of cases: (1) concerning restrictions of access to essential facilities[119] or (2) imposing unfair contractual conditions.[120] In such cases the usual commitments issued by the OPCC consist of: (1) an obligation to change the onerous conditions in the contracts;[121] (2) an obligation to change the terms of contracts concluded by the undertaking concerned;[122] and (3) an obligation to allow competitors to use elements of infrastructure (for instance to use bus stops of the dominant local transport agency).[123] According to the Polish Supreme Court, the President of the OPCC does not have powers to intervene in the 'price policy' of any undertaking in a relevant market.[124] Because of this statement, the President of the OPCC does not use those commitment decisions in the domain traditionally attributed to regulators, namely price and tariff fixing,[125] but the OPCC

---

[119] Cited by Kozieł (n. 21 above) 82; Decisions of 26 November 2009, Case RGD-36/2009 *Białogard City*; and of 7 February 2008, Case RŁO-3/2008 *Łódź City* (access to a bus stop). Cf. also Szydło (n. 11 above) 109 ff.

[120] Kozieł (n. 21 above) 82, cites the following decisions: Decision No. RPZ-7/2009 *Miejskie Przedsiębiorstwo Wodociągów i Kanalizacji Sp. z o. o. w Lesznie* (obliging waste-collecting firms to deliver it to a particular site); Decisions of 16 March 2009, Case RKT-06/2009 *Wodociągi i Kanalizacja 'AKWA' Sp. z o.o. w Nysie*; of 11 June 2008, Case RWR-24/2008 *Przedsiębiorstwo Komunalne, 'PEKOM' S.A. w Żarach*; of 28 August 2007; and Case RWA-27/2007 *Zakład Wodociągów, Kanalizacji i Oczyszczalnia Ścieków 'WOD-KAN' Sp. z o.o. w Mławie* (unfair contractual conditions imposed by dominant undertakings in water supply agreements).

[121] Decisions of the President of the OPCC, Case RPZ-6/2008 ENEA Operator Sp. z o.o. z siedzibą w Poznaniu; and Case RWA-27/2007 Zakład Wodociągów, Kanalizacji i Oczyszczalnia Ścieków 'WOD-KAN' Sp. z o.o. w Mławie.

[122] Decisions of the President of the OPCC, Case RWR-24/2008 *Przedsiębiorstwo Komunalne, 'PEKOM' S.A. w Żarach*; and Case RPZ-13/2007 *Miejskie Przedsiębiorstwo Energetyki Cieplnej, Wodociągów i Kanalizacji sp. z o.o. w Środzie Wielkopolskiej.*

[123] Decision of the President of the OPCC, Case RŁO-3/2008 *Łódź City*. See Miąsik (n. 85 above) 774.

[124] Judgement of the Supreme Court of 17 March 2010, Case III SK 40/09, p. 9.

[125] For example in the energy sector. See Guzik (n. 65 above) 69.

certainly intervenes in the terms of agreements of those undertakings with their clients and consumers.

The majority of commitment decisions in 2012 were issued in matters concerning essential facilities in local markets of energy, gas or water supply or, on a rare occasion, of sewage disposal. In the jurisprudence of the Supreme Court, an essential facility is understood as 'the infrastructure that is necessary for the development of competition because it cannot be replaced and there is no possibility of duplicating it'.[126] In the vast majority of commitment decisions issued in 2012, the probable anticompetitive practice was carried out by dominant undertakings possessing a monopoly over local infrastructures that could be understood as essential facilities.[127] Because a commitment decision can only be issued if the interested undertaking applies for it, one can presume that those concerned came to the conclusion that commitment decisions were the best possible solution – they avoid the statement of infringement for some commitments that might be of regulatory character, for instance by imposing on the undertaking concerned broader obligations towards their customers or competitors. Thus, the President of the OPCC is in fact 'replacing' the regulator in its function of regulating the market. However, the obligations 'imposed' so far were mainly focused on guaranteeing consumer (user) welfare rather than the entry of competitors into the market (though such cases also occurred).[128] Thus those commitment

---

[126] Judgment of the Supreme Court of 17 March 2010, Case III SK 40/09.

[127] Decision of 9 November 2012, Case RKR-47/2012 *Rejonowe Przedsiębiorstwo Wodociągów i Kanalizacji w Brzesku sp. z o.o*; Decision of 25 June 2012, Case RGD-11/2012 *Miejskie Przedsiębiorstwo Infrastruktury KOS-EKO*; Decision of 29 June 2012, Case RŁO-41/2012 *Przedsiębiorstwo Komunalne Konstantynów Łódzki z o.o.*; Decision of 29 June 2012, Case RPZ-12/2012 *Przedsiębiorstwo Wodociągów i Kanalizacji w Nowym Tomyślu sp. z o.o.*; Decision of 12 June 2012, Case RGD-13/2012 *Wodociągi Ustka sp. z o.o.*; Decision of 18 July 2012, Case RGD 14/2012 *Regionalne Wodociągi i Kanalizacja sp. z o.o.*; Decision of 19 July 2012, Case RWR 25/2012 *POMAK sp. z o.o.*; Decision of 23 July 2012, Case RKR-25/2012 *Sanockie Przedsiębiorstwo Gospodarki Komunalnej sp. z o.o.*; Decision of 27 July 2012, Case RKR-28/2012 *Przedsiębiostwo Wodociągów i Kanalizacji sp. z o.o. w Przemyślu*; Decision of 6 August 2012, Case RBG-18/2012 – *Gmina Łukta*; Decision of 21 August 2012, Case RKR-33/2012 – *Gmina Biecz.*

[128] As in a decision upheld by the Court of Appeals – where the dominant undertaking was judged to 'counteract the formation of conditions necessary for creation of competition' – in a judgment of 27 May 2009, Case VI Aca 1404/08 *Katowice Commune*.

decisions mainly introduced elements of 'restorative justice',[129] having as an aim the protection of customers of the offender. One can doubt whether this is an appropriate attitude. The OPCC should 'resist the temptation to use commitments as a means of market regulation' because of their individual and voluntary nature as well as because they are based on the mere plausibility of infringement of competition.[130]

5. CONCLUSION

As demonstrated, the objectives of the APCC allow for an interpretation of the prerogatives of the President of the OPCC such that the competition decisions become decisions with some regulatory flavour, i.e. decisions that modify the market and do not just eliminate an anti-competitive practice. If the ultimate and dominant aim of the APCC is consumer welfare, together with the aim of protection of competition in a given market, such decisions might be perceived as acceptable. However, the division of tasks and competences between the OPCC and regulators is blurred, and might – if no cooperation between those two authorities takes place – lead to incoherence and uncertainty as to the state strategy for rendering a particular market more competitive (or in fact, competitive at all). It may be thus stated that the regulators should retain their *monopoly of action* in two types of situations:

1. The first set of circumstances appears where there is a dominant undertaking not abusing its dominant position. In cases of abuse of a dominant position both the OPCC and the regulators are able to act, doubling their efforts not only to maintain but also to create competition in a relevant market. There is, however, no abuse if for instance an incumbent refuses to grant access to the infrastructure for objectively justified reasons.[131]
2. The second possibility occurs in situations in which the regulator has taken action and imposed on the relevant undertaking such obligations that there is no scope for any autonomous conduct on the part of this undertaking – and thus no scope for the application

[129] Kozieł (n. 21 above) 86, who considers that it is not one of the aims of the APCC.

[130] Kozieł (n. 21 above) 85. The author cites the resolution of the Supreme Court of 23 July 2008, Case III CZP 52/08.

[131] So clearly in the judgment of the Supreme Court of 15 July 2009, Case III SK 34/08.

of competition rules. Otherwise, the very essence of regulation would be endangered, and the logic of regulator's actions would be called into question.[132] However, if the regulator only allows for certain behaviours of the undertaking concerned (for instance and mainly: for the refusal of access to infrastructure) then the application of competition rules should not be blocked.

Thus, it can be stated that in the Polish context it might be legitimate to use competition rules as regulation. The goals of both the APCC and sector-specific acts are similar – they intend to protect and maintain competition and strive for consumers' welfare. However, the aims of regulation are more extensive – the regulators are of course supposed to introduce and maintain competition on certain markets but they should also guarantee continuity, quality and affordability of services, and in some cases impose conditions for the granting of universal services. Therefore, the regulators protect consumers and users in a broader way than the OPCC. One should note that any institutional 'competition' between the regulators and the OPCC is to be avoided. In fact, the pluralism of authorities aiming to protect public interest can be perceived as a solution for the possible regulatory failures[133] of regulators – at least as far as the protection of competition is concerned.

In addition, especially in cases concerning the abuse of dominant position, the actions undertaken by the President of the OPCC are very often not repressive and reactive, but proactive in a sense that the remedies in the form of commitments are often imposed on the undertakings concerned, forcing them both to allow for some competition on the market and to provide a broader protection for users/consumers. The danger connected with such a solution is that the expertise of the OPCC in proactive measures (like measures that should eliminate cross-subsidization) might be less than the expertise of specialised regulators – and thus any such proactive action might turn out to be of more detriment than benefit to competition on the market. The double effort of the OPCC and the regulators directed towards the same practice might be also perceived as breaching the principle of proportionality – the general constitutional principle that stems also from recommendations of the

---

[132] A. Stawicki, *Commentary to Article 3 of APCC*, LEX el. (Wolters Kluwer Polska 2011).

[133] A. Lipowski, 'Ekonomiczna zawodność państwa – krytyczna analiza ujęcia antyetatystycznego' (2002) 2 *Ekonomista* 170.

Council of Europe for administrative actions[134] and from various provisions of primary and secondary EU law.[135]

The possible negative consequences of the regulatory approach to competition rules is mainly linked to the lack of legal certainty for undertakings, connected with the lack of coherence of this part of the Polish legal system. This lack of coherence can create higher costs for undertakings and a general insecurity as to what to expect from the state. The 'state action defence' seems to be an unworkable tool in this context unless a regulator imposes an obligation on the undertaking concerned. It also calls into question the autonomy of regulators as against the President of the OPCC. It should be borne in mind, however, that not all the regulators[136] in Poland are really willing to use their powers to protect and introduce competition and therefore the intervention by the President of the OPCC is a good way to supplement their actions (or mainly their reluctance or failure to take unpopular decisions). The overlap between the competition and regulatory areas of Polish law might thus act as a stimulator for broader procompetitive actions of regulators themselves.

---

[134] Resolution (77) 31 on the protection of the individual in relation to the acts of administrative authorities (adopted on 28 September 1977), available at: http://www.dhv-speyer.de/stelkens/Materialien/Resolution_(77)31.pdf (accessed August 2014); Article 5 Recommendation CM/Rec(2007)7 of the Committee of Ministers to member states on good administration, available at: https://wcd.coe.int/ViewDoc.jsp?id=1155877 (accessed August 2014).

[135] See Article 5(4) TFEU. See also Recital 12 to the Council Regulation (EC) No 1/2003 of 16 December 2002 on the implementation of the rules on competition laid down in Articles 81 and 82 of the Treaty, [2003] OJ L 1, p. 1.

[136] Critically on the energy sector: Szablewski (n. 13 above) 211–256.

8. Enforcement of competition rules in regulated industries: abuse of dominance practices in the new EU Member States, candidate countries and potential candidates

Alexandr Svetlicinii and Marco Botta

1. INTRODUCTION

This chapter analyses the pattern of enforcement of Article 102 TFEU and its national equivalents in regulated industries by the National Competition Authorities (NCAs) of the new EU Member States and candidate countries. While the European Commission enforces Article 102 TFEU in the context of its market liberalization agenda, the NCAs of the selected jurisdictions often enforce Article 102 TFEU and its national equivalents in order to protect final consumers. In particular, while the EU Commission has focused its enforcement on exclusionary conduct and has adopted structural and behavioural remedies via commitment decisions, the NCAs of the selected jurisdictions have mainly sanctioned exploitative conduct, such as excessive pricing and unfair contractual conditions.

The enforcement of competition rules is one of the most important EU policies contributing to the functioning of the EU internal market. In particular, in the industries which have recently been liberalized and opened to competition, the EU competition rules co-exist with the relevant sector-specific regulation. In the context of the EU enlargement process, EU candidate countries have been required to introduce competition rules in their national legislation, as well as to transpose at the national level the EU liberalization Directives. The 'copy-pasting' of the EU competition rules in small, concentrated, emerging economies has provoked some criticisms concerning the functionality of this approach.[1] For various reasons the transplantation of the EU rules and standards did not always translate into their effective enforcement.

The current chapter aims at contributing to the debate concerning the effectiveness of transposition of the EU competition rules in the new EU Member States, candidate countries and potential candidates by analysing the pattern of enforcement of Article 102 TFEU and its national equivalents in these jurisdictions in relation to regulated industries. The chapter builds upon research previously conducted by the authors.[2] In comparison to the authors' previous work, this chapter is based on a new dataset, focusing exclusively on the enforcement of abuse of dominance in regulated industries. Application of Article 102 TFEU is particularly relevant in monopolistic markets, where the former monopolists or current incumbents preserve a large degree of market power even after market liberalization. This chapter thus aims to shed light on the complex relationship between competition law and sector-specific regulation in the new EU Member States, candidate countries and potential candidates for EU accession.

The following analysis primarily focuses on the enforcement of Article 102 TFEU and its national equivalents in network industries, where the ownership of infrastructure or exclusive rights granted by the national or local authorities create uncontested dominance within the relevant market for the former monopolists or current state-owned or privatized incumbents. Network industries are usually characterized by the presence of a National Regulatory Authority (NRA), entrusted with the enforcement of sector-specific regulations which affect the competitive conditions in the relevant markets. The NRAs would normally condition market entry by granting licences to operate, by fixing the retail tariffs of the services provided, by approving the standard agreements and commercial practices including access offers and inter-connection agreements. The network industries covered by this study include telecommunications (i.e. fixed and mobile telephony as well as Internet), TV broadcasting services, electricity supply and distribution, water and sewage services, district heating and natural gas distribution. Other highly regulated industries addressed by this survey include postal services and trade in petroleum products.

---

[1] In relation to the positive and negative effects of transplanting Article 102 TFEU to other jurisdictions, see M. Gal, 'The "Cut and Paste" of Article 82 of the EC Treaty in Israel: Conditions for a Successful Transplant' (2007) 9 *Eur. J. L. Reform* 467.

[2] A. Svetlicinii and M. Botta, 'Article 102 TFEU as a Tool of Market Regulation' (2012) 8 *Eur. Comp. J.* 473.

From a geographical point of view, the comparative study covers nine jurisdictions (i.e. Albania, Bosnia and Herzegovina, Bulgaria, Croatia, Macedonia,[3] Moldova,[4] Montenegro, Romania, Serbia[5]).[6] The selected jurisdictions include both new EU Member States (Bulgaria, Croatia,[7] Romania), as well as candidate countries (Macedonia, Montenegro, Serbia) and potential candidates (Albania, Bosnia and Herzegovina, Moldova) for EU accession. In spite of the different stages of the EU integration process, these jurisdictions share a number of common features in relation to the pattern of enforcement of Article 102 TFEU and its national equivalents in network industries. The enforcement record of the selected NCAs was surveyed in the reference period 2007–2012. This six-year term reflects the most recent developments in the enforcement practices, and it is lengthy enough for identification of prevailing enforcement trends. More specifically, this is the period when Bulgaria and Romania have been acting as EU Member States. For the NCAs in the EU candidate countries and potential candidates this period

---

[3] For a review on competition law enforcement in Macedonia see R. Karova and M. Botta, 'Five Years of Enforcement of Competition Law in the Republic of Macedonia – Time for an Assessment' (2010) 2 *Medit. Comp. Bull.* 56, available at: http://ec.europa.eu/competition/publications/mediterranean/mcb_2.pdf (accessed 30 June 2015).

[4] For a review of competition law enforcement in Moldova see A. Svetlicinii, 'Enforcement of Competition Law in the Republic of Moldova: One Year On' (2008) 29 *E.C.L.R.* 532; A. Svetlicinii, 'New Competition Law of the Republic of Moldova: Prospects and Concerns' (2013) 6 *Österreichische Zeitschrift für Kartellrecht* 210.

[5] For a review of competition law enforcement in Serbia see A. Svetlicinii, 'Competition Law Enforcement in Serbia: Problems and Prospects' (2012) 33 *E.C.L.R.* 273.

[6] Albania (1 decision, NCA: http://www.caa.gov.al/), Bosnia and Herzegovina (4 decisions, NCA: http://www.bihkonk.gov.ba/), Bulgaria (11 decisions, NCA: http://www.cpc.bg/), Croatia (14 decisions, http://www.aztn.hr/), Macedonia (6 decisions, NCA: http://www.kzk.gov.mk/), Moldova (5 decisions, NCA: http://competition.md/), Montenegro (1 decision, NCA: http://www.azzk.me/), Romania (5 decisions, NCA: http://www.consiliulconcurentei.ro/), Serbia (3 decisions, NCA: http://www.kzk.gov.rs/). The websites were last accessed on 30 June 2015. The comments on some of the selected decisions were published in the *e-Competitions Bulletin*, available at: http://www.concurrences.com/

[7] During the period covered by this survey Croatia was an acceding country. The EU and Croatia signed Croatia's EU Accession Treaty on 9 December 2011. Croatia became the EU's 28th Member State on 1 July 2013. See http://ec.europa.eu/enlargement/countries/detailed-country-information/croatia/index_en.htm (accessed 30 June 2015).

has been especially important due to the procedural and substantive reforms of the competition legislation of these countries.

Instead of conducting an overall descriptive review of the enforcement of abuse of dominance in each of the selected countries, we have conducted a cross-country analysis, focusing on four factors. The *first* issue regards the types of infringement of Article 102 TFEU and its national equivalents sanctioned by the NCAs of the selected jurisdictions in regulated industries. In this respect, the study attempts to identify and explain the decisive factors that determined the NCA's decision to intervene and what type of substantive infringements of competition rules have been treated by the NCAs as enforcement priorities. The *second* comparative factor analysed in the study concerns the remedies applied by the NCAs towards undertakings engaged in abusive practices. The overview of the remedies highlights the degree to which the NCAs are prepared to become involved in market regulation. The *third* indicator used in this comparative study concerns the role of the judicial review in the selected jurisdictions. This indicator aims at understanding how the regulatory approach to the enforcement of competition rules is treated by the national courts, and whether the judicial review has any impact on the shaping of the enforcement priorities of the NCAs. Finally, the *fourth* element of our study addresses the issue of coordination between the NCAs and NRAs, where competition rules are enforced by the NCAs in the regulated markets supervised by the NRAs.

In order to place this comparative study in the EU context, this chapter starts with an overview of the interaction of competition and regulation in the regulated industries within the EU. In particular, the paper provides an overview of the patterns of enforcement of Article 102 TFEU in the energy (i.e. electricity and gas) and telecom sectors by the European Commission. Further, the paper engages in a cross-country comparison of the most relevant cases of abuse of dominance sanctioned by the NCAs of the selected jurisdictions on the basis of the four comparative indicators mentioned above.

2. ENFORCEMENT OF EU COMPETITION LAW IN REGULATED INDUSTRIES

2.1 Interaction of Competition Law and Sector-Specific Regulation in the EU

According to Hellwig, the expression 'network industries' refers to the economic sectors which 'involve elements of a natural monopoly, since the provision of services to customers presupposes the use of a fixed network infrastructure the costs of which are largely sunk'.[8] Industries such as telecommunications, electricity, gas, rail transport and postal services fall within this definition: the networks which characterize these industries are natural monopolies, which help to preserve the incumbent's market power and discourage new entrants in the liberalized market. The peculiar structure of network industries thus requires the introduction of 'access regulation' (i.e. third party access), obliging the incumbent operator to guarantee access to its network to its competitors on the basis of fair and non-discriminatory conditions.[9] Access regulation concerns only the parts of the network which cannot be duplicated, due to the presence of insurmountable costs which would not justify such investment. For instance, in the telecom sector access regulation is limited to the 'local loop' (i.e. the last mile of the fixed telephone network), while the duplication of the long-distance lines can be economically feasible for the competitors of the incumbent. Similarly, in the electricity market access regulation is present at the level of electricity transmission (i.e. high-voltage grids) and distribution (i.e. low-voltage grids), while the generation market is often open to competition. The continuous liberalization of network industries has led to a modification of the pattern of regulation: while in the past the state directly regulated the functioning of state-owned monopolies in order to safeguard the interest of final consumers (i.e. command and control regulation), in the liberalized industries regulation aims at fostering competition by granting access to the incumbent's competitors to the remaining monopolistic segments of the market.[10]

Within network industries, EU competition rules and sector-specific regulation share the same goal (i.e. fostering competition within the liberalized markets) and thus their functions within these markets overlap. However, the two sets of rules do not enjoy the same status within the hierarchy of EU norms. In fact, by being enshrined in the EU Treaty, Articles 101 and 102 TFEU enjoy 'primacy' over the sector-specific regulation, adopted via EU secondary legislation and later implemented

---

8 M. Hellwig, 'Competition Policy and Sector-Specific Regulation for Network Industries', Max Planck Institute for Research on Collective Goods, Working Paper 2008/29, 2, available at: http://www.coll.mpg.de/pdf_dat/2008_29online.pdf (accessed 30 June 2015).

9 Ibid., 5.

10 Ibid., 6.

by the EU Member States at the national level.[11] The European Commission explicitly recognized in its *O2* decision the 'parallel and cumulative application' of competition and sector-specific regulation in network industries, subject to the primacy of EU competition rules.[12] Similarly, the Court of Justice of the European Union (CJEU) has also recognized the primacy of EU competition rules in *Deutsche Telekom*, by upholding the Commission's decision sanctioning Deutsche Telekom for exclusionary margin-squeeze practices. In its ruling, the CJEU rejected Deutsche Telekom's claim that the margin squeeze was justified since the wholesale access tariff was regulated, and the tariff had been previously

---

[11] The network industries have been progressively liberalized since the end of the 1980s. One of the first industries to be liberalized was the telecom sector, where the European Commission initially relied on the legislative power granted by Article 106(3) TFEU to adopt directives which forced EU Member States to open certain segments of the telecom sector to competition. However, this 'unilateral' approach was later abandoned, and in the 1990s the Commission proposed a number of directives under the standard legislative procedure, later approved by the Council and the European Parliament. The telecom regulatory framework was consolidated by the 2002 'package', including four directives and one decision. The 2002 telecom package introduced competition law principles; in particular, due to the evolving structure of the telecom markets, it introduced the rule that only the markets where a single operator still enjoyed 'significant market power' after market liberalization were subject to sectorial regulation, while the other markets were subject to ordinary competition rules. The NRA decided at the national level which markets could be open to competition, subject to the review of the European Commission. The 2002 telecom package was strengthened in 2009 by a new package of directives. The liberalization of the energy markets has also proceeded step by step, through the adoption of three energy packages. The energy regulation shares fewer common points with competition law; due to the persistency of vertical integration in the energy markets, the EU directives have introduced the requirement of ownership or legal unbundling in order to separate generation, transmission and distribution activities. The EU has also adopted directives to liberalize the other network industries, although the degree of effective liberalization varies depending on the industry. For an overview of the EU telecom regulatory framework see A. De Streel, 'Interaction between Competition Law and Sector-Specific Regulation' in L. Garzaniti and M. O'Regan (eds), *Telecommunications, Broadcasting, and the Internet: The EU Competition Law and Regulation* (3rd edn, Sweet & Maxwell 2010) 867. For an overview of the process of liberalization of the energy markets in the EU, see S. Hariharan and K. Ghaya, 'Competition Law in the Energy Sector: The European Experience' (2011) 20 *Eur. Energy & Environ. L. Rev.* 197.

[12] Commission Decision of 16 July 2003, Case COMP/38.369 – *T-Mobile Deutschland/O2 Germany: Network Sharing Rahmenvertrag* [2004] OJ L 75, para. 22.

approved by the NRA.[13] The primacy of competition rules over sector-specific regulation is a peculiarity of the EU legal system, and it clearly diverges from the approach adopted by the US Supreme Court in *Trinko*.[14] However, as argued by Petit, the enforcement of EU competition rules in the regulated industries remains *de facto* a 'reserved possibility':[15] the European Commission and the NCAs of the EU Member States, in fact, enforce competition rules in regulated industries only when the regulatory system cannot satisfactorily achieve the goal of safeguarding free competition in the liberalized industries.

2.2 The European Commission's Pattern of Enforcement of Article 102 TFEU in the Regulated Industries – 'Regulatory Antitrust'

During the last two decades, the European Commission has sanctioned a number of cases concerning abuses of dominance in regulated industries under Article 102 TFEU. The type of sanctioned conduct varies due to the specificities of each industry. However, a number of common features can be identified. In particular, the EU Commission has primarily targeted the incumbent's unilateral conduct aiming at excluding its competitors from the market either through long-term exclusive supply contracts[16] or through

---

[13] Case C-208/08 *Deutsche Telekom v Commission* [2010] ECR I-9555.

[14] In this landmark ruling, the US Supreme Court rejected the enforcement of Section 2 Sherman Act to force Verizon to grant access to its telecom network to its competitors. The Court noted that the sector was already subject to access regulation and supervised by the Federal Communications Commission. Therefore, in *Trinko* the US Supreme Court recognized that antitrust rules play a subsidiary role in comparison to sector regulation (i.e. antitrust rules are only applicable if sector regulation does not exist). See *Verizon Communications v. Law Offices of Curtis V. Trinko, LLP*, 540 U.S. 398.

[15] N. Petit, 'Circumscribing the Scope of EC Competition Law in Network Industries? A Comparative Approach to the US Supreme Court Ruling in the Trinko Case' (2004) 5 *J. Netw. Ind.* 361.

[16] The conclusion of long-term exclusive supply contracts concerned the gas and electricity sectors. In particular, the European Commission in a number of decisions has sanctioned under Article 102 TFEU the long-term contracts concluded by the incumbent electricity generator/gas supplier with downstream distributors, which could thus not be supplied by the incumbent's competitors. See, for instance, Commission Decision of 11 October 2007, Case COMP/B-1/37966 – *Distrigaz* [2008] OJ C 9, p. 8; Commission Decision of 17 March 2010, Case COMP/39.386 – *Long-term Contracts France*, available at: http://ec.europa.eu/competition/antitrust/cases/dec_docs/39386/39386_1536_3.pdf (accessed 30 June 2015). For an overview of the EU Commission's enforcement of Article 102 TFEU in energy markets see J. Ratliff and R. Grasso, 'Unilateral Conduct in

margin-squeeze strategies,[17] or by limiting the available capacity of the network.[18] The EU Commission has also sanctioned exploitative conduct of the incumbent (such as withholding capacity in the electricity generation market).[19] However, the 'core' of the abuses sanctioned by the European Commission in network industries concerned exclusionary conduct. In such cases, the incumbent typically circumvents the regulatory obligation to grant its competitors access to its network by either denying access to the network or imposing unfair and discriminatory access conditions. The EU Commission, therefore, sanctioned under Article 102 TFEU the exclusionary conduct which jeopardized the liberalization of the market and which could not be 'caught' by the relevant sector regulation. On the other hand,

---

the Energy Sector: An Overview of EU and National Case Law' (15 March 2012) *e-Competitions* No. 44203, available at: http://awa2013.concurrences.com/business-articles-awards/article/unilateral-conduct-in-the-energy (accessed 30 June 2015).

[17] Margin squeeze is common exclusionary conduct in the telecom sector: the incumbent charges a higher interconnection tariff to its downstream competitors than to its downstream subsidiary. Consequently, the latter can offer retail services at more competitive prices than the incumbent's competitors. The *Deutsche Telekom* judgment recognized margin squeeze as a separate type of abuse of dominance which can be sanctioned under Article 102 TFEU: Case C-208/08 *Deutsche Telekom v Commission* [2010] ECR I-9555, para. 177. Besides the telecom sector, cases of margin squeeze have also been sanctioned in the energy sector, in countries in which the generation activities have not been unbundled from transmission and distribution. For instance, in *RWE*, the European Commission sanctioned RWE for having set its transmission tariffs at an artificially high level in order to squeeze its competitors' margin of profit in the electricity generation market: Commission Decision of 18 March 2009, Case COMP/B-1/39.402 – *RWE Gas Foreclosure*, available at: http://ec.europa.eu/competition/antitrust/cases/dec_docs/39402/39402_576_1.pdf (accessed 30 June 2015).

[18] This type of abuse has been sanctioned in the gas sector. For instance, in the *ENI* case, the European Commission sanctioned the behaviour of the Italian gas incumbent ENI, which refused to invest in its network in order to limit the available capacity for its competitors, or granted access to the network at less favourable conditions: Commission Decision of 29 September 2010, Case COMP/39.315 – *ENI*, available at: http://ec.europa.eu/competition/antitrust/cases/dec_docs/39315/39315_3019_9.pdf (accessed 30 June 2015).

[19] This type of abuse was sanctioned by the European Commission in 2008 in the *E.ON* case. The German incumbent was accused of deliberately withholding available generation capacity in peak moments of consumption in order to increase the electricity wholesale price, to the detriment of final consumers. See Commission Decision of 26 November 2008, Joined Cases COMP/39.388 – *German Electricity Wholesale Market* and COMP/39.389 – *German Electricity Balancing Market* [2009] OJ C 36, p. 8.

the EU Commission has left to NRAs of the EU Member States the task of safeguarding the interests of final consumers by regulating retail tariffs and contractual conditions.

During recent years, the European Commission has closed most of its investigations under Article 102 TFEU in gas and electricity sectors through the adoption of commitment decisions under Article 9 of Regulation 1/2003.[20] The latter provision allows the EU Commission to terminate investigations concerning potential breach of EU competition rules without the finding of an infringement, provided that the undertaking 'voluntarily' accepts a number of remedies aiming at solving the alleged distortion of competition in the relevant market. In the energy sector, the EU Commission negotiated both behavioural remedies, limiting the length of exclusive supply contracts and the ability of the incumbent to limit access to its network to its competitors, as well as structural remedies requiring the divestiture of certain assets in order to decrease the market power of the incumbent.[21] This type of enforcement of Article 102 TFEU has been defined in the literature as 'regulatory antitrust':[22] instead of sanctioning *ex post* the anti-competitive practices which distort competition in the relevant market, the European Commission has relied on *ex ante* commitments as 'can openers', in order to push forward its liberalization agenda in the EU energy markets.[23] In particular, through far-reaching structural commitments, the EU Commission decreased the market power of the incumbent and *de facto* encouraged ownership unbundling in the EU Member States which had opted out of this option in the third energy package.[24]

---

[20] Council Regulation (EC) No 1/2003 of 16 December 2002 on the implementation of the rules on competition laid down in Articles 81 and 82 of the Treaty. [2003] OJ L 1, p. 1.

[21] U. Scholz and S. Purps, 'The Application of EU Competition Law in the Energy Sector' (2013) 4 *J. Eur. Comp. L. & Prac.* 63.

[22] J. Tapia and D. Mantzari, 'The Regulation/Competition Interaction' in D. Gerardin and I. Lianos (eds), *Handbook on European Competition Law* (Edward Elgar Publishing 2013) 588.

[23] Ibid.

[24] For instance, in the 2008 *E.ON* commitment decision (n. 19 above), the European Commission required E.ON to divest a substantial part of its generation capacity in the German electricity market. Similarly, RWE agreed in 2009 to fully divest its gas transportation network in Germany (n. 17 above), while ENI in 2010 agreed to divest its international gas pipelines in order to separate transport and distribution of gas (n. 18 above).

The 'regulatory antitrust' approach followed by the European Commission to liberalize energy markets has been criticized in the literature for its lack of judicial review, and thus lack of legal certainty for the interested parties.[25] Without entering into this debate, it is worth noting that the European Commission has followed this approach not only in the energy markets. As noted by De Streel, in fact, it took a similar approach in the telecom sector in the 1990s.[26] In the absence of the Article 9 procedure, the EU Commission informally negotiated commitments with telecom operators as a condition for an individual exemption under Article 101(3) TFEU.[27] Following the adoption of the 2002 telecom package, the EU Commission has progressively abandoned the 'regulatory antitrust' approach in the telecom sector, and it has focused its investigations on exclusionary conduct that could not be caught by the sector regulation (i.e. margin squeeze). Consequently, we can suppose that the current wave of regulatory antitrust concerning the energy sector is probably a 'transitional' phase, which may be exhausted once the regulatory framework in the energy sector is sufficiently effective to guarantee market liberalization.

To sum up, the European Commission has so far sanctioned primarily exclusionary abuses of dominance in the network industries. The degree of enforcement of Article 102 TFEU depends on the degree of

---

[25] M. Sadowska, 'Energy Liberalization in Antitrust Straitjacket: A Plant too Far?' *EUI Working Paper RSCAS* 2011/34, available at: http://fsr.eui.eu/Documents/WorkingPapers/Energy/2011/WP201134.pdf (accessed 30 June 2015).

[26] A. De Streel, 'Interaction between Competition Law and Sector-Specific Regulation' in L. Garzaniti and M. O'Regan (eds), *Telecommunications, Broadcasting, and the Internet: the EU Competition Law and Regulation* (3rd edn, Sweet & Maxwell 2010) 867.

[27] During the 1990s, the European Commission made the granting of individual exemptions under Article 101(3) TFEU in relation to a number of joint ventures between national telecom incumbents conditional on the adoption of liberalization measures. For instance, in *Atlas* it approved the joint venture between France Télécom and Deutsche Telekom, subject to the condition that the French and German Governments licensed alternative telecom operators in their markets, despite EU legislation requiring this: Commission Decision of 17 July 1996, Case No IV/35.337 – *Atlas* [1996] OJ L 239, p. 23. Similarly, in *British Interactive Broadcasting*, the EU Commission required the divestiture of BT's cable network in order to favour the creation of competition regarding the local network infrastructure in the UK: Commission Decision of 26 August 1997, Case No IV/36.539 – *British Interactive Broadcasting* [1997] OJ C 259, p. 3.

liberalization of each industry. In particular, similar to the telecom sector in the 1990s, in recent years the European Commission has adopted a number of commitment decisions imposing behavioural and structural commitments on energy operators. Such commitments aim at compensating for the modest liberalization progress achieved in the energy markets.

3. COMPARATIVE ANALYSIS OF THE ENFORCEMENT PRACTICE IN SELECTED NEW EU MEMBER STATES, CANDIDATE COUNTRIES AND POTENTIAL CANDIDATES

3.1 Types of Abuses

When identifying the types of unilateral practices sanctioned by the NCAs in the selected jurisdictions we attempt to distinguish between exclusionary and exploitative abuses of dominant position in order to determine the role of the NCAs in protecting and promoting competition in the regulated industries. This distinction also helps us to understand whether the NCAs are pursuing their distinct function of protecting market competition or whether they are merely filling the regulatory gaps where the NRAs do not have competence to act without any effect on actual or prospective competitive conditions in the regulated markets.

Prior to the discussion on the particular types of unilateral practices investigated by the NCAs in the target jurisdictions it should be emphasized that the ensuing picture is heavily affected by the discretion of the NCAs in initiating and conducting investigations preceded by the complaints formulated by the interested parties alleging the existence of competition law infringements. The case of Bosnia and Herzegovina (B&H) represents an illustrative example in this regard. In 2011 the B&H NCA was investigating a complaint by an independent telecom operator alleging that the incumbent had abused its dominant position by delaying the conclusion of an inter-connection agreement mandated by sector regulation. The complainant also alleged discrimination, as the incumbent had already provided access to its infrastructure to another independent telecom company. The B&H NCA opened two separate investigations: one concerning the alleged abuse of dominance and another regarding the alleged anti-competitive agreement. The unilateral practices case failed due to the procedural rule: the B&H Competition Act provides that if the NCA has not issued a decision within a certain period of time (3–4 months from opening the investigation) the parties are entitled to receive a letter of no infringement from the NCA.[28]

Based on the number of cases covered by the present study, the following types of abuses targeted by the NCAs concerned predominantly the exploitation of final consumers: pricing abuses (including excessive and unjustified charges);[29] imposition of unfair trading conditions (including practices of terminating and/or resuming the supply,[30] obliging the consumers to purchase a certain brand of meters for measuring water and gas consumption,[31] and imposing additional unrelated obligations,[32] etc.); and refusals to deal (mainly refusals to conclude the supply agreement or reinstate the connection to the network).[33] The group of exclusionary abuses includes comparatively fewer decisions by number and primarily includes margin-squeeze cases[34] and refusals to deal related to denial of access to network infrastructure ('essential facility' cases).[35]

An attempt to link the types of abuses to the particular regulated industries resulted in the following picture. In the network industries, such as telecommunications and TV services, where there is competition fuelled by the independent providers and access obligations are imposed on the incumbent network owners, claims of exclusionary abuses (refusals to deal, margin squeeze and discrimination) have been quite frequent. At the same time, the utilities markets, often characterized by the presence of a single supplier or distributor, have seen the intervention of

---

[28] Cases BA1, BA2 (Annex to this chapter). The anti-competitive agreement investigation was closed without a finding of an infringement because the Competition Act requires the showing of a restraint of competition by both object *and* effect, while no anti-competitive effect was shown by the complainant to the satisfaction of the NCA. See A. Svetlicinii, 'The Competition Authority of Bosnia & Herzegovina Closes the Investigation into the Alleged Abusive Practices of the Incumbent Telecom Operator without reaching a Decision on the Merits (Telekom RS / Crumb group)', (2011) *e-Competitions Bulletin*, Art. N° 40544; A. Svetlicinii, 'The Objectives of Competition Law and the Effective Conduct of the Infringement Proceedings: Judgments of the Court of Bosnia and Herzegovina in BH Telecom and Telekomunikacije RS' (2015) 8(11) *Yearbook of Antitrust and Regulatory Studies* 241.

[29] Cases MK1, MK2, MK3, MK4, HR1 (Annex to this chapter).

[30] Cases BG6, BG7, BG8, BG10, MD4 (Annex to this chapter).

[31] Cases MD1, MD2, MD3 (Annex to this chapter).

[32] Cases BG5, MD5 (Annex to this chapter).

[33] Cases BG6, BG7, BG8, BG9, BG10 (Annex to this chapter).

[34] Cases MK5, BA1, BA2, HR4, HR13, HR14 (Annex to this chapter).

[35] Cases MK6, RO4, BA4, HR2 (Annex to this chapter).

the NCAs in relation to exploitative abuses directed against the final consumers. Competition enforcement in energy markets has largely targeted exploitative practices such as excessive pricing, imposition of unrelated trading conditions, etc.

The categorization of exclusionary and exploitative abuses can also be instrumental in understanding the overall enforcement priorities in a particular jurisdiction. For example, Bulgaria and Romania have exhibited somewhat different enforcement trends in the field of unilateral practices, at least as far as regulated industries are concerned. The Bulgarian NCA's enforcement record includes a significant number of cases where the NCA prosecuted dominant undertakings for exploitative abuses directed against final consumers.[36] The Romanian NCA, on the other hand, despite the clear acknowledgment that it is not restrained from intervention in the regulated industries, has exhibited a rather cautious approach to these sectors, intervening only in a few instances of established exclusionary conduct.[37] Similar divergence is observed amongst the candidate countries that are formally positioned at the same stage of their EU integration process. The Croatian NCA, which formally joined the ranks of the European Competition Network in the summer of 2013, has traditionally prioritized enforcement against exclusionary abuses where the NCA's intervention could improve the competitive conditions in the relevant market. The enforcement record of the Croatian NCA in the regulated industries clearly supports that preference. The Croatian example has been followed by B&H and Serbia, where the NCAs' intervention in the regulated industries also primarily concerned exclusionary practices such as margin squeeze and other forms of discrimination of competitors. Macedonia and Moldova present contrasting examples: in these countries, the NCAs have primarily targeted exploitative practices of the dominant undertakings, often alongside price regulation and consumer protection. In Albania and Montenegro the collected evidence is inconclusive due to the low number of infringement decisions adopted by the respective NCAs.

3.2 Remedies

When identifying the types of remedies employed by the NCAs as a tool for punishing dominant undertaking for abusive conduct and preventing such conduct from taking place in the future, one should keep in mind

---

[36] Cases BG4, BG5, BG6, BG7, BG8, BG9, BG10 (Annex to this chapter).
[37] Cases RO1, RO2, RO3 (Annex to this chapter).

that the selected jurisdictions may differ with regard to the powers of the NCAs to impose remedies. For instance, unlike the new EU Member States, the candidate countries and potential candidates have only relatively recently entrusted their NCAs with direct sanctioning powers.[38] One should also distinguish between the NCAs' sanctioning powers (to impose monetary fines) and their ability to affect the conduct of the undertakings concerned by imposing behavioural remedies or to change the structure of the relevant market by ordering divestitures.[39] Finally, one should keep in mind that even the NCAs having identical sanctioning and remedying powers may differ significantly in applying these powers, due to their inherent discretion in formulating their own enforcement priorities. The following tendencies have been extracted from the NCAs' decisions finding an abuse of dominance or accepting the commitments proposed by the dominant undertaking.

The extent of the sanctioning powers has significantly affected the outcome of the infringement decisions. In Bulgaria, Macedonia and Romania, fines, calculated as a percentage of annual turnover, have been routinely imposed on undertakings found in abuse of their dominant

---

[38] While in the majority of the jurisdictions covered by the present research the NCAs are authorized to impose fines calculated as a percentage of the annual turnover of the undertaking(s) concerned, there are some notable exceptions. In Montenegro, under the previous law (in force until 8 October 2012) the antitrust fines were expressed as multiples of 'minimum wages' or as a percentage of illegal profits obtained as a result of the infringement. In Moldova, the NCA until 2012 was not authorized to impose fines directly. This power was only vested in the courts. The applicable rules of administrative procedure did not recognize fines calculated as a percentage of the undertaking's turnover. See J. Toskovic, B. Nikolic, S. Vesovic, 'Main News and Challenges in Competition Law and Policy in Montenegro' (2013) 6 *Österreichische Zeitschrift für Kartellrecht* 225.

[39] For example, the Montenegrin competition law specifically provides that in cases of abuse of dominant position the NCA is not authorized to impose structural measures such as divestitures, sales of assets or shares, and termination of existing contracts on disposal of rights that would allow it to exercise decisive influence on the undertaking's conduct. In Serbia, the Competition Act allows the NCA under certain circumstances to impose structural remedies in order to mitigate the anti-competitive effects of an infringement. This power, however, remains to be further specified in the Government's regulation on the matter. In B&H, the Competition Act authorizes the NCA to impose 'other appropriate measures which contribute to competition between undertakings on the relevant market' without further specifying whether this includes structural measures. Forced divestitures are authorized explicitly only in cases where a prohibited concentration was implemented.

position.[40] In Moldova and Serbia, the NCAs until recently did not have the direct sanctioning power to impose fines; these had to be imposed by the court in the course of separate sanctioning proceedings.[41] Finally, in B&H and Croatia, where the majority of the investigations have ended without a finding of infringement, we could not identify any pronounced enforcement tendencies.

The most common remedy ordered by the NCAs in case of an infringement was the order to cease the application of the abusive practices and to undertake certain procedural and/or technical measures that would prevent similar conduct in the future. Since the significant part of the exploitative abuses in the regulated industries concerned an un-identified number of final consumers, the NCAs usually aimed at modifying the internal policies and rules of the dominant undertakings so as to prevent the abusive practices in a systemic manner. In order to achieve this goal, the NCAs frequently required the dominant companies to modify their general terms and conditions,[42] standard agreements[43] and internal commercial practices,[44] as well as to notify consumers about their rights.[45] The same behavioural obligations made their way into the commitments decisions when 'voluntarily' accepted by the dominant undertakings.[46]

3.3 Judicial Review

Judicial review of the infringement decisions delivered by the NCA is available in the competition laws of all of the selected jurisdictions. The most common form of judicial review is carried out by administrative courts specialized in reviewing the decisions of the state authorities.[47] In some of the jurisdictions covered by this research, the review of the

---

[40] Cases BG1, BG2, BG5, BG9, BG10, MK1, MK2, MK3, MK4, MK5 (Annex to this chapter).

[41] Cases MD1, MD2, MD3, MD4, MD5, RS1, RS2 (Annex to this chapter).

[42] Cases HR1, HR6 (Annex to this chapter).

[43] Cases RS1, RS2 (Annex to this chapter).

[44] Case MD4 (Annex to this chapter).

[45] Cases MD1, MD2, MD3 (Annex to this chapter).

[46] Cases BG6, BG7, BG8, RO5 (Annex to this chapter).

[47] Bulgaria (Supreme Administrative Court, http://www.sac.government.bg/), Croatia (High Administrative Court, http://www.upravnisudrh.hr/), Macedonia (Administrative Court, http://www.usskopje.mk/ and High Administrative Court, http://www.vusskopje.mk/), Montenegro (Administrative Court, http://sudovi.me/uscg), Serbia (Administrative Court, http://www.up.sud.rs/). The websites were last accessed on 30 June 2015.

NCA's decisions is carried out by the regular courts,[48] which may have specialized panels for hearing administrative cases. The selected data is far from conclusive because in some of the selected jurisdictions the judicial precedents are not readily accessible. The absence of court decisions from a significant number of the selected jurisdictions can be explained in part by the fact that the courts have not yet reviewed abuse-of-dominance decisions rendered by the NCAs. The following analysis presents the main features of the judicial review of the abuse-of-dominance decisions in the regulated industries in those jurisdictions where they have been identified.

The Bulgarian judicial practice in the field of unilateral practices has been the most extensive among the selected jurisdictions, which is partly due to the longer experience with competition law enforcement as well as the large number of the NCA's infringement decisions that have been challenged before the Supreme Administrative Court (SAC). The court has clearly legitimized the NCA's interventions in the regulated industries. In the 2009 *District Heating Plant Rousse* case, the court confirmed that sanctions imposed by the NCA for the same violation that had already been sanctioned by the NRA under the sector regulation did not violate the *ne bis in idem* principle.[49] In a refusal-to-deal case against a telecom incumbent, the court found simultaneous infringements of the Competition Act (abuse of dominance by refusal of access to essential facility) and the Telecommunications Act[50] (prohibiting operators with significant-market-power status from refusing a request for co-location if it was technically and physically feasible).[51]

When reviewing the NCA's interventions in the regulated industries the Bulgarian judiciary has considered the EU practice in this field. In the *BTC* telecommunications margin-squeeze case the SAC followed the European Commission's decision in *Deutsche Telekom*[52] and held that the existence of tariff regulation exercised by the NRA should not prevent

---

48 Albania (District Court of Tirana, http://www.gjykatatirana.gov.al/), B&H (Court of Bosnia and Herzegovina, http://www.sudbih.gov.ba/), Romania (Bucharest Court of Appeals, http://www.cab1864.eu/). The websites were last accessed on 30 June 2015.

49 Judgment No. 8140/2009 of 18 June 2009, available at: http://www.sac.government.bg/ (accessed 30 June 2015).

50 Article 177(2) Telecommunications Act 2003.

51 Judgment No. 8181/2007 of 28 October 2007, available at: http://www.sac.government.bg/ (accessed 30 June 2015).

52 Commission Decision of 21 May 2003, Case COMP/C-1/37.451, 37.578, 37.579 – *Deutsche Telekom AG*, [2003] OJ L 263, p. 9.

the NCA's intervention under the Competition Act in cases of unfair or excessive prices.[53] At the same time, the direct approval by the NRA of the charges for re-establishing electricity supply after disconnection for non-payment have precluded the NCA from establishing the existence of an excessive-pricing case.[54] Similarly, in telecom margin-squeeze cases, the SAC has held that there could be no margin-squeeze abuse if the access charges have been approved by the NRA.[55]

The Bulgarian judges have approved the interventions of the NCA applying the national equivalent of Article 102 TFEU even against purely exploitative practices and consumer-protection violations. In 2010, the Bulgarian NCA held that by setting an excessive (one hour) downtime programmed into the safety devices of its electrometers, the dominant electricity supplier violated its duties under the Energy Act and abused its dominant position under the Competition Act.[56] The SAC upheld the NCA's decision.[57] The court also agreed with the NCA that termination of electricity[58] or water[59] supply to the whole building when only several residents had defaulted on their payments constituted an abuse of dominant position under the national equivalent of Article 102 TFEU.

The substantial case law on Bulgarian competition enforcement in regulated industries demonstrates that the judiciary does not shy away from a substantive review of the NCA's findings, including the evidentiary support and economic analysis contained in the NCA's infringement decisions. At the same time, the SAC has explicitly endorsed the NCA's interventions in the presence of sector regulation as well as prosecution of dominant companies for exploitative abuses and consumer protection violations.

The Croatian experience with judicial review of the NCA's infringement decisions concerning regulated industries is very limited, partially

---

[53] Judgment No. 2478/2008 of 5 March 2008, available at: http://www.sac.government.bg/ (accessed 30 June 2015).

[54] Judgment No. 5973/2010 of 10 May 2010, available at: http://www.sac.government.bg/ (accessed 30 June 2015).

[55] Judgment No. 4986/2010 of 15 April 2010, Judgment No. 865/2010 of 22 January 2010, available at: http://www.sac.government.bg/ (accessed 30 June 2015).

[56] Case BG11 (Annex to this chapter).

[57] Judgment No. 9994/2010 of 19 July 2010, available at: http://www.sac.government.bg/ (accessed 30 June 2015).

[58] Judgment No. 831/2010 of 21 January 2010, available at: http://www.sac.government.bg/ (accessed 30 June 2015).

[59] Judgment No. 14703/2009 of 3 December 2009, available at: http://www.sac.government.bg/ (accessed 30 June 2015).

due to the number of those decisions. During the reference period of the present study, the Croatian High Administrative Court reviewed two NCA decisions concerning discriminatory pricing in regulated industries.[60] On both occasions, the NCA's decisions were upheld as the court found no error in the NCA's substantive assessment.[61] These precedents tell us little about the judiciary's approach towards the NCA's intervention in the regulated industries. However, they did clarify the general standard of proof in discriminatory-pricing cases.

Macedonia represents a different example of judicial control: here the courts (Administrative Court and High Administrative Court) have focused their review predominantly on the procedural aspects of the NCA's investigation and formal elements of the NCA's infringement decisions. The typical Macedonian scenario of judicial review runs as follows: (1) the Administrative Court quashes the NCA's infringement decision for procedural irregularities (for example, the NCA fails to mention the exact duration of the infringement); (2) the NCA remedies the procedural irregularities and adopts the second decision, which addresses the comments of the court; (3) the Administrative Court rejects the appeal of the parties against the second decision where no procedural irregularities are found; and (4) the High Administrative Court upholds the judgment of the Administrative Court where no procedural irregularities are found. As a result, the substantive test and economic analysis of the NCA remained outside the courts' attention.

The study has identified judicial control of the abuse-of-dominance decisions only in these three out of ten target jurisdictions. The Bulgarian and Macedonian cases represent two different examples of the role and influence of the judiciary on the development of the enforcement practices. In Bulgaria, the NCA's decisions have been subject to substantive judicial review, which has tested the validity of the NCA's substantive assessment and evidentiary support. The Bulgarian jurisprudence has also delineated the competences of the NCA and NRA in relation to the regulation of prices. The Macedonian experience, on the other hand, provides a different picture. In this jurisdiction the attention of the courts has been focused primarily on the procedural aspects of the NCA's investigations and the formal elements of the infringement decisions. As a result, the Macedonian NCA remained largely unrestrained in the

[60] Cases HR1, HR6 (Annex to this chapter).

[61] Judgment No. Us-7153/2011-8 of 9 February 2012, published in *Narodne novine* No. 35/2012 on 23 March 2012 and Judgment No. Us-14370/2009-13 of 20 April 2012, published in *Narodne novine* No. 62/2012 on 4 June 2012, both available at: http://narodne-novine.nn.hr/ (accessed 30 June 2015).

formulation of its enforcement priorities and continued with its interventions in the regulated sectors.

3.4 Relevance of Sector Regulation and Coordination with the NRA

In all of the researched jurisdictions, the enforcement of competition rules goes hand in hand with the regulatory oversight exercised by NRAs. As mentioned throughout the chapter, the NCAs would normally exercise significant discretion in formulating their enforcement priorities, which leads to a certain heterogeneity in the individual NCAs' approaches towards intervention in the presence of sector regulation. As a rule, the NCAs are not formally prohibited from intervening in sectors covered by sector regulation.[62] However, the presence of the NRA has often affected the NCA's decision when conducting its analysis and imposing remedies against abusive conduct of the dominant undertakings.

It should also be mentioned that in the majority of the selected jurisdictions the NCAs have formalized their relationship with the NRAs through a series of memoranda on cooperation (MoC) that provide the basic rules and principles governing the coordination of enforcement activities, information exchange, professional consultations and similar issues related to the NCAs' and NRAs' interventions in the regulated sectors.[63] In Albania, the NCA has entered into a series of MoCs with NRAs in charge of regulating financial markets, energy, telecommunications, water supply and distribution, and public procurement. Similarly, the Montenegrin NCA has concluded MoCs with NRAs in the fields of energy, telecommunications and insurance.[64] The Serbian NCA likewise has entered into MoCs with energy and telecommunications NRAs.[65] In

[62] Article 34(5) of the Moldovan Competition Act contains the following principle regarding the delimitation of the spheres of intervention between the NCA and the NRAs: '[T]he regulatory authorities shall act *ex ante* in the regulated sectors, while the Competition Council shall act *ex post* in order to guarantee competition by applying the competition legislation to all relationships within the national economy that are covered by the current law.'

[63] Bosnia and Herzegovina is a notable exception to this trend; the B&H NCA has not yet entered into any MoCs with the NRAs. The absence of MoCs has been explained by the fact that pursuant to the provisions of the Competition Act the NRAs are obliged to cooperate with the NCA so that no special MoCs are required in this regard.

[64] See http://www.azzk.me/ (accessed 30 June 2015).

[65] See http://www.kzk.org.rs/medunarodne-i-domace-aktivnosti/protokoli-o-saradnji/domaciprotokoli (accessed 30 June 2015).

Macedonia, the NCA has had MoCs with energy,[66] telecommunications[67] and broadcasting[68] regulators in place since 2007. Despite the existence of formalized cooperation mechanisms in some of the selected jurisdictions, it remains difficult to evaluate their effectiveness and impact on cooperation between the competition and regulatory authorities. This is partly due to the fact that cooperation between the NCAs and NRAs under the respective MoCs is largely voluntary, depending on the initiative and good will of the parties.

The research presented in this chapter is primarily based on the analysis of the NCAs' decisions, with some additional feedback provided by the officials of individual NCAs, who cooperated with the authors by offering their interpretations of and comments on the practices of the respective NCAs. As a result, the NCAs' approaches towards intervention in regulated industries and cooperation with the NRAs have been formulated on the basis of the analysed decisions and do not represent the official positions of the respective authorities. As a predominant trend observed in the selected jurisdictions, the NCAs usually acknowledge their autonomy in formulating the enforcement priorities and the NRAs are primarily contacted for professional consultations to assist the NCAs in understanding the competitive situation in the relevant markets, and thus provide the necessary evidence to be used in the infringement decisions concerning unilateral anti-competitive practices in regulated industries.

In the overwhelming majority of the decisions, the NCAs evaluate the presence and role of sector regulation by referring to the applicable regulatory framework. In some cases, the NCAs acknowledge that they have consulted the NRAs for interpretation of the sector legislation. The Croatian NCA is a good example of this, as it routinely mentions the extent of such cooperation in its decisions.[69] On many occasions, the NCAs refer to the market definitions developed by the NRAs. This

[66] Memorandum of Cooperation in the Field of Protection of Competition on the Energy Market, available at: http://www.kzk.gov.mk/images/Vestiimages/430/DOWNLOAD.PDF (accessed 30 June 2015).

[67] Memorandum of Cooperation in the field of Protection of Competition on the Market of Electronic Communications, available at: http://www.kzk.gov.mk/images/Vestiimages/427/DOWNLOAD.PDF (30 June 2015).

[68] Memorandum of Cooperation in the field of protection of competition in the broadcasting activity, available at: http://www.kzk.gov.mk/images/Vestiimages/614/DOWNLOAD.PDF (30 June 2015).

[69] Cases HR1, HR2, HR4, HR5, HR8, HR9, HR11, HR12 (Annex to this chapter).

practice is especially visible in the telecommunications sector, where the NCAs routinely check significant market power (SMP) determinations issued by the respective NRAs.[70] At the same time, the wording of the NCAs' decisions makes it clear that in the absence of express legislative provisions on this issue, the NCAs are not bound by the market definitions adopted by the NRAs.

While the above requests for information and references to the NRAs' market definitions are fairly common in the selected jurisdictions, deference to the NRAs' regulatory powers and coordination of enforcement are not so frequent. The Romanian NCA has on several occasions verified the extent of the NRA's remedying and sanctioning powers and competences in order to determine the extent of its own intervention in the regulated industries.[71] In Croatia the appreciation of the NRA's regulatory powers is commonly present in the NCA's decisions.[72] In an excessive-pricing case in the telecommunications sector, the Albanian NCA noted that the dominant undertakings failed to comply with the recommendation of the NRA concerning price ceilings for various telecom tariffs.[73] This appreciation of the NRAs' competences in several instances has played the key role in the NCA's decision to terminate the investigation or not to intervene in the areas already covered by the NRA. For example, the Serbian NCA terminated its investigation in the cable TV abusive-pricing case due to the remedies adopted by the telecom regulator in order to address the anti-competitive concerns.[74] In Croatia, the NCA has reported several instances where it terminated its investigations due to the price regulation carried out by the NRA (postal services, DTV transmission services, etc.).[75] Active cooperation between the NCA and NRAs in Croatia has also been manifested in several margin-squeeze cases where the NCA has commenced its investigation following a request by an NRA that lacked competence to regulate certain areas in the fields of telecommunications.[76] In other countries such as Macedonia,

---

[70] Cases RO4, AL1, BA4, RS1, RS2, HR5 (Annex to this chapter).

[71] Cases RO2, RO5 (Annex to this chapter).

[72] Cases HR2, HR3, HR4, HR7 (Annex to this chapter).

[73] Case AL1 (Annex to this chapter). The NCA noted that the service prices applied by the dominant undertakings did not have any reasonable relation to their cost. If the undertakings implemented a national termination fee for mobile telephony recommended by the NRA, then the decision of the NCA could be different as the applied tariffs would be set on a cost-basis.

[74] Case RS3 (Annex to this chapter).

[75] Cases HR8, HR9, HR10 (Annex to this chapter).

[76] Cases HR3, HR13, HR14 (Annex to this chapter).

although the NCA has concluded MoCs with all key NRAs, the assessment of the regulatory framework is often absent from the NCA's decisions, which makes it difficult to appreciate whether and how the NCA has accounted for the existing regulatory framework and remedying powers of the NRAs. The survey presented here has also revealed instances where, partially due to the lack of inter-institutional cooperation, the NCA's decisions have expressly condemned certain practices allowed by the NRA. For example, in Moldova the NCA has found that some exploitative practices by the dominant electricity distributor were implicitly approved by the NRA's guidelines on termination of supply to final consumers.[77]

4. CONCLUSION

This chapter has attempted to identify the patterns of enforcement of Article 102 TFEU and its national equivalents in the network industries of the new EU Member States, candidate countries and potential candidates for EU accession. These enforcement patterns appear to be quite different from that followed by the European Commission during the last two decades: while the EU Commission has mainly sanctioned exclusionary conducts that jeopardized the liberalization of the market, some NCAs in the selected jurisdictions have continued to sanction exploitative abuses of dominance, such as excessive pricing and unfair contractual conditions. While the EU Commission has often negotiated over the incumbents' structural commitments aiming at decreasing their market power, the NCAs in the selective jurisdictions have mainly adopted behavioural remedies or imposed fines to sanction exploitative conduct. In addition, while the EU Commission has relied on commitment decisions as 'can openers' in order to support its market-liberalization agenda, the NCAs of the selected jurisdictions have often applied the national equivalents of Article 102 TFEU to sanction unfair commercial practices of the incumbents in network industries in order to protect final consumers.

In the absence of an effective judicial review, the NCAs in some of the target jurisdictions were able to freely develop their enforcement approaches to unilateral practices in network industries. In some of the surveyed countries, the national courts limited their review to the

[77] Case MD4 (Annex to this chapter).

examination of the procedural aspects, without questioning the substantive assessment of the NCAs. Similarly, although most of the NCAs of the selected jurisdictions concluded MoCs with the relevant NRAs, these agreements have not always resulted in effective cooperation between NCAs and NRAs.

A number of reasons might explain the enforcement approaches of the selected NCAs. First of all, the deficiencies in the regulatory frameworks in the network industries might have led to increasing interventions of the NCAs in these sectors. Furthermore, competition enforcement against excessive pricing might also be triggered by the public opinion and publicity objectives of the NCAs and national governments. Due to the long history of price regulation, the general public in the selected jurisdictions often perceives competition rules as a mechanism to restrain excessive profits of dominant companies. The prosecution of excessive pricing also serves the publicity objectives of the newly established NCAs. The latter often do not have the resources and the experience to investigate and to collect evidence against complex competition infringements, such as cartels or exclusionary abuses. Sanctioning excessive pricing thus may represent an 'enforcement shortcut' that allows the NCAs to show concrete enforcement results in their annual reports.[78]

As mentioned in section 2.1 above, within the EU legal system, competition rules enjoy primacy over sector-specific regulation. Therefore, the enforcement of Article 102 TFEU and its national equivalents by the NCAs of the selected jurisdictions in regulated industries is not *per se* problematic. Nevertheless, this type of enforcement should remain a 'reserved possibility'; a possibility that the European Commission has used in order to sanction exclusionary conduct that could not be caught by the relevant sector-specific regulation. Therefore, the EU Commission's enforcement of competition rules in network industries has 'supplemented' sector regulation. In contrast, the NCAs of the selected jurisdictions have been *de facto* 'substituting' the NRAs in their regulatory activities, sanctioning as 'excessive' and 'unfair' the tariffs and the contractual conditions regulated or unregulated by the NRAs.

[78] OECD Secretariat, Working Paper on Excessive Prices, DAF/COMP/WP2(2011)7/REV1, 52, available at: http://www.oecd.org/regreform/sectors/49482277.pdf (accessed 30 June 2015).

ANNEX: COMPARATIVE TABLE OF THE NCAS' DECISIONS

Country/ number	Case ID/date	Economic sector	Form of abuse	Type of abuse	Outcome and/or remedies	Coordination with NRA
BG1	510/05.07.2007	Telecom	Refusal to deal	Exclusionary: refusal to provide interconnection to its own network	Fine	Unknown
BG2	1142/16.12.2008	Electricity	Excessive pricing	Exploitative	Fine	Yes
BG3	624/23.06.2009	Telecom	Margin squeeze	Exclusionary	Unknown	Yes
BG4	600/17.07.2008	Water	Excessive pricing	Exploitative	No infringement found	Yes
BG5	617/03.06.2010	Electricity	Unfair trading conditions	Exploitative	Fine	NCA referred to regulatory framework and tariffs fixed by NRA
BG6	1630/22.12.2010	Telecom: fixed telephony	Refusal to deal	Exploitative	Commitments to adopt new internal guidelines that would prevent future abusive conduct	
BG7	258/11.03.2010	Electricity	Refusal to deal	Exploitative	Commitments to adopt new internal guidelines that would prevent future abusive conduct	
BG8	333/25.03.2010	Electricity	Refusal to deal	Exploitative	Commitments to adopt new internal guidelines that would prevent future abusive conduct	
BG9	585/04.05.2011	District heating	Refusal to deal	Exploitative	Fine	Unknown
BG10	350/22.03.2011	Electricity	Refusal to deal	Exploitative	Fine	Unknown
BG11	307/31.03.2009	Electricity	Unfair conditions	Exploitative	Fine	Unknown

Country/ number	Case ID/date	Economic sector	Form of abuse	Type of abuse	Outcome and/or remedies	Coordination with NRA
MK1	08-102/9/29.10.2012	Mobile telephony	Abusive charges for voicemail	Exploitative	Fine	Yes
MK2	09-13/3/04.03.2011	Telecom: mobile telephony	Abusive charges for voicemail	Exploitative	Fine	Yes
MK3	09-15/8/16.03.2011	Electricity	Abusive charges (fee for issuing monthly bills)	Exploitative	Fine	Yes
MK4	09-5/5/21.04.2011	Telecom	Abusive charges (fee for issuing monthly bills)	Exploitative	Fine	Yes
MK5	07-50/1/26.01.2009	Telecom: leased digital lines	Margin squeeze	Exclusionary	Fine and order to preserve 30% difference between wholesale and retail	Yes
MK6	07-40/14 of 28.06.2007	Telecom: leased digital lines	Refusing access to own network	Exclusionary	Fine and order to cease	Yes, but no direct reference to NRA
MD1	18.09.2008	Water supply and waste water disposal	Requiring consumers to switch to single brand meters, charging for installation of new meters	Exploitative	Order to cease the abusive practices, notify the consumers about their freedom to choose the brand of the meters	Reference to the consumer protection legislation
MD2	03.07.2008	Energy: natural gas distribution	Requiring consumers to switch to single brand meters	Exploitative	Order to cease the abusive practices, notify the consumers about their freedom to choose the brand of the meters	No

MD3	24.04.2008	Energy: natural gas distribution	Requiring consumers to switch to single brand meters	Exploitative	Order to cease the abusive practices, notify the consumers about their freedom to choose the brand of the meters	No
MD4	22.02.2011	Energy: electricity distribution	Automatic termination of supply	Exploitative	Order to modify its termination practices; call to NRA to modify its guidelines	NCA decision runs contrary to the guidelines by NRA
MD5	01.02.2011	Water supply and waste water disposal	Refusing to provide consumers with meters free of charge	Exploitative	Order to cease the infringement	NCA informed the NRA about the infringement
RO1	52/16.12.2010	Postal services	Excessive pricing, price discrimination among clients	Exclusionary	Fine and order to cease and notify new prices	No reference
RO2	1/14.02.2011	Telecom: call termination services	Failure to provide access at regulated tariffs	Exclusionary	Fine	Sector regulation considered
RO3	2/14.02.2011	Telecom: call termination services	Failure to provide access at regulated tariffs	Exclusionary	Fine	Sector regulation considered
RO4	09.04.2012	Telecom: call termination services	Failure to provide quality service and refusal to expand capacity	Exclusionary	No infringement found	NCA considered NRA's market definition and SMP status of the incumbent
RO5	50/05.09.2012	Energy: certification of natural gas installations	Excessive pricing	Exclusionary	Behavioural commitments and monitoring obligations for two years	NCA considered that this segment of the market was not regulated by NRA
AL1	59/09.11.2007	Telecom: mobile telephony	Excessive pricing	Exploitative	Fine	Yes

Country/ number	Case ID/date	Economic sector	Form of abuse	Type of abuse	Outcome and/or remedies	Coordination with NRA
BA1	05-26-2-028-76-II/10/ 12.10.2011	Telecom	Margin squeeze	Exclusionary	No infringement found	Yes
BA2	01-05-26-028-63-II/ 2009/04.11.2010	Telecom	Margin squeeze	Exclusionary	No infringement found	Yes
BA3	01-06-26-056-36-II/08 of 04.06.2009	Postal services	Obstacles to access to relevant market	Exclusionary	No infringement found	Reference to NRA's competence to issue licenses and thus regulate competition in the sector
BA4	05-26-2-028-92-II/10 of 17.11.2011	Telecom: fixed telephony	Discriminating between competitors and delaying interconnection	Exclusionary	No infringement found	Reference to NRA's market definition, SMP status, etc.
RS1	5/0-03-0003/07-13/ 22.03.2007	Cable TV	Promotional action to divert the customers from competitors and lock them in a long-term agreement	Exclusionary	Order to allow customers to terminate agreements	Reference to NRA on the issue of market definition and SMP
RS2	5/0-01-73/08-59 26.12.2008	Cable TV	Exclusivity clause in distribution agreement	Exclusionary	Order to annul exclusivity clauses	Reference to NRA on the issue of market definition and SMP
RS3	22.03.2007	Cable TV	Abusive pricing	Exploitative	No infringement found	Deference to NRA's remedies
HR1	UP/I 030-02/2009-01/ 035 of 19.05.2011	Energy: trade in jet fuel	Price discrimination	Exploitative	Order to adopt objective non-discriminatory pricing formulas	Reference to NRA for data on licences and market shares

HR2	UP/I 030-02/2009-01/030 of 21.04.2011	Energy: natural gas distribution	Refusing inter-connection works on gas distribution installations	Exclusionary	No infringement found	Reference to NRA for information; NRA confirmed that the market is under regulation
HR3	UP/I 030-02/2009-01/034 of 15.12.2011	Telecom: broadband Internet	Retail promotion campaign by incumbent telecom operator with SMP determined by NRA	Exclusionary	No infringement found	NRA referred this case to NCA because it regulated only wholesale promotion campaigns while retail level was not regulated
HR4	UP/I 030-02/2008-01/45 of 31.08.2010	Telecom: leased digital lines	Margin squeeze and predatory pricing	Exclusionary	No infringement found	NRA confirmed that it is regulating the leased lines based on SDH technology; it also assisted in the substitutability analysis for market definition
HR5	UP/I 030-02/2008-01/21 of 16.12.2010	Collection of royalties on copyrighted music and recording products	Price discrimination	Exploitative	No infringement found	Reference to NRA for market definition
HR6	UP/I 030-02/2008-01/41 of 03.11.2009	Collection of royalties on copyrighted music and recording products	Price discrimination	Exploitative	Order to cease the infringements, adopt and announce objective and non-discriminatory royalty rates	No reference

Country/ number	Case ID/date	Economic sector	Form of abuse	Type of abuse	Outcome and/or remedies	Coordination with NRA
HR7	UP/I 030-02/2011-01/ 025 of 27.12.2012	Railway cargo transport	Price discrimination	Exploitative	No infringement found	NRA confirmed that it does not have regulatory competences over rail cargo transporter's and its clients' contracts
HR8	UP/I 034-03/2012-01/ 011 of 14.12.2012	Postal services	Price discrimination, predatory prices	Exploitative	No infringement found	NCA cooperated with NRA, which was competent for price regulation
HR9	UP/I 034-03/2012-01/ 014 of 14.12.2012	Postal services	Price discrimination, predatory prices	Exploitative	No infringement found	NCA cooperated with NRA, which was competent for price regulation
HR10	UP/I 030-02/11-01/ 052 of 12.07.2012	Digital TV transmission services	Pricing abuse	Exploitative	No infringement found	Yes, NCA terminated its investigation partly in deference to NRA's competence
HR11	UP/I 030-02/ 2009-01/11 of 12.07.2012	Telecom: broadband Internet access	Predatory pricing	Exclusionary	No infringement found	NRA assisted NCA in analysing the applicable regulations as well as prices applied by the dominant undertaking
HR12	UP/I 030-02/2011-01/ 038 of 05.04.2012	Energy: natural gas distribution	Take or pay clauses in supply contracts	Exploitative	No infringement found	NRA was consulted but did not want to comment on the rules that it did not adopt

HR13	UP/I 030-02/10-01/ 007 of 09.02.2012	Telecom: termination of calls in own network	Price squeeze	Exclusionary	No infringement found	NRA asked NCA to investigate possible price squeeze because retail segment was not regulated
HR14	UP/I 030-02/10-01/ 012 of 09.02.2012	Telecom: termination of calls in own network	Price squeeze	Exclusionary	No infringement found	NRA asked NCA to investigate possible price squeeze because retail segment was not regulated
ME1	01-I-UP-10/19-11/ 19.07.2011	Energy: maritime petroleum storage	Price discrimination	Exploitative	Order to adopt and announce transparent and non-discriminatory pricing	No

PART 4

Information and telecommunications markets

9. From competition law to sector-specific regulation in internet markets? A critical assessment of a possible structural change*

Rolf H. Weber

1. REGULATION CHALLENGES CAUSED BY INTERNET MARKETS

Though the worldwide triumph of the internet and of the new internet-based services has already lasted about two decades, many competition authorities have taken a hands-off approach with regard to the internet industry for quite some time. This situation, however, is changing and competition authorities are more carefully monitoring the internet sectors.

1.1 Specific Features of Internet Markets

A primordial task for any competition law analysis is the delineation of the relevant market. As far as the internet is concerned, some specific features are to be taken into account.

1.1.1 Two-sided markets and network effects

A particular characteristic of internet markets is the fact that the services offered are normally free of costs for users.[1] Revenue is only generated from one side of the market, more precisely from the advertisers' side. To be attractive for advertisers, the website has to generate as much traffic as

* This chapter has benefitted from the support of my former research assistant Dr. iur. Stephanie Volz, attorney-at-law, and from the valuable comments of my colleague Prof. Dr. Andreas Heinemann, University of Zurich. It includes the relevant literature and case law until autumn 2013.

[1] Except for charges that might be owed to the officials.

possible. A webpage's advertising space value directly correlates with its visits by internet users. Internet markets are, therefore, typically so-called two- or multi-sided markets.

In two- or multi-sided markets, internet service providers enable the parties involved – through reducing the transaction costs of finding each other – to realize gains from the interaction between each other. This usually leads to network effects. Network effects can be of a 'direct' or 'indirect' nature. 'Direct' network effects mean that the more customers use the same service, the higher is the value of that service.[2] 'Indirect' network effects arise if the attractiveness for one side of the market rises with the increasing number of users on the other side of the market, since this increase may attract more potential transaction partners.[3] 'Indirect' effects are characteristic of two-sided markets.[4]

1.1.2 'The winner takes it all' or concentration effects

Network effects may cause strong 'concentration effects', which are also referred to as 'winner-takes-it-all effects'; this means that the biggest player will receive most of the revenues. However, these 'concentration effects' depend largely on the type of network, and are not equally pronounced.[5] Network effects of two-sided markets may also lead to a kind of 'pulling effect', because all users of a market will decide to use the same provider or product. For internet users the existence of one single market place may be efficient, because it reduces searching costs and ensures price transparency.

The mentioned 'winner takes it all' effect is reduced through certain facts: capacity restraints may naturally limit the size of a network. Furthermore, its degree depends on the heterogeneity of a market. The more other providers may differentiate their offerings, the more specificity must be added by a new provider.[6] Finally, the concentration effect has to be put into the perspective of 'multi-homing' possibilities.

---

[2] See R. Whish and D. Bailey, *Competition Law* (7th edn, Oxford University Press 2012) 11; A. Fatur, *EU Competition Law and the Information and Communication Technology Network Industries* (Hart Publishing 2012) 82.

[3] J. Haucap and U. Heimeshoff, 'Google, Facebook, Amazon, eBay: Is the Internet Driving Competition or Market Monopolization?' (2014) 11 *Int'l Econ. & Econ. Pol.* 49.

[4] Whish and Bailey (n. 2 above).

[5] Haucap and Heimeshoff (n. 3 above).

[6] Fatur (n. 2 above) 96. See also Haucap and Heimeshoff (n. 3 above) 7.

1.1.3 Switching costs and multi-homing

Switching costs and multi-homing possibilities may have an influence on network effects and concentration. Switching costs are impediments which may prevent customers from changing supplier. Possible switching costs in internet markets are costs for the adaption to a new technological environment or becoming familiar with a changed infrastructure, but also psychological, emotional and social costs.

Multi-homing refers to the possibility of consuming different services in parallel.[7] The existence of multi-homing mainly depends on the switching costs and the form of payment, i.e. whether user-based or flat rates apply.[8]

1.1.4 Free services for one market side

As mentioned, most online services can be used free of cost. Consequently, users are highly price-sensitive and tend to resist any attempt to impose charges for internet services. If a provider starts to charge for a service, users will switch to an alternative, free service.[9]

The free-of-charge-mentality has two main consequences: First, as one side of the market is not willing to pay for the service, the other has to find funding for the provided service. Second, the non-remuneration for the users' side leads to an increase in the importance of other features of a service. A significant parameter for competition in internet markets is the quality of a service.[10] Therefore, service providers may only attract users if they constantly raise the number and/or quality of the services provided. The users will not accept poor services, since worse quality cannot be compensated for by a lower price.[11]

---

[7] Commission Decision of 7 October 2011, Case COMP/M.6281 – *Microsoft/Skype*, available at: http://ec.europa.eu/competition/mergers/cases/decisions/m6281_20111007_20310_2079398_EN.pdf (accessed March 2014), at para 33; see also Summary Decision, [2011] OJ C 341, p. 2.

[8] Haucap and Heimeshoff (n. 3 above).

[9] Case COMP/M.6281 – *Microsoft/Skype* [2011] OJ C 341, p. 2 (n. 7 above) paras 75ff.

[10] Case COMP/M.6281 – *Microsoft/Skype* [2011] OJ C 341, p. 2 (n. 7 above) para 81.

[11] Cf. D. Geradin and M. Kuschewsky, 'Competition Law and Personal Data: Preliminary Thoughts on a Complex Issue' (12 February 2013), available at: http://papers.ssrn.com/sol3/papers.cfm?abstract_id=2216088 (accessed March 2014).

1.1.5 Entry or exit barriers

Existing or non-existing entry or exit barriers for markets are important for the evaluation of market power. Entry barriers may result from a variety of factors such as investment cost, licensing requirements or customer loyalty.

In general, everybody can easily start doing business online; all you need is a good idea and a website. Moreover, capital costs usually are minimal, except that in technically complex market segments, the required technology may be very costly, both in terms of development and maintenance. The most significant barrier is, however, the aforementioned network effects, since most users are captured by the leading provider. Furthermore, network effects constitute barriers in the sense that the platform requires a certain size to be efficient.

Exit barriers are obstacles which make it difficult for undertakings to leave a market. Exit barriers on the one hand may strengthen competition, because they can actually force undertakings to stay in the market. On the other hand, exit barriers may create entry barriers since undertakings are not prepared to start a business in light of the costly exit. Accordingly, the 'just give it a try' strategy will not work. Exit costs may consist in asset write-offs, closure cost or the loss of customer goodwill.

To date, EU and US competition agencies and courts have not yet established a clear policy on defining the markets for internet businesses.[12] However, looking at the practice of competition authorities as well as at the legal doctrine, a tendency can be identified to distinguish three different kinds of markets:

- *Advertising*: Advertising is the common source of financing for internet service providers. There is a wide diversity of internet advertising, ranging from traditional banners or pop-ups to context-sensitive search advertising.[13] Usually the relevant product or service market for internet advertising is distinguished from offline

---

[12] See G. Gürkaynak, D. Durlu and M. Hagan, 'Antitrust on the Internet: A Comparative Assessment of Competition Law Enforcement in the Internet Realm' (2013) 14 *Bus. L. Int'l* 51–53; see also the summarized statements made by J. Haucap at the 47th Symposium of the Research Institute for Economical Constitution and Competition (FIW) (13 March 2014) *Neue Zürcher Zeitung* 26.

[13] Cf. J. Kagan, 'Bricks, Mortar, and Google: Defining the Relevant Antitrust Market for Internet-Based Companies' (2011) 55 *N.Y. L. School L. Rev.* 285.

advertising.[14] Furthermore, different markets for 'direct sales' and 'intermediate sales' by publishers of web space to advertisers can be differentiated. However, to date, an established court practice for the distinction of online advertising markets does not exist, particularly with regard to a possible further segmentation into search and non-search advertising.[15]

- *Retail*: Online trading platforms or auction sites, such as eBay, sell a wide variety of products and goods. Normally, these products have existing brick-and-mortar substitutes. Accordingly, there are functional alternatives to online auction markets in the offline world. For this reason, a relevant market containing only online auctions would be too narrow. As far as retail products/services are concerned, specific market places could be established, such as direct sales or online auctions.[16]
- *Social networks*: The primary problem is to define the term 'social network', since there is a variety of applicable descriptions. The key features are, however, the possibility of creating a profile which enables persons to connect and socialize with friends, relatives and other individuals. Due to their special features and applications, social networks may constitute an independent market.[17] Nevertheless, the lines are blurry in the online world, and it is unclear whether other interactive websites which enable users to generate and share content may also count as social networks.[18] However, there seems to be no doubt that social networks are a rare online phenomenon with no brick-and-mortar substitute.

---

[14] Commission Decision of 11 March 2008, Case COMP/M.4731 – *Google/DoubleClick*, paras 44–47 and 56, available at: http://ec.europa.eu/competition/mergers/cases/decisions/m4731_20080311_20682_en.pdf (accessed March 2014); see also Summary Decision, [2008] OJ C 184/10; Commission Decision of 18 February 2010, Case COMP/M.5727 – *Microsoft/Yahoo! Search Business* para. 61, available at: http://ec.europa.eu/competition/mergers/cases/decisions/M5727_20100218_20310_261202_EN.pdf (accessed March 2014).

[15] Case COMP/M.4731 – *Google/DoubleClick* (n. 14 above) paras 48–56; Case COMP/M.5727 – *Microsoft/Yahoo! Search Business* (n. 14 above) para. 75.

[16] See Kagan (n. 13 above) 289. See also Gürkaynak, Durlu and Hagan (n. 12 above) 60.

[17] *LiveUniverse Inc. v. MySpace Inc.*, Case CV 06-6994 AHM (RZx) (C.D. Cal. 2008).

[18] See S.W. Waller, 'Antitrust and Social Networking' (2012) 90 *N.C. L. Rev.* 7.

1.1.6 Geographical market

The definition of the geographical market relates to the question of whether consumers can effectively attain any substitutes. In the offline world, the geographical market might be limited through transportation costs, national preferences of consumers or language barriers. Additionally, the requirement of local support or local sale networks may restrict the geographic market, as well as different prices or conditions depending on the location of the consumer.[19]

When assessing the relevant geographic markets in the internet, two specific characteristics of online markets have to be considered: on the one hand, there is de-localization, which makes national borders less significant. For online presence, only the technical infrastructure is necessary;[20] consequently, it is often difficult to locate users.[21] On the other hand, through geo-localization technical instruments enable us to clearly identify where in the real world the internet has been accessed from.

Internet markets are global if a product is available over the internet, since it can be purchased from anywhere in the world. Most of the internet-based services are provided globally. They are hardly limited through technical or legal standards, and users' habits are usually universally identical.[22] Because the services are mostly free – irrespective of the location of the consumer – price differences are also irrelevant. However, some authors and courts require a real 'physical place' which cannot exist without outer boundaries.[23] In fact, for the time being, the European Commission has left the exact geographic scope of 'pure' internet services open.[24]

As soon as brick-and-mortar substitutes are available, the geographic market will also include these alternatives and the market will have to be

---

19 Case COMP/M.6281 – *Microsoft/Skype* [2011] OJ C 341, p. 2 (n. 7 above) paras 64 and 66.

20 Cf. R.H. Weber, *Regulatory Models for the Online World* (Schulthess 2002) 48.

21 Ibid.

22 Case COMP/M.6281 – *Microsoft/Skype* [2011] OJ C 341, p. 2 (n. 7 above) paras 64ff. A partly different opinion is expressed by B. Lundqvist, 'Competition Law as the Limit to Standard-setting', in this volume.

23 Kagan (n. 13 above) 283.

24 Case COMP/M.6281 – *Microsoft/Skype* [2011] OJ C 341, p. 2 (n. 7 above) para 68.

defined in a manner that accounts for these offline locations of the physically available substitutes.[25]

1.2 Competition Law and Sector-Specific Regulation as Intervention Means

Competition law, usually referred to as *ex post* regulation, is characterized by the fact that competition authorities may intervene if abusive behaviour by one or more market participants on a normally well-working market takes place.[26]

In contrast, sector-specific regulation is a form of (at least partial) *ex ante* regulation, which tries to lay the groundwork for basic competition. It is only admissible in those markets in which forces and actors fail to ensure workable competition (for example natural monopolies).

Competition rules are considered to be generally applicable norms that disregard the particularities of a certain market. They are backward-looking (*ex post*), i.e. they rely on historical evidence; for example, evidence of abusive behaviour of a market-dominant enterprise.[27] Sector-related regulation is specifically designed to meet the requirements of a certain market; it is forward-looking (*ex ante*), i.e. it describes regulatory solutions regardless of particular circumstances.[28] Sector-specific regulation can mostly be found in infrastructure and utility sectors, in which – due to the importance of the services – governmentally controlled monopolies exist. In addition, specific regulation is adopted in market segments in which competition pressure is weak or even non-existent, and the systematic abuse of market power is therefore likely.

Both approaches have their strengths and weaknesses; at large, it can be said that competition rules are quite general and normally do not

---

[25] Kagan (n. 13 above) 283.

[26] An exception applies in the case of merger control, allowing competition authorities to pre-emptively block a proposed transaction or attach conditions and obligations thereto.

[27] Cf. P. Alexiadis, 'Balancing the Application of Ex Post and Ex Ante Disciplines under Community Law in Electronic Communications Markets: Square Pegs in Round Holes?' in E. Buttigieg (ed.), *Rights and Remedies in a Liberalised and Competitive Internal Market* (Gutenberg Press 2012) 137, 139, available at: http://www.gibsondunn.com/publications/Documents/Alexiadis-BalancingtheApplicationofExPostandExAnteDisciplines.pdf (accessed March 2014).

[28] Ibid.

provide specific solutions, but are consequently more flexible. In contrast, sector-specific regulation contains precise terms, which offer certainty for regulatory bodies and concerned undertakings; they usually make faster and more effective solutions available.[29]

With regard to the relationship between general competition rules and sector-specific regulation, the existence of certain tensions is obvious. Nonetheless, between the two regimes a certain form of co-existence applies. To clarify the correlation, reference is frequently made to the different goals of the two instruments. Competition rules try to protect competition in general, whereas sector-specific regulation often focuses on promoting entry into markets that are deemed to lack sufficient competition. As a general principle, it may be stated that the existence of – even extensive – regulation does not free an undertaking from the obligation to comply with general competition rules.[30] Sector-specific regulation and competition rules work together. The main problem, though, is to find the most effective and well-functioning balance.

In recent years, the problem of sector-specific regulation was especially discussed with regard to the liberalization of previously publicly monopolized areas, for instance telecommunications. These sectors are often characterized by the existence of a non-duplicable network that is necessary to reach other markets, a so-called monopolistic bottleneck.[31] In these sectors, sector-specific regulation has the function of avoiding undesirable developments and ensuring market entries of interested undertakings.

2. CALL FOR MORE REGULATION

2.1 The Political Call

Regulation of internet markets has not been a topic of international agreements so far, except for technical issues, such as standardization, that have been addressed by the International Telecommunication Union (ITU) since 1865. During the last decade, however, internet governance

---

[29] See Weber (n. 20 above) 116ff.

[30] See Case T-398/07 *Spain v. Commission* EU:T:2012:173; for further details see also M. Siragusa and F. Caronna, 'A Reassessment of the Relationship between Competition Law and Sector-specific Regulation', in this volume.

[31] G. Knieps, 'The Three Criteria Test, the Essential Facility Doctrine and the Theory of Monopolistic Bottlenecks' (2011) 46 *Intereconomics – Rev. Eur. Econ. Pol.* 17.

has attracted more attention, starting from the World Summits of the Information Society (WSIS) of 2003 (Geneva) and 2005 (Tunis), followed by the establishment of the Internet Governance Forum, which has conducted eight annual conferences so far.

Thereby, the bottom-up process has been widened to a so-called multi-stakeholder approach that aims at the equal participation of governments, the private sector, academia and civil society. This multi-stakeholder approach reflects the fact that members of academia and civil society have been responsible for a vast extent of the programming and protocols of the internet; the private sector has provided the backbone (i.e. the technical infrastructure), whereas governments have not played a major role in this context.

However, during the last few years, the situation has changed: many countries claim that the current, mainly private, order of the internet is impairing their national security; these 'cyber sovereignty'-oriented countries advocate that control over the internet must remain in the competence of national governments, which, accordingly, should have the right to decide about the activities occurring in the internet to the extent that the domestic population is concerned by its contents.

These voices were particularly strong during the World Conference on International Telecommunications (WCIT) held in Dubai in December 2012. In fact, the negotiations revealed two different visions of political power: 'Cyber sovereignty'-oriented countries advocated for an extension of the mandate of the International Telecommunications Union (ITU) to include internet governance topics. Liberal democracies, however, pleaded for a privately organized regime allowing the free flow of information without any national interference.

The internet is not limited to national borders, while this is the case for legislation. Although national borders are softened through international legal harmonization, legal differences still exist. This applies even more with regard to different world regions. Therefore, it seems highly unlikely to find a common solution. The ubiquity of the internet services and the national borders of legislation are in a relationship of mutual tension, as the following two examples show.

An important element in the task of managing the internet is the security challenge. Obviously, governmental regulators are interested in reserving potential rights to intervene in the internet for emergency cases, reaching from intelligence services in military matters through supervision for combating criminal activities to the protection of minors against pornography. The problem of the term 'security' lies in its vagueness; apart from the mentioned objectives, the reference to security can also be used for exercising political pressure. The extensive discussions about Article 5 of the International Telecommunications Regulations (ITRs) at the WCIT show how different state interests can be interpreted.[32] Meanwhile, countries such as Russia, China or Saudi Arabia are attempting to subject the management of the internet to governmental control, mainly by referring to issues such as security and public order; in contrast, the United States and some allied countries strongly disapprove of such censorship of the internet for ideological and economic reasons.

A further problem with the ITRs consists in the fact that Iran supported an Internet Resolution submitted by some Arab countries to the plenary session at the WCIT, which called for an inclusion of the 'right to access of Member States to international telecommunications services' in the ITRs' Preamble. The resolution was adopted by majority decision (not unanimously, as is customary for international agreements) and has been included in the Preamble as demanded. Western media have presented this amendment as an attempt to subject the ITRs to governance and content regulation; they additionally argue that such a right could be (mis-)used to force internet application, content and service providers to deliver services to particular organizations.[33] Notwithstanding the fact that the Preamble and therefore the Internet Resolution is legally non-binding, it is part of the ITRs package and can evolve as a standard-setting principle, particularly in case of a re-interpretation over the next few years.[34]

The approach of the cyber-sovereignty advocates leads to a (national) fragmentation of the internet, since each national government under this concept has its own right to decide about the internet activities which are accessible in its area. It seems obvious that national decisions will differ widely and that the 'governance regime' could jeopardize the cross-border flow of information and business activities (for example e-commerce).

---

[32] See W. Kleinwächter, 'Internet Governance Outlook 2012: Cold War or Constructive Dialogue?' (2012), available at: http://news.dot-nxt.com/2012/01/10/ig-outlook-2012-part-one (accessed March 2014).

[33] See, for example, G. Lynch and D. Burstein, 'WCIT Collapses: US, UK, Allies Refuse to Sign Treaty after Africa Wins Floor Vote' (14 December 2012), available at: http://www.commsday.com/uncategorized/wcit-collapses-us-uk-allies-refuse-to-sign-treaty-after-africa-wins-floor-vote (accessed March 2014).

[34] Available at: http://files.wcitleaks.org/public/S12-WCIT12-C-0065!!MSW-E.pdf (accessed March 2014).

2.2 The Economic Call

From the economic side, different voices can be heard. The economic industry especially has expressed its concern about more regulation or surveillance for the internet, as business is concerned that a governmental big-footing in the industry may hinder innovation and new developments. However, it cannot be overlooked that those who urged investigation against Google were mostly Google's competitors, above all Microsoft. It seems that these competitors try to restrain their successful market leader through regulatory methods instead of fighting it through economic methods such as innovation, quality or efficiency.[35]

Net neutrality (also called network neutrality or internet neutrality) has become an important principle in internet debates.[36] According to this principle, internet service providers (ISPs) as well as governments and telecommunications carriers should be bound to treat all data transmissions on the internet equally, without exercising any kind of discrimination against or differentiation in charging any user, content, site, platform, application, and mode of communication. Advocates of net neutrality claim in particular that prices for internet transmissions as well as speed of delivery may not be distinguished along customers' categories.

The imposition of a tiered service model allowing a controlling of the infrastructure could lead to a removal of competition and to the creation of artificial scarcity. Eventually, such a model could also require customers to buy otherwise uncompetitive services. Opponents of net neutrality argue that data discrimination would be able to guarantee the quality of the services and would allow deep packet inspection that avoids the transmission of undesirable contents (pornography, hate speech).

3. CASE STUDIES

Based on the described understanding of the general competition law principles and the mentioned call for more regulation, three case studies will be presented in order to deepen the discussion of the risks of a

[35] See R.H. Bork and J.G. Sidak, 'What Does the Chicago School Teach about Internet Search and the Antitrust Treatment of Google?' (2012) 8 *J. Comp. L. & Econ.* 663.

[36] See Weber (n. 20 above) 203.

structural change in the internet markets. These case studies will examine online sellers, search engines and social networks.

3.1 Online Sellers

One of the first commercial appropriations of the internet was its utilization as a sale channel.[37] Apart from its use as an additional distribution channel, the internet also brought up new business models, such as strictly online sellers and, in particular, the model of online trading platforms. In general, online trading platforms simply utilize the fundamental functions of traditional market places in matching demand and supply.

As a popular representative of the retail market, eBay can be mentioned. Since the beginning of the internet age, eBay has constantly increased its market share. In fact, eBay is not a simple online reseller but an online trading platform, which provides sellers with the possibility of selling their products.

3.1.1 Economic elements and characteristics of the relevant markets

Trading platforms benefit from strong 'indirect' network effects. From the buyers' point of view, the more sellers are active on the platform, the greater is the variety of offered goods and the better the opportunity to compare the offered products. From the sellers' perspective, an online trading platforms' attractiveness is enhanced as more buyers join the platform, since the likelihood of finding a buyer increases and the price resulting from the online auction will be higher. These network effects increase the tendency for concentration, since the existence of one single platform is the most effective option for both sellers and buyers.

The possibility of 'multi-homing' exists especially for buyers, who may easily search for goods on different platforms. For sellers of unique goods, multi-homing is not feasible. The limited possibility of multi-homing strengthens the concentration tendency.

Furthermore, concentration is enhanced through the importance of the reputation on trading platforms. Since everybody may act completely anonymously online, trading platforms are very prone to fraud. Therefore, trust and confidence are an essential issue of all internet transactions. To avoid fraudulent behaviour, most trading platforms have introduced a 'reputational system', which enables sellers and buyers of a

---

[37] See also M. Dolmans and L. Leyden, 'Internet & Antitrust: An Overview of EU and National Case Law' (2012) No. 45647 *e-Competitions Competition Laws Bulletin* 3.

certain transaction to evaluate each other. Especially for sellers, reputation is very important and it depends on the number of successful transactions.[38]

Reputation is platform-specific and may not be transferred to another platform which results in high switching costs and lock-in effects. Although the reputation system also applies to buyers, reputation is generally less important and lock-in effects lower.[39]

3.1.2 Abusive behaviour through rating practices

The mentioned lock-in effects for sellers gave rise to the question of whether eBay is able to abuse its strong market position to foreclose the market for online auctions.[40] The apparently existing market dominance is offset by different factors. On the one hand, despite its strong position on the market for trading platforms, eBay is facing competition not only from other platforms but also from 'traditional suppliers' making use of the direct sale channel and the online distribution of their products. On the other hand, the potential barriers should not be overestimated, since they could be of importance for professional resellers only representing a small part of the participants; for 'normal' sellers, reputation is not of such great importance.[41]

3.2 Search Engines

To assess the relevant competition problem better, it is important to understand how search engines work. Broadly speaking, search engines try to map the contents of the internet by collecting all the information on the different websites through so-called 'web crawlers'. The information found by the web crawler is collected based on the indexes of the search engines.

The majority of the revenues of a search engine depend on advertising, normally through so-called search advertising. This means that the user conducting a search on such a website will see on the result page not only the result of his search, but also a list with some query-related advertisements also known as 'sponsored links'. The ads are bought by the advertisers on the basis of the search words of the user (keywords). The search engines sell the keywords to the advertisers who bid most for

---

38 Haucap and Heimeshoff (n. 3 above) 11.
39 Ibid., 12.
40 Ibid., 11ff.
41 Ibid., 12.

the respective search word.[42] A particular feature of this form of advertisement is represented by the payment terms, as Google earns revenue from the advertisements only if the advertisement was clicked by a user. Therefore, strong incentives exist to make the advertisements useful and valuable for the recipient.[43]

Google is an important search engine as well as a big player in the advertising market in the internet, since the undertaking not only directly sells advertising space to advertisers, but also acts as an intermediary with its own advertising network. On Google's website, advertisers can place their ads through Google's auction-based advertising program 'AdWords' directly on Google's website or on websites of Google's 'AdSense' network. For website publishers Google offers its intermediary program 'AdSense', which places either contextual targeted ads on the publisher's website or 'normal' search ads if the publisher embeds a special Google search box on its website.[44] This sophisticated direct and indirect advertising system makes Google the leading provider of online advertising.

3.2.1 Economic elements and characteristics of the relevant market

The search engine business is characterized by very high fixed costs; the technical infrastructure as well as the development and the necessary constant progression of the search algorithms are cost-intensive (hardware, human capital, IP patents). However, marginal costs are very low, applying to both market sides: costs for providing the search function to users as well as for the advertising possibility to advertisers are quite modest.

As explained above, search engine markets are two-sided markets. First, they provide search functions to users, who are aiming at relevant and accurate search results. Secondly, search engines provide advertising space to advertisers, who are aiming at a large number of users and good visibility for ads. Network effects between the market sides are of a direct nature.[45]

These direct network effects in turn cause economies of scale, which are enhanced through the importance of size for search engines: the more the search function is used by customers, the more data are available. These data are essential for the search engines to improve their search

[42] Case COMP/M.5727 – *Microsoft/Yahoo! Search Business* (n. 14 above) para 35.

[43] See Bork and Sidak (n. 35 above) 6.

[44] Case COMP/M.4731 – *Google/DoubleClick* (n. 14 above) paras 92ff.

[45] Bork and Sidak (n. 35 above) 5.

algorithm quality and provide an accurate and relevant search function to the users, with the result that Google's search gets even more attractive for the users.[46]

Another remarkable feature in the search engine market is the low switching costs.[47] Especially for users, the next search engine is always only 'one click away'. Furthermore, there is no possibility for providers such as Google to prevent users from switching to other search engines or to generate other lock-in effects. The only way to keep users is to provide them with a better service.

3.2.2 The gatekeeper issue

Search engines are often referred to as 'new gatekeepers'. Due to the massive information flood, users need search engines to find the information they are interested in. For businesses it is, therefore, of crucial importance to be found through a search engine. Therefore, a search engine – in practice mostly Google – is often compared with 'mass media', viewed as a bottleneck through which the information has to flow in order to reach the general public.[48]

Sometimes, users only consider the first few sites listed in the search results. Therefore, in order to be found by users, sites have to appear in the top positions.[49] Obviously, this is a problematic requirement because at any given time only a limited number of sites can be displayed on the first page of the search results. The determination of a certain order is indispensable; search engines, therefore, have to make editorial judgments through their search algorithm about the pages' relevance; the same applies to traditional mass media. It is obvious that 'pure objectivity' is not possible; furthermore, the term 'neutrality' even lacks a common understanding. In fact, every medium – be it a conventional newspaper or a search engine – is heavily reliant on editorial judgments

---

[46] Haucap and Heimeshoff (n. 3 above) 9.

[47] See Bork and Sidak (n. 35 above) 7ff. For a different opinion see K.L. Devine, 'Preserving Competition in Multi-Sided Innovative Markets: How Do You Solve a Problem Like Google?' (2009) 10 *N.C. J. L. & Tech.* 59.

[48] See F. Pasquale, 'Beyond Innovation and Competition: The Need for Qualified Transparency in Internet Intermediaries' (2010) 104 *Nw. U. L. Rev.* 7.

[49] See FairSearch Coalition, 'Google's Transformation from Gateway to Gatekeeper: How Google's Exclusionary and Anticompetitive Conduct Restricts Innovation and Deceives Consumers', available at: http://www.fairsearch.org/wp-content/uploads/2011/10/Googles-Transformation-from-Gateway-to-Gatekeeper.pdf (accessed March 2014).

and control.[50] For users, the main goal may be termed 'relevance': relevant results are the ones satisfying the user the most.[51] If the search engine is not able to provide the user with 'relevant' – thus satisfying – search results, it will lose its (dominant or strong) position within a short time, since users will no longer use the service.

3.2.3 Abuse of dominant market position

The primary charge against Google was the preferential treatment of its own vertical services, caused by a major shift in Google's business strategy.[52] While in the beginning Google acted as a pure search engine and tried to help users to find the information they were looking for, in recent years it has expanded its business to vertical search and other specialized content services. Vertical search engines are websites that specialize in specific content, such as travel services, books, local businesses, etc. Vertical search engines are important because consumers are actively searching for something and are, therefore, interesting for advertisers as immediate consumers.[53]

3.2.4 Abuse through privileging own services

Google was accused of displaying links to its own vertical search services in a different way than it did for links to competitors' webpages, and thus steering users to its own services. According to Google's competitors, this may result in preferential treatment compared to those of competing services. Furthermore, Google was blamed for manipulating its search algorithm to exclude any competing sites.[54]

Even if the most often mentioned complaint, that Google privileges its own services, may be true, further questions arise as to whether such preferential treatment constitutes anticompetitive behaviour or whether the preference given to Google's services simply depended on its

---

[50] See E. Goldman, 'Search Engine Bias and the Demise of Search Engine Utopianism' in B. Szoka and A. Marcus (eds), *The Next Digital Decade – Essays on the Future of the Internet* (TechFreedom 2010) 461, 473.

[51] See J. Grimmelmann, 'Some Skepticism about Search Neutrality' in B. Szoka and A. Marcus (eds), *The Next Digital Decade – Essays on the Future of the Internet* (TechFreedom 2010) 435, 439.

[52] For an actual overview R.H. Weber and S. Volz, 'Kartellrechtlicher Handlungsbedarf im Lichte potenzieller Meinungsmacht von Suchmaschinen' (2015) 4 *Wirtschaft und Wettbewerb* 356 ff.

[53] See G.A. Manne, 'The Problem of Search Engines as Essential Facilities: An Economic and Legal Assessment', in B. Szoka and A. Marcus (eds), *The Next Digital Decade – Essays on the Future of the Internet* (TechFreedom 2010) 419.

[54] See FairSearch Coalition (n. 49 above) 6ff.

business acumen and was a consequence of providing a better service. If Google is actually pointing users to its own services, it may really be better for users.[55]

These issues are often discussed under the concept of 'neutrality' of search engines, meaning that search engines should not discriminate among websites.[56] However, the search-neutrality concept causes more problems than it solves. Even the definition of the term 'neutrality' is controversial.[57] Should neutrality be understood to mean equality? Or should it focus more on the requirement of objectivity? Or does it mean that the algorithms used should be made transparent to the users? None of these concepts is the be-all and end-all solution. As shown above, certain judgements between the websites have to be made; furthermore, there are no generally accepted theories about objectivity or relevance, since these terms are confounded by subjective factors. Therefore, transparency is naturally limited by the risk of search engine manipulation through website editors.

In assessing a possible 'neutrality' concept the application of the net neutrality principles developed in telecommunications law could also be considered. However, this approach would not provide a satisfactory solution, since the concept of net neutrality varies among world regions and even the application of the 'net neutrality' principle to internet service providers itself is highly controversial.

3.2.5 Abuse through exclusion of index

In 2006, a lawsuit was filed against Google because it removed a website from its index which had used manipulation to get a better ranking in the search results. Since not appearing in Google's search results is like not existing in the internet, the website's traffic afterwards dropped by 70 per cent. This may lead to the question of whether due to Google's dominant market position – undertakings are entitled to be indexed on Google's website. Furthermore, the question arises whether the exclusion from an index after manipulating websites goes too far, or whether the exclusion should be considered admissible. A right to be readmitted to the index could be based on the essential facilities doctrine as developed by the European Court of Justice.[58] By analogy, the inclusion in the index

---

[55] See Grimmelmann (n. 51 above) 452.

[56] Ibid., 453.

[57] Ibid., 442ff.

[58] The first time this concept was applied was in the *Magill* decision. See Joined Cases C-241/91 P and C-242/91 P *RTE and ITP v Commission* ('*Magill*') [1995] ECR I-743.

must be indispensable for the applicant, the refusal is not objectively justified and the applicant does not have any alternative possibility for rendering its services. However, in practical terms this question does not seem very relevant, since it is in Google's own interest to index all websites.

3.2.6 Investigations in the European Union and the United States

On the basis of the complaints of different online undertakings, the FTC as well as the European Commission opened an antitrust investigation against Google. In the US, the investigation began in 2011; after 20 months of investigation, at the beginning of January 2013, the Federal Trade Commission (FTC) dropped the *Google* case with minimal consequences.[59] According to the FTC, no evidence was found to prove that Google used unfair techniques towards competing sites. Nevertheless, Google agreed to voluntarily change some of its practices to be more open to competitors.

In Europe, the competition authorities were far more successful in achieving concrete concessions from Google. Shortly after the announcement from the FTC that it would close the investigation without prosecution, EU's former Competition Commissioner Joaquín Almunia asked Google to put forward proposals on how to change the presentation of its search results.[60] In early April 2013, Google promised to clearly label the search results of its own vertical service providers and to show at least three results of rival services; the remedies proposed by Google were assessed through a market test, which was concluded by the end of June 2013.[61] According to Google's competitors, as well as to some voices from legal doctrine, the proposed measures were not sufficient and would have a minimal effect with respect to the affected markets.[62] Later Joaquín Almunia asked Google to improve its proposals since the remedies did not go far enough to overcome the existing competition

---

[59] See E. Katz, 'FTC Drops Bias Charges Against Google' (17 January 2013) 249 No. 12 *N.Y. L.J.*

[60] See the statements made by J. Almunia in the Financial Times (11 January 2013), available at: http://ec.europa.eu/commission_2010-2014/almunia/headlines/articles/ft1_en.pdf (accessed 10 September 2014).

[61] Commission Communication of 26 April 2013, Case COMP/AT.39740 – *Google*, available at: http://eur-lex.europa.eu/legal-content/EN/TXT/PDF/?uri=CELEX:52013XC0426%2802%29&from=EN (accessed 10 September 2014).

[62] See T. Höppner and L.J. Davies, 'The EU Competition Investigation of Internet Search' (2013) 14 *Computer L. Rev. Int'l* 107; see also Haucap (n. 12 above).

concerns.[63] In February 2014, Commissioner Almunia announced that Google had realized significant improvements; he was optimistic to make Google's commitments legally binding within the next few months.[64] In an unexpected move, however, the Commissioner told Bloomberg TV on 7 September 2014 that following very negative responses from complainants the antitrust investigation is being reopened.[65] Consequently, Google has not yet escaped the watchful eyes of the European competition authorities. In April 2015, the European Commission issued a Statement of Objections alleging that Google abused its dominant position on the market of horizontal Internet search services to privilege its own vertical search engines. Furthermore, a separate antitrust investigation was initiated with regard to Google's mobile operating system Android.[66]

The reason for the harder line adopted by the European competition authorities may be that Google's market position is even stronger in Europe than in the United States. In Europe, Google has a search share of about 90 per cent compared to about 70 per cent in the United States.

3.3 Social Networks

Social networks are currently one of the most discussed internet phenomena. They constantly gain new market shares, and in 2012 as well as at the beginning of 2013, Facebook was the most visited website.[67]

As explained above, the primary problem with regard to social networks is their definition. Nevertheless, at the time of writing, the market leader in the social network industry is doubtlessly Facebook, a private network that enables users to build up a profile and to interact with friends and relatives.

---

[63] See the statements made by J. Almunia at a news conference (17 July 2013), available at: http://in.reuters.com/article/2013/07/17/eu-google-idINL6N0FN1K120130717 (accessed 10 September 2014).

[64] See J. Almunia, 'Statement on the Google Investigation' (5 February 2014), available at: http://europa.eu/rapid/press-release_SPEECH-14-93_en.htm (accessed 10 September 2014).

[65] See C. Arthur, 'European Commission Reopens Google Antitrust Investigation' (8 September 2014), available at: http://www.theguardian.com/technology/2014/sep/08/european-commission-reopens-google-antitrust-investigation-after-political-storm-over-proposed-settlement (accessed 10 September 2014).

[66] Cf. European Commission Press Release, Memo/15/4781 (15 April 2015), available at: http://europa.eu/rapid/press-release_MEMO-15-4781_en.htm (accessed 29 June 2015).

[67] According to http://www.seomoz.org/top500 (accessed March 2014).

3.3.1 Economic elements and characteristics in the relevant market

What makes social networks special is the fact that they are pure online phenomena and have no brick-and-mortar analogue. Furthermore, social networks are platforms and, therefore, characterized by network effects. From the users' side, network effects of social networks are of a direct nature since the attractiveness of the network increases if more users are part of the same social network. Since the use of social networks is mostly free and funded through advertising, indirect network effects exist from advertisers. The more traffic there is on a social network website, the better is the visibility of an advertisement.

The market concentration level in social network markets is lower than in other online markets. The reasons for this certainly include the fact that markets are less homogeneous; even on the basis of a very narrow market definition, different types of social networks such as business or private networks may be distinguished. Principally, multi-homing is very easy, as setting up a profile in a social network does not entail major effort.[68] Multi-homing may even be necessary, as different networks such as private or business networks are used for different purposes.

3.3.2 Personal data as a cause of market dominance

To date, concerns related to social networks have arisen not only from the competition side, but also from the privacy perspective. Through their services, social networks have the possibility of acquiring a vast amount of personal data about their users. This information may be monetized in different ways.

The availability of personal data can lead to competition advantages. In general, internet service providers often derive substantial revenue from personal data. In particular, data may be used to improve one's own service, for example to better target the advertisements to users.[69] The possibility of targeting users/customers is a decisive advantage compared to other media, such as television advertising.[70] Targeting is an increasing issue of advertising, since advertising is only efficient if it is addressed to its relevant target group. The more information is gathered about a person, the better predictions can be made in view of which advertisements might appeal to the user.[71]

---

[68] See Haucap and Heimeshoff (n. 3 above) 12.

[69] P.J. Harbour and T.I. Koslov, 'Section 2 in a Web 2.0 World: An Expanded Vision of Relevant Product Market' (2010) 76 *Antitrust L.J.* 769, 780.

[70] Geradin and Kuschewsky (n. 11 above) 4.

[71] Harbour and Koslov (n. 69 above) 793.

3.3.3 Abuse of dominance through preventing exportability of data

Some commentators have criticized Facebook's alleged exclusionary conduct leading to the creation of lock-in effects of customers.[72] The gathered personal data may be used to create barriers for potential competitors. In Europe, competition authorities were particularly concerned that Facebook prevented the portability of personal information. According to Joaquín Almunia, the right of data portability stated in the European Data Protection Directive 'goes to the heart of competition policy'.[73]

A particular anxiety with regard to Facebook may arise from the fact that it is very difficult to terminate a Facebook account, since the social network makes it almost impossible to delete the account. Normally, it is only possible to deactivate the account; all the information about the account remains preserved and even if one manages to delete the account completely, Facebook maintains ownership of all the information and images about the user.[74] Through this, users may be obliged to stay with Facebook. Furthermore, it is not possible to transfer data to a competing service. In addition, users will often be reluctant to change a social network, since such a move forces the individual to notify this change to his or her personal community. If users were able to take their former profile, including contacts, applications, pictures, etc. to the other network, switching costs would be reduced.[75] The lack of data portability may therefore constitute entry barriers for new competitors.[76]

If data portability is relatively easy, users might be more likely to switch to another service provider if they are not satisfied with the service offered, particularly in the light of the level of data protection offered by this service.[77] The portability of personal datasets provides strong incentives in terms of both switching costs and the possibility of multi-homing. In markets in which switching costs are low and the possibility of multi-homing is given, it is hard to achieve market

---

72 Cf. C.S. Yoo, 'When Antitrust Met Facebook' (2012) 19 *George Mason L. Rev.* 1147.

73 See the speech delivered by J. Almunia, 'Competition and personal data protection', Speech of 26 November 2012, available at: http://europa.eu/rapid/press-release_SPEECH-12-860_en.htm (accessed March 2014).

74 See Waller (n. 18 above) 17ff.

75 Pasquale (n. 48 above) 153; R.H. Weber, 'Information at the Crossroads of Competition and Data Protection Law' (2014) 12 *ZWeR – J. Comp. L.* 169, 178 et seq.

76 Yoo (n. 72 above) 1155; see also Geradin and Kuschewky (n. 11 above) 10.

77 See Harbour and Koslov (n. 69 above) 796.

dominance and even harder to abuse this dominance. However, complete data portability could also raise privacy concerns, since personal data may be ported easily from one platform to another, which will perhaps not provide an equivalent level of data protection. The new platform may use the transferred personal data in an unjustified manner. For example, the singles site 'power.com' used login data provided by its users to scrap information from third-party websites such as Facebook or Gmail.[78]

4. LESSONS AND NEW APPROACHES FOR COMPETITION REGULATION

4.1 Definition of New Relevant Markets

4.1.1 One market for online advertising

As mentioned above, most internet services are free and sponsored by advertisers; therefore, internet markets are normally two-sided markets. This leads to the question of whether all providers of internet services may be part of the same 'online advertising' market. In general, all advertising is ultimately designed to promote the sale of a product or a service.[79]

Broadly speaking, multi-sided online platforms try to match different parties with contrasting needs. The higher the number of participants on both sides, the higher the likelihood of finding a suitable match.[80] Online platforms usually earn revenues from advertising. They try to attract a large number of users in order to then sell the advertiser the access to users. The content provided by the website is only a tool to attract the users: search engines provide search results to searchers; other websites may attract traffic through other means. Once a website generates enough traffic, the advertising inventory may be supplied to advertisers.[81] Apparently, advertisers are not primarily interested in what kind of content is provided, as long as their advertising seems promising.

Even if advertisements and the kind of advertising differ depending on the different types of platforms being used, they may be considered as substitutes, since advertisers are usually not bound by a certain form of

---

[78] *Facebook Inc. v. Power Ventures*, 91 U.S.P.Q.2d 1430 (N.D. Cal. 2009); see also Yoo (n. 72 above) 1160.

[79] D.S. Evans, 'The Economics of the Online Advertising Industry' (2008) 7 *Rev. Netw. Econ.* 6.

[80] Ibid., 21.

[81] Ibid., 21.

advertisement, such as video or normal banner ads, or a certain kind of advertisement (e.g. search advertising). In most cases, advertisements may be designed for all kinds and forms of advertising; it is only a matter of design.

4.1.2 Influence of data issues

As shown with regard to Facebook, personal data are of great value for internet service providers. Personal data can be applied to a variety of commercial uses, most importantly for providing greater advertising effectiveness through better targeting possibilities. The likelihood that advertising is successful is highly dependent on whether the advertising reaches the relevant target group. Therefore, the more personal information about individuals is accumulated, the more interesting it is for advertisers. For that reason, data issues have a direct influence on online advertising markets.

The relationship between personal data and competition law was analysed by the European Commission in the merger control procedure related to *Google/DoubleClick*, in particular with regard to troubling consequences on competition of the combination of the companies' vast troves of personal data.[82] Ultimately, the Commission considered that this specific combination of gathered data would not result in a competitive advantage; but this fact should not lead to the conclusion that the possession of personal data is not an issue in competition investigations at all. Commissioner Almunia indicated that personal data may under certain circumstances – which were not given in the *Google/DoubleClick* case – be misused to weaken competition.[83]

However, online data protection is also of growing importance for many users who tend to pay more attention to privacy issues online. Therefore, incentives for internet service providers may arise to provide better data protection policies for users, be it through privacy policies or through underlying data protection technologies.[84]

Furthermore, competition can be influenced by the possibility of data portability.[85] If data is transferable from one service provider to another, users may tend to switch if they are not satisfied with the service provided, for instance with regard to the level of data protection. Nevertheless, full data portability can give rise to privacy concerns, since

---

82 See Geradin and Kuschewsky (n. 11 above) 12.

83 Ibid., 13; see Almunia (n. 73 above).

84 See Harbour and Koslov (n. 69 above) 793.

85 See section 3.3.3 above.

the personal data may be misused by the service provider the data are transferred to.

4.1.3 Market for user attention

Going further, the relevant market is eventually not the market for online advertising but for user attention.[86] The value of advertising space highly depends on the traffic of a website. The more users visit a website and the more time they spend there, the greater its likelihood to be noticed. Undertakings therefore try to attract significant traffic on a website to increase their revenue.

Even if people in general spend more time online, time is naturally limited due to offline activities such as working or sleeping. The variety of internet services in the last years has increased dramatically, novel services appearing daily. These services all seek the attention of the users. The services provided, whether search engine services, social networking possibilities or blogs, are only tools for harvesting attention.[87] The internet players compete against each other across boundaries of product or services markets. Once a website loses traffic, it is not attractive for advertisers anymore and they will turn to another internet service provider with more traffic.

The theory of a market for user attention also applies to online providers that are not financed through advertisements but through other channels; user attention is important for strengthening the market presence (market awareness). Furthermore, in consequence of a widespread advertising fatigue, some undertakings are trying to implement other possibilities for awareness-raising and for financing. For example, WhatsApp, a messaging tool for smartphones, is financed through selling subscriptions to its service for 1 dollar a year and is completely advertising-free. Notwithstanding the fact that WhatsApp is mainly known in US and European markets, whereas other countries use different applications (e.g., Line, Kik, Viber etc.), this service could be considered as one of the largest competitors for Facebook. However, by acquiring the shares of WhatsApp in February 2014, Facebook has extended its business scope to a service that combines elements of text messaging and social networking, and has thereby eliminated a fierce competitor.

---

[86] D.S. Evans, 'Attention Rivalry among Online Platforms and its Implication for Antitrust Analysis' (2013) 9 *J. Comp. L. & Econ.* 313.

[87] Ibid., 4.

4.2 Need of New Regulation or Legal Action?

With regard to the regulation issues, two main questions have to be clarified. The first question, in connection with sector-specific regulation, is whether such governmental intervention is justified, because the market suffers from a lack of workable competition and this deficiency cannot be solved with the existing antitrust instruments. Second, one may ask whether competition authorities should – with recourse to traditional competition law instruments – increasingly force the internet players to fulfil certain obligations or whether new approaches are required to provide for a competitive environment.

4.2.1 The Schumpeterian vision of competition

A remarkable factor in all the discussions about the internet and competition is the fact that the concept of the Austrian scholar Joseph Schumpeter, who established the theory that competition consists of one dominant firm being replaced by another dominant firm, seems to be proven again in the online world.[88] The past has shown that internet markets share much of the Schumpeterian vision of competition, as once dominant firms have disappeared from the market.

Furthermore, internet players normally do not restrict their business activities to their core business, but are willing to compete with others in their business area or in emerging business areas. A look at the mobile phone market shows how fast things change: some years ago, Apple's iPhone was the number one in the smartphone market; its software IOS was the state of the art for smartphone software. Now, Google's software Android, along with different mobile phone providers, has caught up and even overtaken Apple in some areas.

However, it should not be forgotten that internet markets are – due to network effects – prone to concentration. Furthermore, network effects may generate market entry barriers. Both facts, firstly that internet markets – up to now – were highly competitive markets in which big players fight each other and market shares may rise from zero to a decent level in only a few months, and secondly that network effects and concentration tendencies may have a positive impact on market foreclosure strategies, must be carefully assessed when analysing internet issues.

---

[88] Weber (n. 20 above) 60; see also Devine (n. 47 above).

4.2.2 State intervention and specific regulation

As explained above, specific regulation is only feasible if a certain market does not have competitive structures, that is, normally, if one dominant undertaking is active in a market and this market is characterized by high and non-transitory entry barriers.

4.2.2.1 Legitimization of sector-specific regulation Regarding online markets, the question can be raised whether one of the internet giants has a dominant position in a certain market and whether the market barriers to enter this market are so high that the implementation of specific regulation is legitimate. As already mentioned, the main characteristics of internet markets are their strong dynamic and their continuous change. Notwithstanding the fact that network effects may cause high market entry barriers, they are neither insurmountable nor non-transitory. Furthermore, since a universal and generally accepted definition of the relevant product or service market has not been established yet, and since new approaches in this area (such as data portability, value of personal data, etc.) should be reflected, far-reaching specific regulations can hardly be legitimated.

Hence, sector-specific regulation will only be necessary under special circumstances; general competition law usually provides the competition authorities with sufficient powers to face the arising problems of online markets. Online business does not generate any entirely new form of anticompetitive behaviour that is not included in the existing legal framework. The need for a new legal framework would only be justified if the problems in the online world were materially different from the ones in offline business.[89]

Nonetheless, the lack of a convincingly established legitimacy for sector-specific regulation of online markets should not lead to the conclusion that traditional competition views can be 'transferred' to the online world in a one-to-one way. The emergence of the internet brought along many new difficulties with regard to competition matters. These special features of internet markets and their influence on the competition situation should not be underestimated.

Accordingly, legal and political theorists should acknowledge that the development of the internet is too fast to be regulated in a 'traditional' manner. Unlike in other sectors, when regulating bodies start to prepare rules for the internet, there is an almost simultaneous reaction from the (potentially) regulated environment. A further challenge lies in the

---

[89] Weber (n. 20 above) 46.

fragmentation of powers within the online world. This makes even 'responsive regulation' inadequate, since the cost of acquiring the relevant information might be very high.[90]

4.2.2.2 The special situation of ICANN When discussing competition issues in the online world, the special situation of the Internet Corporation for Assigned Names and Numbers (ICANN) should be mentioned. ICANN is a private non-profit organization with quasi-governmental power to set policies. It is responsible for implementing and supervising the internet's naming and numbering and has therefore the power to control the architecture of the internet. The role of ICANN in the internet world gave rise to different concerns about legitimacy, accountability and transparency;[91] in recent times, antitrust issues have also been brought up.[92]

Due to its unique character, ICANN was spared antitrust scrutiny. In connection with several lawsuits – mainly that filed by Manwin Licensing – the question of whether ICANN might be held liable under competition law had to be assessed. According to ICANN, its activities are not commercial and therefore competition law does not apply to its conduct. The judge, however, refused to dismiss the lawsuit and stated that ICANN in general can be sued for alleged antitrust violations.

4.2.2.3 Adaption of conventional competition approaches In view of the above assessment, a slight adaptation of conventional competition approaches seems inevitable, in particular with regard to market definitions and the assessment of market power. More importance should be attached to the temporal component, since the success of both alleged anticompetitive behaviour as well as reactions of competitors and consumers must be taken into account. Therefore, the main goal should be to analyse whether the monopoly power is a temporary or non-temporary phenomenon. As the past has shown, market shares in online markets can change very quickly.[93]

At any rate, excessive governmental intervention should be avoided, especially with regard to innovation incentives. It is unquestionable that a

[90] R. Baldwin, M. Cave and M. Lodge, *Understanding Regulation: Theory, Strategy, and Practice* (2nd edn, OUP 2012) 278.

[91] For further details see Weber (n. 20 above) 60ff.

[92] J.T. Lepp, 'ICANN's Escape from Antitrust Liability' (2012) 89 Wash. U. L. Rev. 931.

[93] See J.T. Rosch (former Commissioner of the US FTC), 'Intel, Apple, Google, Microsoft, and Facebook: Observations on Antitrust and the High-Tech

certain amount of competition protection for undertakings is necessary to create incentives to invest time and money in innovation. Innovation has ultimately positive effects on consumer welfare.[94] The main question is how to balance competition and protection.

Consequently, competition authorities should focus more on competition for attention and user time, as well as on data and privacy issues, and less on particular services or products. For advertisers the different websites are substitutes; they are mostly interested in traffic and user attention. User attention may be influenced directly by the level of privacy provided by a certain internet service provider. Since customers' awareness of data protection issues is constantly growing, levels of data protection may constitute a competition parameter of increasing importance.

5. ASSESSMENT AND CONCLUSION

The analysis above shows that internet markets are very challenging for competition authorities. Even in traditional brick-and-mortar markets, the definition of the relevant product market normally creates complications, but internet markets with their special features are even more complex. The rapid technological change, the innovative players and the continuous spread of internet access makes the appreciation of future developments very difficult.

Further problems are posed by the two-sided characteristics of the markets, because the interdependence between the market sides has to be taken into account when assessing interchangeability. Likewise, the widespread lack of cost involvement in internet markets raises problems since conventional antitrust models that distinguish relevant markets are price-based. To put it simply: price is not the sole competition parameter in internet markets.

All these problems lead to the conclusion that traditional views on markets are not appropriate when assessing the relevant product markets. Internet players generate revenue via advertising and therefore try to be attractive for advertisers. As a consequence of multi-sided markets, attractiveness depends on the number of users visiting a website. Hence,

---

Sector' (18 November 2010) 7, available at: https://www.ftc.gov/public-statements/2010/11/intel-apple-google-microsoft-and-facebook-observations-anti trust-and-high (accessed March 2014).

[94] Ibid., 19.

internet service providers endeavour to provide an attractive service with constantly new features to keep users on their website.

As shown above, the political pressure to regulate the internet was mainly based on 'old' sovereignty concepts and might lead to a fragmentation that could become detrimental to the internet markets and business. Consequently, it seems to be doubtful that national security and content norms are more suitable than the strict enforcement of competition by competition authorities. Furthermore, markets are not static but are subject to rapid and substantial changes, which will cause ever-changing competition conditions.

Competition authorities need to act prudently. In this context, one should bear in mind that the mere possession of dominant market power is not an antitrust concern. So far, dominant market players in internet markets have alternated. This means that market forces have solved the problem by themselves. However, to the extent to which dominant internet undertakings compete with other big players in adjacent markets, the competitive environment must be secured – in so far as competition law has the function to avoid anti-competitive behaviour – for example, lock-in situations or cross-subsidization are to be challenged by the competition authorities.

10. The regulatory approach in competition law enforcement for innovation-intensive industries: the case of broadband access regulation in Japan

Toshiaki Takigawa

1. INTRODUCTION

Innovation-intensive industries – those in which innovations play a vital role for consumer welfare – have an ever-growing share in the economy. The market structures of these industries rapidly evolve as new technologies and new products are constantly created. Thanks to these innovations, consumers gain attractive new products while at the same time obtaining lower prices through large cost reductions. The most representative of these are the mobile devices and services industries that make use of high-speed and high-capacity Internet ('broadband').

In spite of their benefits, we cannot simply leave competition to proceed at random in these industries. Competition agencies (governmental agencies in charge of competition law enforcement) need to enforce competition law in order to safeguard consumer interests from anticompetitive conduct. This chapter examines how different a viewpoint the competition agencies need to adopt in dealing with the innovation-intensive industries in contrast to other industries. For this purpose, this chapter takes the example of the broadband industry, which includes not only broadband networks but also products and services (typically mobile devices and services) that make use of those networks.

Broadband stands in contrast to the narrowband network, which uses copper wires, and which for years has offered traditional telephone services. The narrowband network is a stable natural monopoly with little innovation. To reflect this contrast between the two industries, competition agencies also need to find a new way to apply competition laws to the broadband industry.

This chapter focuses on unilateral conduct (that is, exclusionary conduct in particular) because this, rather than cooperative conduct, is what prompts competition agencies to pay particular heed to innovations. Hardcore cartels (which occupy a predominant part of cooperative activities) are condemned as per-se illegal. Unilateral conduct, in contrast, requires competition agencies to balance its exclusionary effects with its pro-competitive effects, both of which are characterized by innovations.

Moreover, unilateral conduct requires more intensive intervention on the part of competition agencies. Whereas they must simply prohibit companies from engaging in cartels, when competition agencies face illegal unilateral conduct, they often have to order the violating company to adopt a specific behaviour. Typically, when a competition agency determines as illegal a refusal to provide access by a dominant telecommunications company ('carrier'), the agency is required to order the carrier to set up specific access conditions, including a specific access charge. This requires very specific knowledge of the market.

Traditionally, telecommunications agencies have regulated the broadband industry concurrently with competition agencies, which enforce the competition law. A telecommunications agency has more detailed knowledge of the broadband industry than a competition agency has. A competition agency, therefore, can learn from a telecommunications agency how to take innovations into account. It is from this perspective that this chapter looks at the telecommunications regulation of broadband networks.

2. STATIC EFFICIENCY VERSUS DYNAMIC EFFICIENCY AS AN OBJECTIVE OF THE COMPETITION LAW

Before analysing the role of innovations in the enforcement of competition law, we have to examine different views on the objectives of competition law. Competition agencies in major countries and regions have largely come to grasp the objective of competition law as being consumer welfare (or consumer surplus), which is achieved through the competition process. Nevertheless, many economists have advocated defining total welfare (the sum of consumer surplus and producer surplus) as the objective. Still, most producer surplus, in the long run, accrues to consumers through the competition process. Thus, the standpoint of recognizing consumer welfare as the objective reflects the position that producer surplus needs to be passed on to consumers more quickly.

Despite the widespread consensus that the objective of competition law should be consumer welfare, notable commentators have criticized the traditional definition of consumer welfare. This criticism emanates from these authors' emphasis on dynamic competition realized through innovations. They criticize the tendency of traditional economic analysis to grasp consumer welfare in a static manner that equates an increase in consumer welfare with a decrease in prices. In order to secure lower prices, according to the traditional view, competition policy has to be concerned about the pricing power of firms.

In most cases, this traditional viewpoint properly guides competition agencies in their merger control. Where competition law enforcement becomes more problematic is in the area of unilateral conduct. Here a competition agency acts against a dominant company when it engages in conduct that obstructs the business of rivals (hereinafter 'exclusionary conduct'). In high-technology or information-technology industries competition evolves dynamically. Some companies, by developing new products, temporarily attain monopolies, but other companies soon launch more innovative products, ushering in new markets.[1] Therefore, market shares in these industries only reflect static and temporary situations, and have a weak relationship with the degree of market power. In innovation-intensive industries, creation of new products and product innovations, rather than gradual price reductions, bring benefits to consumers. Innovations, in the long term, also lead to steep decreases in prices through cost reductions. Competition agencies, then, need to put more emphasis on securing incentives to innovate than on controlling temporary pricing power.[2]

In order to secure innovation incentives, competition agencies need to honour (although not absolutely) property rights in their regulation of

---

[1] See M.L. Katz and H.A. Shelanski, 'Schumpeterian Competition and Antitrust Policy in High-Tech Markets' (2005) 14 *Competition* 7.

[2] See J.G. Sidak and D.J. Teece, 'Dynamic Competition in Antitrust Law' (2009) 5 *J. Comp. L. & Econ.* 581, 582 (dynamic competition should be favoured over static competition).

unilateral conduct.[3] If competition agencies readily condemn dominant companies for refusing to provide rivals with access to their facilities, the value of the invested facilities decreases, thus undermining the innovation incentives of both incumbents and entrants. This leads to a long-term decrease in consumer welfare. When competition law enforcement is thus exercised against unilateral conduct to realize static efficiency, it ends up undermining dynamic efficiency.[4]

In competition law enforcement, the first requirement for determining the illegality of unilateral conduct is to ascertain that the investigated firm holds market power (including a dangerously high probability of acquiring market power through the exclusionary conduct). Competition agencies need to identify market power not exclusively by the firm's market share, but by the overall market conditions, including the possibility of new entries. In innovation-intensive industries, a high market share often does not demonstrate market power.[5] Moreover, a market may not be permanently defined in an industry where innovations have been actively launched, thus rendering market definition difficult.[6] These conditions in innovation-intensive industries make it imperative for competition agencies to reduce the weight of market shares in determining market power.

Prioritizing innovations, however, need not necessarily lead to weaker competition law enforcement; it may rather lead to a strengthening of the

---

3 Ibid., 610 ('The working assumption in dynamic competition analysis is that intellectual property rights are desirable institutional or legal arrangements providing necessary appropriability mechanisms to advance and reward innovation').

4 See H.A. Shelanski, 'Competition Policy for Mobile Broadband Networks' (2004) 3 *J. Telecomm. & High Tech. L.* 97, 108 ('[P]olicy decisions designed to promote or preserve competition will have unintended, negative consequences for technological change'). See also C.S. Yoo, 'Deregulation vs. Reregulation of Telecommunications: A Clash of Regulatory Paradigms' (2011) 36 *J. Corp. L.* 847, 865 ('Denying access would provide the strongest incentives for creating the alternative network capacity. Although denying access would cause static efficiency losses in the short run, stimulating entry by a competitor would promote dynamic efficiency gains in the long run').

5 Sidak and Teece (n. 2 above) 613 ('when innovation is significant, theoretical connections and empirical correlations become even weaker').

6 Ibid., 613 ('innovation can make defining relevant product markets difficult because business executives and government officials alike may not yet know what the future products will be').

enforcement. This is because threats of entry are imperative for incentivizing incumbents to innovate. Competition agencies, therefore, need to block entry-hindering activities of dominant companies.[7]

In summary, competition agencies need to enforce competition law in innovation-intensive industries in order to secure competitive pressures on incumbents. Nevertheless, the characteristics of innovative activities make it less meaningful to define markets, at the same time making it necessary to reduce the role of market shares in determining market power. Competition agencies, then, need to engage in case-by-case analyses, taking into account the characteristics of each innovation-intensive industry.

3. THE TELECOMMUNICATIONS REGULATION OF BROADBAND NETWORKS

Telecommunications agencies and competition agencies largely share the objective of consumer welfare. Both agencies also regard competition as the key to attaining this objective. Traditionally it is telecommunications agencies rather than competition agencies that have regulated business activities in the telecommunications (including broadband) sector. Competition agencies, therefore, can learn from telecommunications agencies' regulation. In particular, telecommunications agencies know more than competition agencies about the role of innovations in broadband industries.

3.1 Open System Versus Closed System for Telecommunications

The telecommunications industry is characterized by two vertically connected markets. The upstream market consists of telecommunications (both telephone and Internet) networks; the downstream market consists of telecommunications services and products, e.g., smartphone services and devices. Downstream companies cannot maintain their businesses without access to telecommunications networks at the upstream market.

---

[7] T. Wu, 'Taking Innovation Seriously: Antitrust Enforcement If Innovation Mattered Most' (2012) 78 *Antitrust L.J.* 313, 316. (It is exclusion, whether practiced by a monopolist or an oligopoly, that restricts or raises the price by which new ideas (embodied in products) get to enter the market.) I. Segal and M. Whinston, 'Antitrust in Innovative Industries' (2007) *Am. Econ. Rev.* 1703. (In innovation-intensive industries, active enforcement of competition law tends to promote innovation.)

This relationship between the upstream and downstream markets gave rise to the idea of separating ownership of the upstream market from that of the downstream market. This separation would result in prohibiting carriers from offering vertically integrated upstream and downstream services.[8] This idea – the 'open system' or the 'separation principle' – led to the proposal of mandating vertically integrated companies to offer equal treatment to their own downstream divisions as well as their downstream rivals.

Proponents of the open system have advocated 'network neutrality', whereby owners of broadband networks are prohibited from blocking certain contents or applications. The owners are also prohibited from discriminating (e.g., regarding speed) between different contents or applications. The US Federal Communications Commission (FCC), in 2015, adopted the principle of 'network neutrality' as part of its Internet regulation.[9]

Courts and antitrust agencies in the US also used to advocate the open-system principle. The court, in its remedy for the AT&T decision,[10] broke up AT&T both horizontally and vertically, thus prohibiting the regional Bell operating companies from entering the market for long-distance telecommunications. Likewise, the US regulation of the telecommunication sector, through the 1966 Telecommunications Act, prohibited the entry of local exchange carriers into long-distance telecommunications markets until competition arose in the regional telecommunications markets.[11]

---

[8] T. Wu, *The Master Switch: The Rise and Fall of Information Empires* (2010) 304 ('[The separation principle] would mean that those who develop information, those who own the network infrastructure on which it travels, and those who control the tools or venues of access must be kept apart from one another.').

[9] Federal Communications Commission, In the Matter of Protecting and Promoting the Open Internet, Report and Order (Open Internet Order), FCC 15-24 (February 26, 2015), available at https://apps.fcc.gov/edocs_public/attachmatch/FCC-15-24A1.pdf (accessed 3 July 2015). Although the FCC advocates the neutrality principle, this policy contains much ambiguity, including opaqueness of the 'reasonable network management' by which network owners can effectively discriminate between contents or applications.

[10] *United States v. American Tel. and Tel. Co.*, 552 F.Supp. 131 (D. D.C. 1982).

[11] 47 U.S.C. §§ 271–275 (2000). The FCC eliminated this 'structural separation' obligation in 1999: *Computer III Further Remand Order*, 14 FCC Rcd (1999).

However, modern antitrust thinking has ceased to advocate vertical separation of dominant companies. Likewise, in the US telecommunications regulation, proponents of the open system have been decreasing in number.[12] This trend reversal was brought about by economic studies showing that vertical integration often enables companies to raise efficiencies; companies, for efficiency reasons, often opt for vertical integrations over market transactions.[13]

The smartphone industry shows that open versus closed is not a binary distinction but a matter of degree. A single platform may contain both open and closed systems. For example, Apple controls the standards and qualities of its platform's applications, but development of the applications is open to companies other than Apple. Likewise, Microsoft Windows is open at the content and software end but closed at the operating-system end.[14]

The information-technology (typically smartphone) industries, with their platforms mixing open and closed systems, illustrate that the governmental policy of forcing a fixed organizational structure on companies decreases consumer welfare through constraining companies from flexibly adapting to market changes.

3.2 The Federal Communications Commission's Departure from the Open-System Regulation

3.2.1 The interconnection obligation under the 1996 Telecommunications Act

In the US, the Federal Communications Commission (FCC) is in charge of the telecommunications regulation under the Telecommunications Act of 1996[15] (hereinafter 'the 1996 Act'). The 1996 Act mainly targets the

---

[12] E.g., the FTC has published a report expressing a negative opinion on net neutrality: Federal Trade Commission (FTC), 'Broadband Connectivity Competition Policy: FTC Staff Report 2007' (2007) 157, available at: http://www.ftc.gov/reports/broadband/v070000report.pdf (accessed 30 September 2014) ('as long as consumers have one or more alternatives to which they can turn, it is difficult to imagine them accepting the blockage or elimination of content that is important to them').

[13] Regarding the merits of vertical integration see P.L. Joskow, 'Vertical Integration' (2010) 55 *Antitrust Bull.* 545, 563–569.

[14] See H.F. Kaiser, 'Are "Closed Systems" an Antitrust Problem?' (2011) 7(1) *Comp. Pol. Int'l* 94, available at: http://papers.ssrn.com/sol3/papers.cfm?abstract_id=1844944 (accessed 6 July 2015).

[15] P.L. No. 104-104, 110 Stat. 56 (1996).

'Regional Bell Operating Companies', which were created by the antitrust decision that broke up AT&T in 1984.

The US legislature designed the regulatory system of the 1996 Act, recognizing that the telecommunications network the Bell Operating Companies inherited from AT&T was a natural monopoly that the rivals of AT&T could not economically duplicate. This insight is the same as that for the electricity grid networks.

Nevertheless, the telecommunications network, as a natural monopoly, could admit new entrants if the government ordered the Bell Operating Companies to provide new entrants with access to their networks. This would result in competition within a single US-wide network. This logic was first revealed by the MCI antitrust decision, which ordered AT&T to provide the new entrant (MCI) with access to its network.[16]

The access provisions in the 1996 Act may be interpreted as a detailed embodiment of the principle espoused by the *MCI* decision. The 1996 Act, however, contains principles more interventionist than under antitrust law. Namely, antitrust enforcement against unilateral conduct (including that of the *MCI* decision) would require a finding of market power before the unilateral conduct can be condemned. By contrast, the 1996 Act obligates every telecommunications carrier to offer access, regardless of the carrier's market power.[17]

The 1996 Act stipulates access as 'interconnections', from the view that each carrier should provide other carriers with access to its network, thus realizing a unified giant network. Indeed, a network operator, in order to be accepted by customers, needs to cover as many customers as possible. Then, each carrier, in order to achieve the network effect, will broaden its network coverage through interconnecting with other carriers' networks.

Such governmental regulation may be regarded as legitimate for the reason that the government, in order to nurture competition, needs to force a dominant network operator to provide other operators with access to its network, because the network coverage of a new entrant is too small to attract customers. A dominant incumbent could perpetuate its dominance by refusing to provide access to its network.[18]

---

[16] *MCI Communications Corp. v. American Tel. and Tel. Co.*, 708 F 2d. 1081 (7th Cir. 1983).

[17] 47 U.S.C. § 251(a)(1) (2000).

[18] H.A. Shelanski, 'Adjusting Regulation to Competition: Toward a New Model for U.S. Telecommunications Policy' (2007) 24 *Yale J. Reg.* 55, 68.

3.2.2 Does the network effect of telecommunications necessitate mandatory interconnection?

A considerable number of commentators have endorsed obligating every carrier (irrespective of its market power) to interconnect with all others. Their argument is based on the grounds that the network effect of telecommunications networks makes it impossible for a new company to enter a market when the incumbent refuses to provide the entrant with access to its network.[19]

When no incumbent holds market power, however, companies are able to enter a market by obtaining access to incumbents' networks. The need to gain the network effect forces every incumbent to broaden its network by interconnecting with other carriers.[20] Thus, when no carrier holds market power, the government need not force interconnections on carriers.

The interconnection obligation increases the carriers' operating costs by necessitating technological and managerial coordination.[21] Therefore, when carriers refuse to interconnect it is not always in order to block rivals' entry. Often carriers dislike interconnection because of the large cost increases caused by being forced to go through technological changes. Interconnections, therefore, have no more rationale than to fulfil the government-imposed access obligation.

In addition to interconnection, the 1996 Act also stipulated 'unbundling', which forced carriers to separate their telecommunications facilities into functional elements (exchange, network, etc.) in order to provide access to other carriers at 'any technically feasible point'. The unbundling obligation thus constrains carriers' freedom of management to a degree greater than the interconnection obligation.

The 1996 Act moreover forced carriers to set interconnection charges at cost-based 'wholesale charges', the costs of which correspond to 'long-run incremental costs'.[22] The interconnection obligation logically leads the government to regulate interconnection charges. Otherwise, carriers could simply charge very high prices, realizing a virtual refusal to interconnect.

---

19 See, for instance, Shelanski (n. 18 above) 68.

20 D.F. Spulber and C.S. Yoo, 'Rethinking Broadband Internet Access' (2008) 22 *Harv. J. L. & Tech.* 1, 29.

21 D.F. Spulber and C.S. Yoo, 'Mandating Access to Telecom and the Internet: The Hidden Side of Trinko' (2007) 107 *Colum. L. Rev.* 1822, 1888.

22 FCC Rule, 47 CFR § 51.505(a) (1997).

'Long-run incremental costs' cover 'a reasonable allocation of forward-looking common costs'.[23] But the costs do not cover risks inherent in new investments, leading to costs lower than the actual costs borne by carriers in real businesses. The interconnection charges based on long-run incremental costs, thus, have put access-giving carriers at a disadvantage against carriers receiving the access. By contrast, competition law principles would argue in favour of competition-neutral charges.

Nevertheless, the unbundling and wholesale charge obligations are applicable only to the Bell Operating Companies (in the terminology of the 1996 Act, the 'local exchange carriers').[24] In limiting the regulation to dominant companies, the 1996 Act follows antitrust principles. Indeed, the 1996 Act contains a clause authorizing the FCC to refrain from enforcing the regulation when new entrants are able to compete effectively without the benefits of unbundling (as well as wholesale charges).[25] The ubiquity of cell phones using the wireless network has made it feasible for consumers to replace landline phones with cell phones. Rivals of the Bell Operating Companies, therefore, may be deemed capable of offering telephone services competitively without benefitting from the unbundling measures. The FCC, however, has not yet exercised this regulatory forbearance (except in the area of broadband).

3.2.3 Liberalization of broadband by the FCC

The 1996 Act remains intact, but the FCC, in 2005, liberated broadband companies from the constraints of interconnection (as well as the unbundling and the wholesale charge) obligations.[26] The basis for this regulatory forbearance is that broadband (in contrast with narrowband)

---

[23] *Verizon Communications Inc. v. FCC*, 535 US 467, 495 (2002).

[24] 47 U.S.C. § 251(c)(3) (2000); 47 U.S.C. § 251(c)(4) (2000).

[25] 47 U.S.C. § 251(d) (2000) ('the Commission shall consider … the failure to provide access to such network elements would impair the ability of the telecommunications carrier seeking access to provide the services that it seeks to offer).

[26] The 1996 Act authorizes the FCC to forbear from regulation when the FCC considers that such regulation is unnecessary and the forbearance will promote competitive market conditions (Section 401: Regulatory Forbearance). This provision enabled the FCC, in 2005, to exempt broadband access from core regulation of the 1996 Act (Appropriate Framework for Broadband Access to the Internet over Wireline Facilities, Report and Order and Notice of Proposed Rulemaking, 20 F.C.C.R. 14853, 14856 ¶ 2 (2005) [hereinafter 'Broadband Access Order']).

has undergone rapid innovations.[27] Consumers already enjoy multiple alternatives for their choice of companies offering broadband services.[28]

Several carriers opposed the regulatory forbearance on the grounds that the cited introduction of competition still leaves many regional markets where competition is restrained. But the FCC criticized this opposition as being too static, in ignorance of the trend of dynamic competition.[29] This stance of the FCC is in harmony with that of the proponents of dynamic competition.

3.3 Access Regulation by the Japanese Telecommunications Agency

An assessment of the access regulation in Japan in comparison with that in the US illuminates further areas where improvements may be made. The access regulation of the Japanese telecommunications agency (the Ministry of Internal Affairs and Communications, MIC) does not distinguish broadband from narrowband, thus applying the same articles of the telecommunications law to the whole telecommunications industry.[30]

The Telecom Law obligates all carriers in possession of telecommunications facilities (both narrowband and broadband) to provide interconnections to all other carriers when they seek interconnections.[31] This universal obligation coincides with the interconnection obligation set by the US 1996 Act.

In addition to the interconnection obligation imposed on all carriers, the Telecom Law imposes an unbundle-based interconnection obligation on dominant carriers. Dominant carriers are defined as carriers possessing 'Category I Designated Telecommunications Facilities',[32] facilities

---

[27] Broadband Access Order, para. 47; Spulber and Yoo (n. 20 above) 25 ('The shift to digital transmission has allowed networks that once were dedicated exclusively to voice or to video to compete with one another').

[28] Broadband Access Order, para. 47.

[29] Ibid., para. 50 ('We find that an emerging market, like the one for broadband Internet access, is more appropriately analyzed in view of larger trends in the marketplace, rather than exclusively through the snapshot data that may quickly and predictably be rendered obsolete as this market continues to evolve').

[30] Telecommunications Business Law (Law No. 86 of 25 December 1984) (hereinafter 'the Telecom Law'), as amended most recently by Law No. 125 of 24 July 2003, Art. 33(4)(ii), available at: http://www.soumu.go.jp/joho_tsusin/eng/Resources/laws/2001TBL.pdf (accessed 30 September 2014).

[31] Article 32 Telecom Law.

[32] Article 33 Telecom Law.

with more than 50 per cent market share.[33] The MIC obligates the 'dominant carriers' to set uniform interconnection charges that are calculated based on the carriers' long-run incremental costs. This standard is basically the same as that set by the US FCC.

The idea of imposing a special interconnection obligation on dominant carriers is shared by the Japanese MIC and the US FCC. Also, Nippon Telegraph and Telephone Corporation (NTT) (which has been designated as the sole carrier possessing the Category I Designated Telecommunications Facilities) is the equivalent of each of the US Bell Operating Companies.

Nevertheless, the MIC's dominant-position regulation is at odds with the dominant-position regulation conducted by the competition agencies in major countries, because the MIC designates the dominant carriers as carriers with more than 50 per cent market shares. The 50 per cent share threshold is too low for identifying companies holding market power. Moreover, market power should not be identified solely from market share, ignoring overall market conditions including the possibility of new entries.

Furthermore, against refusals to provide access, the competition agencies in major countries have adopted a standard more lenient than that set against other exclusionary practices. This standard consists in the 'essential facility' doctrine, by which competition agencies oblige dominant companies to provide rivals with access to their assets only when economically feasible alternatives are not available.[34] According to this standard, a 50 per cent market share is clearly insufficient for determining essentiality.

In spite of these constraining clauses, the Telecom Law equips the MIC with general clauses for exemptions, both for the interconnection obligation on all carriers and for the special unbundle-based interconnection obligation. The former authorizes the MIC to exempt carriers from the interconnection obligation when 'the interconnection is likely to hinder telecommunications services from being smoothly provided', etc. (Article 32(i) (ii) (iii)). The latter authorizes the MIC to exempt the dominant carriers from the unbundle-based interconnection obligations when '[the interconnection conditions set by the dominant carriers] have

---

[33] The MIC Notice, which is based on Article 33(1) Telecom Law as well as the Article 23-2 Telecom Law Implementing Regulations.

[34] See European Commission, Guidance on the Commission's enforcement priorities in applying Article 82 of the EC Treaty [now Article 102 TFEU] to abusive exclusionary conduct by dominant undertakings (hereinafter 'Article 102 Guidelines'), [2009] OJ C 45, p. 7, para. 81.

a comparatively small effect on improvement of user convenience and on comprehensive and reasonable development of telecommunications' (Article 33(3)).

This exemption authority given to the MIC is equivalent to the authority given to the US FCC by which the FCC exempts carriers from interconnection obligations when the exemption benefits the public and enhances competition. Thus the MIC is capable of implementing deregulation from considerations on innovations, without going through amendments of the Telecom Law.

Nevertheless, the MIC has shown no sign of initiating deregulation. The MIC has little incentive to deregulate, because it would curtail the roles and authorities of its own MIC. Deregulation of telecommunications in Japan needs to be initiated by the government.

3.4 Summary

Telecommunications access regulation in both the US and Japan has basically maintained the traditional common-carrier regulation whereby carriers are obligated to give non-discriminatory access to their networks. Concurrently with this common-carrier regulation, the US and Japanese agencies both have imposed special access regulation on dominant carriers. Competition law shares this concern for dominant positions. But the regulation of dominant positions by the telecommunications agencies is at odds with the control of market power by competition agencies. First, the telecommunications agencies have found dominant positions in a considerably wider range of companies than those holding dominant market power. Second, the telecommunications agencies' regulation of dominant positions, characterized by the unbundling-based access obligation, is much more interventionist than that conducted by the competition agencies.

If telecommunications networks form natural monopolies (in the same way as electricity grids do), the telecommunications-specific regulation on carriers' business activities has a rational basis. Innovations, however, have ushered in competition to telecommunications networks, enabling customers to choose from multiple networks. This phenomenon is most marked in the broadband sector, which has been going through rapid industrial changes due to incessant innovations. These two points should convince governments to replace telecommunications regulation with competition law enforcement, at least for this broadband sector.

Moreover, governments should refrain from obligating carriers to vertically separate into network and service divisions. Nor should governments force carriers to adopt non-discriminatory treatment between the carriers' own divisions and rivals. Experiences in competition law enforcement, as well as economic analyses, have shown that obligating companies to vertically separate (or to treat downstream companies non-discriminatorily) causes a great increase in costs. Thus, the disappearance of natural monopoly in telecommunications networks should prompt governments to replace telecommunications regulation with competition law enforcement to deal with unilateral conduct and mergers.

4. COMPETITION LAW ENFORCEMENT OF ACCESS TO BROADBAND NETWORKS

Competition agencies, not telecommunications agencies, should regulate telecommunications' access issues when effective competition prevails in the telecommunications industry. This is because, first, from the perspective of business freedom, competition law enforcement has the merit of limiting regulation to *ex post* control of anticompetitive acts. Such limited regulation contrasts with more constraining telecommunications regulation, which uniformly imposes specific conduct obligations (e.g., unbundle-based interconnections) on carriers *ex ante*, irrespective of the individual situation.

A second merit of regulation by competition agencies is grounded in considerations of the political economy. A regulatory agency in charge of a single industry can be captured by the interests of the incumbents.[35] A competition agency, by contrast, is in charge of a cross-section of industries which makes it more immune to industry capture and guarantees that it will indeed promote consumer welfare.

Among various telecommunications sectors, at least the broadband sector is no longer a natural monopoly because consumers already enjoy a choice of multiple providers. Competition agencies, therefore, should exclusively be in charge of the regulation of broadband.[36] Telecommunications agencies should cease regulating competition-related business

[35] G.J. Stigler, 'The Theory of Economic Regulation,' (1971) 2(1) *Bell J. Econ. & Manag. Sci* 3.

[36] Regarding telecommunication sectors in general (not restricted to broadband) see H.A. Shelanski, 'Adjusting Regulation to Competition: Toward a New Model for U.S. Telecommunications Policy' (2007) 24 *Yale J. Reg.* 55, 57 ('*ex ante* regulation that depends for its rationale on monopoly market structure should give way to *ex post* intervention against specific, anti-competitive acts on the model of conventional antitrust and competition policy, with resort to *ex ante* rules only where experience provides a compelling case that such rules are

activities in this sector, limiting their regulation of it to other issues such as the allocation of spectrum, consumer data protection, etc.

4.1 Competition Law Enforcement against Vertical Foreclosures

Governments need to refrain from obligating carriers to vertically separate into upstream networks and downstream services. Competition agencies, then, need to deal with individual exclusionary acts of vertically integrated carriers.

Access to telecommunication networks, in competition law enforcement, concerns exclusionary acts in vertically related markets. This type of conduct – 'vertical foreclosure'– consists of acts by dominant companies leveraging their dominance in upstream network markets to exclude (or raise the costs of) rivals in downstream markets. Representative types of vertical foreclosures include refusal to deal (including refusal to provide access), tying and exclusive dealing.

For a time, competition agencies and courts treated vertical foreclosures severely, but the 'severe tradition' disappeared during the 1970s as the Chicago School and the post-Chicago micro-economists, as well as management scholars, showed that vertical foreclosures often augment economic efficiencies.

Major competition agencies now evaluate each vertical foreclosure from the viewpoint of consumer welfare, comparing its competition-restraining effects with its efficiency effects. When this evaluation leads to a determination of illegality, competition agencies have to design remedies that best secure consumer welfare while at the same time minimizing intrusion into corporate decision-making. In spite of this basic convergence, competition agencies in major countries and regions are not uniform regarding how they conduct specific evaluations. Nor are they uniform in differentiating treatments between innovation-intensive industries (e.g. broadband) and other industries.

Competition agencies apply competition law to vertical foreclosures in two stages. At the first stage, a competition agency examines whether the investigated company holds market power in the upstream market. If

---

necessary to protect consumer welfare'). See also A.E. Kahn, 'Telecommunications: The Transition from Regulation to Antitrust' (2006) 5 *J. Telecomm. & High Tech. L.* 159, 164 ('preference for an interpretation of the antitrust laws as prohibiting anti-competitive behavior and the intent that can reasonably be inferred from it, as opposed to economic evaluations of either the structure of the markets involved or of their economic performance or results').

the company does not hold market power, the agency terminates the inquiry, not proceeding to the second stage. The reason for this termination is that the downstream companies are deemed to have alternative companies in the upstream market that are able to provide them with necessary inputs. In other words, a company without market power in an upstream market does not have the leverage to exclude rivals in downstream markets.

The rationale for requiring a competition agency to identify market power before intervening in unilateral conduct is to prevent excessive intervention. Market power, therefore, is a necessary condition but not a sufficient condition for intervention. This limiting standard is even more important for innovation-intensive industries because considerations on innovation (as discussed above in section 2) argue for a less interventionist attitude on the part of competition agencies.

The smartphone industry buttresses this argument. Google, Apple and Microsoft preside over the three competing smartphone platforms, each of which consists of several layers: devices, applications and content. Consumers have the freedom to choose the most appealing platform; each platform risks being driven out of the market if it fails to become more efficient and fails to appeal to consumers.

Each of the three, Google, Apple or Microsoft, therefore, in the lower layers of its platform, is obliged to deal with a rival if this will increase the platform's efficiency. Otherwise, a less efficient platform will lose business to its rivals and be forced out of the market. Conversely, an owner of a platform needs to decline to deal with a rival when this would decrease the platform's efficiency. For example, Apple has not obstructed iPhone users from using Skype, which competes with Apple's own FaceTime. Nor has Apple declined to adopt the Kindle app on iPads.

Thus, effective competition among platforms pressures the platform owners to calibrate the degree of openness (or closedness) of their platforms in order to appeal to consumer preferences. This insight supports the notion that competition agencies should not intervene in a vertical foreclosure when there is no company active in the upstream market that holds market power.

Moreover, even when a monopoly prevails in an upstream market, Chicago School scholars proclaim that a monopolist does not wish the downstream market to become less efficient through competition restraints. If it has already obtained a monopolistic profit from the upstream market, then a less competitive downstream market will lead to a decreased profit.[37] This thinking has led Chicago School proponents to advocate a standard of per-se legality for vertical foreclosures.

However, downstream rivals are often capable of entering the upstream market, as the US *Microsoft* case showed. Here, the appellate court found that Microsoft maintained its market power in the upstream operating-system market by excluding a rival in the downstream browser market.[38] This insight has influenced competition agencies in the US and other regions towards not adopting the 'per-se legal' treatment for vertical foreclosures. Still, this Chicago-School concept strengthens the argument that competition agencies should not intervene in vertical foreclosures when no company holds market power in the upstream market.

Identification of market power in an upstream market fulfils only one of two requirements for determining as illegal a vertical foreclosure. In order to fulfil the second requirement, a competition agency must show that competition-restraining effects in the downstream market outweigh pro-competitive effects. In the case of telecommunications, inputs from an upstream network market are indispensable for providing services (and products) in downstream markets. A large majority of vertical foreclosures, therefore, restrain competition in downstream markets. Nevertheless, when the dominant upstream company convincingly shows that pro-competitive efficiency effects outweigh competition-restraining effects, competition agencies must tolerate the foreclosures for the sake of consumer welfare.

After determining a competition law violation in a vertical foreclosure scenario, the competition agency needs to design a remedy. The agency first needs to determine whether it should impose a structural remedy such as divestiture of a corporate division on the violating company. Formerly, competition agencies widely supported structural remedies on the grounds that they needed to remedy the market structures giving rise to competition restraints. However, in recent years, competition agencies have usually eschewed structural remedies. This attitude reflects a new understanding of the merits of vertical integration.[39] When a violating company appeals a structural remedy to a court, the competition agency will find it difficult to convince the court of the merits of that remedy.

---

[37] J. Farrell and P.J. Weiser, 'Modularity, Vertical Integration, and Open Access Policies: Towards a Convergence of Antitrust and Regulation in the Internet Age' (2003) 17 *Harv. J. L. & Tech.* 85, 104.

[38] *United States v. Microsoft Corp.*, 253 F.3d 34 (D.C. Cir. 2001).

[39] J. Farrell and P.J. Weiser (n. 37 above) 121.

The US *Microsoft* case testifies to this difficulty.[40] Behavioural remedies are the rule, therefore, excepting rare cases in which the merits of structural remedies clearly outweigh their demerits.

4.2 Competition Law Enforcement against Refusals to Deal

The US antirust agencies and courts have established a rule-of-reason treatment (an overall assessment of consumer welfare) for vertical foreclosures. Nevertheless, for refusal-to-deal cases (including refusal to provide access), the Supreme Court has established a standard with an extremely narrow definition of illegal conduct: virtually no cases of illegality may be found among refusals to enter into new deals, as distinct from terminations of existing deals.[41]

The Court's standpoint emanates from the principle of honouring property rights (both physical and intellectual), which the Court considers imperative for securing innovation incentives. From the static view of consumer welfare, an obligation to deal leads to an increase in welfare through lower prices. However, an obligation to deal also decreases innovation incentives by lowering the values of the invested assets, which in the long run leads to a decline in consumer welfare.[42]

The same concern for innovation incentives may on the other hand lead to a standpoint contrary to that of the Supreme Court. This is because a virtual 'per-se legal' standard for refusals to deal would hinder new entries, thus reducing competitive pressure on dominant companies, resulting in a decrease in innovative activities.[43]

Indeed, concern for innovation incentives has not led competition agencies and courts to soften their stance against vertical foreclosures

---

[40] In the *Microsoft* decision, the Court of Appeals reversed the District Court's final judgment (decision on the remedy to structurally break up Microsoft), stating: 'One apparent reason why courts have not ordered the dissolution of unitary companies is logistical difficulty. ... [A] corporation, designed to operate effectively as a single entity, cannot readily be dismembered of parts of its various operations without a marked loss of efficiency' *United States v. Microsoft*, 253 F.3d 34, 106 (D.C. Cir. 2001).

[41] *Verizon Communications Inc. v. Law Offices of Curtis V. Trinko, LLP*, 540 U.S. 398 (2004) (the Court referred to its earlier decision in *Aspen Skiing* [a case regarding a termination of continuing dealing] as 'at or near the outer boundary of § 2 liability').

[42] See Katz and Shelanski (n. 1 above) 8.

[43] See H.A. Shelanski, 'Unilateral Refusals to Deal in Intellectual and Other Property' (2009) 76 *Antitrust L.J.* 369, 383 (citing a survey regarding theory and evidence on the relationship between competition and innovation).

(except refusals to deal). In the US *Microsoft* decision, the Court of Appeals expressed a neutral position on whether the regulation against exclusionary conduct should be softened in high-technology markets where innovations spread dynamically (and network effects exist).[44] The Court of Appeals then went on to determine that Microsoft's exclusionary conduct regarding its restrictive licensing conditions towards PC manufacturers (Original Equipment Manufacturers) was illegal.[45]

In summary, regarding vertical foreclosures (including refusals to provide access), competition agencies need to honour property rights in order to secure innovation incentives. 'Honouring' them should not be elevated to an absolute level, however; an extremely soft stance against refusals to deal (as shown by the US Supreme Court) would lead to a greater risk of too little enforcement of competition law as against the risk of too much enforcement.

In the US, active exercise of treble-damage private suits augments the risk of too much enforcement of antitrust laws. In contrast, in the EU and Japan, private suits occur only rarely. Competition agencies are principally responsible for enforcing competition law; therefore, the risk of too much enforcement in refusal-to-deal cases is considerably lower in these jurisdictions than in the US.

Moreover, vertical refusals to deal, in contrast to refusals to deal with direct competitors (horizontal refusals to deal) have been exercised in order to extend dominant companies' market powers from upstream markets to downstream markets. Dominant companies have also engaged in vertical refusals to deal in order to prevent downstream rivals from entering the upstream markets. These considerations would prompt competition agencies to adopt the same rule-of-reason standard for vertical refusals to deal as for other vertical foreclosures.[46]

As to the rule-of-reason standard for vertical refusals to deal, the 'essential facility doctrine' adopted in the *MCI* decision is deemed to strike a proper balance between the need for honouring property rights (for the sake of innovation incentives) and the need for securing opportunities for new entries. This is because the essential facility doctrine demands that a competition agency find (as a condition for identifying illegal conduct) that an incumbent upstream company holds a

---

[44] *United States v. Microsoft Corp.*, 253 F.3d 34, 50 (D.C. Cir. 2001).

[45] Ibid., 62 and 64.

[46] See S.C. Salop, 'Refusals to Deal and Price Squeezes by an Unregulated, Vertically Integrated Monopolist' (2010) 76 *Antitrust L.J.* 709, 711 (stating that refusals-to-deal and price squeezes by vertically integrated monopolists should be evaluated under the rule of reason).

greater than usual market power, resulting in a lack of economically alternative channels of inputs for downstream rivals.

To fulfil this condition, competition agencies must first investigate whether downstream rivals have economically feasible alternative channels of inputs other than those of the dominant company. When competition agencies determine that such an alternative is not available, they then compare the competition-restraining effects of the refusal to deal with its efficiency-increasing effects before ultimately finding the refusal illegal.

4.3 The European Commission's Competition Law Enforcement against Refusals to Provide Access

Regarding vertical refusals to deal, the European Commission, in the same way as the US Supreme Court, states that it will honour companies' freedom to choose their trading partners. This fits the principle of securing incentives to invest and innovate.[47] Nevertheless, unlike the US Supreme Court, the Commission has not adopted a standard of virtual per-se legality on refusals to deal.

Specifically, the Commission states that a vertical refusal to deal will be examined in accordance with the standard commonly applied to vertical foreclosures when it is clear that prohibition of the refusal to deal will not undermine incentives for new investments. As an example the Commission cites a situation where an upstream dominant position was developed under the protection of the state.[48] This situation arises when a state-authorized monopolist has installed a telecommunications network.

The Commission has in common with the US antitrust agencies (as well as the courts) the method of examining unilateral conduct in two steps, the first of which is devoted to examining whether an investigated company holds market power.[49]

Regarding the second step (on whether the examined exclusionary conduct is anticompetitive or harms consumer welfare), the Commission has expressed an opinion that refines the essential facility doctrine formulated by the US *MCI* decision. Namely, the Commission is likely to determine illegality if three conditions are fulfilled: (i) the refused input is objectively necessary to effectively compete in the downstream market;

---

[47] Article 102 Guidance (n. 34 above) para. 75.

[48] Ibid., para. 82.

[49] Ibid., para. 9 ('The assessment of whether an undertaking is in a dominant position and of the degree of market power it holds is a first step in the application of Article 102').

(ii) the refusal is likely to lead to the elimination of competition in the downstream market; (iii) the refusal is likely to lead to consumer harm.[50] The last point coincides with the modern rule of reason adopted by the antitrust agencies in that mere showing of exclusionary effects does not suffice to condemn unilateral conduct.[51]

As to the evaluation on consumer welfare, the Commission emphasizes the importance of innovation for consumer welfare: 'The Commission considers that consumer harm may… arise where the rivals that the dominant undertaking forecloses are, as a result of the refusal, prevented from bringing innovative goods or services to market.'[52] This stance coincides with one in the US regarding the regulation of unilateral conduct in innovation-intensive industries, namely, the opinion supporting active competition law enforcement in innovation-intensive industries.

Nevertheless, the Commission also expresses an opinion similar to the one in the US that opposes aggressive competition law enforcement in innovation-intensive industries: a stance in sympathy with dominant companies, that a refusal to deal is necessary to preserve innovation incentives.[53] This stance would prompt the Commission to refrain from forcing incumbents to provide rivals with access to their facilities until the incumbents recover the costs incurred for building their facilities.

4.4 Japan's Fair Trade Commission and Supreme Court Decisions in *NTT East*

The Japanese competition agency – the Fair Trade Commission (JFTC) – expressed its view on broadband access in its *NTT East* decision.[54] This

---

[50] Ibid., para. 81.

[51] It has to be noted, however, that in contrast to the Commission's Guidance on Article 102 (n. 34 above), the CJEU refuses to apply any consumer harm criterion. See Case C-95/04 P *British Airways v. Commission* [2007] ECR I-2331, para. 106 (stating that the prohibition of abuse of dominance does not only aim at 'practices which may cause prejudice to consumers directly, but also to those which are detrimental to them through their impact on an effective competition structure'). This approach was also confirmed by the Court of First Instance (now General Court) for refusals to license in Case T-201/04 *Microsoft v. Commission* [2007] ECR II-3601, para. 664

[52] Article 102 Guidance (n. 34 above) para. 87.

[53] Ibid., para 89.

[54] JFTC hearing decision, 53 Shinketsushu 776 (26 March 2007); available (only in Japanese) at: http://www.jftc.go.jp/houdou/pressrelease/kako/07032904.html (accessed 3 July 2015).

case concerns access conditions that the dominant company (in both its upstream broadband network and downstream services) provided to a rival in the downstream market.[55] In 2007, the JFTC found that the access conditions provided by NTT East were detrimental to the rival, thus constituting illegal exclusionary conduct, in violation of the monopolization clause of the Antimonopoly Act.[56] In 2010, the Supreme Court upheld the JFTC decision.[57]

The broadband network that NTT East installed consists of optical fibres. NTT East was formerly the state-owned Telegraph and Telephone Corporation, which, under the government-authorized monopoly, had installed the copper-wire telecommunications network across Japan. In contrast, NTT East, after its privatization (and introduction of competition) in 1985, took a business risk in investing in the optic-fibre network. A competition agency, therefore, must pay heed to innovation incentives in this case.

4.4.1 Market definition and evaluation of NTT East's market power

This case concerns a vertical foreclosure, which requires a competition agency to determine first whether the investigated company holds market power in an upstream network market. Examination of market power requires the agency to define the relevant market, which the JFTC defined narrowly, limiting it to include only the optic-fibre networks.

Broadband networks, however, contain not only optic-fibre networks but also DSL (or ADSL, which enables copper-wire networks to perform broadband services), cables and Wi-Fi broadband networks. Consumers generally do not care about differences in technologies as long as they can enjoy broadband services. Hence, it would seem logical to define the market as composed of all broadband networks. This is how the US FCC defined the broadband market.

---

[55] NTT East, being designated as a dominant carrier, is subject to regulation by the MIC for the special access obligations under the Telecom Law. In spite of the telecommunications regulation, this case went to the JFTC because the MIC did not intervene in NTT's access pricing due to a controversy regarding a technical issue on access methods.

[56] Act on Prohibition of Private Monopolization and Maintenance of Fair Trade (Act No. 54 of April 14, 1947), known as 'Antimonopoly Act', available at: http://www.jftc.go.jp/en/legislation_gls/amended_ama09/index.html (accessed 3 July 2015).

[57] Supreme Court decision (17 December 2012), available (only in Japanese) at: http://www.courts.go.jp/hanrei/pdf/20101217113923.pdf (accessed 3 July 2015).

Yet, as the main reason for defining a market as composed of only the optic-fibre networks, the JFTC states in its finding: 'Those customers who opted for optic fiber have rarely switched to ADSL or cable.'[58] The Supreme Court stated a similar reasoning in detail:

> Some customers evidently opted for the optic-fibre-based service because of its superiority in speed and other merits, regardless of the level of its price. For those customers, demand substitution did not exist between the optic-fibre-based service and other broadband services; therefore, the optic-based broadband service independently constitutes a relevant market.[59]

Both the JFTC and the Supreme Court defined the relevant market focusing on demand substitution between similar services. Their method, therefore, is basically in harmony with the globally accepted method for market definition – the 'hypothetical monopolist test'[60] – although the test has developed a much more elaborate method to examine demand substitutability. Nevertheless, the JFTC and the Supreme Court, when examining demand substitution between the optic-fibre based service, ADSL and other services, made the error of examining only the customers who had already adopted the optic-fibre service and ignoring possible new customers of broadband services.

This constitutes an error because companies compete not only in retaining existing customers but in attracting new customers. In rapidly expanding industries like this one, companies' competition strategy in fact prioritizes the acquisition of new customers over exploiting existing customers. If customers who have adopted optic-fibre broadband switch to another broadband technology, they cannot recover the cost they paid for having the last-mile network facilities installed inside their homes (or offices). Due to this sunk cost, those customers have become 'locked in' to optic-fibre broadband, and therefore will not switch, not only to the old technologies (ADSL or cable broadband), but not even to the cutting-edge Wi-Fi broadband, for several years to come. This is why the companies operating in the broadband industries focus on acquiring new customers, not on retaining existing customers.

---

[58] 53 Shinketsushu 776, 809 (2007).

[59] Supreme Court (n. 57 above) 12.

[60] See *United States v. H & R Block, Inc.*, 833 F.Supp.2d 36, 51 (DCC 2011) ('[The hypothetical monopolist test] is to ask hypothetically whether it would be profitable [by raising prices for those products by five percent or more] to have a monopoly over a given set of substitutable products. If so, those products may constitute a relevant market'). See also Federal Trade Commission and US Department of Justice Horizontal Merger Guidelines (2010) § 4.1.1.

Hence, also in running the hypothetical monopolist test, a competition agency would commit an error if it interviewed only the existing customers of optic-fibre broadband, asking them whether they would switch to a neighbouring service in response to a price raise of 5 to 10 per cent.[61] A competition agency needs to interview, in addition, possible new customers of broadband services. These potential customers are crucial in defining the relevant market. A market definition including them would be expanded to include all the networks that provide broadband services.

In support of this reasoning, technologies for broadband (and their appeals to consumers) have been rapidly evolving under competitive pressure. It is not appropriate to define a market narrowly as consisting of only the optic-fibre network on the basis of its current technological superiority. As a cutting-edge technology, Wi-Fi broadband has recently been rapidly expanding in major countries and regions. At the time of the *NTT East* case, the Wi-Fi broadband technology in Japan was nascent, just being briefly mentioned by the respondent in *NTT East*. But since the case, Wi-Fi broadband has been rapidly accepted by consumers.

When all networks realizing broadband services are included in the relevant market, the market share of NTT East will be greatly reduced from the 92 per cent the JFTC determined from its narrow definition of the market consisting of only the optic-fibre networks. Moreover, the market power of NTT East should not be determined solely from its market share, but from the overall market conditions. In innovation-intensive industries, a competition agency needs to foresee the possibility of new entries. Wi-Fi technologies, even if they are not included in a relevant market, need to be taken into account as a market-power mitigating factor. The JFTC, therefore, needs to reduce the degree of a market power held by NTT East, compared to that estimated from its market share.

4.4.2 Determination of an undue refusal to deal or a price squeeze

In order to determine as illegal an exclusionary act, a competition agency must identify not only market power but also the undue nature of the exclusionary act, namely, that the act is restraining competition without redeeming efficiencies.

---

[61] See *United States v. Engelhard Corp.*,126 F.3d 1302, 1306 (11th Cir. 1997) ('No matter how many customers in each end-use industry the Government may have interviewed, those results cannot be predictive of the entire market if those customers are not representative of the market').

The JFTC, in its decision, determined that NTT East's conduct was of predatory nature by identifying the conduct as a price squeeze, based on the finding that the downstream rival (Tokyo Electric Power Co) was not able to make a profit at the combination of the wholesale price (the access charge) and the retail price both set or controlled by NTT.

The JFTC, without an explanation, directly linked the identification of a price squeeze to the undue nature of NTT East's conduct. A question, however, remains as to whether a company's engaging in a price squeeze should be found illegal even when the company may legally refuse to deal. Concerning this point, the Supreme Court suggests that a common element exists between a refusal to deal and a price squeeze by stating: 'This case concerns a unilateral refusal-to-deal or predatory pricing.'[62]

The Supreme Court could clarify its position by stating that a price squeeze constitutes a refusal to deal (as shown by the EU Article 102 Guidelines). For a downstream rival, to be given a deal (although with a price squeeze) is still more advantageous than to be confronted with a refusal to deal. Accordingly, a price squeeze should not be deemed illegal when a refusal to deal is not illegal.[63]

In this case, NTT East engaged in a price squeeze, and therefore is deemed to have virtually refused to deal with the downstream rival. In the next stage of the examination, the vertical refusal to deal should be examined based on the essential facilities doctrine. As shown above, the relevant market needs to be broadened to include all broadband networks, and so the essential nature of NTT East's optic-fibre networks is likely to be denied.

Even if the networks were identified as an essential facility, forcing a deal would increase NTT East's operating costs. This cost increase must then be taken into account in comparing competition-increasing effects and efficiency-decreasing effects.

4.4.3 A remedy issued in collaboration with a telecommunications agency

Following its decision against a refusal to deal, a competition agency needs to order a remedy to the respondent company. If the agency merely orders the company to cease refusing to deal, the company is able to set an access charge at a very high level, resulting in a virtual refusal to deal.

---

[62] Supreme Court Decision (n. 57 above) 10.

[63] See *Pacific Bell Telephone v. Linkline Comm.*, 129 S. Ct. 1109, 1119 (2009) ('*Trinko* … makes clear that if a firm has no antitrust duty to deal with its competitors at wholesale, it certainly has no duty to deal under terms and conditions that the rivals find commercially advantageous').

The competition agency, therefore, is pressed to stipulate an access charge together with other access conditions.

Nevertheless, in this case, the JFTC merely stated that NTT East engaged in illegal conduct, without ordering a remedy. This is because NTT East had ceased the price squeeze before the JFTC issued the decision. The background to this case is that the Japanese telecommunications agency (MIC) regulates access conditions including access charges; therefore the JFTC did not need to stipulate access conditions as a remedy. This case indicates that, when a competition agency issues a decision against a regulated company, it may leave the task of setting a remedy to the regulatory agency.

A telecommunications agency is more knowledgeable about the telecommunications industry than a competition agency. As long as a telecommunications agency exists, administrative efficiency is achieved by leaving the task of setting the remedy to this agency. Nevertheless, this view presupposes that the competition agency and the telecommunications agency share the same standard for regulating dominant companies. Such sharing of common standards has been formed in Japan, as evidenced by the issuance of the joint guidelines on anti-competitive activities in the telecommunications industry.[64]

However, the joint guidelines list a range of anticompetitive activities that are broader than those stipulated as illegal by the current consensus view in competition law. This discrepancy is largely explained by the fact that the JFTC regulates unilateral conduct not only through the monopolization clause but also through the unfair trade practices clause of the Antimonopoly Act.[65] The latter clause does not require the JFTC to identify market power before condemning a company, and yet the market-power requirement is indispensable as a safeguard against overregulation of unilateral conduct. The JFTC is advised to cease using the unfair trade practices clause against unilateral (exclusionary) conduct.

Competition has spread not only to broadband sectors but also to telecommunications in general. A competition agency in the near future

---

[64] Fair Trade Commission and Ministry of Internal Affairs and Communications, Guidelines for Promotion of Competition in the Telecommunications Business Field (30 November 2001; Amendment: 25 December 2002), available at: http://www.jftc.go.jp/en/legislation_gls/imonopoly_guidelines.files/telecom.pdf (accessed 3 July 2015).

[65] Article 2(9) Antimonopoly Act. Regarding deficiencies in the unfair trade practices clause, see T. Takigawa 'Chapter 2 Japan' in M. Williams (ed.), *The Political Economy of Competition Law in Asia* (Edward Elgar Publishing 2013) 37–38.

will be capable of replacing a telecommunications agency as the agency in charge of regulating the business activities of carriers. On that occasion, the JFTC would need to set up access conditions as remedies against dominant carriers engaging in illegal refusals to deal (or price squeezes). Competition agencies, including the JFTC, will be able to choose the appropriate conditions by recruiting economists who are knowledgeable about telecommunications issues.

5. CONCLUSION

New communication technologies and services, particularly the mobile ones, have considerably invigorated competition in telecommunication markets, not only in downstream services markets but also in upstream networks. The broadband networks, in particular, evidently are no longer natural monopolies. Therefore, companies operating in broadband networks and services markets should no longer be subjected to *ex ante* telecommunications regulation. This view is buttressed by the major policy change enacted by the US FCC of removing uniform access regulation from the broadband sector.

The international comparative analysis conducted in this chapter leads to several policy implications regarding the enforcement of competition law in innovation-intensive industries. First, a competition agency is well advised to place the requirement of identifying market power as a safeguard against overregulation of unilateral (exclusionary) conduct. Correct examination of market power necessitates correct definition of the relevant market, which should include not only 'locked-in' customers but potential new customers. Moreover, a current market share should not be treated as the exclusive indicator of market power; a competition agency must also grasp innovation trends in order to make a forward-looking assessment of a firm's market power.

Second, a competition agency needs to base its examination of a refusal to deal (or a price squeeze) regarding access to a broadband network on a standard that balances innovation incentives against chances of new entries. The refined essential facility doctrine properly reflects this balancing consideration. Still, a competition agency must not only identify the essentiality of a facility but also engage in a balancing evaluation between anticompetitive effects and efficiency effects.

Third, a competition agency may let a telecommunications agency do the task of setting a behavioural remedy against a company that has committed a competition law violation. This arrangement leads to administrative efficiency, but it presupposes that the same regulatory standard is shared between the competition agency and the telecommunications agency. When regulatory standards differ between the two agencies, the competition agency should set up a specific behavioural order against the violating company. As competition spreads across telecommunication industries, a competition agency should replace the telecommunication agency as the sole regulator of competition in the telecommunications sector.

11. Abuses of information and informational remedies: rethinking exchange of information under competition law

Fabiana Di Porto

1. INTRODUCTION

Traditionally, the way competition law has viewed the exchange or sharing of information among competing firms has been mainly[1] negative, at least from the supply side.[2] Under present market conditions, an excessively transparent market where operators exchange detailed and (potentially) commercially sensitive data on a regular basis, sharing can amount to a practice facilitating collusion, or itself constitute an anticompetitive agreement violating Article 101 TFEU.

Interestingly, though, while a great deal of literature and case-law reflects on the difficult relationship between the exchange of information and Article 101 (collusive scenarios and oligopolistic interdependence), the relationship between the exchange of information and Article 102 is a much less scrutinized issue.

[1] See F. Wagner-von Papp, 'Information Exchange Agreements' in D. Geradin and I. Lianos (eds), *Research Handbook on EU Antitrust Law* (Edward Elgar Publishing 2012) 130, also available at: ssrn.com/abstract=2015674 (accessed 31 December 2013), for a critical assessment of the pro-competitive arguments in favour of exchange of information.

[2] From the demand side, despite competition authorities acknowledging that information dissemination may benefit consumers (e.g., reducing consumers' search costs, easing their choice while increasing price competition), the consideration paid to the argument is mainly confined to the 'pass on to consumers' analysis under Article 101(1) TFEU, while finding limited scope in the 'efficiency gains' assessment under 101(3). See the example provided by the Commission's Guidelines on the applicability of Article 101 of the TFEU to horizontal co-operation agreements, [2011] OJ C 11, p. 1, para. 100.

A closer look at the Article 102 case-law suggests a less strict and sceptical approach towards information exchange than that on Article 101: it is the *lack* of information exchange or the *misuse* of information by dominant firms that is deemed anticompetitive and abusive. At the same time, this closer look reveals that many Article 102 cases are adjudicated via remedies *imposing an exchange of information or a duty to disclose information*. Such behavioural remedies bear a strong resemblance – as regards the rationale of intervention, the institutional resources employed and the powers exercised – to traditional regulation: I therefore propose to call them 'para-regulatory',[3] to distinguish them from pure, traditional regulatory interventions.

In such a scenario, a risk may arise of conflicts with existing information-based regulation (e.g., access and disclosure regulation), leading to legal uncertainty, conflicting decisions and inconsistency; furthermore, information exchange obligations to remedy informational abuses under Article 102 can come under suspicion, under Article 101, of easing unlawful collusion.

Based on these reflections, this chapter is organized as follows. Section 2 reviews a selection of decisions on Article 102 and corresponding norms in other jurisdictions that deal with information exchange. In particular, two lines of cases are presented: those in which exchanges of information *are the subject-matter of abuse cases* (at section 2.1 below), and those where such exchanges *are the object of 'para-regulatory' remedies* enforced pursuant to Article 102 (at section 2.2 below). Section 3 focuses on the different treatment that exchange of information receives under Articles 101 and 102 TFEU and then analyses possible internal clashes between these two branches of competition law. After a comprehensive assessment in section 4, the conclusion explores the theoretical possibility of reconciling such clashes and suggests a framework for competition agencies to intervene appropriately where exchange of market information is concerned.

---

[3] From the Greek prefix παρά (para), beyond, alongside of, also resembling.

2. THE GROWING RELEVANCE OF INFORMATION IN ABUSE-OF-DOMINANCE CASES

Issues of access and information are said to be shaping competition law in the twenty-first century.[4] The trend, so the argument goes, although most visible in the information-based network, media, software and IT industries, is also expected to grow in other sectors.[5] The European Commission has, since the *Google/DoubleClick* merger,[6] begun to acknowledge that there is a need to investigate more deeply when competition concerns arise from data collection,[7] and that personal data may, under certain circumstances, be misused to weaken competition.[8] On the other hand, the debate around the proposed General Data Protection Regulation[9] has stressed the pro-competitive virtues of data 'portability' (the right to migrate one's own personal data from one service provider to another), which might reduce switching costs and therefore improve competition.[10]

Competition law scholars are also showing a growing interest in the relationship between competition law and information flows. While some suggest inaugurating a new line of research on the intersection between *data portability* and competition,[11] others call for a re-consideration of

---

[4] S.W. Waller, 'Access and Information remedIes in High-Tech Antitrust' (2012) 8 *J. Comp. L. & Econ.* 575, 593.

[5] Ibid., 575.

[6] Commission Decision of 11 March 2008, Case COMP/M.4731 – *Google/DoubleClick*, [2008] OJ C 184, p. 6.

[7] See the speech by J. Almunia, 'Competition and Personal Data Protection', SPEECH/12/860, 26 November 2012, available at: http://europa.eu/rapid/press-release_SPEECH-12-860_en.htm (accessed 31 December 2013).

[8] Ibid., para. 12: 'The line between the sensible use and the abuse of this kind of information is very thin. New problems will probably appear and become systemic.'

[9] See the Commission's Proposal of 25 January 2012 for a Regulation of the European Parliament and the Council on the protection of individuals with regard to the processing of personal data and on the free movement of such data (General Data Protection Regulation), COM(2012) 11 final.

[10] Article 18 of the proposed General Data Protection Regulation.

[11] See, for instance, D. Geradin and M. Kuschewsky, 'Competition Law and Personal Data: Preliminary Thoughts on a Complex Issue', available at: papers.ssrn.com/sol3/papers.cfm?abstract_id=2216088 (accessed 31 December 2013); European Data Protection Supervisor, Preliminary Opinion, 'Privacy and Competitiveness in the Age of Big Data: The Interplay between Data Protection, Competition Law and Consumer Protection in the Digital Economy' (March 2014), available at: https://secure.edps.europa.eu/EDPSWEB/webdav/site/my

traditional antitrust concepts (which consider information not as a good or service in itself, but as an input to goods or services),[12] so as to adapt them to the assessment of new anti-competitive issues stemming from information-related markets.[13] Furthermore, antitrust investigations of the major Internet-based companies[14] have fuelled the debate over 'emerging competition concerns in digital platform markets',[15] with the control of

---

Site/shared/Documents/Consultation/Opinions/2014/14-03-26_competitition_law_big_data_EN.pdf (accessed 31 May 2013). See also J.P. Sluijs, P. Larouche and W. Sauter, 'Cloud Computing in the EU Policy Sphere: Interoperability, Vertical Integration and the Internal Market' (2012) 1 *J. Intel. Prop., Inf. Tech. & Elec. Comm. L.* 12 (suggesting that a dominant cloud-computing provider could increase the customer acquisition costs of rivals by raising customer switching costs and lock-in, leading to anti-competitive foreclosure and consumer harm).

[12] See M.R. Patterson, 'Antitrust and Informational Restraints' in Fordham Competition Law Institute (ed.), *International Antitrust Law & Policy* (2013) Ch. 26.

[13] Ibid., remarking that, because information can be delivered at low cost, notions like market shares fail to provide a strong basis for the definition of dominance or market power.

[14] See, e.g., the European Commission's investigation of Google's allegedly abusive conduct (Case AT.39740, initiated on 30 November 2010); and subsequent negotiation of commitments pursuant to Article 9 of Regulation 1/2003, summarized in the speech by J. Almunia, 'Statement on the Google investigation', SPEECH-14-93, 5 February 2014, available at: http://europa.eu/rapid/press-release_SPEECH-14-93_en.htm (accessed 31 May 2014). Following failure of negotiations, the Commission sent a Statement of Objections to Google: see European Commission, 'Antitrust: Commission sends Statement of Objections to Google on comparison shopping service; opens separate formal investigation on Android', Press Release IP/15/4780 of 15 April 2015, avalable at: http://europa.eu/rapid/press-release_IP-15-4780_en.htm (accessed 6 July 2015). On the other side of the Atlantic, more investigations were initiated with regard to Google (see Federal Trade Commission, file n. 111-0163, and 'Statement of the Federal Trade Commission Regarding Google's Search Practices. In the Matter of Google Inc.', 3 January 2013, available at: http://www.ftc.gov/system/files/documents/public_statements/295971/130103googlesearchstmtofcomm.pdf, accessed 31 May 2014); and consent orders resulting from FTC action against Facebook (Beacon) and Google (Buzz): see F. Pasquale, 'Privacy, Antitrust, and Power' (2013) 20 *George Mason L. Rev.* 1009, 1018.

[15] See J. Haucap and U. Heimeshoff, 'Google, Facebook, Amazon, eBay: Is the Internet Driving Competition or Market Monopolization? (2014) 11 *Int'l Econ & Econ Policy* 49. See also R.H. Weber, 'From Competition Law to Sector-specific Regulation in Internet Markets? A Critical Assessment of a Possible Structural Change', in this volume.

databases of user data being seen as a source of monopolistic dominance.[16]

As far as enforcement is concerned, a position that merits support suggests widening the focus from collusion and Article 101 to dominant firms' conduct and Article 102 (or equivalent norms).[17] Such a wider view of informational profiles converges in the observation that antitrust authorities, both at US and EC levels, are remedying infringements of both Articles 101 and 102 through the adoption of 'highly complex behavioural remedies', mandating access to or disclosure of market information.[18]

---

16 See N. Newman, 'Search, Antitrust and the Economics of the Control of User Data' (13 August 2013), available at: http://ssrn.com/abstract=2309547 (accessed 31 May 2014); F. Pasquale, 'Paradoxes of Digital Antitrust: Why the FTC Failed to Explain Its Inaction on Search Bias' (July 2013) *Harv. J. L. & Tech. Occasional Paper Series*, available at: http://jolt.law.harvard.edu/antitrust/articles/Pasquale.pdf (accessed 31 May 2014); and Pasquale (n. 14 above) 1015, who speaks of a 'self-reinforcing data advantage of dominant firms'. *Contra*: D.F. Spulber and C.S. Yoo, 'Antitrust, the Internet, and the Economics of Networks' in R.D. Blair and D. Sokol (eds), *Oxford Handbook of International Antitrust Economics* (Oxford University Press, forthcoming 2015), also available at: http://papers.ssrn.com/sol3/papers.cfm?abstract_id=2370050 (accessed 31 May 2014).

17 Reference can be found in or inferred from both Waller (n. 4 above) and Patterson (n. 12 above); but see also A.L. Wait, 'Competitor Information Exchanges: Practical Considerations from FTC Consent Decrees', Hunton&Williams (May 2011), available at: http://www.hunton.com/files/Publication/37824b3f-67a0-48d5-9211-712846a587e0/Presentation/PublicationAttachment/1740fa96-1c76-40bb-909f-74c0f7ee0687/Competitor_Information_Exchanges.pdf (accessed 31 December 2013).

18 Waller (n. 4 above) 576 (contending that highly complex behavioural remedies are being adopted, especially in cases involving network industries, telecommunication, broadcasting, software platforms and other high-tech industries, leading to a revival of the essential facility doctrine). See also Newman (n. 16 above) 15–16 (positing that effective antitrust behavioural remedies 'for reducing monopoly power of players like Google' could also include 'requiring greater data portability … and promoting greater common carrier responsibilities by dominant companies'). The author also considers regulation to help 'remov[e] incumbents in technology markets': 'early intervention by regulators is better than trying to dethrone an embedded incumbent like Google'. *Contra* Spulber and Yoo (n. 16 above) 21, suggesting that 'forcing network owners to share the benefits of their investments with their competitors … would dampen the incentives to invest in alternate network capacity'; therefore antitrust should rather 'tolerate some degree of *static inefficiency* in order to promote *dynamic efficiency*' (author's emphasis).

This chapter adds two further aspects to this informational *nouvelle vague*. The first is that competition agencies are increasing their efforts to assess exchanges of information under unilateral conduct rules such as Article 102. This growing category of practice leads to a variety of different liability standards for 'informational' abuses. Since the effect-based approach to Article 102 entered the scene,[19] 'atypical' conduct[20] not included in the list of possible abuses in Article 102 has become more important, confronting undertakings with legal uncertainty. Therefore, some categorization of the legal theories applied in new and old 'informational' abuse cases would seem useful.

Secondly, and in a way confirming one of the positions reviewed above, when applying Article 102 to informational abusive conduct, competition agencies tend to adopt 'para-regulatory' remedies[21] obliging firms to exchange information. This observation adds to the ongoing

[19] Under the Commission's Guidance on Enforcement priorities in applying Article 82 of the EC Treaty to abusive exclusionary conduct by dominant undertakings, [2009] OJ C 45, p. 7, conduct that has actual or even potential exclusionary effects can amount to a violation of Article 102 if those effects are demonstrated 'in context', unless efficiency gains are demonstrated.

[20] As is well known, the effect-based approach requires a case-by-case, facts-specific assessment that takes into consideration all circumstances in the specific market context (from which a harmful effect on competition can derive, if efficiency gains are not demonstrated), without regard to what the formal, legal and typical conduct might be. See G. Ghidini and E. Arezzo, 'L'assalto fallito? Riflessioni sulla proposta rivisitazione in chiave "più economica" dell'abuso di dominanza' (2010) *Mercato concorrenza regole* 115.

[21] The ascent of the 'para-regulatory' antitrust wave is not unique to the realm of information-related conduct. Accounts abound of a non-negligible amount of competition decisions with a regulatory tone, especially after the adoption of Regulation 1/2003/EC. See, e.g., P.L. Parcu, 'On the Convergence of Antitrust and Regulation' (2013) *Concorrenza e mercato* 321. With specific reference to a regulatory bias in competition agencies' commitment decisions, see G. Monti, 'Managing the Intersection of Utilities Regulation and EC Competition Law' (2008) 4 *Comp. L. Rev.* 123; D. Geradin (ed.), *Remedies in Network Industries: EC Competition Law vs Sector-specific Regulation* (Intersentia 2004); W.P.J. Wils, 'Settlements of EU Antitrust Investigations: Commitment Decisions under Article 9 of Regulation No. 1/2003' (2006) 29 *World Comp.* 345; G.S. Georgiev, 'Contagious Efficiency: The Growing Reliance on U.S.-Style Antitrust Settlements in EU Law' (2007) *Utah L. Rev.* 971, also available at: http://papers.ssrn.com/sol3/papers.cfm?abstract_id=1115120 (accessed 31 December 2013). More generally on the legal foundations of remedies in competition law see I. Lianos, 'Competition Law Remedies in Europe' in I. Lianos and D. Geradin (eds), *Handbook on European Competition Law: Enforcement and Procedure* (Edward Elgar Publishing 2013) 362.

discussion of the relationship between competition rules and regulation,[22] providing insights on how to reconcile such decisions with, specifically, access and disclosure regulation.[23]

To explore these two aspects, a selection of informational abuses derived from the EU, US and Italian practice will be presented in the following. Two main groups of cases are distinguished, depending on whether *information exchanges are the subject matter* of Article 102 (at section 2.1 below) or whether it is rather *the chosen 'para-regulatory' remedy that involves information exchanges* (at section 2.2 below). Of course, a combination of the two is possible, so that, for instance, timely disclosure of complete information is imposed to remedy a delay or a refusal to supply information to competitors. Such cases are divided along more artificial lines, with considerations on the conduct confined to section 2.1, and reflections on remedies and their interference with regulation in section 2.2, below.

2.1 When Information Flow Is the Subject Matter of Article 102 Cases

Exchange of information with competitors takes place every day between firms in every market. This is especially the case for vertically integrated firms owning facilities (be they operating systems, telecommunication or

[22] The literature on this topic is overwhelmingly abundant. Among the many, see J. Temple Lang, 'European Competition Policy and Regulation: Differences, Overlaps, and Constraints' in F. Lévêque and H. Shelanski (eds), *Antitrust and Regulation in the EU and US: Legal and Economic Perspectives* (Edward Elgar Publishing 2009) 20, and J. Tapia and D. Mantzari, 'The Regulation/Competition Interaction' in D. Geradin and I. Lianos (eds), *Research Handbook on European Competition Law* (Edward Elgar Publishing 2013) 588.

[23] The rationale for *disclosure regulation* is commonly associated with two types of market failure: information asymmetry and externalities. Disclosure regulation may consist of both *ex ante* information-related obligations and *ex post* control of false or misleading information. It can take the form of a general mandate (e.g., requiring transparency in pre-contractual terms and conditions), but it can also impose the exchange of technical information between vertically integrated firms and their downstream competitors to enable interoperability, or between network operators to ensure interconnection. In these latter cases intervention can also require the standardization of content and format of every single piece of data concerned. See R. Baldwin, M. Cave and M. Lodge, *Understanding Regulation* (2nd edn, OUP 2012) especially 117; A. Ogus, *Regulation* (OUP 1994) 121 ff.; S. Breyer, *Regulation and its Reform* (Harvard University Press 1982) 161ff. Existing information duties at EU level are summarized in the Commission Staff Working Document – Report on Consumer Policy (July 2010–December 2011), 22 May 2012, SWD (2012) 132 final, 11ff.

energy networks, software platforms, standards, etc.) that are essential inputs to competitors in aftermarkets. Providing competitors with access to those inputs implies constant two-way information flows that are either made mandatory by regulation or negotiated on a voluntary basis in unregulated sectors.

In the first case, regulatory duties will typically set out the conditions for (technical and economic) information to flow between firms in transparent and non-discriminatory ways.[24] Such duties to share information are pro-competitive and essential to let the market evolve from monopolistic to competitive arrangements, and should be relaxed as the markets become increasingly competitive.[25]

In the second case (of unregulated industries), firms are only in principle free to negotiate economic and technical conditions for providing access to their informational assets, subject to general contract law. To the extent that they enjoy an informational advantage amounting – alone or together with other elements – to a dominant or super-dominant position,[26] they may still be forced to share information with their competitors, in accordance with the 'exceptional circumstances' requirement.

2.1.1 Informational abuses in unregulated (or slightly regulated) markets

All vertically integrated firms that provide access to their informational facilities have huge amounts of data moving to and from their competitors on a daily basis. From these exchanges they can learn a lot about their competitors (e.g., their production capacity and volume, the number of clients served, the prices they charge). Such knowledge may give them

---

[24] Obligations of this kind are copious in the telecom and energy sectors, where EU Directives specify in great detail what sort of information national regulatory authorities (NRAs) may oblige network operators to share with their competitors. See, e.g., Article 9 of Directive 2002/19/EC of the European Parliament and of the Council of 7 March 2002 on access to, and interconnection of, electronic communications networks and associated facilities (Access Directive), [2002] OJ L 108, p. 7, as modified by Directive 2009/140/EC of the European Parliament and of the Council of 25 November 2009, [2009] OJ L 337, p. 37, on transparency remedies.

[25] F. Di Porto, 'La disciplina delle reti nel diritto dell'economia' in E. Picozza and E. Gabrielli (eds), *Trattato di diritto dell'economia*, Vol. VI (Cedam, 2008) 95, for a discussion of the pro-competitive relevance of access and transparency obligations in liberalized utility markets.

[26] See AG Fennelly, Joined Cases C-395 and C-396/96 P *Compagnie Maritime Belge v. Commission* [2000] ECR I-1365, para. 137.

an 'informational advantage' vis-à-vis their competitors, which they may have an incentive to use to weaken competition in the market they dominate or in other related markets.[27] Whenever the 'informational advantage', solely or (more frequently) together with other elements, gives rise to market power, competition agencies may seek to address potential abuses under unilateral conduct rules such as Article 102 TFEU.

Abusive conduct in this realm, as we shall see, can consist of an outright refusal to supply information to competitors; however, most frequently, it consists of delaying the supply of the requested information, restricting the quantity or frequency of the supplied information or degrading the quality of data supplied. Such abuses normally have the exclusionary effects of raising rivals' (information) costs[28] or enticing rivals' customers away.[29] Conduct with such effect falls within the – still loosely defined – category of 'constructive' refusals to deal, 'characterized by the dominant firm's offering to supply its rival on unreasonable terms, such as extremely high prices, degraded service, or reduced technical interoperability'.[30] However, exploitative abuses are also possible, as we shall see, as the informational advantage may be used to directly harm consumers (e.g., locking them in by raising their information and search-for-alternative costs).

---

[27] R. O'Donoghue and A.J. Padilla, *The Law and Economics of Article 82 EC* (Hart Publishing 2006) 168, claiming that a high degree of market power provides its holder with a greater incentive to commit an abuse.

[28] The daily exchange of information is a necessity for doing business. Low quality data provided to downstream competitors makes for extra processing costs that the vertically integrated firm does not necessarily incur.

[29] Wait (n. 17 above) 3.

[30] Commission Guidance on Article 82 (n. 19 above) para. 79: '"Constructive" refusal cases are heavily fact-dependent, making it difficult to draw general evaluative criteria.' See also International Competition Network, Report on the Analysis of Refusal to Deal with a Rival Under Unilateral Conduct Laws (April 2010), available at: http://www.internationalcompetitionnetwork.org/uploads/library/doc616.pdf (accessed 31 December 2013); J. Drexl, 'Refusal to Deal: Answers to the Questionnaire of the ICN Unilateral Conduct Working Group' (2010), available at: http://www.internationalcompetitionnetwork.org/uploads/questionnaires/uc%20refusals/drexl.pdf (accessed 31 December 2013).

*2.1.1.1 Monopolists' refusal to exchange information in the IT and media markets (*Magill, Microsoft I, Auditel *and* Audipress*)* The way firms wield information can contribute to their establishment of a dominant position, and informational advantage in unregulated markets usually tends to coincide with (informational) 'super-dominance' or quasi-monopoly.

Already in *Magill* the ECJ acknowledged that three broadcasters enjoyed a *de facto* monopoly over the provision of relevant information.[31]

Similar considerations were made in *Auditel*[32] and *Audipress*,[33] in which the Italian competition authority (AGCM) considered that the two Joint Industry Committees[34] held a quasi-monopoly in the markets for surveying and releasing data on, respectively, TV audiences[35] and reading figures of daily and periodical press[36] at the national level.

As regards the *type of information* that is relevant to create informational advantage, a rather 'functional' definition emerges based on the case-law. In short, all information (not just commercial or strategic data)

---

[31] See Joined Cases C-241/91 P and C-242/91 P *RTE and ITP v Commission* ('*Magill*') [1995] ECR I-743, para. 47: 'By force of circumstance, RTE and ITP, as the agent of ITV, enjoy, along with the BBC, a *de facto monopoly over the information* used to compile listings for the television programmes received in most households in Ireland and 30% to 40% of households in Northern Ireland. … The Court of First Instance was therefore *right in confirming the Commission's assessment that the appellants occupied a dominant position*' (emphasis added).

[32] AGCM, Case A422 – *Sky Italia/Auditel*, decision No. 23112, 14 December 2011, *Bull.* No. 50, 2011.

[33] AGCM, Case A424 – *E polis/Audipress*, decision No. 22320, 20 April 2011, *Bull.* No. 16, 2011.

[34] Auditel's shares are owned by: the public broadcaster (RAI: 33%); private broadcasters (Mediaset, Telecom Italia Media and FRT: 33%); advertisers (UPA, Assap Servizi and Unione Nazionale Imprese di Comunicazione: 33%); and publishers (FIEG: 1%). Audipress is owned by the major data users, namely: publishers (FIEG: 49.5%); advertising agencies (UPA: 24.75%; Assap Servizi: 16.5%; Unione Nazionale Imprese di Comunicazione: 8.25%); and Auditel (1%).

[35] AGCM (n. 32 above) para. 173: 'Auditel – whose corporate governance includes the main Italian TV operators – is the sole entity in charge of surveying and releasing reliable and shared audience data. Indeed, the existence of reliable and shared data on TV audience is an indispensable requirement for companies operating in the TV market.' In addition, AGCM considered the probability of new operators entering the market as almost nil, due to high financial barriers to entry and the long-lasting reputation of the incumbent.

[36] In the end, AGCM did not conclusively assess Audipress's dominant position, as it closed the case after accepting commitments (that remedied the allegation that Audipress refused to release its sample surveys).

coming into consideration in abuse cases is functional because it is 'indispensable', whether for operating in the market (thereby preventing anti-competitive foreclosure), for enabling interoperability (for the sake of efficiency), or for creating a new product (for the sake of promoting innovation).

Relevant information is information that can help a competitor to manufacture a new product, such as the TV programme listings in *Magill*;[37] or the information that makes up a strategy to compete in an aftermarket, such as the interface information for work group server operating systems in *Microsoft I*, or the information on viewers and readers that is needed to attract advertising customers, as in *Auditel* and *Audipress*.

As far as the specific *conduct* is concerned, all kinds of refusal to deal can be found with regard to information,[38] and in no case was an objective ground found to justify them. In *Magill*, the abuse consisted in an actual refusal by broadcasters to supply information 'duly in advance': it was primarily the delay in releasing such information that impeded Magill's production of its own comprehensive weekly TV guide. In *Microsoft I*,[39] the Redmond giant, among other things, failed to provide its downstream competitors with the necessary information to allow interoperability and to enable them to develop and distribute competing products. AGCM deemed as abusive and sanctioned Auditel's practice of delaying and impeding the release of daily data concerning the audience, listed by channel and by TV platform (analogue, digital, pay-TV, etc.) as requested by the plaintiff (Sky Italia).[40] The conduct had the effect of distorting competition in the advertising market as it did not allow downstream competitors to duly assess the value of advertising slots.

---

[37] See *Magill* (n. 31 above) para. 47.

[38] We adopt the classification proposed by the European Commission's Guidance on Article 82 (n. 19 above), in which the concept of refusal to supply covers: (1) refusal to supply products to existing or new customers; (2) refusal to license intellectual property rights (3) including when the licence is necessary to provide interface information; or (4) refusal to grant access to an essential facility or a network.

[39] Commission Decision 2007/53/EC of 24 March 2004, Case COMP/C-3/37.792 – *Microsoft* [2007] OJ L 32 p. 23. See also the judgment of the former European Court of Justice: Case T-201/04 – *Microsoft v. Commission* [2007] ECR II-3601. See also N. Economides and I. Lianos, 'The Quest for Appropriate Remedies in the EC Microsoft Cases: A Comparative Appraisal' in L. Rubini (ed.), *Microsoft on Trial. Legal and Economic Analysis of a Transatlantic Antitrust Case* (Edward Elgar Publishing 2010) 393.

[40] AGCM fined Auditel over €1 million.

Similarly, Audipress impeded the circulation of data (sample surveys) relating to the number of readers of daily press and periodicals. Access to this data was essential, especially to free-of-charge press operators in order to value advertising slots; thus, the practice prevented them from capitalizing on their position in the market and from competing.[41]

2.1.1.2 The financial services data sector (Standard & Poor's and Thomson Reuters) The importance of adequate information exchange in the financial markets is well phrased by the Commission: 'Well-functioning financial markets rely on access to information and the availability of high quality and timely market data on the price and structure of financial instruments.'[42]

Markets for the provision of financial information typically have *de facto* standards for financial identifiers and indices that may provide the global financial institutions and information services that own them with significant market power.

The Commission accepted commitments in two cases where access to accurate and timely financial data by market participants was allegedly prevented by Standard & Poor's[43] and Thomson Reuters.[44] The *information at stake* in both cases consisted of codes identifying securities and

[41] Another market concerned is that of Internet search engines, in which most notably the European Commission initiated proceedings against Google (n. 14 above).

[42] European Commission, Report on Competition Policy 2011 (30 May 2012), COM(2012) 253 final, p. 8 (emphasis added).

[43] See European Commission, 'Antitrust: Commission opens formal proceedings against Standard & Poor's concerning securities identification number', MEMO/09/6 of 12 January 2009, available at: http://europa.eu/rapid/press-release_MEMO-09-6_en.htm?locale=en (accessed 31 December 2013). The case was closed through commitment decision of 15 November 2011, Case COMP/39.592 – *Standard & Poor's*, C (2011) 8209 final.

[44] See European Commission, 'Antitrust: Commission Opens Formal Proceedings against Thomson Reuters Concerning Use of Reuters Instrument Codes', Press Release IP/09/1692 of 10 November 2009, available at: http://europa.eu/rapid/press-release_IP-09-1692_en.htm?locale=en#PR_metaPressRelease_bottom (accessed 31 December 2013). The case was also closed through a commitment decision of 20 December 2012, Case COMP/39.654 – *Reuters Instrument Codes (RICs)*, C (2012) 9635 final.

their trading locations: the ISIN (international securities identifier number)[45] and RIC (Reuters instrument code),[46] respectively.

Securities identifiers are essential for a number of activities in the financial sector ('interbank communications, asset and portfolio valuation, clearing and settlement … reporting to authorities, the management of financial institutions' database on securities in their portfolio, etc'),[47] and 'in order to correctly assess investment opportunities, market participants need to access accurate and timely financial data'.[48]

Both identifiers belong exclusively to private firms, allowing them to exercise market power.[49] As far as the *conduct* is concerned, the supposed abuses consisted in prohibiting customers or competitors from migrating data into alternative datafeed services, with exclusionary intent (*Thomson Reuters*); or in exploiting the users of codes (outside the US) by charging them extra fees for licensing (*Standard & Poor's*).

As we shall see (at section 2.2.1 below), para-regulatory remedies adopted in both cases are strongly influenced by the Commission's view of the role information should play in markets for securities' identifiers. Any intervention should ensure the widest access possible to relevant market information; allow the highest interoperability between different products and services; and ensure the portability of information – as with personal data, cited above in section 2 – especially that encapsulated in *de facto* standards or IPRs.

---

[45] Standard & Poor's owns ISIN, the most-used code identifying securities traded worldwide. ISINs are allocated and distributed by national numbering agencies (NNAs). In the US, S&P has been designated by the American Bankers Association (ABA) as the competent NNA and as such enjoys a monopoly for the issuance and the first-hand distribution of US ISINs. See the Commission's commitment decision (n. 43 above) para. 24.

[46] Thomson Reuters owns RICs, codes that identify securities and are used by financial institutions to retrieve data from Thomson Reuters' consolidated real-time datafeeds (providing real-time market data, which is used by financial institutions worldwide in their day-to-day business). See the Commission's press release (n. 44 above).

[47] Commitment decision in *Standard & Poor's* (n. 43 above) para. 13.

[48] See the speech by Commissioner Almunia as reported by European Commission, 'Antitrust: Commission renders legally binding commitments from Thomson Reuters Reference', Press Release IP/12/1433 of 20 December 2012, available at: http://europa.eu/rapid/press-release_IP-12-1433_en.htm?locale=en (accessed 31 December 2013).

[49] In *Standard & Poor's*, the Commission considered that the company enjoyed 'a *monopoly* for the issuance and the first-hand distribution of US ISINs', while Thomson Reuters had a '*dominant position* in the market for consolidated real-time datafeeds' (emphasis added).

2.1.2 Misuse of information exchanges in regulated markets: electronic communications and energy

Vertically integrated network operators in liberalized utility markets can use the informational advantage they derive from managing the network to harm downstream competition. Since access to and interconnection among networks is pivotal to ensuring workable competition, a second group of decisions includes dominant firms' refusal with exclusionary intent to supply information to downstream competitors. Besides actual refusals, vertically integrated dominant firms often downgrade the quality of information exchanged or delay exchanging information with competitors.

In doing so, firms may simultaneously contravene regulations (although not necessarily) and be sanctioned by sector regulators, and harm competition and be sanctioned for that under competition law, the application of which is not pre-empted[50] (see also at section 2.2.3 below). Whether the breach or evasion of regulation (be it pro-competitive or not) may itself be regarded as abusive under competition law is an issue that will be discussed further below (at section 2.1.3).

In the electronic communication sector abuses involving information flows include the Italian *Telecom Italia* case[51] and the EU case of *Telekomunikacja Polska*,[52] while in the energy market supposed informational abuses took place in *Exergia/Enel*[53] and the five *Sorgenia* cases.[54] All Italian cases (in both the energy and telecom markets) were closed through the acceptance of para-regulatory commitments (at 2.2.2 below), while only in *Telekomunikacja Polska* did the Commission impose a fine of €127.5 million.

The Commission challenged Telekomunikacja Polska's provision of non-reliable so-called 'general information', which was indispensable for

---

[50] See Case C-280/08 *Deutsche Telekom v. Commission* [2010] ECR, I-9555, paras 80–96; Case T-271/03 *Deutsche Telekom v. Commission* [2008] ECR II-477, para. 113.

[51] AGCM, Case A426 – *Telecom Italia – Gare affidamento servizi telefonia fissa e connettività IP*, decision No. 23677, 19 June 2012, *Bull.* No. 25/2012.

[52] Commission decision of 22 June 2011, COMP/39.525 – *Telekomunikacja Polska*, C(2011) 4378 final, [2011] OJ C 324, p. 7.

[53] AGCM, Case A410 – *Exergia/Enel – Servizio di salvaguardia*, decision No. 20549, 10 December 2009, *Bull.* No. 49/2009.

[54] The five *Sorgenia* cases are: AGCM, Case A411 – *Sorgenia/A2A*; Case A411-A – *Sorgenia/Acea*; Case A411-B – *Sorgenia/Italgas*; Case A411-D – *Sorgenia/Iride*; Case A411-C – *Sorgenia/Hera*: the first four were decided on 8 September 2010, *Bull.* No. 35/2010; the last, weeks later, on 21 October 2010, *Bull.* No. 41/2010.

alternative operators to make sound decisions regarding access to Telekomunikacja Polska's wholesale broadband products at specific locations.[55] A further abuse consisted in providing inaccurate and incomplete information (data were sometimes transmitted in paper format), that made it particularly difficult and costly for alternative operators to process it and therefore efficiently access Telekomunikacja Polska's network.[56]

A very similar practice was challenged in *Telecom Italia*, in which the incumbent refused to supply alternative operators (especially alternative virtual operators) with technical and economic information needed to fruitfully participate in a tender procedure for the provision of telecom services to big clients (namely, Enel and Consip). At issue were, for example, network configuration data (which typically change over time) and technical limitations to the provision of wholesale access services (some posts are overloaded and cannot handle more data traffic).

In the energy sector, AGCM considered as possibly exclusionary the exploitation of the information monopoly by network incumbents. In particular, in *Enel Exergia*, Enel provided Exergia with inaccurate, incomplete and delayed information on customer data (violating regulatory rules on switching and on taking over the default service).[57] Similar to the decision in *Telekomunikacja Polska*, AGCM considered that the supply of incomplete information and incorrect data greatly increased Exergia's costs, as extra resources had to be devoted to make data ready to use. This artificial raising of the new entrant's costs reduced its ability to compete and, at worst, could have forced it out of the market. In the *Sorgenia* cases, AGCM contested the practice of five vertically integrated

---

[55] D. Kamiński, A. Rogozińska and B. Sasinowska, 'Telekomunikacja Polska Decision: Competition Law Enforcement in Regulated Markets' (2011) 3 *Comp. Pol. Newsletter* 3.

[56] Indeed, no specific channels (e.g., IT interfaces such as dedicated portals) were set up by Telekomunikacja Polska to help alternative operators to efficiently process such information and implement their business. However, such facilities were made available to Telekomunikacja Polska's subsidiary PTK Centertel, resulting in fewer orders being rejected and cheaper treatment of 'general information'. In the Commission's view 'such behaviour of [Telekomunikacja Polska] forms part of the incumbent's strategy aimed at hindering [alternative operators] from efficiently accessing the incumbent's network and using its wholesale broadband products'. See *Telekomunikacja Polska* (n. 52 above) para. 565.

[57] Exergia won the tender for the provision of the *servizio di salvaguardia* (default service), set forth in Law Decree No. 73/2007, and was thus expected to succeed Enel. For this switch to work, all information about consumers once served by Enel had to rapidly and completely migrate to Exergia.

energy distributors of providing incomplete information and adopting inefficient procedures for the provision of customer data to downstream competitor Sorgenia. Again, the abusive conduct was exclusionary, as its effect in the downstream market was to delay the entry of a competitor by raising its costs.

Defendants in all cases claimed that the information under scrutiny could not be provided because it exceeded the disclosure obligations already established by the sector regulator,[58] with which they were already complying (except in *Telekomunikacja Polska*).[59] In all cases the argument was dismissed with reference, first, to *Deutsche Telekom*[60] and, second, to the fact that exclusionary effects arose from wider strategies, not just the informational abuses, which were aimed at delaying or impeding access to networks, thus restricting downstream competition.

2.1.3 Misuse of information flows to distort regulatory procedures

Relevant case-law on possible abuse of regulatory procedures in the US dates back to the 1960s.[61] However, for our discourse, the most important case is probably *AT&T*, regarding which competition scholars have long debated whether distorting a regulatory process could constitute an antitrust liability under Section 2 of the Sherman Act.[62] Allegations

---

[58] E.g., in *Telecom Italia*, reference was made to the Italian Communications Authority (AGCOM) Regulation No. 718/2008/CONS making binding commitments presented by the incumbent Telecom Italia to implement a functional separation of the local fixed network and establishing the *Organo di Vigilanza* to oversee the correct implementation of network access commitments. On this see also at section 3.2.

[59] In *Telekomunikacja Polska*, the allegedly infringing incumbent admitted having violated access regulation, but considered this, by relying on a *ne bis in idem* argument, as a further reason for advocating the non-application of competition rules to the same conduct. On the *ne bis in idem* argument see also at section 2.2.3 below.

[60] *Deutsche Telekom* (n. 50 above).

[61] In the US, the leading cases are *Eastern Railroad Presidents Conference v. Noerr Motor Freight*, 365 U.S. 127 (1961), and *United Mine Workers v. Pennington*, 381 U.S. 657 (1965), which inaugurated the notorious Noerr-Pennington doctrine, establishing immunity from antitrust liability for parties petitioning benefits granted by the government, which was further expanded by the 'sham litigation' exception. See P.E. Areeda and H. Hovenkamp, *Antitrust Law: An Analysis of Antitrust Principles and Their Application*, Vol. I (3rd edn, Aspen 2006) 240.

[62] See, e.g., R.G. Noll and B.M. Owen, 'The Anti-competitive Uses of Regulation: United States vs AT&T (1982)' in J.E. Kwoka and L.J. White (eds), *The Antitrust Revolution* (Harper Collins 1989) 328.

included AT&T's refusal to provide the Federal Communications Commission (FCC) with information on its costs, a strategic withholding to protect its interest and keep prices in competitive markets unreasonably high.

Regulatory procedures are heavily dependent on the information provided by undertakings; therefore questioning whether a strategic use of such flow may, alone or together with other elements, amount to a violation of Article 102 is anything but trivial. Sometimes the provision or exchange of information among market participants is mandated by regulation in an aim to foster competition (as regards network access duties cited above). Therefore, a refusal to supply information, which infringes such pro-competitive regulation, may also constitute an abuse of dominant position. We present below cases where the misuse of information is rendered in the context of a regulatory procedure, but it does not necessarily (although it can) amount to an infringement of that regulation, as in *AT&T*.[63] Here, dominant firms, whether formally complying with regulatory requirements or not, alter information flows that are needed to make a regulatory procedure work, using the margins left by regulation to distort the regulatory process with exclusionary goals.

2.1.3.1 Providing misleading information in regulatory procedures is an abuse (AstraZeneca) Regulatory procedures aimed at releasing patents or extending authorizations for commercializing pharmaceuticals require applicants to submit technical information.[64] Providing several national patent offices with 'highly misleading' information, characterized by 'a manifest lack of transparency', was found to be an abuse of dominant position in AstraZeneca,[65] because it fell outside the scope of competition on the merits. The 'first abuse' consisted principally in the release of

---

[63] Where the FCC's orders to disclose cost information were long ignored by AT&T.

[64] See Council Regulation (EEC) No. 1768/92 of 18 June 1992 concerning the creation of a supplementary protection certificate for medicinal products [1992] OJ L 182, p. 1.

[65] Commission decision of 15 June 2005, Case COMP/A.373507/F3 – AstraZeneca [2006] OJ L 332, p. 24, upheld by the General Court (Case T-321/05 – AstraZeneca v. Commission [2010] ERC, II-02805) and the CJEU (Case C-457/10 P – AstraZeneca v. Commission EU:C:2012:770). For commentaries see M.T. Maggiolino and M.L. Montagnani, 'AstraZeneca's Abuse of IPR-Related Procedures: A Hypothesis of Anti-Trust Offence, Abuse of Rights, and IPR Misuse' (2011) 34 World Comp. 245.

distorted or 'inaccurate'[66] information to obtain supplementary protection certificates (SPCs) that unduly extended the duration of AstraZeneca's patent protection for the anti-ulcer drug Losec.[67] The practice harmed competition since AstraZeneca engaged in 'artificially maintaining market dominance by extending the term of patent protection',[68] and had (potential) exclusionary effects, as it was aimed at preventing market entry of competing generic products.[69] The significance of such abusive practice has been so high that the decision has already found an echo at the national level.[70]

2.1.3.2 Refusal to supply information in regulatory procedures (Italgas and Bayer) Unlike AstraZeneca, in which the provision of misleading information could not be scrutinized by the administrative bodies, which could not but release the SPCs,[71] there are cases in which information is not released at all or its release is delayed, preventing the recipient public administration from accomplishing its duties. Whenever the public procedures at stake consist of some pro-competitive intervention (such as an auction implementing competition for the market), a delay or refusal to provide the administrative body with the information it needs to proceed may amount to an abuse of dominant position if it has exclusionary effects.

---

[66] Patterson (n. 12 above).

[67] On strategic patent filing and its relevance under EU competition rules see J. Straus, 'Patent Application: Obstacle for Innovation and Abuse of Dominant Position under Article 102 TFEU?' (2010) 2 J. Comp. L. & Pract. 189.

[68] J. Drexl, 'AstraZeneca and the EU Sector Inquiry: When Do Patent Filings Violate Competition Law?' in J. Drexl and N. Lee (eds), *Pharmaceutical Innovation, Competition and Patent Law* (Edward Elgar Publishing 2013) 290, 293.

[69] The case ended with AstraZeneca being fined €60 million. The amount was slightly reduced by the General Court on appeal.

[70] See the Italian AGCM, Case A431 – Ratiopharm/Pfizer, decision No. 23194, 11 January 2012, Bull. No. 2/2012, especially para. 179.

[71] The General Court made clear that misleading an authority can be an abuse ('liable to raise regulatory obstacles to competition') depending in part on whether the public body lacks discretion or is not obliged to verify the 'accuracy or veracity of the information provided'. See T-321/05 AstraZeneca (n. 65 above) para. 357.

The leading Italian case is *Italgas*,[72] regarding the renewal procedure of franchise bidding for exclusive gas service provision in two municipalities. The incumbent, Italgas, whose concessions were about to expire, refused to provide the municipalities of Rome and Todi with the information they needed to design the auction (concerning the state of the networks, public funds already enjoyed by Italgas, the identity of gas consumers connected to the network and other very detailed technical data). The data were at the sole disposal of Italgas, making it an 'informational monopolist' in AGCM's view. By refusing to provide these data to local administrations, Italgas artificially kept full control over the infrastructure and impaired its competitors' ability to participate in the auction, with exclusionary intent.[73]

AGCM did not directly classify the conduct as abuse of regulatory procedures; rather, it regarded the relevant information as an essential facility and condemned Italgas' refusal to provide it accordingly.[74] Nonetheless, the refusal had in the first place the effect of altering a pro-competitive regulatory procedure (the auction), whose outcome would otherwise have been enhanced competition *for* the market.

In 2011, the pharmaceutical company *Bayer*[75] was found to have abused its dominant position by refusing to provide its toxicological studies to competing generics producers.[76] In its decision, AGCM

---

[72] AGCM, Case A432 – *Comuni vari – Espletamento gare affidamento servizio distribuzione gas*, decision No. 23114, 14 December 2011, *Bull.* No. 50, 2011.

[73] See also AGCM, Case A433 – *Messinambiente – Affidamento del servizio di gestione integrata dei rifiuti solidi urbani nel Comune di Messina*, decision No. 23396, 14 March 2012, *Bull.* No. 13/2012; and Case A435 – *Comune di Prato-Estra Reti Gas*, decision No. 23243, 25 January 2012, *Bull.* No. 4/2012 (where liability under Article 102 was established on similar grounds). For further comments see A. Candido, A. Canepa and V. Carfì, 'La tutela della concorrenza nei mercati regolati: le decisioni dell'AGCM in materia di servizi di interesse economico generale (Anno 2012)' (2013) *Concorrenza e mercato* 497; M. Zuppetta, 'Abusi di posizione dominante (Anno 2012)' (2013) *Concorrenza e mercato* 410.

[74] In AGCM's view, the denied information was indispensable to municipalities and competitors, and non-replicable; Italgas enjoyed an 'informational monopoly'; its refusal to provide information was not justified; and the refusal was deemed abusive under Article 102 TFEU, because it had the effect of potentially excluding competitors.

[75] AGCM, Case A415 – *Sapec Agro/Bayer-Helm*, decision No. 22558, 28 June 2011, *Bull.* No. 26, 2011.

[76] Bayer refused to provide two scientific reports concerning the effects of fosetyl-aluminium on humans and the environment to the European Union

invoked *AstraZeneca* to establish that the exclusive possession of vertebrate studies gave Bayer a dominant position, since this information was indispensable to fungicide producers for accessing the market.[77] In contrast to *AstraZeneca* and *Italgas*, in *Bayer* the immediate recipients of information were not administrative bodies but competitors. However, what the cases have in common is that pro-competitive regulatory procedures were indeed distorted. In addition, Bayer's refusal was also illegal, since a specific procedure was dictated to force the studies' holder to find an agreement with generics producers requesting an authorization.[78] And the factual findings demonstrated that Bayer's strategy was precisely to 'alter' the procedures for the release of its studies to its competitors,[79] with exclusionary goals and to the detriment of consumers.

Consequently, despite sailing the safe harbour of essential facility in both *Italgas* and *Bayer*,[80] AGCM left room for consideration of abusive

---

Fosetyl-Aluminium Task Force (an association of manufacturers of fosetyl-based products). Such provision was compulsory (pursuant to Legislative Decree No. 194 of 1995 implementing Directive 91/414/CEE) and needed by Task Force members to obtain authorization to market their generic fosetyl-based fungicides.

77 According to AGCM, 'owning vertebrate studies puts Bayer in a position to fix the conditions for accessing the relevant market, and thus, to make barriers to entry stemming from the authorization procedure even higher' (translation by the author.) See *Sapec Agro/Bayer-Helm* (n. 75 above) para. 228.

78 Council Directive 91/414/ EEC of 15 July 1991 concerning the placing of plant protection products on the market, [1991] OJ L 230, p. 1, implemented by Legislative Decree No. 194 of 1995, provides for a procedure requiring pharmaceutical producers that have already conducted studies on vertebrates to share the results of such studies with other producers requesting an authorization. In the absence of an agreement, the scientific study's holder can be obliged to share its data with its competitors according to procedures (consisting of an arbitration and conciliation led by the Ministry of Health) that take into account the interests of all parties.

79 Bayer imposed extra conditions for the release of vertebrate data that were not provided for in Directive 91/414/CEE, hampering the Task Force's access to Bayer's data. Subsequent negotiations led by the Ministry of Health failed due to Bayer's obstructionism and the Task Force exited the market, resulting in an overall increase in prices for final customers. See *Sapec Agre/Bayer-Helm* (n. 75 above) para. 135. In conclusion, AGCM qualified Bayer's refusal as abusive and, while rejecting commitments offered by the party, imposed a fine of €5.124 million.

80 The refusal to supply this information forced the competition out of the market; thus AGCM considered the toxicological reports as an essential facility on the basis that: (1) Regulation 1107/2009/EC bans repetition of toxicological studies; (2) access to such reports was the legal prerequisite for marketing authorization; (3) without access, Task Force members had no alternative but to

conduct as strategic informational misuse of regulatory procedures. Indeed, the exclusionary effect in all cases derives from the distortion of a pro-competitive regulatory procedure, enacted through a strategic use of information.

2.1.4 Beyond the exchange of information to collude: collusion to provide misleading information (outside regulatory procedures) – the US Libor case

Providing misleading information outside a regulatory procedure could still cause competition concerns if the data concerned are able to affect the market dynamics and ultimately consumer interests.

Attempts to apply rules on conspiracy (largely similar to Article 101 TFEU) have been made with regard to *collusion to provide misleading information* in the US *Libor* case.[81] The antitrust claims were dismissed by Judge Buchwald on 29 March 2013. However, plaintiffs can still demonstrate on appeal (or in an amended lawsuit) that the banks' conduct (collusive rate-rigging) does breach federal antitrust laws and harms competition.[82]

US antitrust claims were dismissed based on findings that the banks were not acting as competitors, but rather were cooperating when submitting manipulated Libor interest-rate information to the British Bankers' Association (BBA), which is responsible for setting the Libor based on the data provided by the BBA's member banks.[83]

---

buy the products from Bayer; (4) given access to the reports, the Task Force members would have eventually developed new and innovative products; (5) the refusal to supply could not be justified by the mere presence of IPRs; (6) the elimination of competition was more than a risk, since Bayer's refusal forced the Task Force members out of the market; and so (7) the 'damage to final consumers' condition is met, since the reduction of supply resulted in an overall increase in prices for final customers.

[81] *Libor-Based Fin. Instruments Antitrust Litig.*, 802 F. Supp. 2d 1380, 1381 (J.P.M.L. 2011).

[82] See A. Frankel, 'New Yen Libor Ruling is Bad Omen for Rate-rigging Antitrust Claims' (31 March 2014), available at: http://blogs.reuters.com/alison-frankel/2014/03/31/new-yen-libor-ruling-is-bad-omen-for-rate-rigging-antitrust-claims/ (accessed 31 March 2014), reporting that 'Other Libor plaintiffs, like the National Credit Union Administration, are counting on the 2nd Circuit [Court of Appeals] to overturn Buchwald's interpretation of antitrust injury'.

[83] In Judge Buchwald's words, 'collaboration among banks is not meant to be competition'. Nor could rules on collusion be applied – according to Judge Buchwald – because the financial harm suffered by plaintiffs was not directly related to the harm to competition caused by collusion; the 'injury would have

As suggested by Patterson, Libor rates, which are often used as a benchmark for loan agreements, should be seen as a product market itself, and banks' estimates should be considered as informational inputs to that product. Therefore, by lowering the quality of information provided to the BBA, the banks engaged in a restraint of trade in the antitrust sense (trade in the market for Libor estimates, not in that for Libor-based securities). However, it is to be acknowledged that there is still too little support for making *Libor* a case of collective exploitation of informational market power.[84]

According to a different reasoning, the banks' 'collusive' collective dominance (in the market for Libor estimates, as suggested) could be derived from standards set forth in *Piau* (concerning FIFA),[85] the only case thus far that applies the *Airtours* standards to an abuse of collective dominance. Indeed, the BBA statute, like FIFA's, could be considered a factor establishing the banks' collective dominance; but most decisively, although collusion is not required for the inference of collective dominance, the latter could be established in *Libor*, since collusion is the only ascertainable fact.[86]

Alternatively, *Libor* could be built and understood as a case of abuse of (collective) dominant position 'à la *AstraZeneca*'. This could be the case if misrepresentation and estimates subversion were part of a regulatory

resulted from defendants' misrepresentation, not from harm to competition'. See: Memorandum and order 11 MD 2262 (NRB), Case 1:11-md-02262-NRB, Document 286, Filed 29 March 2013.

[84] Patterson (n. 12 above) 23. Manipulation cannot be abusive because it derives not from the banks' collective market power, but from the 18 banks being selected as members of the US dollar Libor rate board. Moreover, banks are not bound to refer to the Libor index in their loan agreements but are free to do so.

[85] Case T 193/02 *Laurent Piau v. Commission* [2005] ECR II-209, para. 113.

[86] Indeed, collusion was at the heart of recent European Commission decisions to fine eight banks for participating in illegal cartels in the interest rates derivatives industry: Commission Decisions of 4 December 2013, Case AT.39914 – *Euro Interest Rate Derivatives* and Case AT.39861 – *Yen Interest Rate Derivatives* (both unpublished); see also European Commission, 'Antitrust: Commission Fines Banks €1.71 Billion for Participating in Cartels in the Interest Rate Derivatives Industry', Press Release IP/13/1208 of 4 December 2013, available at: http://europa.eu/rapid/press-release_IP-13-1208_en.htm (accessed 31 May 2014). D. Samà, 'Cartel Detection and Collusion Screening: An Empirical Analysis of the London Metal Exchange' (2014), available at: http://ssrn.com/abstract=2425320 (accessed 31 May 2014), claims that 'the cartel aimed at manipulating the pricing process of the Euribor and the Libor, distorting the competition in the underlying trading of interest rate derivatives'.

procedure, that is, if the *Libor* setting-up process were run or overseen by a regulator, or if the index had some publicly recognized effect. In presence of such circumstances, the submission of fake estimates could probably be considered as abusive.[87]

Other promising routes for assessing the case might derive from considering Libor as a *de facto* standard index, similarly to Standard & Poor's ISIN. This would help to overcome the difficulty of considering the (collectively deployed) conduct as abusive, since, as in *Standard & Poor's*, the harm to competition would be of exploitative nature (see section 2.1.1.2).

As mentioned above, the antitrust claim has been dismissed and the case continues under securities regulation and fraud theories, though for sure it deserves greater attention. But the point to be made here is that if it is unquestionable that a unilateral misuse of informational market power can amount to a violation of antitrust rules, the same should be true, at least under EU competition rules, with regard to a misuse of collective informational advantage.

2.2 When Information Flow Is the Object of a 'Para-Regulatory' Remedy

Remedies to cope with informational abuses may well include fines and cease-and-desist orders, but also often behavioural remedies ordering the sharing of information, in the form of disclosure obligations or fair and transparent conditions established for information access and sharing. Such complex behavioural remedies regarding information are imposed, or respective commitments are accepted, in competition law decisions[88] that look para-regulatory, as detailed forward-looking rules are set and continuous monitoring (sometimes requiring the establishment of *ad hoc* compliance bodies) is necessary.[89]

---

[87] Of course, the theory of harm remains unclear, and much depends on the facts, which might demonstrate an effect on quality or price of Libor-related products.

[88] Waller (n. 4 above) 576ff. differentiates between access, disclosure and protection of information remedies in abuse and merger cases.

[89] S.W. Waller, 'Past, Present and Future of Monopolization Remedies' (2009) 76 *Antitrust L.J.* 11, 26. For the argument that by making use of Article 9 commitments 'the Commission is departing on a regulatory venture' see E Hjelmeng, 'Competition Law Remedies: Striving for Coherence or Finding New Ways?' (2013) 50 *C.M.L. Rev.* 1007, 1020. In the same vein, see M. Sadowska, 'Energy Liberalization in an Antitrust Straitjacket: A Plant Too Far?' (2011) 34 *World Comp.* 449.

2.2.1 Informational remedies in unregulated (or slightly regulated) markets

In *Magill*, the Commission required national broadcasters 'to suppl[y] each other and third parties on request and on a non-discriminatory basis with their individual advance weekly programme listings'.[90] In *Microsoft I*, the Commission ordered Microsoft to disclose interoperability information on its Windows operating system to its competitors in the market for work group operating system programs, with the objective of providing greater access to competing application developers.[91] In *Microsoft II*, the must-carry commitment was 'more seamless access to the super-dominant Microsoft operating system';[92] the ballot screen remedy[93] was an alternative to a hardly sustainable obligation to sell rival browser products. Commitments involving duties to share information among competitors in the gaming market were made binding by AGCM in *Giochi/Sisal*,[94] thus allowing competitors to access Sisal's information regarding all bets and to appear in Sisal's website.[95] Also, in *Audipress* commitments were accepted establishing the conditions for Audipress to conduct and release sample surveys to downstream press operators.

To remedy concerns relating to substantial barriers for customers to switch from Reuters Instrument Codes (RICs) to alternative providers for consolidated datafeeds, and, therefore, to increase the interoperability between RICs and rival services, Thomson Reuters agreed to 'allow third parties to develop and maintain a switching tool that allows RICs and

[90] *Magill* (n. 31 above) para. 2 of the operative part of the judgment.

[91] The Court of First Instance (Grand Chamber) upheld the decision, ordering Microsoft to license its IPRs on interoperability information in a transparent and non-discriminatory way: *Microsoft I* (n. 39 above).

[92] Commission decision of 16 December 2009, Case COMP/C 3/39.530 *Microsoft II*, available at: http://ec.europa.eu/competition/antitrust/cases/dec_docs/39530/39530_2671_3.pdf (accessed 31 December 2013. See Waller (n. 4 above) 579.

[93] Microsoft agreed – and the Commission made this commitment binding to distribute a ballot screen to European users of Windows OS allowing them to choose among different browsers in addition to the Explorer.

[94] AGCM, Case A419 – *Giochi24/Sisal*, decision No. 22301, 13 April 2011, *Bull.* No. 15/2011. Sisal, the national legal monopolist for numerical games, refused to provide its downstream competitors with the technical information needed to access its IT platform, effectively preventing the latter from offering online games on a competitive basis.

[95] In AGCM's view, such information-sharing duties (allowing access to essential knowledge about gamblers, their tastes and the market in general) were meant to reduce technical barriers to entry in the market and to facilitate the release of new and innovative products.

rival services to interoperate, by translating RICs into the financial identifiers of other datafeed providers. Subject to a monthly license fee, third party developers can use and keep RICs in the switching tools they develop.'[96]

In addition, an artificial cooperation among Thomson Reuters' competitors was established, so that '[t]hird-party developers and competing datafeed vendors can share information (with the exclusion of RICs themselves) and cooperate closely in building, maintenance, selling and advertising such switching tools'.[97]

Para-regulatory remedies were also adopted in the only exploitative abuse case, relating to the fixing of licensing fees for the use of Standard & Poor's ISINs by direct and indirect end users.[98]

2.2.2 Informational remedies in regulated network industries (electronic communication and energy sectors)

In *Telecom Italia*,[99] AGCM accepted commitments by the former incumbent to provide technical and economic information to alternative virtual operators as competitors in the downstream market, so as to allow them to offer competitive services to big clients. A further obligation was made binding to provide all configuration data regarding access services whenever a tender promoted by one of Telecom Italia's big clients was at stake.

Enel Exergia[100] and the *Sorgenia* cases were closed through acceptance of very similar and complex commitments affecting information exchange in the energy distribution and retail markets. In sum, all major distributors agreed to provide complete and updated information to

---

[96] European Commission, 'Antitrust: Commission Renders Legally Binding Commitments from Thomson Reuters Reference', Press release IP/12/1433 of 20 December 2012, available at: http://europa.eu/rapid/press-release_IP-12-1433_en.htm?locale=en (accessed 31 December 2013).

[97] Ibid.

[98] For five years starting in November 2011 'indirect end users will no longer have to pay licensing fees to S&P for the use of ISIN records; secondly, S&P will also offer a new service consisting only of ISIN records, at a price of USD 15,000 per annum for the provision of the new service to Information Service Providers and direct end users' (European Union, Report on Competition Policy 2011, available at: http://ec.europa.eu/competition/antitrust/cases/dec_docs/39592/39592_2152_5.pdf, p. 21). See European Commission MEMO (n. 43 above).

[99] *Telecom Italia* (n. 51 above).

[100] *Exergia/Enel* (n. 53 above).

retailers, to set up an information portal dedicated to suppliers to manage information flows regarding clients' consumption and distribution data so as to ease switching procedures, to establish a pre-check procedure to improve the quality of data transferred, to avoid costly procedures to streamline the data and reduce the number of switching failures, to make available a list of all contestable sites (i.e. those withdrawing points that are currently not served, and thus available to alternative providers) and to provide access to computer systems at the same conditions the parent companies apply to their subsidiaries.

2.2.3 Some remarks on para-regulatory remedies in information abuse cases

For all remedies reported here, competition agencies engaged in the design of highly complex and long-lasting behavioural remedies aimed at compelling dominant undertakings to disclose (*Audipress* and *Magill*) or to share (all other cases) information with their competitors. The convergence of attitudes[101] of competition law and regulation when dealing with market information flows is thus impressive.

One possible explanation for this type of remedy is that the conduct at stake is in most cases identified as a refusal to deal, *rectius* to provide information (*Audipress*, *Microsoft I* and *II*, *Magill*, *Sisal* and *Telecom Italia*), and it is known that when remedying a 'refusal to deal, the agencies and courts have to act very much like regulatory agencies'.[102]

Whenever the conduct consists in delaying or downgrading the quality of information supplied (*Exergia/Enel* and *Sorgenia*) and the response is not a penalty (*Telekomunikacja Polska*, *Auditel* and *Bayer*), the set of positive economic behaviour to which undertakings commit is even wider. In this respect there is no great difference between formal decisions (*Microsoft I*) and commitment decisions (e.g., *Telecom Italia*), both being very detailed.[103]

---

[101] Parcu (n. 21 above).

[102] Drexl (n. 30 above) 6, claiming that here the enforcement cannot consist of a ban; rather, it 'imposes a "duty to act" in a particular way', in other words, a positive obligation.

[103] G. Monti, 'Limits to Effective Remedies', Speech given at the 18th Annual Competition Law and Policy Workshop, Fiesole, EUI, 19–20 July 2013.

Super-dominance might be a further explanation,[104] considering that in all cases the information at stake is at the sole disposal of dominant firms. Not only are these monopolists of information; also, the contribution of such monopoly to the overall dominant position is paramount. And as is known, such circumstances justify, in a case of a refusal to supply, the widest information sharing (*Microsoft*, *Audipress*, *Sisal*, *Magill*, *Thomson Reuters*, *S&P*, etc.). Indeed, as the theory of harm is most frequently anti-competitive foreclosure in the meaning of the Guidance paper on ex-Article 82,[105] it is no surprise that duties to supply information to any actual or potential competitor are imposed as the most appropriate remedy.[106]

Ensuring compliance with complex behavioural remedies, like in the framework of regulation, calls for continuous monitoring and requires the power to settle disputes arising from their implementation. This explains the recourse by the Commission (not AGCM) to monitoring trustees to supervise compliance with disclosure and sharing obligations in both formal (*Microsoft I*, although partly annulled)[107] and commitment decisions (*Microsoft II* and *Thomson Reuters*). Most frequently, however, competition agencies retain the discretion to monitor compliance, possibly imposing penalties where information-sharing and disclosure obligations are breached.

It is not clear whether 'outsourcing compliance' with informational remedies, while keeping responsibility for it, is effective or not; nor is it

---

[104] E. Szyszczak, 'Controlling Dominance in European Markets' (2011) 33 *Fordham Int'l L.J.* 1738, 1756.

[105] H. Zenger and M. Walker, 'Theories of Harm in European Competition Law: A Progress Report' in J. Bourgeois and D. Waelbroeck (eds), *Ten Years of Effects-Based Approach in EU Competition Law* (Bruylant 2012) 185 and 25.

[106] For criticism that by doing so competition agencies engage in regulating markets rather than removing a market failure caused by dominant players, see Monti (n. 103 above) 12. Critical towards 'regulatory decrees' especially in high-tech markets: W.H. Page and S.J. Childers, 'Software Development as an Antitrust Remedy: Lessons from the Enforcement of the Microsoft Communications Protocol Licensing Requirement' (2007) 14 *Mich. Telecomm. Tech. L. Rev.* 77, available at: http://www.mttlr.org/volfourteen/page&childers.pdf (accessed 31 May 2014), at 81 (positing that 'courts are ill suited … to monitor market conditions continuously').

[107] *Microsoft I* (n. 39 above) paras 1251ff. Waller (n. 4 above) 587ff. discusses the use of a monitoring trustee to supervise compliance with disclosure obligations in *Microsoft I*.

demonstrated which of the two strategies (keeping or outsourcing compliance) is the most effective. In any event, this makes competition agencies similar to regulators, as continuous monitoring requires long-term intervention, while it is not demonstrated that competition agencies are well equipped to perform this task. Indeed, sector regulators may also fail to perform monitoring of commitment decisions, as evidence from the 2013 *Telecom Italia* case demonstrates,[108] thus leaving the question of which of the two bodies may be the best suited unresolved.

Whether the sectors concerned are regulated or not, duties to disclose or share information are used by competition agencies to remedy refusals to provide it. This in turn creates problems of coordination with access and disclosure regulation and the bodies in charge of enforcing it.

As anticipated (at section 2.1.2 above), in the two telecom cases, former monopolists put forth a regulatory defence, claiming that existing national regulation pre-empted the competition agencies from requiring either a commitment to more information exchange (*Telecom Italia*)[109] or a fine for failing to provide it after the domestic sector regulator had already sanctioned this behaviour (Telekomunikacja Polska).[110]

---

[108] Pursuant to AGCOM's Regulation No. 718/2008/CONS (n. 58 above), a new branch of Telecom Italia was established (the Open Access branch) under the joint control of Telecom Italia and AGCOM to run the access network. A compliance body called OTA was also established to oversee the implementation of Telecom Italia's commitments and to deal with conflicts among operators arising from access to the network. To be sure, such regulatory measures proved insufficient to prevent Telecom Italia from abusing its dominant position in the market for access to the network. In 2013, despite functional separation and detailed regulation, AGCM condemned Telecom Italia under Article 102 for limiting access to its networks (AGCM, Case A428 – *Wind-Fastweb/Condotte Telecom Italia*, decision No. 24339, 9 May 2013, *Bull.* No. 20/2013). For comments, see M. Orofino, 'Gli impegni presentati da Telecom (ed accettati dall'Agcom) tra parità di accesso alla rete fissa e lo sviluppo di reti di nuova generazione' (2009) *Astrid Rassegna*.

[109] Such reference was made in AGCOM's Regulation No. 718/2008/CONS (n. 58 above): Telecom Italia claimed that such commitment exceeded the disclosure obligations already established by the sector regulator, with which it was already complying.

[110] Telekomunikacja Polska was found in breach of national regulation and thus fined by the Polish telecom regulator UKE. The incumbent argued that, since the practice had already been sanctioned by UKE, the Commission could not adjudicate it again under EU competition rules.

The *ne bis in idem* argument was dismissed in both cases[111] by reference to the CJEU judgment in *Deutsche Telekom*[112] and subsequent cases. However, the Commission took into consideration the partial overlap of facts with those of national regulatory decisions and deducted the fines Telekomunikacja Polska had already paid from the total amount of the penalty.

A completely different outcome was reached in the energy cases, where the incumbent Enel (Exergia/Enel) expressly agreed to provide complete and updated information to retailers, other than that prescribed by regulatory obligations, thus recognizing the power of AGCM to 'correct' (weak) sectorial regulation. That AGCM has long been acting as a fully functioning sector regulator, defining detailed rules for information sharing in the retail and distribution energy markets, is confirmed by the fact that commitments made by Enel in *Exergia/Enel* and those agreed upon by the five distributors in the *Sorgenia* cases are substantially identical, and concern, if considered altogether, the vast majority (over 90 per cent) of Italian energy distribution. The cumulative effect of para-regulatory commitments in the *Exergia/Enel* and the *Sorgenia* cases is the introduction of a non-ritual sectorial regulatory function by the competition agency.[113]

---

[111] AGCM affirmed that the para-regulatory commitments 'widen[ed] the scope' of those already imposed on Telecom Italia by the existing sector-specific regulation, and 'broaden[ed] the content of information at the disposal of alternative virtual operators'. See *Telecom Italia* (n. 51 above) paras 79ff. Incidentally, the decision gave rise to a conflict between the competition agency and the regulator, with the latter refusing to provide its compulsory, though not binding, opinion on the proposed commitments (ibid., para. 98).

[112] *Deutsche Telekom* (n. 50 above).

[113] Italian administrative courts have repeatedly affirmed that AGCM has only sanctioning competence and does not enjoy any direct regulatory power: See, *ex multis*, Regional Administrative Court (*Tribunale amministrativo regionale*) Lazio, Chamber I, 8 May 2009, No. 4994, and comments by L. Torchia, 'Il diritto antitrust di fronte al giudice amministrativo' (2013), available at: http://www.irpa.eu/wp-content/uploads/2011/07/relazione-cds-def.pdf (accessed 16 June 2015). It should be noted, however, that from 2012 the number of cases closed with commitments has sharply decreased; therefore, we should expect fewer para-regulatory decisions in the future: F. Di Porto, 'Recent Developments in Italian Competition Law' (2013) *Concorrenza e mercato* 377.

3. EXCHANGE OF INFORMATION UNDER ARTICLES 101 AND 102 TFEU: AN INTERNAL CLASH?

The attention given by both competition scholars[114] and antitrust enforcers[115] to exchange of information in the context of collusion has traditionally been immense.

---

[114] L.R. Fullerton, 'Antitrust Liability for an Exchange of Price Information: What Happened to Container Corporation?' (1977) 63 *Va. L. Rev.* 639; S. De Santi and E. Nagata, 'Competitor Communications: Facilitating Practices or Invitations to Collude? An Application of Theories to Proposed Horizontal Agreements Submitted for Antitrust Review' (1994) 63 *Antitrust L.J.* 93; K.U. Kühn and X. Vives, 'Information Exchange Among Firms and their Impact on Competition' (1995), available at: http://blog.iese.edu/xvives/files/2011/09/Information-Exchanges-and-their-Impact-on-Competition.pdf (accessed 31 December 2013); A. Capobianco, 'Information Exchange under EC Competition Law' (2004) 41 *C.M.L. Rev.* 1247; X. Vives, 'Information Sharing: Economics and Antitrust' (2007), IESE occasional papers, available at: http://www.iese.edu/research/pdfs/OP-07-11-E.pdf (accessed 16 June 2015). In Italy, most recent commentaries on information exchange and collusion originated from the *IAMA* case: Council of State, VI Section, judgment No. 9565 of 29 December 2010, *AGCM v. Iama et al.* This literature includes A. Giannaccari, 'Il caso Iama al Consiglio di Stato: Indietro tutta!' (2011) *Mercato Concorrenza e Regole* 145–150; M Grillo, 'Il caso Iama al Consiglio di Stato: avanti tutta!' (2011) *Mercato Concorrenza e Regole* 151; L. Di Via, 'Osservazioni sulla sentenza del Consiglio di Stato sul caso Iama' (2011) *Mercato Concorrenza e Regole* 159–162. The OECD devoted an entire policy roundtable to the topic. See OECD, 'Information Exchanges between Competitors under Competition Law' (2010), available at: http://www.oecd.org/competition/cartels/48379006.pdf (accessed 31 December 2013), with valuable contributions by A. Heimler, 'The Legal Significance of Economic Evidence in Antitrust Cases: Some Comments Based on the Italian Experience, at 400, K.U. Kühn, 'Designing Competition Policy Towards Information Exchanges – Looking Beyond the Possibility Results', at 416, and J. Padilla, 'The Elusive Challenge of Assessing Information sharing among Competitors under the Competition Law', at 434.

[115] In a nutshell, information exchange among competitors can be part of either a broader cartel infringement (price or quantity fixing, other hard core restrictions) which it facilitates, or a wider cooperation agreement not amounting to a cartel (such as a joint venture or an R&D or standardization agreement). Alternatively, information exchange can be a stand-alone practice that, under particular market conditions (highly concentrated oligopolistic market in which competition is already greatly reduced) and characteristics of the information (precise information exchanged at short intervals, concerning the operation of the market and revealing the market positions and strategies of the various individual competitors), may amount to a restrictive practice in violation of Article 101. Reviews of the relevant case-law are copious. See, e.g., OECD (n. 114 above);

Recently, the revised version of the European Commission Guidelines on Horizontal Co-operation Agreements[116] has put at the forefront the exchange of information among competitors, recognizing that this represents the very basis of any horizontal agreements.[117] In parallel, the cases reported in section 2 of this chapter testify to an increasing attention of competition agencies towards abusive conduct related to market information exchanges.

3.1 Article 102 Versus Article 101: Conflicting Views on Exchange of Information?

A quick look at the Article 102 practice analysed above seems to reveal *an internal conflict* between the ways Articles 101 and 102 TFEU treat market information exchanges: the first aims at forbidding what the latter tries to enhance, and vice versa.[118]

To put it less cryptically: at first sight, Article 101 tends to treat the exchange of information with suspicion, possibly forbidding it, while Article 102 tends to condemn practices aimed at worsening that exchange, and may compel firms to implement it as a remedy.

Horizontal Guidelines (n. 2 above). The leading cases referred to in the Guidelines are: Joined Cases 40–48, 50, 54–56, 111, 113 and 114/73 – *Suiker Unie and Others v. Commission* [1975] ECR 1663; Case 172/80 – *Züchner v. Bayrische Vereinsbank* [1981] ECR 2021; Joined Cases C-89/85, 104/85, C-114/85, C-116/85, C-117/85 and C-125/85 to C-129/85 – *Ahlström Osakeyhtiö and Others v. Commission* (‘*Wood Pulp II*’) [1993] ECR I-1307; Case T-35/92 – *John Deere v. Commission* [1994] ECR II-957; Case T-34/92 – *Fiatagri UK and Others v. Commission* [1994] ECR II-905; Case C-238/05 – *Asnef-Equifax v. Ausbanc* [2006] ECR I-11125; Case C-8/08 – *T-Mobile Netherlands* [2009] ECR I-4529.

[116] Horizontal Guidelines (n. 2 above) paras 55ff.

[117] See V.H.S.E. Robertson, ‘A Counterfactual on Information Sharing: The Commission’s Horizontal Guidelines 2011 Applied to the Leading Cases’ (2013) 36 *World Comp.* 459. The Guidelines also clarify the many advantages information exchange can bring about, such as: the reduction of information asymmetries, fostering innovation, economies of scale, risk sharing, enhancement of product quality and variety (para. 2). However, it can also lead to severe competition concerns: it may facilitate collusion or be the subject of an agreement aimed at fixing prices or quantities (para. 59).

[118] A similar question (‘Which of these views is correct: the condemnation or the exaltation of information exchanges?’) can be found in Wagner-von Papp (n. 1 above).

3.2 Exchange *Versus* Unilateral Provision of Information

The conflict implied cannot be overcome by simply considering that Article 101 deals with practices concerning information *exchange*, while Article 102 concerns mostly a *one-way* information dispatch.[119] The restrictions analysed above, as well as the access and disclosure duties, require information on technical access (*Microsoft I*) or consumers (*Telecom Italia* and *Exergia/Enel*) to be *exchanged* among competitors, which entails a reciprocal flow of information. This is also the case when the downgrading (*Sorgenia*, *TP*) or withholding of information has been condemned in network industries, where the exclusionary effects derive precisely from the impossibility of data to *flow both ways* from one system to another.

3.3 Is the Type of Information that is Exchanged any Different?

Conceivably, one could contend that what differs is the *type* of information that is exchanged: to fall within the scope of Article 101 it must be data on *prospective* strategies, while Article 102 is rather on *past or current* data. To be sure, this argument also sounds weak, as what is relevant in both cases is the ability of the information that is exchanged to reduce the strategic uncertainty regarding the 'market positions and strategies of the various individual competitors' that are involved, that is, the functional notion of information (see also at 2.1.1.1 above).[120]

Whenever interconnection and interoperability among systems, platforms or networks must be granted, the markets are necessarily characterized by (or tend toward) the widest transparency. For instance, in telecom access markets, due to daily interconnection relationships, all operators can easily observe how open their competitors' access networks are and what retail prices are reciprocally charged by network operators; from the websites and heavy advertising campaigns they can also learn which deals each competitor is offering its clients; from the requests for switching, every operator can learn the characteristics of clients, the

---

[119] According to the Commission, indeed, truly unilateral disclosure of information involving competitively sensitive information may still fall within the scope of Article 101: Horizontal Guidelines (n. 2 above) para. 62. See also AG Kokott, Case C-8/08 *T-Mobile Netherlands* [2009] ECR I-4529, para. 54.

[120] See Commission Decision of 17 February 1992, Joined Cases IV/31.370 and 31.446 – *UK Agricultural Tractor Registration Exchange* [1992] OJ L 68, p. 19, para. 91; Horizontal Guidelines (n. 2 above) para. 62.

position in the markets, etc.[121] So in a tight oligopoly like the Italian mobile telecommunication market, 'commercial and industrial policies can be easily observed and compared by all participants, allowing them to adopt common strategies ... and to discover and punish any deviations.[122]

In contrast to a common conception, not even the age (i.e. relative to prospective, yet not actual business strategies) or the level of detail (not aggregated)[123] of the information that is exchanged are sufficient criteria to definitely exclude a potential conflict between Articles 101 and 102: Article 102 also applies to, or can require firms to exchange, data whose degree of disaggregation is paramount[124] (think of the *Sorgenia* commitments);[125] and, nonetheless, 'there are no general criteria for determining the minimum level of aggregation required to prevent an antitrust investigation'.[126] As regards the age, also under Article 102, data exchanged can concern future business strategies (i.e. trends of prices,

---

121 These were the AGCM's arguments in opening an investigation of the three main Italian mobile telephone companies for abuse of collective dominance. See AGCM, Case A357 – *Tele2/Tim-Vodafone-Wind*, decision No. 14045 of 23 February 2005, *Bull.* No. 8/2005, para. 67. The case was later split, that against Tim and Wind being closed through commitments, while Vodafone was fined in 2007.

122 Ibid., para 66.

123 Data can only be regarded as genuinely aggregated if it is sufficiently difficult to recognize individual companies. Therefore, only highly detailed, non-aggregated information 'allows competitors to identify each other's future strategies' and 'reduce uncertainty about rivals' conduct'. See OECD (n. 114 above) 48.

124 Possibly, the only remaining difference is that under Article 101 exchange of information is voluntary (i.e. as part of an agreement), while in Article 102 it is imposed as a para-regulatory remedy by competition agencies. However, even with the latter, one could contend that commitments (allegedly the main source of para-regulation) are agreed upon by the parties and the competition agency. See also OECD (n. 114 above) para 5.2.5. On the legitimacy of information exchange through intermediaries in the context of Article 101, see O. Odudu, 'Indirect Information Exchange: The Constituent Elements of Hub and Spoke Collusion' (2011) 7 *Eur. Comp. J.* 205.

125 Where data that distributors need to exchange with electricity retailers are individualized, customized and refer to specific customers and not just aggregated.

126 OECD (n. 114 above) 48: only a case-by-case approach will allow competition agencies to assess this.

sales and capacity);[127] and in any event 'information about past behaviours may still be used to achieve a collusive understanding'.[128]

This clarified, the argument that Article 102 is more benevolent than Article 101 towards exchange of information is still not convincing. Indeed, it may prove over-inclusive for several reasons. First, one cannot say that Article 101 always forbids the exchange of information: if there is no risk of collusion or if the information exchanged is aggregated and retrospective, no violation of Article 101 would exist. Additionally, the pro-competitive virtues of exchanges of information are as relevant as anti-competitive risks in the assessment of any exchange under Article 101(1).[129] In this sense a dichotomy can be found within Article 101 too. Also, even if a risk of harming competition exists, but efficiency gains outweigh that risk, and a fair part of such gains is passed on to consumers, an exchange of information may still account for an individual exemption. Not only, but at least in truly competitive markets, exchanges of information should be regarded as pro-competitive and therefore not in violation of Article 101.[130]

Interestingly, the statement also remains over-inclusive with regard to abusive conduct. Indeed, it is not always true that, in the case of an informational abuse, the competition agency's response under Article 102 would necessarily be to compel an exchange of information. As we have seen, in some (albeit few) cases the response is an injunction and the imposition of a fine.[131]

However, even considering these nuances, it still remains to be explained, from a theoretical point of view, why exchange of information is favoured and protected under Article 102 but regarded with suspicion under Article 101. Only a comprehensive assessment of the exchange of

---

[127] In electricity pools, for instance, communication of forecasts about power production and consumption (in terms of prices and quantities) must be made on a daily basis.

[128] OECD (n. 114 above) 49.

[129] A point particularly stressed by M. Bennett and P. Collins, 'The Law and Economics of Information Sharing: The Good, the Bad and the Ugly' (2010) 6 *Eur. Comp. J.* 311. More generally on the benefits of information exchange from an economic perspective: Kühn and Vives (n. 114 above).

[130] See *Fiatagri UK* (n. 115 above) para. 91. In the Court's words: 'An agreement creating an information exchange system which does not concern prices and does not underpin any other anti-competitive arrangement is likely, *on a truly competitive market*, to lead to the intensification of competition between suppliers' (emphasis added).

[131] This occurred in *AstraZeneca*, *Italgas*, *Messinambiente*, *Estra Reti*, *Bayer*, *Auditel*.

information, one that rests on both pillars of competition law, may provide the answer. And such a comprehensive approach requires inquiring into the market conditions in which the exchange of information takes place and the 'intensity' of information asymmetry that is at stake.

4. A COMPREHENSIVE ASSESSMENT OF EXCHANGE OF INFORMATION

When dealing with exchanges of information among competitors a comprehensive assessment has different outcomes depending on whether it occurs in recently liberalized sectors (such as the network industries) (at section 4.1 below) or in unregulated (or slightly regulated) markets (at section 4.2 below).

4.1 Exchange of Information in Liberalized (But Still Regulated) Markets

Typically, formerly monopolistic, vertically integrated utility markets take time to become truly competitive. At the inception of the liberalization process, when the need to establish competition is highest, regulation usually requires that access to the networks and interoperability be ensured through the establishment of obligations to grant access and to exchange information on a transparent, non-discriminatory and equal basis. As such obligations are widely employed for pro-competitive goals, these markets tend to have the greatest transparency (see also at section 3.3 above). Figure 11.1 synthesizes the comprehensive assessment of exchanges of information in markets whose structure is meant to evolve from a (vertically integrated) monopolistic situation to competition.

It follows that whenever information sharing is mandated by regulation with an aim to reduce information asymmetries and to allow interconnection and interoperability, competition rules on restrictive agreements should not be applicable (exemption), because information exchange should be seen as pro-competitive and transparency as a desired feature. Markets are still dominated by incumbents, often operating both upstream (typically running a network) and downstream, where they face competition by other firms. The benefits of increased transparency should outweigh its costs in terms of ease of collusion.

In the words of Robert Bork, antitrust would be 'at war with itself' if, under the circumstances just described, competition agencies scrutinized the exchange of information under the rules on restrictive agreements. In

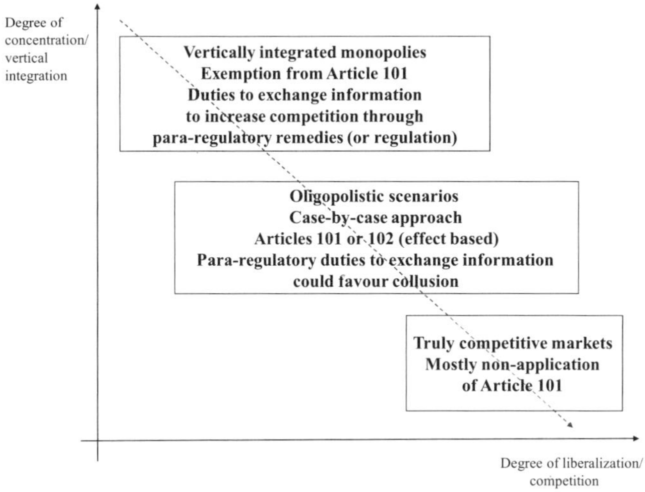

Figure 11.1 Comprehensive assessment of exchange of information

other words, the urge to encourage competition requires competition agencies to put most of their efforts into ensuring that information flows run correctly from the dominant firm to its competitors and vice versa. In order to enhance exchange of information in such markets, competition agencies may apply Article 102 TFEU to ensure that firms do not exploit their informational advantage to harm existing weak competition. To this end, competition agencies may adopt para-regulatory remedies that *complement* and reinforce pure regulation.[132]

The European Guidelines on Horizontal Co-operation Agreements make minor reference to this interesting issue when they affirm that:

> It cannot be excluded that information exchange may also lead to anti-competitive foreclosure of third parties in a related market. For instance, by gaining enough market power through an information exchange, parties exchanging information in an upstream market, for instance vertically integrated companies, may be able to raise the price of a key component for a market downstream. Thereby, they could raise the costs of their rivals downstream, which could result in anti-competitive foreclosure in the downstream market.[133]

---

132 Monti (n. 21 above) would probably speak of an undue 'correction' of regulation by competition law intervention.

133 Horizontal Guidelines (n. 2 above) para. 71.

However, the safe harbour from Article 101 should only be in place as long as the duty to share information (no matter whether para-regulatory or purely regulatory) is truly pro-competitive, that is, if without this remedial obligation to circulate information, markets would not likely work. When markets become truly competitive, theoretically such obligations should no longer exist (nor should Article 101 be applied, as the chances to ease collusion are very low);[134] but if they still do exist, then, in principle, they should no longer provide a sufficient ground for an exemption from Article 101(1), and a case-by-case approach should prevail.

What is interesting, though, is everything that can happen in between.

It is almost commonplace that before (if ever) turning competitive, formerly monopolistic markets evolve into oligopolies (examples are numerous in the telecom or energy sectors).[135] In such circumstances, an exchange of information, even if mandated through regulation, could increase transparency to an excessive extent, and eventually set the basis for collusion.[136] In this limited sense, the assumed clash between Articles 101 and 102 re-emerges: a remedy meant to terminate anticompetitive conduct (i.e. the informational abuse) and prevent its recurrence can pave the way for other violations (i.e. easing collusion).[137] Discussion within the International Competition Network provides evidence of this risk,

---

[134] This statement is largely accepted. However, criticism is expressed in OECD (n. 114 above) 47: 'No clear answers [are provided by competition agencies] to the question of whether an exchange of information may be deemed anticompetitive in a competitive market situation'; in non-concentrated markets 'where the cost of collecting information on competitors is higher' exchange of information may still be the best way to 'ensure the stability of a collusive agreement'.

[135] See, e.g., M. Stoyanova, *Competition Problems in Liberalized Telecommunications: Regulatory Solutions to Promote Effective Competition* (Kluwer Law International 2008) 168 (referring to the telecoms market segments as having an 'oligopolistic structure').

[136] As supposed by AGCM in its 2005 investigation of Tim, Vodafone and Wind (n. 121 above).

[137] See Stoyanova (n. 135 above) 168–169 (discussing the relevance, besides the oligopolistic structure of telecommunications markets, of the type of data supplied, its level of detail and the regularity of meetings between the parties to an interconnection agreement as factors allowing competitors to identify each other's sales and commercial strategies. At the same time, the author highlights the importance of requiring oligopolists to exchange information, e.g. on modifications of technical interfaces constituting access to essential facilities. Indeed, when imposing an antitrust para-regulatory remedy, competition agencies should be 'careful not to make information sharing obligations disproportionate

stating that a behavioural remedy (e.g., requiring a minimum margin for margin-squeeze cases) that necessitates an information exchange between the dominant firm and its (wholesale) customers may in turn 'increas[e] the risk of collusion'.[138]

As is known, a competition law remedy mandating an exchange of information would not pre-empt further scrutiny under either Articles 101 or 102. Indeed, since the very exchange of information could be regarded as a collusive agreement (and thus fall under Article 101) or be caught by Article 102 as an abuse of a collusive collective dominant position, undertakings can still 'engag[e] in autonomous conduct which prevents, restricts or distorts competition'.[139]

No matter which of the two provisions applies,[140] in the circumstances described, transparency-enhancing interventions (i.e. para-regulatory remedies) should be set aside, or else designed very carefully to avoid the risk of creating the conditions for easing collusion.

A question could then be whether regulation or competition law would be the best tool to avoid the risk that an imposed exchange of information will lead to collusion, for instance by setting firewall duties or harmonizing the type of information to be exchanged, or else establishing third

---

to the competition concern [they seek] to address'. For instance, a non-discrimination para-regulatory obligation may be attached to a regulatory disclosure or access duty, provided that it covers only 'information which would confer a substantial competitive advantage and is not readily and equally available elsewhere by [other] service providers'. Under this approach 'the obligation to assist competitors is confined to the strictly necessary and relates to an input which is indispensable for competitors to remain in the market'.)

[138] See ICN Unilateral Conduct Workshop, Remedies Breakout Session Guide (2–3 December 2010), available at: http://www.internationalcompetitionnetwork.org/uploads/library/doc811.pdf (accessed 31 December 2013).

[139] See Joined Cases C-359/95 P and C-379/95 P *Commission and France v. Ladbroke Racing* [1997] ECR I-6265, paras 33–35.

[140] M. Filippelli, *Collective Dominance and Collusion: Parallelism in EU and US Competition Law* (Edward Elgar Publishing 2013) 275, claiming that '[i]n the area of collusive collective dominance … it makes no difference whether to apply the one rule or the other [i.e. Articles 101 or 102]; indeed, any distinction between them appears formalistic as … they perfectly overlap – formally two utterances, but substantially one rule'. Less radically, E. Rousseva, *Rethinking Exclusionary Abuses in EU Competition Law* (Hart, 2009) 431, makes out an increasing convergence in the application of Articles 101 and 102, while I. Lianos, *La transformation du droit de la concurrence par le recours à l'analyse économique: l'exemple des restrictions verticales* (Bruylant, 2007) 1307, speaks of 'continuity' between Articles 101 and 102, allowing for an application of either of the two rules to collective dominance.

bodies to ensure compliance.[141] According to Kühn, 'restrictions on communication', which he suggests are 'among the more powerful instruments to fight collusion', should be made through some form of regulation.[142]

4.2 Exchange of Information in Unregulated (or Slightly Regulated) Markets

In unregulated (or slightly regulated) sectors, whenever the market is neither fully competitive nor oligopolistic, full exemption of exchange of information from Article 101(1) should be avoided, and a case-by-case approach should be preferred. In barely regulated sectors, regulatory obligations to share information among competitors should not exist, as the need to grant interoperability or access to competitors' information should be less likely than in regulated network industries.

However, super-dominance cases teach us that para-regulatory remedies are possible under Article 102. Again, a potential clash between the two norms can resurge. Looking at the market conditions, cases like *Microsoft*, *Auditel*, *Audipress*, *Standard & Poor's* and *Bayer*, in which a sole company enjoys an absolute informational monopoly, grounds for imposing para-regulatory obligations to exchange information are strong. Such cases much resemble those in network industries, as market failures are prominent and, absent any regulation, competition agencies must foster access and interoperability in order for competition to work. The increase of transparency caused by such para-regulatory intervention would, in the short run, hardly lead to market conditions that are prone to collusion. Thus investigations should not lead to the conclusion that there is a violation of Article 101.

Theoretically, if the informational advantage is not absolute (or evolves from absolute to relative, e.g., due to a modification of the legal framework or to technological innovation making alternative standards emerge), and market conditions favour collusion, exchanging information could lead to a violation of Article 101, if all conditions for establishing such a violation set forth in the European Guidelines on Horizontal Co-operation Agreements are met.

In these circumstances, the very presence of a stand-alone agreement on information exchange (or an indirect exchange through a common

---

141 On monitoring trustees as a feature of para-regulatory remedies, see section 2.2.3 above.

142 K.U. Kühn, 'Fighting Collusion by Regulating Communication Between Firms' (2001) 16(32) *Econ. Pol'y* 169, 171.

partner[143] or a common agency)[144] would leave little room for para-regulatory remedies imposed by competition agencies, which would compel such exchange. Indeed, Article 9 of Regulation 1/2003 does not permit commitment decisions in cases of hard-core restrictions such as cartels, nor could para-regulatory remedies be adopted on the basis of Article 102, as a dominant position due to the fact that mere informational advantage would be hard to demonstrate.

5. CONCLUSION: RECONSTRUCTING THE ASSESSMENT OF EXCHANGE OF INFORMATION UNDER COMPETITION LAW

Legal and economic scholars have extensively studied the risks and benefits of information exchange among market participants, drawing with more or less certitude the legal boundaries of such an exchange, as opposed to an illegal exchange of information leading to collusion.

Much less attention has been devoted to unilateral or collective abuse of information exchange under Article 102 TFEU or equivalent norms in other jurisdictions. Yet there is an increasing number of cases drawn from EU, US and Italian practice that condemns abuses of information flows and, often, adopts complex behavioural remedies that strongly resemble disclosure and access regulation: they are therefore para-regulatory (section 2).

The legal theory applied in such abuses is composite, as the conduct is assessed in a case-by-case approach (as purported by supporters of the effect-based approach). Thereby, the informational abuse is often part of a wider anticompetitive strategy (this happened in all cases but *Magill*, *Italgas*, *Auditel* and *Audipress*). By challenging established orthodoxies, this prevailing de-constructivist approach does not help to define a standard of legality of dominant firms' conduct affecting information. Nor does it more generally help to understand the contradictory use of information: under competition law it may be used to violate antitrust rules (under both Articles 101 and 102) and, at the same time, to remedy such violations.

In an effort to provide some guidance, this chapter has suggested that informational abuses can consist in three practices. First, in the majority

143 Commission Guidelines on Vertical Restraints, [2010] OJ C 130, p. 1, para. 211.

144 Horizontal Guidelines (n. 2 above) para. 55.

of cases they consist in *actual refusals* (e.g., *Magill*, *Microsoft I* and *II*, *Audipress*), *constructive refusals to provide information* (*Exergia/Enel*, *Sorgenia*, *Telekomunikacja Polska*) or both (*Auditel*, *Telecom Italia*) with exclusionary effects. In a second set of cases *information is misused* by dominant firms *to distort regulatory procedures* with an aim of preventing competition (*Italgas*, *Messinambiente*, *Estra Reti*) and/or exclude competitors (*AstraZeneca* and *Bayer*). Third, only one (US) case (*Libor*) related to *collusion to provide misleading information*, and this one, though closed on antitrust allegation, could establish a separate class of informational misconduct, namely, that of abuse of informational collusive collective dominance.

The analysis of cases in the first group suggests a resurgence of the 'special responsibility' of informational dominant and super-dominant firms. Most frequently, competition agencies recognize that the informational advantage amounts to a real informational monopoly or quasi-monopoly (e.g., *Microsoft*, *Auditel*, *Audipress*, *Standard & Poor's*, *Italgas*, *Bayer*, *Telekomunikacja Polska*), providing its owner with market power that it can use to harm competition and consumers in related markets. A special relationship bundles super-dominant firms to the holding of (functional)[145] information and, therefore, justifies a strong remedy consisting in the imposition of specific para-regulatory, continuous obligations. With the exception of *Standard & Poor's* (which ended with price para-regulation of licence conditions), such obligations imply the sharing of information (e.g., *Microsoft I* and *II*, *Sisal*, *Thomson Reuters*, *Telecom Italia*, *Exergia/Enel*, *Sorgenia*) and/or access to market information (*Magill*, *Audipress*) in transparent and non-discriminatory ways.

These para-regulatory remedies can sometimes overlap with sectorial regulation (e.g., *Telekomunikacja Polska*), or be wider in scope (*Exergia/Enel*), leading to a *ne bis in idem* argument and conflicting visions about the same conduct, such as in *Telecom Italia*. However, in line with *Deutsche Telekom*, competition agencies will not be prevented from intervening if firm conduct is in compliance with sectorial regulation. Yet, at the same time, competition agencies quite rightly take into account sanctions already imposed for a violation of the sector-specific rules, for instance, by deducting the fines already imposed by the sector regulators (*Telekomunikacja Polska*).

---

[145] On the 'functional' character of information implied in Article 102 cases see section 2.1.1.1 above.

Interestingly, para-regulatory remedies adopted in one case (*Exergia/Enel*) tend to bind successive decisions in similar cases (as in the *Sorgenia* cases). Although this benefits the industry since it signals, with some certainty, the standard of liability; at the same time, it may overlap or conflict with existing sectorial regulation. A *ne bis in idem* problem can thus emerge, which is not limited to the single case, but rather refers to the whole regulated market. This effect, which could replicate itself in other markets as well, generates the risk of a (doubtfully legitimate) substitution of regulators by competition agencies, without competition law necessarily being a strong legal basis.

Further considerations on the competition/regulation relationship stem from a second group of cases involving informational misuse of regulatory procedures. This is possibly the new frontier of this relationship. As this chapter has shown, despite sailing the safe harbour of the essential facility doctrine,[146] competition agencies (e.g., AGCM in *Italgas* and *Bayer*) do leave room for considering the abusive conduct as one of strategic informational misuse of regulatory procedures[147] (e.g., by referring to *AstraZeneca*).

In these cases, it is the *distortion* of regulatory procedures, made possible by the strategic use of information, that dominant firms aim at realizing. Then, questioning the nature and goals of such regulatory procedures might prove useful in order to establish a legal principle. It is one thing to breach the general rules of sector regulation; it is quite another to breach a rule of sector regulation that is specifically designed to enhance competition for or in the market. Indeed, the exclusionary effect derives most likely from the distortion of a pro-competitive regulatory procedure; the distortion is achieved through a strategic use of information; and these data are in turn needed to accomplish the regulatory goal. To sum up, antitrust liability can be established provided that: (1) the informational advantage amounts to super-dominance in the sense clarified above; (2) the regulatory procedure that is misused pursues a pro-competitive goal (e.g., a tender as in *Italgas*); (3) the misuse is implemented through strategic use (e.g., misleading conduct as

[146] Waller (n. 4 above) 577, speaks of a 'return of the essential facility doctrine', referring to the increasing use of access behavioural remedies in high-tech antitrust decisions.

[147] The essential facility doctrine seems too strict a standard for liability, and may be an overly stretched one too. For instance, the relevant market tends to artificially coincide with the information facility (e.g., Bayer's toxicological studies), which makes it relatively easy to demonstrate that its owner dominates that market.

in *AstraZeneca*) of the information required to achieve the regulatory goal; (4) the informational misuse pursues exclusionary goals; and (5) harm to competition is proven. If, in contrast, the misused information is rendered in regulatory procedures that are not designed for pro-competitive goals, the analysis should necessarily include other and additional factors.[148]

A third and final consideration on the interaction of competition and regulation arises from the problematic relationship between para-regulatory remedies and the risk of collusion. Any duty to share or disclose information can result in an 'invitation to collude'.[149] Indeed, para-regulatory remedies mandating information sharing and disclosure can increase transparency to an extent that they favour collusion.[150] Hence, a clash may still arise, since information disclosure and exchange can at the same time be pro-competitive (as remedies under Article 102) and anti-competitive (under Article 101).

In order to ensure an appropriate balance and to avoid conflicting views when assessing such information exchanges and disclosures, this chapter has proposed that authorities use a comprehensive approach (at section 3 above). Accordingly, for establishing whether and when either of the two rules (Articles 101 or 102) should be applied, this chapter recommends examining the market conditions, taking into account whether the market in which the information exchange or disclosure takes place is regulated or not, this market's level of concentration and the pervasiveness of information asymmetry in particular.

---

[148] Competition agencies may want to inquire whether, as in *AstraZeneca*, the administration enjoys any discretion on releasing its decision (which is based upon the misused information). In *Italgas*, in contrast, it was not up to the discretion of the municipalities to make a tender (it was mandated by the law), but without information, no tender could be released, which was precisely the exclusionary goal of Italgas.

[149] See the background paper by A. Capobianco in OECD, 'Unilateral Disclosure of Information with Anticompetitive Effects' (2012) 12, available at: http://www.oecd.org/daf/competition/Unilateraldisclosureofinformation2012.pdf (accessed 31 December 2013).

[150] The Australian competition law system specifically addresses the issue of pro and anti-competitive effects of information disclosure and exchange that is mandated by regulation (e.g., in the banking sector). OECD (n. 149 above) 99.

PART 5

Competition law as regulation in IP-related markets

12. Competition law as an instrument of IP regulation? The case of strategic patent filings

Emanuela Arezzo

1. INTRODUCTION

As many have recently observed, competition law enforcement seems to be somehow merging into a form of market regulation. This is surely true as far as innovation is concerned. Indeed, competition law has progressively acquired the role of an IP 'watchdog', with the mission of curtailing the scope and use of IP rights in cases where their exploitation seems to worsen rather than promote innovation.

Indeed, significant steps have been taken in certain areas of the intersection of competition policy and IPRs, such as that relating to the application of Article 101 of the Treaty, where a block-exemption regulation has been adopted.[1] In the other two main areas of competition law, however, mergers and unilateral practices, no legislative instruments have been adopted, leaving the Commission and the Courts considerable room to manouvre in developing their own case-law.

This chapter argues that the shaping of a common core of guiding principles concerning the intersection of competition law and intellectual property rights in the area of unilateral practices has become a necessity considering that not only the number of abusive practices involving the use of IPRs has recently increased, but also that new kinds of practices have emerged, posing increasingly complex issues to analyse. Among such new practices, this work will focus on the conduct of so-called strategic patent filings, pursued by dominant firms for the purpose of keeping competitors off the market. This conduct has become extremely

[1] Commission Regulation (EU) no. 316/2014 of 21 March 2014 on the application of Article 101(3) of the Treaty on the Functioning of the European Union to categories of technology transfer agreements, in OJ L 93, pp. 17–23.

frequent in the pharmaceutical sector, and its assessment by competition authorities is particularly complex because, on the one hand, the act of strategic patenting pertains to behavior which is permitted by patent law, hence perfectly legal according to this branch of the legal system. On the other hand, it does not imply alleged or actual *(ab)use* of the IPRs, as it typically involves the preliminary stage of patent filing (i.e. the acts aimed at obtaining the protection).

2. INTELLECTUAL PROPERTY RIGHTS AND MARKET POWER

That each IPR confers a certain degree of market power, understood as power over prices, is without doubt. Whether such market power poses a threat to competition in a competition-law sense is, however, a question of degree. Generally speaking it is very unlikely that IPRs *alone* are capable of granting the degree of market power that turns into dominance[2] and therefore attracts the attention of competition agencies.[3] It is indeed widely accepted that IPRs allow competition by substitution, while preventing competition by mere imitation.[4]

---

[2] See Joined Cases C-241/91 P and C-242/91 P *RTE and ITP v Commission* ('*Magill*') [1995] ECR 1141, para. 46, where the European Court of Justice expressly held that 'so far as dominant position is concerned, it is to be remembered at the outset that mere ownership of an intellectual property right cannot confer such a position'. A similar conclusion was later also reached by the US Supreme Court in *Illinois Tool Works, Inc v. Independent Ink, Inc*, 547 U.S. 28, 126 S.Ct. 1281 (2006).

[3] See G. Ghidini and E. Arezzo, 'On the Intersection of IPRs and Competition Law with Regard to Information Technology Markets' in C.D. Ehlermann and I. Atanasiu (eds), *European Competition Law Annual 2005: The Relationship Between Competition Law and Intellectual Property Law* (Hart Publishing 2006) 105. Yet this may rarely happen in the case of genetic inventions due to the 'uniqueness' – hence, the lack of duplicability – of such resources. See extensively in this sense R.C. Dreyfuss, 'UniqueWorks/Unique Challenges at the Intellectual Property/Competition Law Interface' in C.D. Ehlermann and I. Atanasiu (eds), *European Competition Law Annual 2005: The Relationship Between Competition Law and Intellectual Property Law* (Hart Publishing 2006) 119, 122.

[4] This conclusion is widely shared among European scholars. See, *inter alia*, J. Drexl, 'The Relationship between Legal Exclusivity and Economic Market Power: Links and Limits' in I. Govaere and H. Ullrich (eds), *Intellectual Property, Market Power and the Public Interest* (PIE-Peter Lang 2008) 13, 16.

This generous attitude towards the limited degree of market power generally conferred by IPRs, together with the pro-competitive stances built into the IP paradigms,[5] should not lead us to downplay the complexities of cases in which IPRs intersect with competition law and the need to fine-tune more properly competition-law tools used to assess such cases. In fact, experience has shown – and is increasingly showing – that despite the fact that IPRs by themselves only confer a modicum of market power, there may be *other* market factors or circumstances that can well lead IP holders to reach the level of dominance and *then* use IPRs as strategic tools to pursue anticompetitive goals and obtain returns that exceed by far those that the very same IP laws were meant to facilitate.[6]

In such cases, notwithstanding the reassuring vision of commonalities of goals between the two disciplines,[7] the application of competition rules has proved to be a rather complex task. First of all, this is precisely because competition law has traditionally been poorly equipped to make assessments capable of taking into account dynamic efficiency. Competition-law tools employed in 'traditional' competition-law cases, from market-definition tools to instruments to measure dominance, were not designed to take innovation and IPRs into account, nor do they seem any different today.[8] Quite on the contrary, the assessment of intersection

[5] See the exhaustive analysis performed, for each of the main IP paradigms, by G. Ghidini, *Innovation, Competition and Consumer Welfare in Intellectual Property Law* (Edward Elgar Publishing 2010). In particular 33–89 (regarding patents); 98–146 (regarding copyright); 156–204 (regarding trademarks).

[6] See also E. Arezzo, 'Intellectual Property Rights at the Crossroad between Monopolization and Abuse of Dominant Position: American and European Approaches Compared' (2006) 24 *John Marshall J. Comp. & Inf. L.* 455, 493ff.

[7] In this sense see, *inter alia*, L. Peeperkorn, 'IP Licences and Competition Rules: Striking the Right Balance' (2003) 26 *World Comp.* 526, 527; M.A. Lemley, 'A New Balance Between IP and Antitrust' (2007) 13 *Sw. J. L. & Trade in the Americas* 237, 248ff.; S. Anderman, 'The IP and Competition Interface: New Developments' in S. Anderman and A. Ezrachi (eds), *Intellectual Property and Competition Law – New Frontiers* (Oxford University Press 2012) 3, 4 (arguing that there is a natural overlap in the aims of the two fields of law); C. Madero Villarejo and T. Kramler, 'Intellectual Property Rights and Competition Rules, a Complex but Indispensable Coexistence' in S. Anderman and A. Ezrachi (eds), *Intellectual Property and Competition Law – New Frontiers* (Oxford University Press 2012) 61.

[8] See M.A. Lemley and M.P. McKenna, 'Is Pepsi Really a Good Substitute for Coke? Market Definition in Antitrust and IP' (2012) 100 *Geo. L.J.* 2055 (highlighting the fallacies likely to emerge from a rigid application of the so-called 'SSNIP' test to define the relevant market in intersection cases).

cases often requires predictions of what effects a likely finding of a competition violation will have on incentives to innovate for both the incumbent and its rivals:[9] predictions that competition authorities are still poorly equipped to make.[10]

Moreover, the tension between the two sets of laws does not stem merely from the circumstance that they cherish different kinds of efficiencies, but also from the fact that they pursue their respective efficiency goals in different ways. Namely, while IPRs are grounded on complex sets of statutory norms that *as a system* promote dynamic efficiency (i.e. innovation), hence, do not require proof that each granted IPR actually promotes technological progress, on the contrary, the assessment of competition law – whose normative architecture rests on a relatively small set of provisions – is based on a factual economic-based evaluation of the circumstances of each case and is intended at proving *in concreto* competitive harm.[11]

This is a crucial consideration that brings about two important conclusions that may seem – but are not – at odds. On the one hand, the case-by-case analysis performed by competition authorities may risk undermining the incentive system underlying IP legislations. A facts-oriented assessment aimed at demonstrating the actual anticompetitive effects on the market, as called for by the novel *effects-based approach*,[12]

---

[9] See J. Drexl, 'The Real Knowledge is to Know the Extent of One's Own Ignorance: On the Consumer Harm Approach in Innovation-Related Competition Cases' (2010) 76 *Antitrust L.J.* 677, 685ff. (arguing that a correct approach should focus on foreclosure effects in such a way as to preserve open markets and rivalry as sources of competitive pressure).

[10] On this difficulty and the risk that competition authorities might privilege static anticompetitive effects, which are easily proven, over dynamic anti-competitive effects based on prospective and theoretical analysis see J. Kallaugher, 'Existence, Exercise, and Exceptional Circumstances: The Limited Scope for a More Economic Approach to IP Issues under article 102 TFEU' in S. Anderman and A. Ezrachi (eds), *Intellectual Property and Competition Law – New Frontiers* (Oxford University Press 2012) 113, 116–117; in a similar sense see I. Rahnasto, *Intellectual Property Rights, External Effects and Anti-trust Law: Leveraging IPRs in the Communication Industry* (Oxford University Press 2003) 39ff.

[11] See Kallaugher (n. 10 above) 116ff.

[12] The new approach towards exclusionary abuses has been promoted by the European Commission in its recent Communication on enforcement priorities. See Communication from the Commission – Guidance on the Commission's enforcement priorities in applying Article 82 of the EC Treaty to abusive exclusionary conduct by dominant undertakings, [2009] OJ C 45, p. 7. For a

inevitably factors in a high degree of unpredictability (hence, uncertainty), which may exert negative effects on the incentive system lying at the heart of IP legislations.[13] On the other hand, exactly because competition agencies perform such broad analysis of the market, taking into consideration all the legal and economic factors that contribute to promoting or hampering the competitive structure of the market, they may well be in the very best position to test the limits of IPRs and see whether the restriction of competition caused by their use might find a justification in the dynamic efficiencies they are supposed to promote; or rather, whether the conduct not only is contrary to competition rules but amounts to an employment of the right contrary to what the very same IP legislations demand.

We believe that competition authorities and competition law in general have an important role to play in intersection cases. This is especially true today, in consideration of the so-called expansionist trend embraced by IPR holders.[14] Nonetheless, unconstrained competition-law intervention based on a case-by-case assessment and proof of consumer harm, as advocated by the proponents of the modern *effects-based approach*, may be detrimental in intersection cases. A guiding principle should be set to limit competition-law intervention to exceptional cases and avoid the recent tendency whereby each intersection case achieves results so inextricably linked to the factual circumstances of the case that it will be almost impossible to use it as a guide in future cases.

3. THE ANTICOMPETITIVE POTENTIAL OF STRATEGIC PATENT FILINGS

Today, the already complex interplay between competition law and IPRs seems to be moving to a new phase with new types of conduct posing even more complicated issues to assess. This is the case for a series of

---

critical assessment of the effects-based approach as advocated by the Commission in this document see G. Ghidini and E. Arezzo, 'L'assalto fallito? Riflessioni sulla proposta rivisitazione in chiave "più economica" dell'abuso di dominanza' (2010) no. 1 *Mercato Concorrenza Regole* 115.

[13] See A. Ezrachi and M. Maggiolino, 'European Competition Law, Compulsory Licensing, and Innovation' (2012) 8 *J. Comp. L. & Econ.* 565, 599 (noting that the case-by-case approach causes a constant change in the intervention formula which translates into a loss of certainty as to the degree of protection granted by IPRs).

[14] H. Ullrich, 'Expansionist Intellectual Property Protection and Reductionist Competition Rules – A TRIPS Perspective' (2004) 7 *J. Int'l Econ. L.* 401.

practices consisting in the abuse of regulatory procedures and, in particular, of the rules dictated by the patent system. For the purpose of this chapter, I will limit the analysis to the practice of *strategic patent filing*, focusing my attention on the pharmaceutical sector.

With the term 'strategic patent filings' the European Commission refers to 'all strategies of a company concerning the *use of the patent system to the benefit of the company in relation to generic competition*' (emphasis added), including in particular 'strategies on the timing and scope of filing as well as the manners in which patents are applied for'.[15] This is a very broad definition of the concept of strategic patent filing, to which the Commission adds some specific examples.[16] Among them, the Commission includes the creation of *patent clusters* or *thickets*,[17] arising from multiple filings presented simultaneously or soon after the deposit of the 'main' patent, each filing elaborating on a sliver of knowledge

---

[15] See European Commission, Pharmaceutical Sector Inquiry, Final Report, 8 July 2009, para. 467, available at: http://ec.europa.eu/competition/sectors/pharmaceuticals/inquiry/index.html (accessed 31 January 2014).

[16] The Commission tries to make a distinction between strategic patent filings and *defensive* patent filings. The latter relates to practices whereby the application for a patent is filed for the purpose of blocking the development of a new innovative product of a competitor, hence in the case of competition between originators. See European Commission (n. 15 above) paras 1090ff., and, especially, paras 1117, 1118 and 1122. In particular, the Commission explains: 'defensive patent applications usually refer to inventions which the applying company considers to have little or no prospect of being developed and/or commercialized and/or which, once granted, the company holds primarily to protect itself against actual or potential competition' (ibid., para. 1118). Such distinction, however, is somehow difficult to support. Indeed, the case in which the originator company files for an invention knowing that it will not meet the patentability requirements (so-called *vexatious patenting*) could also happen for the purpose of deterring entrance by generics when the originator's drug is about to expire. In this sense see D. Schnichels and S. Sule, 'The Pharmaceutical Sector Inquiry and its Impact on Competition Law Enforcement' (2010) 1 *J. Eur. Comp. L. & Pract.* 93, 103.

[17] On the phenomenon of *patent thickets* in general see, *inter alia*, J. Bessen, 'Patents Thickets: Strategic Patenting of Complex Technologies' (2002), available at: http://www.researchoninnovation.org/thicket.pdf (accessed 31 January 2014); C. Shapiro, 'Navigating the Patent Thicket: Cross Licenses, Patent Pools, and Standard-Setting' in A.B. Jaffe, J. Lerner and S. Stern (eds), *Innovation Policy and the Economy 1* (MIT Press 2001) 119; W.M. Cohen, R.R. Nelson and J.P. Walsh, 'Protecting their Intellectual Assets: Appropriability Conditions and Why US Manufacturing Firms Patent (or Not)', NBER Working Paper no. W7552 (2000), available at: http://www.nber.org/papers/w7552 (accessed 31 January 2014).

embedded in the first patent,[18] and the so-called *evergreening* of the patent,[19] described as the filing of dependent patents after the filing of the primary patent, typically when the latter is about to expire.[20]

The Commission has pointed out the potential anticompetitive effects such conduct may have:[21] in fact, the joint deposit of several patents would surely reinforce the protection of the main innovation, granting originator companies a multi-layered shield against competitors;[22] in much the same way, derivative patents could be used by originators as a means to unduly prolong the duration of the first patent well after its 20-year protection term with the purpose of perpetually avoiding competition.[23]

However – and this is one of the two factors that makes strategic-patent-filing cases so intriguing and complex to analyse – while the category of conduct studied by the Commission surely has a potential excluding effect (as does every act of patenting) and may well be used within a broader anticompetitive strategy, all such conduct is permitted by patent law. As for divisional applications, patent law expressly envisages the possibility of the examiners of the patent office requesting the patentee to file a divisional application whenever they realize that the

---

[18] The Commission refers to the fact that firms in the pharmaceutical sector customarily deposit several patents around the main innovation constituting the base for the drug. Often through divisional patents, they deposit patents on the isolated compound, on the process to isolate or otherwise make the compound, on the reformulation of the compound in other forms, on new therapeutical uses, etc. These practices are permitted by patent law, as far as each patent covers (even a tiny sliver of) an innovation. Nonetheless, the Commission has drawn attention to the likely negative effects such practices can exert on competitors. Indeed, the simultaneous filing of several patents vests the originator company with a multi-layered protection that makes it harder for competitors to access the market. See European Commission (n. 15 above) paras 476ff.

[19] Ibid., para. 480.

[20] The filing of derivative patents when the main patent is about to expire is a valuable tool for originators as it creates a situation of uncertainty that deters generics' entry. Ibid., paras 987ff.

[21] It is worth noting that the final version of the Interim Report has endorsed a more cautious approach in proclaiming the anticompetitive nature of certain IP-based conduct. This is probably due to the harsh criticism the provisional version of the Interim Report drew from the pharmaceutical companies that received the questionnaires. See M. Ramondino and C. Stothers, 'Aftermath of AstraZeneca and the Pharmaceutical Inquiry: The Big Chill?' (2011) *E.C.L.R.* 591.

[22] See European Commission (n. 15 above) paras 476ff.

[23] Ibid., para. 480.

innovation embedded in the first patent application contains information pertaining to more than one invention.[24] The same may occur when the patentee herself realizes that her application contains more than one innovation. In the latter case, provided that certain requirements are satisfied, the patentee may voluntarily submit a divisional patent application.[25] As for the patentability of derivative inventions, this practice also represents a common routine for all sectors in which innovation has an incremental nature.[26]

The second cause of concern in a competition-law assessment of strategic patenting arises from the fact that such conduct (i.e. the patent filing) relates to the coming into being of the right and, hence, to the very 'existence' of the IPR, a realm that has been traditionally foreclosed to competition authorities' intervention, upon the well-known distinction between existence and exercise of the IPR.[27]

---

[24] On the principle of the unity of the invention see n. 38 below.

[25] The Commission has pointed out that only 20% of divisional patents released by the EPO in 2008 were actually requested by the Office, while the remaining 80% were voluntary divisionals, hence highlighting an increasing use of such patent-filing tool by pharmaceutical firms. European Commission (n. 15 above) para. 510.

[26] It is worth noting that the possibility of filing a derivative patent is not reserved to the holder of the main title of protection, but is also granted to her competitors. The second derivative invention, however, will often be 'dependent' on the first one, meaning that its commercial exploitation cannot take place without authorization by the first patent holder. On this issue see Ghidini (n. 5 above) 71ff.

[27] According to this doctrine, only the exercise of an IPR may constitute the object of assessment under competition law rules, while the latter cannot interfere with the coming into being of the right, normally regulated by national laws. See Case 24/1967 *Parke Davis* [1968] ECR 76, where the Court stated: 'since the *existence* of patent rights is at present a *matter solely of national law*, the *use* made of them can only come within the ambit of Community law where such use contributes to a dominant position, the abuse of which may affect trade between Member States' (emphasis added). On this topic see G. Marenco and K. Banks, 'Intellectual property and the Community rules on free movement: discrimination unearthed' (1990) *Eur. L. Rev.* 224, 226; A. Geiger, 'Patents, Trade-marks, Copyrights – A Mission for Article 82 EC' (2004) *E.C.L.R.* 311, 312.

4. STRATEGIC PATENT FILINGS BETWEEN EXISTENCE AND EXERCISE OF THE RIGHT

In the light of the above considerations, one might question whether the simple deposit of a patent could be claimed to be part of an abusive exclusionary strategy in which the very objective of obtaining a patent is to prevent competitors from exploiting the patented subject-matter. This is a cumbersome question to which economists would respond with a straightforward 'no'. If a positive answer were to prevail, the innovation process would be at a great risk, as the disincentives flowing from the punishment of conduct which seems to but does not harm competition (so-called *false positives*)[28] would exceed by far those typically associated with the punishment of *false positives* in refusal-to-deal cases: here, indeed, we are – supposedly – not discussing ways of using the right, but the possibility of allowing competition authorities to have a say in the coming into being of the right itself.[29]

But is it really so different? It is to be noted that on the one hand a competition authority would not question the properness of the evaluation conducted by patent offices as to whether or not an invention satisfies patentability requirements.[30] On the other hand, as the Commission has pointed out, the patent offices' duties are strictly limited to the assessment of formal and substantive patentability requirements, but they are not asked to perform any *ex ante* evaluations about the likely *strategic* use the right owner might make of the patent, nor *a fortiori* to perform an *ex post* control on the likely *non-use* of the patent, such as characterizes

---

[28] The Chicago School maintains that the sanctioning of *false positives* has much more severe effects on the market than permitting conduct that seems lawful at first sight but then reveals an anticompetitive nature (so-called *false negatives*). See the seminal article by F.H. Easterbrook, 'The Limits of Antitrust' (1984) 63 *Tex. L. Rev.* 1, 3.

[29] See L. Kjølbye, 'Article 82 EC as Remedy to Patent System Imperfections: Fighting Fire with Fire?' (2009) 32 *World Comp.* 163, 176 et seq. According to this author, given the key role played by the patent system in the pharmaceutical sector as a means to recoup investments in innovation, a presumption should be introduced that the refusal to license patent rights in such a market is always objectively justified.

[30] See, for example, Case T-201/04 *Microsoft v. Commission* (2007) ECR II-3601, para. 289, where the Court explained that the assessment of the case '*must* proceed on the *presumption* that the protocols in question, or the specifications of those protocols, are covered by intellectual property rights or constitute trade secrets and that those secrets must be treated as equivalent to intellectual property rights' (emphasis added).

the cases in which patent protection is filed only for defensive purposes.[31] *Ex post* evaluations about whether the patent has been filed for strategic or defensive purposes, then, may well be placed with a competition authority that could be in the best position to assess, in the light of the factual circumstances of the case, whether a validly granted title of protection has been filed for the exclusive purpose of being used as part of a broader anticompetitive exclusionary strategy, rather than for protecting investment in R&D.

Given these premises, we do not see any reason why, in principle, competition authorities should not intervene in these cases. Furthermore, note that the act of patenting and then using the patent only for defensive purposes, *without concretely working the patent*, is a form of exercise of the right.[32] In fact, the very same patent system devotes attention to specific circumstances of non-use of the granted patent, to which it attaches precise legal consequences: namely, the imposition of a compulsory licence in favor of third parties willing to work the patent and eventually the forfeiture of the patent itself.[33] In conclusion, even if we assume that the old dichotomy between the existence and the exercise of the right is still valid today,[34] competition-law intervention should be permitted, as it would not interfere with the former.[35]

---

[31] European Commission (n. 15 above) paras 270ff., 500, 523 (n. 375) and 1091.

[32] However, for a contrary view see J. Straus, 'Patent Application: Obstacle for Innovation and Abuse of Dominant Position under Article 102 TFEU?' (2010) 2 *J. Comp. L. & Prac.* 189, 193 (observing that the act of filing does not yet constitute a form of use or exploitation of the right, but rather represents the first step for establishing the specific subject of the patent 'without which … once the invention has been published … it is no longer possible to allocate the economic benefits arising from the exploitation of the invention'.

[33] More broadly on this topic see E. Arezzo, 'Strategic patenting e diritto della concorrenza: riflessioni a margine della vicenda Ratiopharm – Pfizer' (2014) *Giurisprudenza Commerciale* 424 (arguing that the instrument of patent forfeiture, if revitalized, may be an effective weapon to combat strategic and defensive patenting where the invention covered by the title of protection has often never been worked by the patentee).

[34] For a historical reconstruction of this doctrine see Kallaugher (n. 10 above) 120ff. (describing the existence/exercise dichotomy as a 'device for determining regulatory competence': namely, between on the one side the Commission and the European Courts, entitled to apply EU law, and on the other side national Member States, which retain the power to enact IP legislation).

[35] Note that several authors have expressed skepticism towards such a doctrine, observing that even depriving the IP owner of the capability of freely exercising his right would create a prejudice to the very existence of the right. In

However, in these cases, even more than in refusal-to-deal cases, it has to be clear that such conduct can *exceptionally* be punished by competition authorities if the overall conduct shows an anticompetitive nature. And again in this context, as in refusal-to-deal cases, it would be necessary to have a test explaining when the exercise of particular conduct may result in a restriction of competition and can therefore be punished through competition-law remedies.

In the following, the soundness of the above reasoning will be tested against the backdrop of a recent Italian case.

5. THE *RATIOPHARM V. PFIZER* CASE

The *Ratiopharm v. Pfizer* case did not involve any misleading representations of facts or information to national patent offices, nor any form of 'patent fraud', but a more complex exclusionary strategy. In September 1989, the Swedish firm Pharmacia A.B., later acquired by Pfizer, filed a European patent application on a certain class of molecules – including latanoprost – that showed therapeutic capabilities to cure eye hypertension and glaucoma. In February 1994, Pharmacia obtained a European patent and promptly validated it in several Member States of the European Union,[36] where it also asked for supplementary protection certificates (SPCs).[37] Only in Italy, however, did Pharmacia validate the

this sense see A. Frignani and M. Waelbroeck, *Disciplina della concorrenza nella CEE* (UTET 1996) 724; F.-K. Beier, 'Industrial Property and the Free Movement of Goods in the Internal European Market' (1990) 21 *Int'l Rev. IP & Comp. L.* 131; G. Friden, 'Recent Developments in EEC Intellectual Property: the Distinction between Existence and Exercise Revisited' (1989) 26 *C.M.L. Rev.* 193.

[36] As is well known, the patent procedure envisaged by the European Patent Convention (EPC) allows the inventor to file a centralized 'European patent application', which is processed by the examiners of the European Patent Office located in Munich. The term 'European patent' is, however, somehow improper since the protection released does not give rise to a common European title but to a bundle of national rights. In fact, at a certain stage of the procedure, the EPO asks the inventor to select the Member States where she wants the patent to be effective ('validation' of the patent application) such that, once protection is granted, it is tantamount to a set of national patents. Broadly on the subject: G. Sena, 'I diritti sulle invenzioni e sui modelli di utilità' in A. Cicu, F. Messineo, L. Mengoni and P. Schlesinger (eds), *Trattato di Diritto Civile e Commerciale* (4th edn, Giuffrè 2011) 215ff.

[37] As a common rule, patent term cannot be extended for any reason. The only exception to this rule is found in the pharmaceutical sector, where the EU

patent without asking for an SPC: hence, Italy was the only country with shorter patent protection.

Knowing that the term of protection for latanoprost would expire in 2009, Ratiopharm developed an equivalent drug and in November 2007 began the administrative process to get the market authorization needed to distribute the product. Ratiopharm, however, was not aware of the fact that in 2002, 13 years after the filing of the main patent, Pharmacia had filed a voluntary divisional application[38] with claims including latanoprost.[39] In January 2009, Pfizer, which had succeeded Pharmacia by that

legislature – harmonizing the laws of the Member States – has introduced a specific tool called the supplementary protection certificate (SPC). Since medicinal products must wait for a market authorization before entering the market, it often happens that a considerable time span elapses between the filing of the patent and its actual exploitation. The SPC was expressly conceived as an instrument to extend patent duration in such a way as to give back the inventor some of the time (up to a maximum of five years) she has lost waiting for the market authorization to be released. See Regulation no. 469/2009 of the European Parliament and of the Council of 6 May 2009 concerning the supplementary protection certificate for medicinal products (codified version), [2009] OJ L 152, p. 1.

[38] The European patent system has codified a principle, contained in Article 82 of the European Patent Convention (EPC), known as the principle of the unity of the invention. According to this principle each patent may only contain one invention; therefore, if the examiner realizes that the patent contains material and information capable of supporting more than one invention, she will require the applicant to present a second patent application called a 'divisional' application. The divisional patent, being derived from a previously presented application, takes the date of filing and the date of expiry from the first patent, although it has actually been filed later (see Article 76(1) EPC). Sometimes, the inventor herself may realize that the application for a separate patent is needed. Therefore, the patent system also allows for a voluntary filing of divisional patents. In both cases, however, a divisional patent can only be granted if the application demonstrates inventive elements contained and described in the first patent to be subject of a separate invention. On this see more extensively Sena (n. 36 above) 233ff. and 272ff. On the principle of the unity of the invention see also V. Di Cataldo, 'I brevetti per invenzione e per modello di utilità: i disegni e modelli: artt. 2584–2594' in F.D. Busnelli (ed.), *Il Codice Civile – Commentario* (3rd edn, Giuffrè 2012) 28ff.

[39] The patent application originally filed by Pharmacia related to the molecule latanoprost (claim number 2). Upon request by the European Patent Office (EPO), Pharmacia withdrew some of the claims supposed to be lacking innovative features beyond what was already contained in the main patent; claim number 2 regarding latanoprost was among these claims. Nonetheless, this molecule was also covered by a different claim, pertaining to a broader group of

time, eventually obtained the divisional patent, which it only validated in Italy, where it then asked for an SPC so as to extend protection until July 2011. As the procedure for marketing authorization was still pending before the competent Italian authority (Agenzia Italiana del Farmaco, AIFA), Pfizer commenced actions both against AIFA and against the generics producer to prevent the former from granting the authorization[40] and the latter from entering the market (threatening to sue it for infringement of the divisional patent). The market authorization was granted in September 2009. Yet Ratiopharm decided to postpone the sale of the generics in the market and lodged a complaint before the Italian Competition Authority.

The Italian Competition Authority found that the overall conduct amounted to an abuse of dominant position according to Article 102 TFEU and imposed a very high fine. According to its assessment, Pfizer had engaged in conduct that could be regarded as competition on the merits, namely, making abusive use of administrative procedures[41] and instituting sham/vexatious litigation.[42] More specifically, the Authority argued that both forms of conduct were part of a unitary and complex

---

molecules, which remained in the patent application. The latanoprost molecule was therefore protected by the divisional patent. See Italian Competition Authority (Autorità Garante della Concorrenza e del Mercato), case A431 – *RATIOPHARM/PFIZER*, provv. n. 23194, Bollettino Settimanale, no. 2/2012, 30 January 2012, para. 79. The decision was also published in (2012) II *Riv. Dir. Ind.* 529.

[40] Pfizer also tried to pressure AIFA into leaving the latanoprost molecule off the so-called 'transparency list'. As explained by the Italian Competition Commission, the insertion of the molecule in such a list, which normally takes place right after the generic company has notified AIFA that it has the drugs in stock, ready to enter the regional market, immediately causes a drop in the prices of all drugs containing the same molecule (i.e. a drop in the price of the drug borne by the national health system). *Ratiopharm v. Pfizer* (n. 39 above) paras 38 and 40.

[41] Regarding the abuse of administrative procedures, the conduct at issue consisted in the filing of divisional patent EP 168, the validation of such patent only in Italy (so that Pfizer could apply for the SPC and align the Italian expiry date with the other national patents), the further request for an extension of protection for paediatric experimentation (which, if granted, would have extended the length of protection for six more months, until January 2012). See *Ratiopharm v. Pfizer* (n. 39 above) para. 176.

[42] The analysis of the anticompetitive potential of vexatious litigation is beyond the scope of this paper. On the topic see S. Vezzoso, 'Towards an EU Doctrine of Anticompetitive IP-Related Litigation' (2012) 3 *J. Eur. Comp. L. & Prac.* 521, including references to the *Ratiopharm v. Pfizer* case.

exclusionary strategy that was aimed at creating a situation of uncertainty that would prevent generic companies from entering the market with their equivalent drugs.[43]

Based on a different approach to the case, the Regional Administrative Tribunal (Tribunale Amministrativo Regionale, TAR), before which Pfizer had lodged an appeal, overturned the decision of the Competition Authority. The Tribunal found that the competition authority had reached the finding of competition-law liability by simply putting together a series of lawful acts, all permitted by both patent law and constitutional law. On the contrary, the Tribunal argued, in order to deem such conduct anticompetitive the competition authority *must* show a *manifest intent to exclude* in the light of a *quid pluris* that adds to the mere tallying of different forms of lawful conduct.[44] Such *quid pluris* was missing in the Authority's reasoning. According to the Tribunal, the Authority had wrongfully concluded proof of the illicit intent from the sole circumstance that Pharmacia had filed the divisional patent application 13 years after the original application. Nonetheless, the Tribunal did not mention the circumstance that the filing of a divisional patent such a long time after the filing of the initial patent application was no longer permitted by European patent law.[45]

---

[43] See *Ratiopharm v. Pfizer* (n 39 above) paras 175–177. For a critical comment on the case see G. De Stefano, 'Tough Enforcement of Unilateral Conduct at the National Level: Italian Antitrust Authority Sanctions Bayer and Pfizer for Abuse of Dominant Position (aka AstraZeneca Ruling and Essential Facility Doctrine in Italian Sauce)' (2012) 3 *J. Eur. Comp. L. & Prac.* 396, 400.

[44] See Jugdment of the Administrative Regional Tribunal of Latium, Italy, *Pfizer Italia s.r.l. et al. v. AGCM*, 3 September 2012, no. 7467, para. 4.1.

[45] At the time when the Administrative Tribunal decided the case the EPO Administrative Council had amended rule 36 of the EPC Implementing Regulation and introduced a specific time constraint so that the patentee willing to file for a divisional patent had to deposit it within 24 months from the receipt of the Written Opinion sent by the EPO examiner. See EPO, Implementing Regulations to the Convention on the Grant of European Patents of October 1973, as adopted by decision of the Administrative Council of the European Patent Organisation of 7 December 2006 and as last amended by decision of the Administrative Council of the European Patent Organisation of 26 October 2010 (CA/D 2/09 of 25 March 2009) [2009] EPO OJ 296. The new Regulations entered into force on 1 April 2010. The EPO Administrative Council has recently re-amended rule 36 once again to cancel the time limit constraint and restore the previous scenario where patentees could file for divisional patents at any time, provided that the parent application is still pending. See new rule 36, as amended by decision of the Administrative Council of the European Patent Organisation of 16 October

6. STRATEGIC PATENTING AND THE LATEST EUROPEAN CASE-LAW: THE *ASTRAZENECA* JUDGMENT

Although one can certainly agree with the Tribunal's proposition in the *Ratiopharm v. Pfizer* case that a *quid pluris* needs to be proven in order to punish the conduct, the Italian Competition Authority does not seem to have erred in finding an abuse. On the one hand, pursuant to what the new effects-based approach to unilateral exclusionary conduct advocates, the Italian Competition Authority relied on two important elements: (i) concrete anticompetitive foreclosure[46] (indeed generics were prevented from entering the market); and (ii) proof of anticompetitive harm to consumers,[47] who were damaged directly in that they could not benefit from equivalent drugs at lower prices, and indirectly because the Italian national health system, funded by Italian tax payers, had to bear high prices during the time in which the violation persisted (with an estimated loss of €14 million).[48]

2013 (CA/D 15/13 of 16 October 2013) [2013] EPO OJ 501, entered into force on 1 April 2014.

[46] The definition of 'anticompetitive foreclosure' was introduced by the aforementioned Commission Guidance (n. 12 above) in para. 19: a 'situation where effective access of actual or potential competitors to supplies or markets is hampered or eliminated as a result of the conduct of the dominant undertaking whereby the dominant undertaking is likely to be in a position to profitably increase prices ... to the detriment of consumers'. On the topic see Ghidini and Arezzo (2010) (n. 12 above) 130ff.

[47] According to the Commission, competition authorities' intervention should be aimed at punishing exclusionary practices that, in the light of convincing evidence, cause anticompetitive foreclosure to the prejudice of consumers. See Commission Guidance (n. 12 above) para. 20. The finding of an abuse would then depend on a showing of both anticompetitive foreclosure and consumer harm. In this sense G. Bruzzone and M. Boccaccio, 'Impact Based Assessment and Use of Legal Presumptions in EC Competition Law: The Search for the Proper Mix' (2009) 32 *World Comp.* 465, 459; N. Petit, 'From Formalism to Effects? The Commission's Communications on Enforcement Priorities in Applying Article 82 EC' (2009) 32 *World Comp.* 483, 489.

[48] The structure of the pharmaceutical market indeed shows several peculiarities. Not only is the price of the drugs determined by the regulator and not as a result of the intersection of demand and supply curves, but the choice of the product is highly influenced by doctors who prescribe drugs, while the costs are usually borne by the consumers and, in large part, by the national health care system. For an in-depth analysis of the structure of the pharmaceutical market see Schnichels and Sule (n. 16 above), 95 et seq. Such high level of regulation

Moreover, the Italian Competition Agency correctly referred to the most recent EU case-law in the field, relying on the principle recently confirmed by the Court of Justice of the EU (CJEU) that the fact that the abusive conduct is regulated by other branches of law that pursue different goals and that such laws might entail their own mechanism of sanctioning is irrelevant for the purpose of applying competition law.[49] The only thing that matters is that the conduct is of an anticompetitive nature according to the principles of competition law.[50]

Ironically, both decisions rely on the most recent European case-law on unilateral practices in the pharmaceutical sector:[51] namely, the *AstraZeneca* judgment. But what does this case say?

---

makes the industry particularly prone to practices known as 'regulatory gaming', or conduct that tries to exploit the fallacies of the regulatory system to the disadvantage of competitors. On this point see S.L. Dogan and M.A. Lemley, 'Antitrust Law and Regulatory Gaming' (2009) 87 *Tex. L. Rev.*, 2009, 685, 687 and 709ff.

[49] See *Ratiopharm v. Pfizer* (n. 39 above) para. 181 (referring to the *AstraZeneca* case).

[50] Ibid. In this regard, it is worth noting that the most recent European case-law does not demand proof of intent in abuse-of-dominance cases, as wrongly required by the Italian Regional Administrative Tribunal. See, more recently, Case C-549/10 P *Tomra v. Commission* [2012] ECR I-0000, para. 11 (not yet officially reported). The idea of the irrelevance of intent in abuse-of-dominance cases is also shared within the community of European scholars. See, for example, R. O'Donoghue and A.J. Padilla, *The Law and Economics of Article 82 EC* (Hart Publishing 2006) 225–227. With specific regard to intersection cases, in its *AstraZeneca* judgment, the General Court extensively explained that there is no need to prove anticompetitive intent of the firm nor the dominant undertaking's bad faith in order to substantiate the finding of abuse: for the latter, the following suffice: (i) a conduct integrating a form of competition which is not based on the merits; and (ii) the conduct's capability to hamper competition. See Case T-321/05 *AstraZeneca v. Commission* [2010] ECR II-2805, paras 356, 672, 817, 824 and 845. This does not mean that any evidence showing a company's wilfulness to pursue an anticompetitive exclusionary strategy will be irrelevant for the assessment. Such evidence, as clarified by the General Court, may contribute to corroborating the finding of an abuse which, however, must primarily rest 'on an objective finding that the abusive conduct actually took place'. Ibid., paras 356–359. The reasoning of the General Court has been upheld by the CJEU. See case C-457/10 P *AstraZeneca v. Commission* [2012] ECR I-0000, para. 63 (not yet officially reported).

[51] There was actually another interesting case opened by the Commission after its decision in *AstraZeneca*. In 2007, the Commission opened proceedings against Boehringer, an originator pharmaceutical company that, *inter alia*, sold drugs for lung diseases, for abuse of dominance because the company had filed

The *AstraZeneca* case concerned two unilateral practices that aimed at excluding generic drugs from the market. The abusive character of both forms of conduct was recently confirmed by the CJEU.[52] The first form of conduct involved the provision of false information to national patent offices and courts regarding the date on which the first marketing authorization for Losec (AstraZeneca's best-selling drug based on the compound omeprazole) was granted, for the purpose of acquiring national SPCs for which AstraZeneca did not qualify. The second type of conduct related to the deregistration of the marketing authorization for Losec capsules, following AstraZeneca's decision to convert its production from capsules to tablets.[53] This conduct had the effect of delaying the market entry of generics, as they could not benefit from the abridged (market authorization) procedure with regard to the marketing of capsules.[54]

---

and later used blocking patents to exclude potential competitors from the market. The case was finally settled by the Commission, and unfortunately not much information is available on it. See Case COMP/B2/39246 – *Boehringer*, Communication from the Commission (opening of proceedings), 29 March 2007, available at: http://ec.europa.eu/competition/antitrust/cases/dec_docs/39246/39246_951_10.pdf (accessed 31 January 2014); Commission, Antitrust: Commission welcomes improved market entry for lung disease treatments, Press Release IP/11/842, 6 July 2011, available at: http://europa.eu/rapid/press-release_IP-11-842_en.htm?locale=en (accessed 31 January 2014).

[52] CJEU in C-457/10 P *AstraZeneca* (n. 50 above). For a comment on the case see P.A. Van Malleghem and W. Devroe, 'AstraZeneca: Court of Justice Upholds First Decision Finding Abuse of Dominant Position in Pharmaceutical Sector' (2012) 4 *J. Eur. Comp. L. & Prac.* 228.

[53] The reformulation of pharmaceutical products is a strategy commonly used by originator companies to impede generics competition. Reformulation often takes place when the patented drug is about to expire, but with a sufficient time span to allow the originator to withdraw the first branded product from the market and start advertising the new reformulated drug. Such time lapse between patent expiry and the market entry of generics has to be sufficiently large to allow physicians to shift to the new product and to persuade them that the new drug is an ameliorated version of the older one. On product reformulation see, *inter alia*, S.D. Shadowen, K.B. Leffler and J.T. Lukens, 'Bringing Market Discipline to Pharmaceutical Product Reformulations' (2011) 42 *Int'l Rev. IP & Comp. L.* 69; M. Carrier, 'A Real-World Analysis of Pharmaceutical Settlements: The Missing Dimension of Product Hopping' (2010) 62 *Fla. L. Rev.* 1009; J. Cheng, 'An Antitrust Analysis of Product Hopping in the Pharmaceutical Industry' (2008) 108 *Colum. L. Rev.* 1471, 2008.

[54] The third paragraph of Article 4(2)(8)(a) of Council Directive 65/65/EEC of 26 January 1965 on the approximation of provisions laid down by Law, Regulation or Administrative Action relating to proprietary medicinal products

Both practices have some aspects in common with the facts in the Italian *Ratiopharm v. Pfizer* case but, at the same time, the circumstances are substantially different.

As far as the first type of conduct is concerned, the fact that the European Court found illegitimate the practices aimed at obtaining an exclusive right that AstraZeneca was entitled to obtain or was entitled to obtain for a shorter period of time, may lead commentators to think that, for the first time, Courts proclaimed abusive the mere act of obtaining an IPR.[55] This, however, does not seem to be the case. The Courts indeed found that the provision of false information – for the purpose of obtaining an IPR that the applicant was not entitled to obtain or with a longer duration than that permitted by the law – was an abuse of dominant position.[56] Interestingly, the accent was placed on the continuous and deliberate release of misleading information to patent offices and national courts,[57] whereas the grant of the title of protection was considered as the anticompetitive *effect* produced by the conduct.[58] The

([1965] OJ L 22, p. 369) establishes that '[t]he applicant shall not be required to provide the results of pharmacological and toxicological tests or the results of clinical trials if he can demonstrate: … the proprietary medicinal product is *essentially similar* to a product which has been authorised within the Community, in accordance with Community provisions in force, for not less than six years and is marketed in the Member State for which the application is made'. The Directive has been amended, *inter alia*, by Council Directive 87/21/EEC of 22 December 1986, [1987] OJ L 15, p. 36.

55 In this regard, it is worth recalling a passage from the judgment of the General Court where it overturned the argument raised by AstraZeneca that in order to exert an effect on competition the right-holder must *use* the patent. See Case T-321/05 (n. 50 above), paras 362, 364 and 366.

56 Ibid., paras 355–357; confirmed by the CJEU in *AstraZeneca* (n. 50 above) paras 105–113.

57 This can be inferred from the *AstraZeneca* judgment of the General Court (n. 50 above) paras 356 and 357, where it explained that '[i]t follows from the objective nature of the concept of abuse … that *the misleading nature of representations* made to public authorities *must be assessed on the basis of objective factors*' and 'that the question whether representations made to public authorities for the purposes of improperly obtaining exclusive rights are misleading must be assessed *in concreto* and that assessment may vary according to the specific circumstances of each case' (emphasis added).

58 See, in this regard, the eloquent words of the CJEU in *AstraZeneca*, C-457/10 P (n. 50 above) para. 108, explaining that 'the appellants cannot deny the *anti-competitive effect* of *those representations* on the ground that the applications for the SPCs were filed between five and six years before the entry into force of those SPCs and that, until that time, AZ's rights were protected by

implicit assumption here was that while an IPR in itself has the intrinsic effect of preventing competitors competing by imitation, to the benefit of technological progress, the acquisition by fraudulent means of rights to which the party is not entitled has the effect of unfairly and unduly distorting competition, and that cannot be regarded as competition on the merits.[59]

It seems from the wording of the judgments that European bodies deemed AstraZeneca's conduct so unfair that they did not even feel the need to delve into a discussion of the intersection of competition law and intellectual property, except for quickly observing that 'such misuse of the patent system potentially reduces the incentive to engage in innovation, since it enables the company in a dominant position to maintain its exclusivity beyond the period envisaged by the legislator'.[60]

The second contested abuse, although not related to the acquisition or the exploitation of an IPR, resembles more closely the arguments raised by the parties in the Italian *Ratiopharm v. Pfizer* case. Indeed, AstraZeneca contested the Commission decision as well as the General Court judgment on the basis that the mere legitimate exercise of a right granted by EU law, such as the right to deregister a market authorization pursuant to Directive 65/65 on medicinal products, could not amount to anti-competitive behaviour.[61] According to AstraZeneca, such conduct might constitute an abuse of dominance only when certain exceptional circumstances were proven, specifically, where there was an elimination of all effective competition, and a mere likelihood to distort competition was not sufficient for that purpose.[62]

---

lawful patents. *Not only do such unlawful SPCs lead*, as the General Court observed at paragraphs 362, 375 and 380 of the judgment under appeal, to a *significant exclusionary effect* after the expiry of the basic patents, but they are also liable to *alter the structure of the market* by adversely affecting potential competition even before that expiry' (emphasis added).

59 Case T-321/05 (n. 50 above) paras 355 and 375.

60 Ibid., para. 367. Note that the CJEU did not raise the subject at all.

61 Case C-457/10 P (n. 50 above) para. 125.

62 Ibid., para. 142. According to AstraZeneca, the General Court should have referred to the case-law on compulsory licences as set forth in Case C-418/01 *IMS Health* [2004] ECR I-5039, since the effect of the judgment would amount to an expropriation of the right to deregister the market authorization and the prohibition on deregistration has to be regarded as a form of a compulsory licence. The argument was not accepted by the CJEU, which held that the possibility of revoking the market authorization pursuant to Directive 65/65 does not amount to a property right. See Case C-457/10 P (n. 50 above) para. 148.

The CJEU was not persuaded by these arguments and, finally, confirmed the findings of the General Court, stating that an undertaking may not '[mis]use regulatory procedures in such a way as to prevent or make more difficult the entry of competitors on the market, in the absence of grounds relating to the defence of the legitimate interests of an undertaking engaged in competition on the merits or in the absence of objective justification'.[63] The Court did not accept as objective justification the argument put forward by AstraZeneca that the maintenance of a market authorization would entail onerous pharmacovigilance obligations upon the firm, as, on the one hand, such argument was raised for the first time before the General Court and there was no mention in the undertaking's internal documents of the heavy burden arising from those obligations. On the other hand, the Court inferred the anticompetitive character of the conduct by the circumstance that AstraZeneca had only pursued its abusive strategy (regarding the deregistration of its market authorizations) in the countries where it feared entrance by generics (namely Denmark, Sweden and Norway).[64] This marks an important parallel with the Italian *Ratiopharm v. Pfizer* case, where the Competition Authority similarly inferred the anticompetitive nature of the conduct from the circumstance that Pfizer had only validated the divisional patent in Italy, where, due to the shorter length of patent protection, generics' entrance was imminent.[65]

7. AN INNOVATION-BASED TEST FOR STRATEGIC PATENTING CASES

Clearly, both *AstraZeneca* and *Ratiopharm v. Pfizer* relate to the pharmaceutical sector and both cases involve a misuse of the patent system and regulatory procedures in general. However, the facts in *Ratiopharm v. Pfizer* appear more complex to assess, given the absence of any manifest fraudulent behaviour before the EPO or the courts, which makes the line between legitimate enforcement of rights and abusive conduct fuzzier.

The problem with the *AstraZeneca* judgment arises from the fact that the circumstances of the case were very facts-specific. Therefore, it is

---

[63] Case C-457/10 P (n. 50 above) para. 134.

[64] In fact, AstraZeneca did not deregister its market authorization in Germany, Spain, France, Italy, Netherlands and Austria, where entrance by generics was not a risk. Ibid., paras 137–138, confirming the General Court judgment, case T-321/05 (n. 50 above) para. 689.

[65] See *Ratiopharm v. Pfizer* (n. 39 above) para. 176.

very difficult to extrapolate from it a holding that is applicable to future cases.[66] However, an important *dictum* can be inferred from the analysis of the European Courts in *AstraZeneca*, which has been stated with regard to both kinds of conduct. In particular, the Courts considered that 'in the majority of cases, abuses of dominant positions consist of behaviour which is otherwise lawful under branches of law other than competition law'.[67] Accordingly, the Courts state the general principle that 'the illegality of abusive conduct under Article 82 EC is unrelated to its compliance or non-compliance with other legal rules'; this even in cases where such rules envisage 'specific remedies which make it possible to rectify, or even annul, patents and SPCs granted unlawfully'.[68]

The principle that competition-law enforcers should not take into account, as a justification for the anticompetitive conduct, the fact that that such practice complies with other sets of law, appears both rational and logical. And in fact if compliance with specific sector-made rules would be sufficient to avoid liability for competition law infringements then lots of abusive conduct could not be sanctioned. Much in the same way, one will agree on the irrelevance of the fact that such sets of law might contain internal mechanisms to constrain certain misuses of their own norms. This is because, if and when they exist, these instruments – which pertain to different bodies of law, with other goals than those pursued by competition law – function in such a way as to cure the malfunctions of their own system and not to eliminate distortions of competition. Hence, these mechanisms will probably not succeed in eliminating the anticompetitive effect brought about by such conduct. This is especially the case, for a number of reasons, as far as IPRs are concerned. First of all, the means to rectify errors in the procedures for the patent grant or to annul patents unduly granted may be not as effective as one might think. The judicial assessment of the validity of

---

[66] See also J. Drexl, 'AstraZeneca and the EU Sector Inquiry: When do Patent Filings Violate Competition Law?' in J. Drexl and N. Lee (eds), *Pharmaceutical Innovation, Competition and Patent Law: A Trilateral Perspective* (Edward Elgar Publishing 2013) 290, 291 (observing that the specific circumstances of the *AstraZeneca* case are not likely to arise again in practice).

[67] See the judgment of the General Court Case T-321/05 (n. 50 above) para. 672; upheld by the CJEU, Case C-457/2010 (n. 50 above) para. 132.

[68] See General Court judgment in *AstraZeneca*, Case T-321/05 (n. 50 above) para. 366; upheld by CJEU in Case C-457/2010 (n. 50 above), para. 154. The Italian Competition Authority expressly referred to the judgment of the General Court in *Ratiopharm v. Pfizer* (n. 39 above) para. 181.

patents is costly and lengthy, and sometimes leads to different results in different jurisdictions. Secondly, and most importantly, a title of protection that has been validly granted pursuant to the requirements set forth by patent law may still be used – or rather not used – for the sole purpose of excluding competitors, with no real benefits in terms of innovation, just as happened in the *Ratiopharm v. Pfizer* case.

Having said that, it seems, however, that even such a holding as the *AstraZeneca* case proves to be too far-reaching to be generally applied to all cases at the intersection of competition law and intellectual property. Indeed, the principle that competition law must not take into account the compliance of supposedly anticompetitive conduct with other sets of laws, if literally applied, would always allow, with no caveats, competition-law intervention in intersection cases. Quite the contrary, competition-law intervention in IP-related cases must be carefully deliberated; this even more so in strategic-patenting cases where drawing the line between illicit conduct and routine patent filing is extremely difficult. In this area, competition-law intervention should be limited to cases that are characterized by exceptional circumstances.[69] Such exceptional circumstances should be argued where, as result of the practice, no real advances to innovation have been made or released to the market and, consequently, the underlying conduct only causes a market-foreclosing effect with no likely benefits for consumers.[70]

Though not framed in these terms, the reasoning of the Italian Competition Authority in *Ratiopharm v. Pfizer* seems to embrace this

---

[69] In favour of an approach requiring further elements to support the finding of an abusive conduct in strategic patent cases see H. Ullrich, 'Strategic Patenting by the Pharmaceutical Industry: Towards a Concept of Abusive Practices of Protection' in J. Drexl and N. Lee (eds), *Pharmaceutical Innovation, Competition and Patent Law: A Trilateral Perspective* (Edward Elgar Publishing 2013) 241; G. Sena, 'Esclusiva brevettuale e strategia escludente' (2012) II *Riv. Dir. Ind.* 626, 628; M. Maggiolino and M.L. Montagnani, 'AstraZeneca's Abuse of IPR-Related Procedures: A Hypothesis of Anti-Trust Offence, Abuse of Rights, and IPR Misuse' (2011) 34 *World Comp.* 245, 248; Kjølbye (n. 29 above) 179.

[70] In a similar sense see H. Ullrich, 'Intellectual Property: Exclusive Rights for a Purpose – The case of Technology Protection by Patents and Copyright' in K. Klafkowska-Waśniowska et al. (eds), *Problemy polskiego i europejskiego prawa prywatnego* (Wolters Kluwer Polska 2012) 425, 430 (drawing a distinction between mere defensive patenting and patenting for blocking purposes, arguing that the distinction between the two should rest on whether the patents forming the cluster are or are not really necessary to protect a firm's incentive to invest in innovation).

approach. Indeed, the Authority inferred the strategic nature as well as the excluding purpose of the conduct (hence its overall anticompetitive nature) from the fact that the divisional patent application did not protect any new invention, as shown by the facts that (i) the divisional patent was only validated for Italy and (ii) not even in this country has the validation of this new exclusive right brought about the release of a new drug, a new formulation thereof, or even the provision of the same drug in a slightly different composition or dosage.[71]

The reasoning of the Competition Authority, in particular with regard to this latter point (i.e. lack of actual working of the divisional patent through the release of a new drug in the market, as further proof of the intention of the overall conduct) has been recently affirmed by the Italian Supreme Administrative Court (*Consiglio di Stato*), which overturned *in toto* the sentence of the Regional Administrative Tribunal.[72] Interestingly, the *Consiglio di Stato*, after stating the irrelevance for a competition law analysis of the circumstance that the divisional patent was validly requested and obtained, explained that the abuse of dominance is, in its essence, nothing more than a specification of the broader category of the abuse of a right that assumes (i) the existence of a right and (ii) its use at odds with the goal for which the right was granted in the first place: a form of exploitation causing an unjustified disproportion between the benefit obtained by the right holder and the sacrifice imposed on her counterpart.[73]

The aforementioned argument regarding the lack of a real innovation being put on the market as a result of the patent grant seems in line with the position of the Commission in the Sector Inquiry Report where it distinguished between abusive exclusionary conduct based on misuse of the patent system and legitimate recourse to lawful patent practices. The Commission argued that if the use of the patent system lacks any innovation-based justification, i.e. when it is only 'aimed at excluding competition and not at safeguarding a viable commercial development of

---

71 *Ratiopharm v. Pfizer* (n. 39 above) paras 193, 198, 199 and 203.

72 *AGCM v. Pfizer s.r.l. et al.*, Italian Supreme Administrative Court, Case n. 9181/2012, Doc. N. 693/2014, 14 January 2014, deposited on 12 February 2014, published in *Il Foro Italiano*, 2014, III, 507, with a comment by M. Colangelo.

73 Ibid., at V. C. Eloquently, the Supreme Administrative Court added that the abuse of right, instead of presupposing a formal violation of the law, implies 'l'utilizzazione alterata dello schema formale del diritto, finalizzata al conseguimento di obiettivi ulteriori e diversi rispetto a quelli indicati dal legislatore'.

own innovation',[74] this may suggest that patent law has been misused for the sole purpose of creating entry barriers to generics.

8. CONCLUSION

Competition authorities in the European Union have acquired the role of 'IP watchdogs', playing a pivotal role in the regulation of markets where innovation is a key determinant. Thereby, they directly contribute to the shaping of innovation policies. On the one hand, this trend has to be welcomed. Through recourse to competition law, the European Commission and the national competition authorities indeed try to constrain the expansionist trend recently experienced by IP legislation and courts worldwide. Not only does European IP legislation lack sufficiently strong internal mechanisms to limit firms' strategic use of its rules, but there is also no common European law on unfair competition that could help to address some of these unfair practices. On the other hand, however, competition-law intervention in IP-related cases has to entail a balanced approach. Otherwise there is the opposite risk that there might be an over-intervention of competition law into IPRs and that could exert detrimental effects on innovation.

Strategic-patenting cases, in particular, must be analysed much more thoroughly than traditional refusal-to-deal cases or, in general, cases where dominance does not arise from mere IP ownership but rather from a combination of the IP right and a complex set of market factors such as network effects. When such market-related 'plus-factors' are absent and dominance exceptionally arises only from IP ownership, the application of competition law will be in need of a very careful consideration of the specific circumstances of the case. Intervention should only take place in the exceptional case where there is proof that the IP system has been misused for the exclusive purpose of restricting competition with no real consumer benefits in terms of innovation.

---

[74] The Commission points out that 'both patent clusters and divisionals seemingly serve to prevent or delay generic entry. While this, during the period of exclusivity, is generally in line with the underlying objectives of patent systems, it may in certain cases only be aimed at excluding competition and not at safeguarding a viable commercial development of own innovation covered by the clusters.' See European Commission (n. 15 above) para. 523.

13. Competition law as the limit to standard-setting

Björn Lundqvist

1. INTRODUCTION

Standards, and especially standards produced by standard-setting organizations (SSOs), are a growing phenomenon, especially in connection with the New Economy.[1] There are several reasons for this. First, we are (still) continuously developing the infrastructure of the New Economy, and since this is done through cooperation among the relevant stakeholders, rather than unilaterally by governmental organs, collaboration is essential. Second, firms' specialization is also profound in, for example, the information and communication technology (ICT) sector and therefore, agreed-upon and transparent technology interfaces, decided through standard-setting between firms, are necessary for the industry to work efficiently. Third, globalization demands global joint solutions, implemented through collaboration, rather than national and regional ones decided by public organs. In fact, it seems that standard-setting is quickly becoming part of the core business practice of any firm aspiring to operate globally, and thus an essential part of firms' competitive global strategies. Finally, several markets within the New Economy are affected by network effects, and those markets that are characterized by the presence of network effects tend to migrate towards single standards,[2]

[1] According to Castells' pioneering three-volume work from the 1990s, *The Information Age*, the network society and the New Economy tie together several developments: new technological paradigms, globalization, social movements and the demise of the sovereign nation-state. M. Castells, *The Rise of the Network Society*, Vol. I of *The Information Age: Economy, Society and Culture* (2nd ed, Cambridge, MA; Oxford, UK: Blackwell 2000).

[2] Shapiro and Varian were among the first researchers to identify that markets in the New Economy tend to tip in favour of one technology due to network effects. C. Shapiro and H.R. Varian, *Information Rules* (Harvard Business School Press 1999) 173–174. Drexl rightly states that markets with

firms active on such markets have an incentive to agree on single standards that include their technology, while otherwise a *de facto* standard originating from a single firm might develop.

The aim of this chapter is to provide an analysis of the application of EU competition law to standards, by looking at case law under both Articles 101 and 102 TFEU. I will try to show that there is, and should be, a difference in competition law treatment of standards and standard-setting conduct depending on whether the market exposed to the standard is plagued with network effects or not. For markets with network effects, collaboration to create standards is benign, even pro-competitive, while access to such standards, if covered by intellectual property rights, may, in exceptional circumstances, be granted by the antitrust agencies. On the other hand, agreements to decide standards for markets which do not display network effects should benefit from a heightened antitrust scrutiny, because these standard agreements may cause exclusionary anti-competitive effects. The chapter also provides, in the end, some suggestions for how the standard-setting procedure, given this difference, should be treated under competition law.

The starting point, in section 2, is to identify what technical standards are of interest from a competition law perspective. Such identification should be based on economic and legal research identifying the antitrust harm and effect. The main point of the discussion in the section is that Article 101 TFEU should only prohibit those standard-setting collaborations that actually cause anticompetitive exclusionary effects, while Article 102 TFEU should deal with accessing standards, SEPs and even SSOs, on fair terms under the exceptional circumstance doctrine.

Identifying a dominant position to the point that the requirements of the 'exceptional circumstance' doctrine are met will only be likely when the standard scrutinized has been agreed upon and adopted by the market. Only then will implementers be locked in, with the result that Article 102 TFEU may be used to enable access for, for example, potential and willing licensees to SEPs. On the other hand, standard-setting agreements could cause anticompetitive exclusionary effects under Article 101 TFEU when an agreed-upon standard causes exclusionary effects due to a misuse of the standard-setting procedure, while a court would still need, in the circumstances just described, to take into consideration the natural exclusionary effects originating from network effects and tipping.

network effects 'migrate' towards single standards. J. Drexl, 'Intellectual Property in Competition: How to Promote Dynamic Competition as a Goal' in J. Drexl et al. (eds), *More Common Ground For International Competition Law?* (Edward Elgar Publishing 2011) 212ff.

Collaborations to create standards on interoperability on markets with network effects are, thus, benign under competition law. These markets would naturally migrate towards one *de facto* standard even without an agreement on a *de jure* standard. Taking the counterfactual situation into consideration, generally, only in markets where there are no network effects could agreements on standards have an exclusionary anti-competitive effect.

From that outset, in section 3 I examine the scant case law regarding standard-setting agreements under Article 101 TFEU. The aim is to see whether the EU case law matches the ideas put forward in the preceding section. US case law is also visited in order to find arguments and support for identifying a legal test to judge standard-setting agreements under EU competition law. In section 4, I turn to case law referring to standard-setting as unilateral conduct assessed under Article 102 TFEU. The section ends with an analysis of the latest EU Commission decisions in *Samsung* and *Motorola* from 2014.[3] In these cases, the Commission seems to purport that when the effect of the standard is that a holder of an SEP is in a monopoly position on a market displaying network effects (i.e., when lock-in effects emanate from this standard), Article 102 TFEU should be applicable if the patentee is not giving a willing licensee access to the standard. This finding also seems to confirm the ideas put forward in section 2.

I conclude in section 5 with a gentle plea for creating guidelines and perhaps a block exemption for standard-setting activities, so as to identify a safe harbour and even a test to determine when standard-setting conduct can be prohibited under Article 101 or 102 TFEU. Such a test should be based on the prior identification of the economic effects of the standard at issue, followed by a case-by-case analysis aimed at establishing whether the conduct under scrutiny causes or is likely to cause any anticompetitive effects.

---

[3] Commission decision of 29 April 2014, Case AT.39939 *Samsung – Enforcement of UMTS Standard Essential Patents*. http://ec.europa.eu/competition/elojade/isef/case_details.cfm?proc_code=1_39939 (accessed 28 September 2014). Commission decision of 29 April 2014, Case AT.39985 *Motorola Enforcement of GPRS Standard Essential Patent*. http://ec.europa.eu/competition/elojade/isef/case_details.cfm?proc_code=1_39985 (accessed 28 September 2014).

2. LIMITS TO COMPETITION POLICY AND LAW

The theories of static competition, or von Hayek's and Schumpeter's concepts of competition as a discovery process and as creative destruction, respectively, are difficult to apply to certain standard-setting procedures since standard-setting often entails collective cooperative efforts and not a competitive process.[4] There are many different forms of standards and likewise different forms of standard-setting procedures. Under the International Standardization Organization (ISO) classification, standards may be divided into eight groups:[5]

(i) Basic standards have a broad effect in a particular field. (These standards are also called infrastructure standards.)
(ii) Terminology standards define words permitting representatives of an industry to understand and communicate with each other.
(iii) Testing standards define the test methods to be used to assess the performance or other characteristics of a product.
(iv) Product standards establish qualities or requirements for a product (or related group of products) to assure that it will serve its purpose effectively.
(v) Process standards specify requirements to be met by a process, such as an assembly line's operation, in order to function effectively.
(vi) Service standards, such as for servicing or repairing a car, establish requirements to be set in order to achieve the designated purpose effectively.
(vii) Interface/interoperability standards, such as the point of connection between a telephone and a computer terminal, are concerned with the compatibility of products.
(viii) Standard on data: The last type provides a listing of characteristics for value of data specifying a product, service, etc.

---

[4] Cf. generally F.A. von Hayek, *New Studies in Philosophy, Politics, Economics, and the History of Ideas* (Routledge and Kegan Paul 1978) 185; J. Schumpeter, *Capitalism, Socialism and Democracy* (George Allen & Unwin first published in 1942, new edn 1976) 81.

[5] See L. Zhang, *Standardization and Patent Licensing in the European Union* (Oy Nord Print Ab 2012) 26, with references. For a discussion regarding these groups see B. Lundqvist, *Standardization under EU Competition Rules and US Antitrust Laws – The Rise and the Limits of Self-Regulation* (Edward Elgar Publishing 2014) 35–39.

In addition to the above, product and service standards, but also other forms of standards such as interoperability standards, may be divided into performance (also called general uniformity or non-product standards) and prescriptive standards (also called design or product standards). A performance standard implies that the standard only mandates a certain performance that the product or service should meet to fulfil the standard, while a product or prescriptive standard stipulates specific requirements for the goods.[6]

Performance standards cause little or no anticompetitive exclusionary harm and are thus of little or no interest to competition authorities or competition courts.[7] Such standards leave it up to the undertakings to select a technology or product to present to the market as long as it fulfils the standard. Performance standards thereby leave undertakings room to compete with different technical solutions to fulfil the requirements mandated in the standard. One example of a performance standard would be that a building material, e.g. cement, should be able to withstand a certain pressure and weight, while the undertakings may still decide on the content of the material and the process for creating it, as long as the performance requirements are fulfilled. Product or prescriptive standards, on the other hand, mandate specific technical requirements, often in reference to content, so that only one solution or technology fits the standard. That may cause exclusionary effects that may amount to anticompetitive harm, should the procedure for deciding the standard have been misused.

In other cases, standards may represent the basic groundwork on which competition thrives, like standards on the width of railroad tracks or which telecommunication technology should be used to connect our mobile phones. These standards reflect infrastructure or interoperability standards in the ISO list above. There are several interoperability standards, such as the protocols and tools for the virtual infrastructure we call the Internet.[8] Interoperability is the linking of systems, networks or services so that they can work together successfully.[9] It seems that the

---

[6] See Lundqvist (n. 5 above) at 35–39, 116–148.

[7] G. Tassey, 'Standardization in Technology-Based Markets' (2000) 29 *Res. Pol'y* 587, at 589ff.

[8] Standardization of basic protocols and interfaces were the prerequisite for the development of the Internet. See M. Glader, 'Open Standards: Public Policy Aspects and Competition Law Requirements' (2010) 6 *European Competition Journal*, 611.

[9] There is no clear definition of interoperability. See C. Tapia, *Industrial Property Rights, Technical Standards and Licensing Practices (FRAND) in the*

notion of interoperability is spreading. For example, standards for the railway system (e.g. for the gauge, couplings, brakes and signalling), and standards for public safety (e.g. fire-fighting material) or for the armed forces are today perceived as interoperability standards, while previously they were considered basic or infrastructure standards.[10] These standards stipulate the requirement of interoperability, which indicates the interface between different forms of products and technologies, similar to adopting a technology to be the infrastructure for markets. Such standards may create not only new markets but also increased competition and wealth on and from such markets. The demand for basic infrastructure as well as for interoperability technologies is network-driven, implying that when a market implements an infrastructure or interoperability standard the demand tends to migrate towards one solution, i.e. one technical solution tends to become a *de facto* standard, if no standard-setting agreement, i.e. *de jure* standard, is made.

On the contrary, the product or prescriptive standards often reflect the joint effort or agreement of specialized firms to market a jointly developed technology or product on an already existing relevant market. A product or prescriptive standard is a bundle of requirements on how a product should be designed, function or work, e.g. a list of ingredients and requirements for, for example, cement or for the production process of cement, the size and technical specifications for radiators, or even for the ingredients of pasta. They often limit product variety on the downstream market, as the requirements exclude certain products. Of course, the reason for implementing such a standard can be to exclude certain products as not being safe or environmentally friendly. However, they can also be implemented to make markets more efficient or to exclude competing products.

Prescriptive product standards must be judged differently from interoperability standards, since they limit the variety of products, i.e. product variations on a market or a future market, while infrastructure or interoperability standards facilitate or create new markets. In fact, product standards are common on markets that do not display network effects. Where different products, possibly reflecting different standards, compete on a market an exaggerated effort to regulate and implement a product

---

Telecommunications Industry (Carl Heymanns Verlag 2010) 9, esp. at n. 22, for references.

[10] See Zhang (n. 5 above), at 26, with references.

standard may limit product variety with the consequence that, if the market is not network-driven, anticompetitive harm and effects on the relevant product market may appear.

However, the question may arise why interoperability standards in the network-driven industries should not be considered as causing similar anticompetitive harm and effect as a prescriptive product standard may cause.

Competition as a procedure for developing markets and for creating wealth does not seem to be the best procedure for developing some classical infrastructure or interoperability standards, such as the width and size of railroad track. Implementing such an infrastructure implies selecting one solution for an industry, market or society. Inevitably, infrastructure standards are not efficiently and effectively developed through a trial-and-error method, where the consumers are exposed to different solutions, and then through selecting and re-selecting to choose the best alternative. Infrastructure standards are rather developed through a standard-setting process in which the relevant stakeholders negotiate and agree upon the infrastructure while conducting R&D to develop the standard. Hence, these standards should not be considered as similar to those goods and services Arrow, von Hayek and Schumpeter discuss.[11] Indeed, they seem to discuss markets where the consumers have a choice and where consumer welfare is increased by making selections. Here, the consumer may select a good, try it out, and purchase another good if the first one is not to his or her liking. The fundamental assumption of von Hayek's, Schumpeter's and Arrow's work[12] – that consumers can always enjoy freedom of choice among products and that innovation and competition is a process of trial and error – is not readily applicable to infrastructure or interoperability standards.

However, in the New Economy or the high-tech, network-driven industries, certain technologies that are currently being standardized are, perhaps short-lived, but still infrastructures. Thus, society needs to agree, *de jure*, on such a standard, and it will be unlikely that the parties affected by these standards, including suppliers, content providers and consumers, will be able to back-track when the technology or standard has been selected. They will all have to accept and invest in the new

[11] K. Arrow, 'Economic Welfare and the Allocation of Resources for Invention' in R. Nelson (ed.), *The Rate and Direction of Inventive Activity: Economic and Social Factors* (National Bureau of Economic Research 1962) 620–625; Von Hayek (n. 4 above), at 185–188; Schumpeter (n. 4 above), at 81–85.

[12] Arrow (n. 11 above).

standard. Possibly, a new technology or standard will soon develop that may overtake the old standard, but that does not contradict the fact that the industry or markets connected to the standard can hold only one standard at a time. For these standards, as well as classical infrastructure standards, competition as a process does not suffice as a theoretical groundwork to select the best technology for society. First, trial and error could be a very costly method for selecting infrastructure.[13] Second, if standards are not agreed upon, *de facto* standards will soon emerge. The connected markets will tend to select one infrastructure or interoperability technology to become the standard. However, *de facto* standards created through network effects and tipping could very well be inferior to a *de jure* standard.[14] The notion of tipping implies that markets with network effects may have a limited form of product competition in the beginning of a new technology or product cycle. However, soon thereafter, when one technology or product acquires more users then the others, the greater number of users will attract more users, and finally the whole market will tip towards a monopoly for that one technology or product, and, thus, for one firm only.[15] In the New Economy, due to network effects and tipping, a single solution may become a global solution, though this *de facto* standard may not be as good for society as the other solutions. In such circumstances, the solution will be in the hands of one monopolistic firm. Instead, stakeholders should be allowed not only to choose between available technologies, but also to discuss the advantages and disadvantages of different technical solutions, while individually continuing their R&D efforts, and to reach a compromise on the technology to standardize. The result will be a compromise between different stakeholders, often including technologies from different sources. In these circumstances, the standard-setting process must be understood as a form of collective innovation and also 'collective competition', where the end result

---

[13] Private standard-setting organizations advance consumer welfare on several levels. See generally M. Lemley, 'Antitrust Intellectual Property and Standard Setting Organizations' (2002) 80 *California Law Review* 1889.

[14] C. Shapiro and H.R. Varian, *Information Rules* (Harvard Business School Press 1999) 173–185.

[15] For a definition of tipping see M. Katz and C. Shapiro, 'Systems Competition and Network Effects' (1994) 8 *Journal of Economic Perspective* 93, 105–107.

is a standard that meets the demands of the stakeholders as a whole.[16] In theory, what may be created through a standard-setting process is a standard that uses technology from several firms (most likely an oligopoly situation), while a *de facto* standard in the New Economy may wind up in the hands of one firm (monopoly situation).[17]

The question is then: what does this have to do with EU competition law? Selecting technologies for standards seems to fall, generally speaking, outside the competitive process. If the above, rather theoretical, discussion is accepted as valid, the application of competition law should be limited, yet there should still be some room for it. In reference to standard-setting, competition law needs to be applied differently depending on whether there are network effects on the market or not, and whether the standard is an interoperability standard or a prescriptive product one.

Indeed, competition law agencies and courts are not well suited to review the selection of a technology to become a global infrastructure standard. They should, however, scrutinize whether the standard creates anticompetitive exclusionary effects that would not have *de facto* materialized without the standard-setting agreement. The courts then have a limited scope to scrutinize the procedure used to establish the standards, and the terms of accessing these standards, once the standards have been established. A 'misuse of the standard-setting process' may produce anticompetitive harm, e.g. by excluding a technology from a relevant market that may hold competing technologies. However, competition agencies and courts will seldom find anticompetitive harm when dealing with interoperability or infrastructure standards and the substantial result of the standard-setting process in itself, i.e. the technology.

---

[16] J. Drexl, 'Anticompetitive Stumbling Stones on the Way to a Cleaner World: Protecting Competition in Innovation without a Market' (2012) 8 *Journal of Competition Law and Economics* 507. See also S. Anderman and J. Kallaugher, *Technology Transfer and the New EU Competition Rules* (Oxford University Press 2006) 252, esp. at n. 32.

[17] For a very interesting scholarly work regarding the driving forces of the old and the New Economy and what kind of markets may be created, see Shapiro and Varian (n. 14 above), at 173–185.

3. APPLICATION OF THE PROHIBITION OF ANTICOMPETITIVE AGREEMENTS TO STANDARD-SETTING

3.1 The Assessment of Product and Prescriptive Standards under Competition Law

In the *EMC* case,[18] EMC Development AB (EMC) challenged a Commission decision[19] rejecting a complaint against a group consisting of some European cement producers (European Portland cement producers, the European Cement Association (Cembureau) and the European Committee for Standardization (CEN)), for creating a cartel, facilitated by an industrial standard, aimed at creating barriers to entry to the European cement market. EMC's challenge was based on the fact that its cement product would not fit the five prescriptive product standards (EN 197-1 standard) that had been developed and decided upon by the standard development organization (SDO)[20] named CEN.[21] EMC had marketed its

---

[18] Case T-432/05 *EMC Development AB* [2010] ECR II-01629. The case is also discussed in Lundqvist (n. 5 above) at 201–205, 372–375.

[19] Commission decision of 28 September 2005, Case COMP/F-2/38.401 *EN 197-1 Standard- EMC/European Cement*, http://ec.europa.eu/competition/antitrust/cases/dec_docs/38401/38401_35_5.pdf (accessed 6 March 2014).

[20] The term 'standard development organization' (SDO) has a specific meaning when discussing standardization both under EU and US Competition law. Under US law, an SDO is a standard-setting organization (SSO) that has been accredited with the International Standardization Organization (ISO) or the International Electronic Commission (IEC). Under EU law, the Commission formally acknowledges that both the European standards organizations (e.g. CEN), which are also SDOs, and national standard-setting organizations (NSOs) are SDOs in the international system. An SSO is therefore a larger term, including not only SDOs but also, for example, private consortia of firms joining together to advance a technical solution to an issue. See Lundqvist (n. 5 above) at 116–118, 149–166.

[21] According to the CJEU in Case T-432/05 (n. 18 above), paras 12–13:

> The EN 197-1 Standard ('the Standard') was adopted in April 2000 by the 19 national standards bodies that were members of CEN at that time. It was developed by a CEN technical committee, CEN/TC 51 'Cement and building limes' (CEN/TC 51), under mandate M/114 which was granted by the Commission and the European Free Trade Association (EFTA) pursuant to Directive 89/106. That mandate defined the scope of application of the Standard, set out the list of products that had to be taken into consideration and stated that the Standard would be expressed, as far as practicable, in product-performance terms, having regard to the interpretative documents.

cement product, Energetically Modified Cement (EM Cement), since it was developed in the 1990s, and claimed that its product had been *de facto* excluded from the European cement market due to the EN 197-1 standard. EMC also claimed that Cembureau and the head of the technical committee in CEN had conspired to create barriers to entry to the cement market, barriers which also excluded or, at least, manifestly restricted, entry.

The Union Courts rejected EMC's claim that an anticompetitive agreement was at hand and that the EU Commission should have made a more in-depth analysis before dismissing the complaint. The Commission and the Courts found that the safe harbour for standardization agreements established in the Horizontal Guidelines[22] was applicable, and that EMC had not shown that there was a cartel. Furthermore, the Commission and the Courts did not agree that the EN 197-1 standard created lock-in effects, since the latter was not *de facto* a mandatory standard, provided that there were other ways to enter the cement market and to obtain the sought after 'EC mark'. More generally, the Commission and the Courts did not agree with EMC regarding the existence and weight of the evidence presented.

The Commission also rejected the argument that the technology and products developed and patented by EMC were, at least, of similar quality or even 'better' than the technologies agreed upon under the standard.[23] EMC seems to have claimed, at least in front of the Commission, that the cement it had developed was superior to the cement

---

The Standard defined each of the 27 common cement products, that is to say, the common cements described by the various national standards bodies within CEN as traditional and well tried. Those products are further grouped into five main cement types (CEM I to CEM V), according to the proportions in which the main constituents were to be combined to produce those distinct products in a range of six 'strength classes'. Each main cement type was composed of a certain percentage of Portland cement clinker combined with varying levels of constituents. That definition included requirements which the constituents have to satisfy, and mechanical, physical, chemical and durability requirements of the 27 common cement products and 'strength classes'. According to the applicant and Cembureau, 'real' Portland cement corresponded to products of the main cement type CEM I, as defined by the Standard. Blended cements corresponded to cements of the four other main types, CEM II to CEM V.

22 Guidelines on the application of Article 101 of the Functioning of the European Union to horizontal co-operation agreements, OJ C 11, 14/01/2011, 1 (Horizontal Guidelines).

23 Case COMP/F-2/38.401 (n. 19 above), at paras 48, 50, 51, 54, 72.

detailed by the EN 197-1 standard. According to EMC, the reason why the latter was established as a prescriptive product standard rather than a performance standard was possibly to exclude better cement products. Allegedly, the European standard excluded EMC's technology from gaining access to the market on equal terms, and prevented the creation of a level playing field between the standardized technologies and EMC's technology. The Commission and the Courts seem to have found this line of argument to be outside the ambit of the proceeding when establishing that the safe harbour was applicable for CEN. In fact, neither the Courts nor the Commission seriously considered the claim that the EN 197-1 standard should at least have been a performance rather than a prescriptive standard.[24] If the standard had been drafted so as to encompass all methods that enabled the cement to reach certain quality thresholds, i.e. as a performance standard, EMC's technology, according to EMC's claim, would have been in accordance with the standard, and would have gained access, on equal terms, to the customers/consumers. The Commission instead distanced itself from this discussion and stated that this assessment was outside the scope of the proceeding.[25] According to the Commission, the discussion over whether a standard should be prescriptive or performance-based 'cannot be reopened in a framework concerning the application of Articles 101 or 102 EC Treaty'.[26]

As discussed in the preceding section, the Commission and courts should seldom deal with the substance of the standard. Perhaps what EMC needed to show, or the Commission needed to find, was that the cement producers 'gamed' or misused the standard-setting process so that a competitor (or competition) was excluded. EMC seems to have claimed that there were cement producers that through the trade association had 'gamed' the technical committee at CEN, and also put forward evidence to that effect, but the Commission, on the other hand, seems not to have agreed that the weight of these findings amounted to a misuse of the standard-setting procedure. Without such a finding of misuse, the plaintiff was, according to the Commission, in reality asking the Commission and the courts to scrutinize the standard-setting process itself, i.e., the semi-regulatory process put in place to create standards.[27]

---

[24] The Court did not elaborate on this point. However, see the Commission decision (n. 19 above), at para. 111.

[25] Ibid., at para. 107.

[26] Ibid., at para. 111.

[27] In the *EMC* case (n. 18 above), it seemed clear that the dominant position of the involved firms and the exclusionary effect of the standard were present. However, since the involved firms had complied with the by-laws and the good

The US Department of Justice (DoJ) has reached very similar conclusions. For example, in a Business Review Letter of 2002, *American Welding Society*, the DoJ stated that it does not consider whether one standard is better than another; rather, it only assesses whether the standard-setting process has been abused or not.[28] Likewise, in other patent pool Business Review Letters, like *MPEG-2*, the DoJ did not analyse the technology as such, but was satisfied that the technology was standardized by an SDO.[29]

The Court's decision in *EMC* and the US DoJ's letter in *American Welding Society* reflect a position according to which reviewing and deciding on the substance of the standard, i.e. what constitutes the 'best' technology, is outside the scope and ability of the antitrust agencies and courts.[30] This may be a sensible position: neither the competition authorities nor competition courts indirectly may have the ability to judge

---

governance for standard-setting rules, there was no misuse or breach of 'competition on the merits'. According to Hovenkamp, the courts should be very reluctant to become embroiled in evaluating complex technical concepts, but there are times when the courts are forced to do so. When an antitrust plaintiff has shown that one standard was chosen over others, that *prima facie* the other technologies were rejected for anticompetitive purposes, and that this had relevant economic effects on the market, by making the market less competitive, it is likely that the standard was not selected on technical merits. Then, the defendants should be able to argue that the selected technology is still superior and that it was selected because of its merits. The burden of proof is on the defendant. See H. Hovenkamp et al., *IP and Antitrust: An Analysis of Antitrust Principles Applied to Intellectual Property Law* (Aspen Publishers 2010) para. 35.4, p. 35-35.

[28] See C. James, Department of Justice, *American Welding Society Business Review Letter to Douglas Macdonald* of 7 October 2002, http://www.justice.gov/atr/public/busreview/200310.htm (accessed 5 March 2014), where the Department of Justice states that it does not consider whether one standard is better than the other, but only whether the process of standard-setting has been abused. The American Welding Society's letter is discussed in P. Plompen, 'The New Technology Transfer Guidelines (TTG) as Applied to Patent Pools and Patent Pool Licensing: Some Observations Regarding the Concept of "Essential Technologies"' in C.D. Ehlermann and I. Atanasin (eds), *European Competition Law Annual 2005: The Interaction between Competition Law and Intellectual Property Law* (Hart Publishing 2005) at 300. See also Lundqvist (n. 5 above) at 372–375.

[29] See *MPEG-2 Pool Business Review Letter to Gerrard Beeney* of 26 June 1997, 6: http://www.usdoj.gov/atr/public/busreview/215742.htm (accessed 3 May 2009).

[30] Generally speaking, the majority of commentators seem to agree on this point. See e.g. Anderman and Kallaugher (n. 16 above), at 252.

and decide on substantive issues of a technology.[31] This explains why competition authorities have been reluctant to judge the technical merits of standards.[32] The standard in *EMC* (EN 197-1) seems to have been classified as a prescriptive product standard, decided and implemented on an existing product market (cement), where the alleged claim of anti-competitive effect that product variety was lessened was dismissed. The standard, according to the Commission, was not *de jure* or *de facto* mandatory, since there were other means to obtain access to the market and access to the EC mark. EMC maintained that numerous contracting authority procurement regulations were specifically drafted only in terms of cement products set out under the EN 197-1 standard, thus excluding the other cement products bearing the EC mark. Moreover, EMC claimed that the fact that Portland cement complying with EN 197-1 represented between 85 and 90 per cent of the total sales of cement in Europe demonstrated that the EN 197-1 was *de facto* mandatory. The Commission did not recognize these arguments, and thereby set a high threshold for establishing anticompetitive harm and effect. In fact, this would imply that the standard did not, according to the Commission, have lock-in effects.

Anticompetitive harm and effect may exist if a firm selling a competing product is excluded from the market due to an anticompetitive agreement entered into by its competitors. Such exclusion may lead to higher prices and a reduction in quality. The EU Commission and the Courts seem to have rejected the evidence put forward by EMC with reference to the misuse. If EMC had been able to prove that there was an agreement between its competitors to exclude EMC and its product from the cement market, through the standard agreement in CEN, then the Commission could have identified a violation of Article 101 TFEU, irrespective of whether the standard was *de jure* or *de facto* mandatory. The test to show anticompetitive effect should focus on whether cement prices were likely to increase and product variety to decrease due to the implementation of the standard. A dominant prescriptive product standard like the EN 197-1 may cause that effect without being *de jure* or *de facto* mandatory. Thus, the Commission in this respect appears to set the bar too high. The standard does not need to be mandatory for anticompetitive

---

[31] Hovenkamp asserts that courts may get entangled in a discussion of what technology is superior in cases where the defendant (e.g., the SSO) submits that the selected standard has a technology bias due to superiority: Hovenkamp et al. (n. 27 above), at para. 35.4, p. 35-35.

[32] M. Glader, 'Open Standards: Public Policy Aspects and Competition Law Requirements' (2010) 6 *European Competition Journal* 611, 615.

effects to appear when a non-network-driven market is being regulated with a prescriptive product standard that has been decided upon so as to exclude a competitor.

3.2 The Assessment of Interoperability and Infrastructure Standards under Competition Law[33]

When dealing with interoperability (or infrastructure) standards, many of the disputes regarding the selection of a standard involve neither significant effect on prices or output, nor significant reduction in incentive for future innovation. Such disputes, according to Anderman and Kallaugher, would establish which set of rights holders should be able to benefit from rents attributable to an interoperability standard. According to these authors, Article 101 TFEU is not a good platform to judge this issue. Presumably, this is the case because the courts need then to analyse the substance of the standard. It is therefore important to identify a 'real' competitive harm, e.g. the exclusion of a product or technology or increased prices on a relevant market (that is able to hold competing products or technologies).[34] Only if a plaintiff is able to demonstrate that several technologies or standards could prevail on the market and that the standard-setting process was misused so as to exclude a competing technology or product, may the plaintiff be successful in showing an anticompetitive harm, which may cause anticompetitive effects under the Anderman and Kallaugher formula.

In light of the above, it is clear that the competition authorities and courts need to preserve competition by focusing on the procedural aspects of standard-setting. Seldom can a court venture in to decide whether the technology selected is the best technology or not.[35] So competition can only be upheld indirectly, by stipulating rules for the standard-setting process, by prohibiting the misuse of the procedure in those circumstances where competition by substitution is feasible.

The scant (and mostly US) case law regarding the horizontal effects of standard-setting diverges depending on what sort of technology is scrutinized. As concerns standard-setting cases, most of the successful horizontal cases have been brought by plaintiffs regarding markets that

---

[33] For a more lengthy discussion regarding the case law discussed in this sub-section see Lundqvist (n. 5 above) at 149–228.

[34] Anderman and Kallaugher (n. 16 above), at 251ff.

[35] See however Hovenkamp's claims: Hovenkamp et al. (n. 27 above), at para. 35.4, p. 35-35.

may hold several different standards or technologies, and where competition by substitution may exist, while the SSOs in these cases have been misused or misled when selecting one technology as the standard, thereby excluding other technologies[36] and limiting product variation. Also, in these cases there are mechanisms that make the selected technology or standard become dominant and work as a barrier to trade for any other technology to penetrate the market, i.e. there are lock-in effects on the stakeholders. The misused SSO thereby creates a standard that limits competition by substitution, which could have prevailed if the standard had not been implemented.

The same goes for patent pools. The few patent pool cases where the authority or court have found an antitrust violation normally revolved around exclusion of competing technologies from markets where the plaintiff and the court agree that the market should be able to hold competing technologies.[37]

There are cases in the US concerning members of SSOs in reference to both collusive and joint exclusionary conduct. Historically, the US antitrust case law books were (and still are) fairly filled with cartels thinly disguised as standard-setting organizations or patent pools. For example, the *Standard Sanitary* case[38] concerned a cartel where the ringleader licensed the finishing process to other cartel members. Products produced under the licensed process were sold at agreed prices in the US, while the products that did not meet the US standard needed to be sold outside the US. The effect of the collaboration was to set prices, but the standard facilitated the cartel by decreasing product variety. Products that did not meet the standard could not be sold in the US, presumably because they would have been sold at a lesser price. Interestingly, many of these old cartels or patent pool cases also included agreements on technology standards.[39]

---

[36] See *Allied Tube and Conduit Corp. v. Indian Head, Inc.* 817 F2.d 938 (2d Cir 1987) aff'd 486 U.S. 492, 500 (1988), 817 F.2d at 947.

[37] See for example the VIXS patent pool: In re *Summit Tech. Inc.*, 127 F.T.C. 208 (1998), In re *VIXS Inc.*, 127 F.T.C. 136 (1999).

[38] *Standard Sanitary Mfg. Co. v. United States*, 226 U.S. 20 (1912).

[39] Even *Standard Oil* (*Standard Oil Co. v. United States 283* U.S. 163 (1931)) concerned a standard: *Standard Oil* is a complicated and contradictory case concerning several issues. The history of the Standard Oil patent pool may be briefly stated. For about half a century before 1910, gasoline had been manufactured from crude oil exclusively by distillation and condensation at atmospheric pressure. When the demand for gasoline grew rapidly with the widespread use of the automobile, methods for increasing the yield of gasoline from the available crude oil were sought. It had long been known that from a

There are also cases from the 1960s and 1970s concerning product standards. These cases concern prescriptive product standards rather than interoperability standards and display antitrust harm such as collusive conduct, in the form of buyer or seller cartels, or group boycotts of competing technologies. There is, for example, the famous *Macaroni* case,[40] in which the defendants responded to a temporary shortage of durum semolina wheat by setting a product standard for pasta that required only 50 per cent durum semolina and 50 per cent of an inferior wheat. Hovenkamp argues that by changing the standard, the defendants intended to suppress the price of durum semolina wheat input, and, of course, their own costs.[41] In fact, it was a buyer cartel using the standard to decrease input prices.

The *C-O Two* decision[42] and the *Household Radiators* case[43] revolved around the issue that creating a narrow product standard diminished product differentiation either completely or at least to the extent that

---

given quantity of crude, additional oils of high volatility could be produced through so-called 'cracking', i.e. a technology and *de facto* standard by applying heat and pressure to the residuum after ordinary distillation. But a commercially profitable 'cracking' method and apparatus for manufacturing additional gasoline had not yet been developed. The first of such processes was perfected by the Indiana Company in 1913; and for more than seven years this was the only one practised in the US. During that period, the Indiana Company not only manufactured cracked gasoline on a large scale, but also had licensed the technology to 15 independent firms to use that process. Meanwhile, since the phenomenon of 'cracking' was not controlled by any patent, other firms had been working independently to develop commercial processes of their own. Most prominent among these were the three other primary defendants, the Texas Company, the New Jersey Company, and the Gasoline Products Company. Each of these firms secured numerous patents covering their respectively particular 'cracking' process. Beginning in 1920, conflict developed among the four companies concerning the validity, scope and ownership of issued patents. The primary defendants asserted that these difficulties led to their executing the three principal agreements making up a patent pool, which the DoJ attacked for being a cartel; and that their sole object was to avoid litigation and losses incident to conflicting patents.

40 *Nat. Macaroni Mfrs. Ass'n.*, 65 FTC 583 (1964), enforced, 345 F.2d 421 (7th Cir. 1965).

41 Hovenkamp et al. (n. 27 above), at para. 35.4, p. 35-35.

42 *C-O-Two Fire Equip. Co. v. United States* 197 F2d 489 (9th Circ), cert. denied, 344 U.S. 892 (1952).

43 *United States v. Am Radiator and Standard Sanitary Corp.* 433 F2d 174, 185 (3rd Cir 1970), cert. denied, 401 U.S. 948 (1971).

prices (and costs) among the members aligned to the point that the Courts found the collaborations to amount to seller cartels.

There are several similar cases from this 20-year period, and Hovenkamp affirms that while one or two of them were too far-reaching under current antitrust theory, these cases most probably still reflect accurate antitrust law and policy. They carry an important message according to Hovenkamp: that product differentiation is still an important antitrust value, and thus, 'standards that do no more than reduce product differentiation in order to facilitate price matching do not provide a social benefit'.[44]

In the early 'patent ambush' cases where the notion of 'patent trolls' originates, there was a discussion that firms were actually victims of buyer cartels, monopsonies, where mainly vertically integrated (telecommunication) firms collectively tried to decrease the royalty rate by colluding under the notion of FRAND and also what FRAND supposedly meant when it came to royalty rates. Patent trolls were no 'trolls' but victims of buyer cartels that did not let the patent assertion entities (PAEs) obtain royalty rates reflecting their monopoly positions.

The difference between the patent troll cases and the cases above is the 'interoperability' character of the relevant telecom standards. GSM and UMTS (3G) standards are both interoperability and, to some extent, infrastructure standards which need to be accessible to product manufacturers. They are standards for markets with network effects, while, for example, *Standard Sanitary* and *Macaroni* display standards that *de facto* limited choice on the relevant product markets in an effort to increase or decrease prices on the market. The markets in *Standard Sanitary* and *Macaroni* were able to accomodate different technologies or solutions. Since, generally speaking, there can only be one infrastructure standard in the telecom market, exclusion of one technology cannot produce an anticompetitive harm, whereas not giving access to the standard may amount to an anticompetitive harm. The counterfactual scenario is still one (*de facto*) standard. Thereby, the patent trolls went from being victims of buyer cartels to being violators of competition law for not giving access to their SEPs. Thus, the argument that PAEs were exposed to anticompetitive monopsonies in the telecom sector, which was mainly put forward in Europe, and had no or very limited success[45] and for those

[44] H. Hovenkamp, 'Standard and Ownership Policy' (2007) 48 *Boston College Law Review* 87, at 95.

[45] See D. Geradin, 'Standardization and Technological Innovation: Some Reflections on Ex-ante Licensing, FRAND, and the Proper Means to Reward Innovators' (2006) 29 *World Competition* 511.

seeking a court injunction due to infringement of a SEP in the telecom sector generally, is now considered to be an abuse under Article 102 TFEU. In fact, the doctrine seems to be that patent troll activities, e.g. seeking injunctions and not abiding by FRAND commitments (cf. *Motorola* and *Samsung* cases *infra*) may be in violation of Article 102 TFEU.

Most cases concerning standards and standard-setting outside the field of intellectual property law (e.g. patent ambush or other cases based on unilateral actions by patentees), concern firms whose technology was denied the status of standard or part of the standard.[46] These cases border on group boycott or collective refusal to deal, and many of them concern membership or acceptance from various accreditation boards. However, mainly the concern is an SSO selecting a product standard that *de facto* excludes competing or substitute technologies.

The leading US case regarding exclusionary standard is *Radiant Burners*,[47] where the Supreme Court seems to indicate that the intent of the defendants, i.e. the members of the boycott group, is what determines whether there might be anticompetitive exclusion. Unlawful combination and conspiracy by the members of a SSO enacted through a refusal to certify a specific burner, and through the lack of provision of gas for the same, constituted an antitrust offence in *Radiant Burner*, where anti-competitive harm and effect were proven.

The *Allied Tube* case also fits this category. In this case, the plaintiffs were able to show that the standard-setting procedure had been abused, causing the exclusion of a competing technology and competition. In *Allied Tube*, the National Fire Protection Association (NFPA) – a private SSO – had only allowed for electrical conduits made of steel under a fire hazard standard. NFPA sets and publishes fire protection standards through a member voting process. Standards approved by a majority of NFPA members are generally adopted as state law and codified in the National Electric Code. In 1980 this Code permitted the use of steel, but not plastic electrical conduits. The defendant was the nation's largest steel conduit manufacturer and an NFPA member. Allied Tube, a plastic electrical conduit manufacturer, had proposed the inclusion of plastic electrical conduits in the 1981 Code and received preliminary approval by an NFPA panel. Prior to the 1980 meeting, at which the final NFPA vote occurred, however, the defendant and other steel industry and NFPA

---

[46] Hovenkamp et al. (n. 27 above), at para. 35.4, p. 35-35.

[47] *Radiant Burners, Inc v. People's Gas and Coke Comp. et al.* 364 U.S. 656, 81 S, Ct. 365 (1961).

members agreed to 'pack' the NFPA with new members in order to defeat the proposal. The proposal was rejected by a membership that included 230 of such 'new' members.

Allied Tube successfully sued in Federal district court, alleging unreasonable restraints on trade, in violation of the Sherman Act. After that decision was overturned on appeal, the Supreme Court held for Allied Tube, rejecting the defendant's argument that it was immune from the antitrust laws under what is commonly referred to as the 'Noerr-Pennington doctrine' (which effectively, makes 'concerted efforts to restrain or monopolize trade by petitioning government officials' immune from the antitrust laws).[48]

There are similar cases also under EU competition law. In the *IAZ* case,[49] the EU Commission was confronted with something which was very similar to the US *Radiant Burners* case. The Belgian trade association CEG and other Belgian trade associations of manufacturers and sole importers of dishwashers and washing machines, concluded an agreement with the National Association of Water Suppliers (ANSEAU) to monitor compliance with Belgian regulations regarding water quality. The legislation stipulated that only devices complying with Belgian standards were to be connected to the water supply system. To that end, CEG issued a label of conformity and ANSEAU ensured that only machines bearing the label would commercially available. ANSEAU also drew the attention of dealers and consumers to the possible consequences of failure to comply with the standard and the regulation. The Court found that this was a private attempt to re-establish national borders inside the internal market by restricting parallel trade.[50] Regarding the intent to restrict competition, the Commission declared that it did not need a showing of intent, but that the parties had clearly in their correspondence declared their intention to use the standard as a weapon against parallel traders.[51] The effect on trade and competition was

---

[48] Ibid., 511. For an older case see *Radiant Burners, Inc. v. Peoples gas Light & Coke Co.*, 364 U.S. 656, 659ff. (1961), where a *per se* violation of Section 1 of the Sherman Act was found. See H.R. REP. 108-125, reprinted 2004 U.S.C.C.A.N. 609, 613.

[49] Joined cases 96 to 102, 104, 105, 108 and 110/82 *IAZ and others v. Commission* [1983] ECR 3369.

[50] For a comprehensive analysis, see H. Schepel, *The Constitution of Private Governance – Product Standards in the Regulation of Integrating Markets* (Hart Publishing 2005), 290.

[51] See Joined cases 96 to 102, 104, 105, 108 and 110/82 *IAZ and others v. Commission* [1983] ECR 3369, 3391.

proven, since the restriction under the standard at least potentially restricted parallel trade.[52]

3.3 Some Critical Remarks

Interestingly, all the successful (old) cases concern prescriptive product standards in the 'old economy' and not standards on interoperability or infrastructure. In fact, they involve an SSO's members, primarily, and an SSO, secondarily, deciding to promote one substitute or competing solution above the others on a relevant market (by selecting it as the standard), and thereby excluding a competing technology. These cases tell us that this may be in violation of competition law. It is therefore difficult, to say the least, to draw any form of conclusion from these cases when scrutinizing infrastructural or interoperability standards under competition law. Nonetheless, they show that members of an SDO may abuse or misuse the 'governance rules' or the standard-setting process, and 'game' the SSOs, to exclude competition.

The unsuccessful (horizontal) cases regarding alleged exclusion of competing technologies often revolve around the New Economy, infrastructure or true interoperability standards, where the market is not able to bear several competing technologies, and, thus, exclusion of competition cannot be proven and no anticompetitive effect exists. In these cases, competition law may only uphold competition by imitation under the selected standard.[53] Thus, access to the standard and/or the technology becomes an antitrust value, and limitation to access an antitrust harm. On the contrary, for markets where there may exist different competing technologies or standards, denied access to an essential standard or technology is not an antitrust harm.

4. APPLICATION OF THE PROHIBITION OF ABUSE OF DOMINANT POSITION AND MONOPOLIZATION TO STANDARD-SETTING

The US *Rambus* case was a monopolization case, but the Court seems to be occupied with the dichotomy between markets where exclusion and anticompetitive effects can be identified and markets where such effects

---

[52] H. Schepel (n. 50 above), 289, at 311ff.

[53] Generally, on the dichotomy between competition by substitution and by imitation, see Drexl (n. 16 above), at 507ff.

may not be proven. In this case, the FTC investigated Rambus for unfair competition and unfair deceptive acts or practices in violation of Section 5 of the FTC Act and Section 2 of the Sherman Act. The FTC alleged that Rambus violated the US antitrust laws by not letting the concerned SDO know about its patents, and also by amending patent applications in accordance with the discussion in the technical committee to make them fit with the description of the standard as it was presented to Rambus while it was still a member of the relevant SDO. Rambus' conduct (which could be regarded as patent ambush) increased its monopoly power according to the FTC, which, in the end, imposed on Rambus an obligation to license its essential patents for reasonable royalty rates.

On appeal, the D.C. Circuit found Rambus' arguments persuasive and set aside the Commission's order.[54] The Court used the rule of reason and demanded a showing of anticompetitive effect. A plaintiff, according to the D.C. Circuit, must show that the SDO would have selected another technology but did not because of the nondisclosure or deceptive behaviour of the defendant. This is a heavy burden and implies that the plaintiff needs to show that there existed a competing (non-proprietary) technology, that the SDO would possibly have selected, 'but for' the deceptive act of the patentee. Only then may anticompetitive effects on price be proven.[55] Furthermore, the D.C. Circuit based its judgment on the possibility that Rambus would have been allowed to hold a lawful monopoly. It used the *NYNEX* case[56] regarding deceptive pricing behaviour for exclusion of competitors, rather than the *Microsoft* case regarding deceptive behaviour to gain a monopoly position.

The *Rambus* saga also had an EU twist.[57] The European Commission started investigating Rambus under Article 102 TFEU for patent ambush.

---

[54] *Rambus, Inc. v. F.T.C.* 522 F.3d 456 (D.C. Cir 2008), cert. denied.

[55] As stated above, when dealing with interoperability (or infrastructure) standards, many of the disputes regarding the selection of a standard involve neither significant effect on price or output for consumers, nor significant reduction in incentive for future innovation. The disputed issue in these cases, according to Anderman and Kallaugher, is instead which set of rights holders should be able to benefit from rents attributable to a standard. Article 101 or Section 1 of the Sherman Act is not a good platform to judge these issues since they need anticompetitive effects to be triggered. Anderman and Kallaugher (n. 16 above), at 251ff.

[56] *NYNEX Corp. v. Discon, Inc.* 525 U.S. 128 (1998).

[57] See Press Release of 9 December 2009, http://europa.eu/rapid/press-release_IP-09-1897_en.htm (accessed 13 July 2013), where the EU Commission also stated that it concurred with the DOJ regarding the benefits of IP policies generally and *ex ante* unilateral statements of licensing terms. See also the

The case was settled when Rambus agreed to lower its royalty rates. It should be mentioned that Rambus neither in the US cases nor with the Commission denied that it held a dominant position. Thus, the EU *Rambus* case seems to have been based, at least in part, on a theory of excessive pricing as the anticompetitive harm.

The need to show anticompetitive effect under the US *Rambus* case seems to imply that a plaintiff needs to show, first, a misuse of the standard-setting process, and second, that the selection of the standard excluded a competing technology, causing anticompetitive harm.[58] Only a showing of a misuse of the process is not enough under *Rambus*. Moreover, under *Rambus*, it is not entirely clear that a plaintiff only needs to show that the SSO selected the technology for the standard under false premises and that a competing technology existed. Perhaps, a plaintiff also needs to prove it likely that the competing technology would have been selected and that prices are likely to increase due to the patentee's misuse. All this to show an anticompetitive effect.

The technology standardized in the US *Rambus* case and to which Rambus held patent rights seems to have been an interoperability technology. The standard covered DRAM technology. DRAM chips are a type of electronic memory primarily used in computer systems, but also used in a wide range of other products which need to temporarily store data, including servers, workstations, printers, PDAs and cameras. The interface technology allows interoperability between a DRAM chip and other computer components which need to access the data stored in the DRAM chips. The *Rambus* case seems therefore to be a case where the relevant market displays network effects, and where there most likely is no competing technology, apart from the standardized technology. There may be rival technologies before the standard is decided. However, that depends on the level of migration that goes on before the SSO makes its decision.

If the D.C. Circuit demanded a showing of anticompetitive effect by means of demonstrating what technologies have been excluded, it is interesting to discuss how the FTC should have gone about showing such anticompetitive effect. Since the market is not yet in existence when the SSO makes its selection, any anticompetitive effects need then to be

---

speech given by former Commissioner N. Kroes, SPEECH/09/575 of 9 December 2009, http://europa.eu/rapid/press-release_SPEECH-09-575_en.htm?locale=en (accessed October 2014).

[58] See Hovenkamp et al. (n. 27 above), at para. 35.4, p. 35-35.

identified on the 'future goods or technology market'.[59] However, considering that the D.C. Circuit does not discuss a 'future goods market', where else should the anticompetitive effect discussed by the Court materialize? In other words, the FTC had to show that Rambus by its conduct in the technical committee eliminated the development of competing (non-proprietary) technologies. If a 'future goods' market concept is not accepted, the Court is instead forced to use a per se rule and to accept that patent ambush, irrespective of the existence of competing technologies, is not 'competition on the merits' and may harm the private standard-setting procedure as such and therefore is a violation of antitrust law.

After *Rambus*, there have been several cases in the telecom sector both in the US and in Europe regarding the application of, on the one hand, Section 5 of the FTC Act or Section 2 of the Sherman Act and, on the other hand, Article 102 TFEU.[60] They deal with different conduct: patent ambush situations, where FRAND terms agreed upon by the original patentee are transferred when the SEPs are transferred or assigned,

---

[59] Under EU competition law, patent ambush fits poorly since the abuse happens before dominance and not the other way around. In fact, it is a problem similar to the one the *Rambus* court was facing. As Drexl has stated, the term 'innovation market' is theoretically misguided (n. 16 above, at 516ff.). However, in certain cases, primarily in the pharmaceutical sector, mergers and collaborations between firms that both have developed drugs with the same or similar effect that are close to being marketed (perhaps in phase III studies) may be seen as creating a dominant position on a future goods market or to diminish innovative competition, or competition between R&D poles to the effect that it violates merger law or the prohibition against anticompetitive agreements. For the difference between innovation market and future goods market, and for cases regarding future goods market, see M. Glader, *Innovation Markets and Competition Analysis* (Edward Elgar Publishing 2006) 90ff., 189ff.; M.A. Carrier, *Innovation for the 21st Century: Harnessing the Power of Intellectual Property and Antitrust Law* (Oxford Scholarship Online, May 2009) 297ff. and L.B. Landman, 'Competitiveness, Innovation Policy and the Innovation Market Myth: A Reply to Tom and Newberg on Innovation Markets as the "Centerpiece" of "New Thinking" on Innovation' (1998) 13 *St. John's Journal of Legal Commentary*, 223. Perhaps a similar analysis can be made in patent ambush cases regarding interoperability standards. When an influential SDO or the technical committee in the SDO is deciding on a specific technology for a standard it is *de facto* creating a (future) market. When a patentee commits patent ambush it abuses its dominant position by not acknowledging that it now holds SEPs under that standard, when the technical committee has decided what technology should be standardized.

[60] For a lengthy discussion, see Lundqvist (n. 5 above), at 299–360.

defining FRAND and, generally, the terms for accessing SEPs.[61] One of the main current discussions is whether and when a holder of an SEP who has committed to license on FRAND terms may deny access to a willing licensee. In other words, the issue at stake seems to be when the court should grant injunctions on the SEP-infringing but willing licensees, or when the courts should deny injunctions due to competition law. Two of the main cases in these litigations are *Samsung* and *Motorola*, where these firms were accused of abusing their dominant position by seeking injunctions against a firm (Apple) that willfully infringed their SEPs, while it still sought to obtain licences from Samsung and Motorola.

The FTC was first to deal with the situation and reached a settlement with Motorola in 2013,[62] while the European Commission reached a settlement in the *Samsung* case in 2014[63] and then delivered a decision in the *Motorola* case on the same day.[64]

For the purpose of our discussion, the findings of the Commission in its *Samsung* and *Motorola* decisions are most interesting. The Commission starts in both cases by stating that standards ensure 'compatibility and interoperability' and goes on to describe the role of ETSI and SEPs. The Commission, in both these decisions, reached the finding that Samsung and Motorola were each dominant on their similar but separate relevant markets. The Commission stated in both cases that an implementer of a standard has to use the technology protected by an SEP when manufacturing a standard-compliant product and is therefore locked into the technology. According to the Commission, the relevant product markets encompass the licensing of the technologies as specified in the (UMTS or GPRS) standard technical specifications on which Samsung's UMTS SEPs and Motorola's Cudak GPRS SEP, respectively, read.[65] There was no demand-side substitutability in either case. Each company

---

[61] Ibid.

[62] FTC decision of 3 January 2013, *Statement in the Matter of Google Inc.*, FTC File No. 121-0120. http://www.ftc.gov/os/caselist/1210120/130103googlemotorolastmtofcomm.pdf (accessed 11 July 2013).

[63] Commission decision of 29 April 2014, Case AT.39939 *Samsung – Enforcement of UMTS Standard Essential* Patents. http://ec.europa.eu/competition/elojade/isef/case_details.cfm?proc_code=1_39939 (accessed 28 September 2014).

[64] Commission decision of 29 April 2014, Case AT.39985 *Motorola Enforcement of GPRS Standard Essential Patent*. http://ec.europa.eu/competition/elojade/isef/case_details.cfm?proc_code=1_39985 (accessed 28 September 2014).

[65] Geographic markets were at least EEA-wide. See e.g. ibid., at paras 214–220.

held 100 per cent of the respective market. Dominance was also assured due to widespread adoption of these standards through market penetration and the legal requirement to use the standards.

The Commission established that seeking preliminary and permanent injunctions against a 'willing' licensee was an abuse following the 'exceptional circumstance' doctrine.[66] The Commission stated in *Samsung*: 'the exceptional circumstances in this case are: (i) the UMTS standard-setting process; and (ii) Samsung's commitment to ETSI to license its UMTS SEPs on FRAND terms and conditions'.[67] Thereafter, the Commission in the *Samsung* case, building on the commitments given by Samsung, establishes a safe harbour, i.e. a procedure for how potential licensees may obtain licence agreements based on FRAND terms without the risk of facing injunctions.[68]

The *Samsung* and *Motorola*[69] cases show that if the interoperability standard has been accepted in the market to the point that there is no substitute and the users are locked in, then access to single SEPs may be granted. Each SEP represents a separate market.

Indeed, the application of competition law to standard-setting should, generally, be divided into at least two groups: (i) 'infrastructure' or 'interoperability' standards (or otherwise on markets where there are market failures);[70] and (ii) standards that are present on markets where

---

[66] See *Samsung* (n. 63 above), at paras 52, 55–56, 66 and 68. Apple's alleged unwillingness to enter into a licence agreement for Samsung's UMTS SEPs on FRAND terms and conditions was taken into account as a potential objective justification.

[67] See *Samsung* (n. 63 above), at para. 56.

[68] See *Samsung* (n. 63 above), at paras 121–122.

[69] The Commission *Motorola* case dealt with Motorola's SEPs relating to the ETSI GPRS standard, part of the GSM standard. When this standard was adopted in Europe, Motorola Mobility declared some of its patents as essential to the standard and gave a commitment that it would license these patents on FRAND terms. The Commission in its decision found that Motorola abused its dominant position by seeking and enforcing an injunction against Apple in Germany on the basis of an SEP which it had committed to license on FRAND terms and where Apple had agreed to take a licence and be bound by a determination of the FRAND royalties by the relevant German court. The Commission also found it anticompetitive that Motorola insisted, under the threat of the enforcement of an injunction, that Apple give up its rights to challenge the validity or infringement by Apple's mobile devices of Motorola SEPs. See *Motorola* (n. 64 above).

[70] See generally Drexl (n. 16 above), at 507ff.

there may be substitute technologies or products available for the consumer to choose from.[71]

If the underlying market can only hold one standard (i.e. there is no room for competition by substitution), the horizontal result of that standard (i.e. the agreement on the standard) falls outside the ambit of competition law.[72] Thus, it will be very difficult to demonstrate an anticompetitive effect based only on the fact that the 'wrong' technology was selected. However, as the *Motorola* and *Samsung* decisions show, these situations trigger the 'exceptional circumstance' doctrine under Article 102 TFEU. Holders of SEPs must grant access to their SEPs under these standards, if the standards reflect the basic technologies that are implemented for connected markets, when they have committed to license on FRAND terms to the relevant SSO and they are confronted by a willing licensee.[73] In these situations, the Commission decisions map out a procedure for how to reach a licence based on FRAND terms. This procedure is based on 'good governance' rules, i.e. regulations under competition law for how these parties may and may not act, such as when to seek court injunctions. Moreover, excessive royalty rates and the *Rambus*-style patent ambush may amount to abuse of dominant position in these circumstances.

The opposite holds true for group (ii): if the standard is a prescriptive product standard on a market that may hold several competing solutions, then courts might want to scrutinize in more detail the standard setting procedures, considering whether they are horizontal collusive agreements and have exclusionary effects, while the 'exceptional circumstance' doctrine should not be as readily available as it would be for interoperability standards. Access should only be granted if there is some form of market failure creating a monopoly standard. Apart from these situations, competition by substitute should be given room to develop.

---

[71] See Lundqvist (n. 5 above) at 389–393.

[72] Likewise, if the standard is not a design standard but more of a performance standard, then the collaborations should fall outside Section 1 of the Sherman Act or Article 101 TFEU.

[73] See also AG Wathelet opinion in Case C-170/13, *Huawei Technologies v. ZTD*, delivered on 20 November 2014.

5. CONCLUSION: DEVELOPING MORE NUMEROUS AND STRINGENT PROCEDURAL RULES WHEN SCRUTINIZING STANDARD-SETTING ORGANIZATIONS?

Standard-setting is quickly becoming part of the core business strategy of many firms and the antitrust agencies need to develop a policy towards these forms of collaborations. In this chapter I have argued that such policy or guidelines must take into account the difference between various markets and diverse standards, and that antitrust authorities and courts should judge standard-setting agreements as well as the conduct of SEP-holders different depending on whether the technology and market being standardized are plagued by network effects or not.[74]

Competition agencies and courts need to devise indirect rules on how to regulate standard-setting. Clearly, the development under US antitrust law is that competition law plays only a minor role in regulating standard-setting and unilateral conduct under standards. Nonetheless, the business activity of standard-setting is quickly becoming a core business for firms, so competition agencies and courts need to establish tests to evaluate these collaborations.

A policy must take its point of departure from the fact that different standards create different competitive effects; therefore, different rules must be created depending on whether the effect creates market failures or not.

It is clear that courts and agencies should be reluctant to decide on the substance of standards. This is the prerogative of SSOs, while agencies and courts should try to protect and uphold the good governance procedural rules of the SSOs under competition law. These rules should protect competition indirectly, by regulating so that the integrity of the standard-setting procedure is upheld. Competition law must, however, be detached from the by-laws of the SSOs, and create its own set of norms on how firms may compete and interact in SSOs. Competition law can develop such rules under the notions of 'competition on the merits' and anticompetitive harm and effect. Such rules should have a firm basis in what may cause anticompetitive effects, while aiming to protect the integrity of the standard-setting procedure. These rules must be focused

---

[74] For a more lengthy discussion with more in-depth suggestions see Lundqvist (n. 5 above) at 365–412, 413–418, 419–424.

on the transparency of the standard-setting procedure. Access to membership and standards must be upheld, especially when dealing with standards where competition is based on imitation; thus, interoperability standards.

The chapter in the European Commission's Horizontal Guidelines on standard agreements is a good start. However, since we are dealing with an area in which there are no markets when the standard is being decided, and the idea of an innovation market is conceptually wrong, the standard-setting procedure and thereby the innovation process must be protected indirectly by rules stipulating openness and access to the SSO. In fact, the WTO principles regarding standard-setting[75] may be used as a point of departure to identify what good governance rules should be used under competition rules.

Since standards come in such a multitude of different forms, these rules must take into consideration the aim and ambit of the proposed standards and the market being regulated. There may be markets where standards can be implemented, but there is still room for competition by substitution. Competition law should then protect such competition; if that is not possible, competition law should be used to gain access to the downstream markets, e.g. markets regulated by the respective infrastructure or interoperability standard. In such cases, assessing the SSO's

---

[75] See Articles 2 and 5 and Annex III to the WTO/TBT Agreement and connected decisions. Annex III of the TBT Agreement is the Code of Good Practice for the Preparation, Adoption and Application of Standards, known as the WTO Code of Good Practice. In accepting the TBT Agreement, WTO Members agree to ensure that their central government standardizing bodies accept and comply with this Code of Good Practice and agree also to take reasonable measures to ensure that local government, non-governmental and regional standardizing bodies do the same. The Code is therefore open to acceptance by all such bodies. In addition, the TBT Agreement is reviewed annually and triennially and the reviews become important interpretations of the document. Under the TBT, decisions and recommendations have been issued that set out criteria defining the principles of an international standards-developing organization. These decisions/principles came out of the Second Triennial Review (23 May 2002) and specify that the WTO-TBT criteria for an 'international standards developing organization' are: transparency, openness, impartiality, effectiveness, relevance, consensus, use of performance-based standards, coherence, due process and technical assistance. See WTO, *Decisions and Recommendations adopted by the WTO Committee on Technical Barriers to Trade since 1 January 1995*, G/TBT/1/Rev.10, 46, 48. See http://ec.europa.eu/enterprise/tbt/index.cfm?fuseaction=library.viewLibrary&section_id=6&dspLang=EN (accessed 6 March 2014).

procedural rules under competition law is thus the only way to maintain competitive pressure.

For example, the FTC *Google* settlement order[76] may be criticized in many respects, but it clearly establishes rules for when injunctions may be used, and is a safe harbour for when injunctions may not be used. It actually stipulates quite delicate and detailed procedural rules for identifying FRAND, including arbitration. The *Samsung* decision by the European Commission is in many ways similar to the FTC *Google* settlement order. It stipulates a similar mechanism for injunction immunity and a FRAND procedure: (i) five years of immunity for infringement suits; thereafter (ii) 12 months of negotiations and, if the negotiations do not render any result; (iii) a court or arbitration to settle the FRAND level.[77] These are clearly procedural rules regarding when access to SEPs must be given, and possibly, in the area of standard-setting, such sophisticated governance or procedural rules need to be developed under competition law if the latter is to be used to supervise SSOs.

Moreover, AG Wathelet has recently given an opinion in the standard-setting case *Huawei v. ZTD*,[78] where a similar mechanism or procedure for accessing SEPs are drawn up. ECJ's judgement is decisive but the AG's Opinion is interesting in multiple respects:

(i) It is clearly arguing for a *per se* use of Article 102 TFEU when a holder of an SEP does not give access to a willing licensee. If the requirements for the test of abuse are fulfilled, then *ipso facto* it is to the detriment of consumers and competitors. For example, an SEP-holder must provide the opportunity to enter into a FRAND license irrespective of the number of licensees already appointed or the market share held by the SEP-holder or potential licensee.
(ii) The requirement to negotiate FRAND also implies that there are naked restrictions that may not be used (e.g. it would constitute an abuse if the SEP holder required a non-challenge clause to be incorporated in the license agreement).
(iii) Generally, and more importantly, the whole FRAND procedure drawn up by the AG is very indebted to a legal, procedural/governance frameworks. It is somewhat different from what we are

[76] See FTC, *Statement in the Matter of Google Inc*. (n. 62 above).

[77] See European Commission Press release on Samsung Electronics' proposed commitments, http://europa.eu/rapid/press-release_IP-13-971_en.htm and http://europa.eu/rapid/press-release_MEMO-13-910_en.htm (accessed 28 February 2014).

[78] Opinion by the AG Wathelet in Case C-170/13, *Huawei Technologies v. ZTD*, delivered on 20 November 2014.

accustomed to in antitrust law: a clear test which identifies anti-competitive conduct and/or effect.

Lately, Lemley and Shapiro also argue for a set of rules for members of SSOs when setting reasonable royalties, which are quite similar to the FTC *Google* consent order.[79] These authors imply that there is room for competition law, should these rules not be followed. Competition law may act as an incentive and a threat for adhering to the good governance rules. In fact, as Lemley and Shapiro suggest, when the rules of the SSO are 'gamed', antitrust law should step in.

This applies to both the members of an SSO and the SSO itself. If the SSO does not set clear rules or establishes rules that can easily be manipulated, the SSO may be in breach of competition law due to the collusive effects these vague rules facilitate. So patentees that game these rules by patent ambush, FRAND ambush, or by selling SEPs to PAEs with the intention of raising royalty rates or eliminating competitors may be in breach of competition law. SSOs, on the other hand, can be in breach of competition law if the rules are so vague that they facilitate collusion or patent hold-up.[80] An SSO should have, for example, stringent IP policies.

Notwithstanding this, competition law practitioners still need to remember the markets where competition between a variety of products and/or different standards may prevail. On these markets, a suit where a firm alleges that the standard reflects a misuse of the standard-setting procedure, where that firm's competitors have jointly tried to exclude the firm and its technology through the standard-setting organization, should still be considered a benign and valid antitrust suit, if the firm meets the needed burden of proof.

However, not all standards are interoperability standards even in the telecommunications or IT sector or for the worldwide web. In fact, given the multitude of different standards and collaborations the industry holds, joint guidelines for standard-setting would certainly benefit the 'New Economy' and the 'Old Economy' as a whole.

---

[79] M.A. Lemley and C. Shapiro, 'A Simple Approach to Setting Reasonable Royalties for Standard-Essential Patents' (2013) 28 *Berkeley Technology Law Journal* 1135, also available at http://btlj.org/data/articles/28_2/1135-1166_Lemley&Shapiro_112613_Web.pdf (accessed August 2014).

[80] Ibid.

Index